THE ASTROTWINS'
2022
HOROSCOPE

Authors: Tali Edut, Ophira Edut
Art Direction: Rosie Dienhart
Contributing Editors: Felicia Bender, MizChartreuse, Matthew Swann
Managing Editor: Lisa M. Sundry
Copy Editors: Amy Anthony, Jasmmine Ramgotra
Consulting Editors: Jess Garcia, Jennifer Karnik

Cover Illustration © 2021 by Bodil Jane. www.bodiljane.com
Book Design: Rosie Dienhart
Interior Illustrations: Will Dudley

CONTENTS

A MESSAGE FROM THE ASTROTWINS

DEAR READER,

What do you get when you cross a mer-person, an alien and a tiger-suited woman? Well, 2022's cosmic alignment, that's what. As we enter the third year of the Aquarian Decade, there's disruption on every dimension, from outer space to the deep sea to the heart of the disappearing forests and jungles.

This is the 10th Anniversary Edition of our yearly horoscope guide, we're proud and a bit stunned to say. Yep, we've been tracking cosmic trends since 2013, the first full year of the new Mayan calendar, when it was prophesied that life as we knew it would never be the same. (Little did we know how true that would be.)

Once again, it's time to change our stripes. The Lunar Year of the Water Tiger begins February 1, setting a softer tone than the past two Metal-ruled years. Empathy is back, with a dose of nurturing from the 6 Universal Year (2+0+2+2).

The 2022 stars still serve plenty of fierceness and fight! Unpredictability reigns supreme, carving space for innovations to emerge. With supply chains in disarray and systems shifting on every level, we've dubbed 2022 the Year of the New Abnormal.

So, come get weird with us! We might all be boarding a flight to Mars (or traveling interdimensionally to Pleiades) soon. Meantime, let's enjoy our earthly pleasures sustainably and responsibly.

Ophi & Tali

2022 *THE NEW*
ABNORMAL

Nothing's been the same since the new decade began—and it probably won't ever be again. In 2022, we'll start getting used to this "new abnormal."

As old systems break down, space for new ones emerge. Call it entropy: Nothing ever disappears but, like wood burning to ash in a fire, it does change form.

Astrologers have been sending up smoke signals since before this decade began. We observed that major planets were moving from classical Capricorn into avant-garde Aquarius and knew this would spark a seismic shift. Our *2022 Horoscope* book even predicted a "black swan event" that would overturn the economy, supply chains and life as we knew it.

Two years later, the next evolution of humanity is calling. And, in a weirdly Aquarian way, it involves going backward and forward at the same time. Restructuring the way we "do life" is part of the New Abnormal.

While researching this book, we found a striking similarity between 2022 and 1962 in their planetary patterns. Sixty years ago, Saturn was also in Aquarius while Jupiter transited between Pisces and Aries. The Chinese Water Tiger ruled the Lunar Year, uniting empathy with strategy.

Impactful breakthroughs were a hallmark of 1962. New York City introduced its first automated subway car. Worldwide broadcasting debuted with the first transatlantic TV signal. Civil Rights activist James Howard Meredith was the first Black student to attend the University of Mississippi. Bob Dylan released his first album. Walmart opened its doors.

The Jetsons aired, treating us to TV's pre-millenium interpretation of the Space Age. While we're still waiting for Elroy's flying jetpack to hit the shelves, the Musk-Bezos-Branson trio is sending civilians on rocketship rides. Today's A.I. gives Rosie the Robot, The Jetsons' machine-operated maid, a run for her Roomba. (Siri, search "sex robots." Wait—no, don't.)

The excitement of progress has swelled to high tide since 1962, warming our oceans in the process. As you'll read in the pages ahead, 2022 is both a year of reckoning and one that's ripe for ingenuity.

We don't have to stop innovating and creating—as if we could curb that human impulse! The challenge is to work with what we've already got, whether we're upcycling secondhand denim, reforesting acres of wildlife using permaculture or figuring out how to capture carbon from the air to achieve Net Zero by 2030.

There's plenty of support from the stars with such matters. The karmic South Node heads into resourceful Scorpio, alchemizing "trash" into treasure. Expansive Jupiter gets spiritual alongside boundary-dissolving Neptune in Pisces—then advances into trailblazing Aries, inspiring fearless action. Saturn and Uranus keep disrupting the system, drawing attention to disparities and helping us engineer innovative solutions.

Hoarding all the toys isn't cool on the Aquarian playground, but oligarchs and dictators may tighten their iron grips one final time as Pluto draws its last few breaths in Capricorn between now and January 2024.

Venus and Mars both have retrograde phases, echoing this "stick with it" sentiment in love. Rather than endlessly swiping the apps, 2022 wants us to assess our patterns, heal from traumas and forge deeper connections. Simultaneously, unconventional arrangments for loving and living (apart and together) continue making "relationship anarchist" a viable status.

We've got it all covered in the *2022 Horoscope*—including an in-depth forecast for every zodiac sign. Here's to a decade of mapping the yearly stars together, and to many decades more. ✹

THE *Inner* PLANETS

IN 2022

SUN

MOON

MERCURY

VENUS

MARS

The inner planets are the faster moving heavenly bodies, nearest to the Sun (plus the moon and the Sun itself). United by their rocky cores, they include Mercury, Venus and Mars. Their journey through the zodiac shapes the intimate areas of our lives including family, friendship, love and sex. Because they hit on matters so close to home, astrologers refer to them as the "personal planets." We've tracked their movements for you in 2022, to help you make decisions that are close to your heart!

THE SUN

THE SUN IN ASTROLOGY

The Sun is the center of our solar system. It literally gives us life, providing the light, heat and energy that sustains us. Since all other planets revolve around it, we'd say the Sun has earned its well-deserved place as our primary sign in the astrology chart. Your birthday—called your "solar return" in astrospeak—always occurs when the Sun is in your sign.

The Sun doesn't actually orbit anywhere at all. But Western astrology is geocentric, meaning it's calculated from our vantage point down here on Earth. From that perspective, the Sun does appear to travel like the other planets. Every 30 days or so, el Sol moves into a new zodiac sign, kicking off a new zodiac "season." This prevailing energy colors the world for all of us. It's as if the Sun slips on a pair of colored glasses—golden yellow for Leo season, smoky amber for Scorpio—and casts its light on us through the mood of that filter.

Planning WITH THE SUN

In our Hotspots section, you can learn how to work with the energy of every Sun sign season. We thought we'd share another one of our favorite ways to plan with el Sol using the three zodiac modalities: cardinal, fixed and mutable. When the Sun travels through one of these positions, it directs our energy accordingly. Should you initiate, hunker down or spread the word? Here's how to know.

THE SUN IN CARDINAL SIGNS

Aries, Cancer, Libra, Capricorn

The cardinal signs start off every season and dovetail with major heavenly events:

Sun in Aries — equinox
Sun in Cancer — solstice
Sun in Libra — equinox
Sun in Capricorn — solstice

During these month-long solar cycles, we should initiate projects, taking on leadership (and ownership) to get them in motion. Map out your ideas, woo supporters and get all hands on deck!

THE SUN IN FIXED SIGNS

Taurus, Leo, Scorpio, Aquarius

Production is underway! The tenacious fixed cycles occur at the middle of each season and help us move from idea to action. You might feel more like a drone than a queen bee during these times, but that's okay. Fixed phases are essential for getting the job done. Stay focused, hustle and pay attention to the bottom line.

THE SUN IN MUTABLE SIGNS

Gemini, Virgo, Sagittarius, Pisces

Time to walk your talk! The mutable signs finish each season, helping us bring our work into the world. Time to start buzzing, evangelizing and arousing interest. These solar cycles are highly social and interactive. You might not get much sleep, but hey, the conversations will be life-changing!

the Sun IN 2022

AQUARIUS
JAN 19 (9:39PM)

PISCES
FEB 18 (11:43 AM)

ARIES
MAR 20 (11:33AM)
Equinox

TAURUS
APR 19 (10:24PM)

GEMINI
MAY 20 (9:23PM)

CANCER
JUN 21 (5:14AM)
Solstice

LEO
JUL 22 (4:07PM)

VIRGO
AUG 22 (11:16PM)

LIBRA
SEP 22 (9:04PM)
Equinox

SCORPIO
OCT 23 (6:36AM)

SAGITTARIUS
NOV 22 (3:20AM)

CAPRICORN
DEC 21 (4:48PM)
Solstice

times listed are Eastern US Time Zone

AKA THE ZODIAC SEASONS

THE MOON

THE MOON IN ASTROLOGY

The moon is the Sun's favorite companion, holding space for all the private matters el Sol doesn't care to shine a light on. These are things like our deepest feelings, secret desires, and the security blankets that we reach for to comfort ourselves. Home and family affairs, how we nurture others and what kind of caretaking we crave are also #MoonMatters. Our society is just starting to truly honor the importance of lunar topics, perhaps because they tend to fall into the archetypally feminine category. As the world grows to respect women's perspectives and issues, the moon's power is being felt more and more!

THE MOON IN 2022

The first new moon of 2022 is in Capricorn, setting a somewhat serious tone for our emotions this year. And it's probably a good thing! While Jupiter and Neptune shoot us off on flights of fancy, this new moon reminds us to touch down at base. There, we must weigh fantasies against our present-day realities. How will our new ideas affect the existing structures in our lives? What will the emotional impact be on our loved ones?

There's a goal-getter vibe to years that begin with a new moon in Capricorn! (It's a real contrast to years that begin with a wildly experimental and visionary Aquarius new moon, which is the only other kickstarter new moon that's possible, astrologically.) Career and family matters will be front and center. Be patient! The moon is "in detriment" in Capricorn, which is a more challenging position on the zodiac wheel. As such, it may take a minute to get systems working and the right players in place. While the process can be frustrating, make like the Capricorn Goat and keep forging ahead. This prestige-boosting lunar lift practically guarantees that your dreams will take shape, bringing material world success as a reward for your tenacity.

Planning WITH THE MOON

Each month, we complete a multi-phase moon cycle, as la luna disappears into the darkness of the new moon, then swells into a full moon two weeks later. During the weeks in between, there are quarter moons. While the moon doesn't "go retrograde" like Mercury or the other planets, these waxing and waning spells are just as important to track for planning each month. There are four eclipses in 2022, occurring as two solar (new moon) eclipses and two lunar (full moon) eclipses.

2022 NEW MOONS

New moons occur when la luna is perfectly positioned between the Earth and the Sun. As such, the "backside" of the moon is lit, and it becomes invisible from our view down here. Because everything goes dark, it's as if we have a blank canvas on which to create. In "nothingness" there is a sense of limitless possibilities. That is the gift of the new moon, a great time for setting intentions, making wishes, and taking the first bold step towards a new goal. We may actually start to see the first signs of these lunar requests two weeks later, when the next full moon on the calendar lights up the night skies.

Astro-geek fact: The new moon occurs in the same zodiac sign as the Sun each month.

the New Moon

CAPRICORN (12°20)
JAN 2, 1:33PM

AQUARIUS (12°20)
FEB 1, 12:45AM

PISCES (12°07)
MAR 2, 12:34AM

ARIES (11°31)
APR 1, 2:24AM

TAURUS (10 °28)
APR 30, 4:27PM
Partial Solar Eclipse

GEMINI (9°03)
MAY 30, 7:30AM

CANCER (7°23)
JUN 28, 10:52PM

LEO (5°39)
JUL 28, 1:55PM

VIRGO (4°04)
AUG 27, 4:16AM

LIBRA (2°49)
SEP 25, 5:55PM

SCORPIO (2°00)
OCT 25, 6:49AM
Partial Solar Eclipse

SAGITTARIUS (1°38)
NOV 23, 5:57PM

CAPRICORN (1°33)
DEC 23, 5:16AM

times listed are Eastern US Time Zone

2022 FULL MOONS

It's harvest time! During a full moon, you reap the seeds that were sown six months prior during the corresponding new moon. These cosmic manifestation moments can be cause for celebration or major eye-openers. During this lunar phase, the moon is on the exact opposite side of the Earth from the Sun. That explains why it's such a brightly lit spectacle for us to enjoy—and why the full moon is always in the opposite sign from the Sun each month. Contradictions stand out in stark reality during full moons, which can stir up intense passion and fierce head-butting. You may realize that you're done with one path and ready to find whatever's next. No matter what, emotions and overall intensity will be amplified. Stay aware of how much energy you're exuding and how people are responding to you.

the Full Moon

times listed are Eastern US Time Zone

CANCER (27°51)
JAN 17, 6:48PM

LEO (27°60)
FEB 16, 11:56AM

VIRGO (27°40)
MAR 18, 3:18AM

LIBRA (26°46)
APR 16, 2:54PM

SCORPIO (25°18)
MAY 16, 12:14AM
Total Lunar Eclipse

SAGITTARIUS (23°25)
JUN 14, 7:52AM

CAPRICORN (21°21)
JUL 13, 2:38PM

AQUARIUS (19°21)
AUG 11, 9:35PM

PISCES (17°41)
SEP 10, 5:59AM

ARIES (16°33)
OCT 9, 4:55PM

TAURUS (16°01)
NOV 8, 6:02AM
Total Lunar Eclipse

GEMINI (16°02)
DEC 7, 11:08PM

QUARTER MOONS

First Quarter Moon (Waxing)

The first quarter moon comes about a week after each new moon. This marks the halfway point between the new moon and the forthcoming full moon. Since the moon is waxing (growing fuller), it brings a reminder to pick up the pace and make sure that our actions match our words. After all, what's the point of making those new moon wishes if we don't actually do something about them? Grab the baton...but no need to burst into a full-on sprint! Since quarter moons are balancers, measured, thoughtful action is key (and haste makes waste). The first quarter moon is a stellar time to map out a plan and take the first few steps.

Third Quarter Moon (Waning)

The third quarter moon comes approximately a week after the full moon, as we are reaping and harvesting, but also winding down to the next new moon. This is a time for sorting the crops. Not every pick is a keeper! During this phase, we might shed a few elements that aren't the right fit. This curating process creates the right setting to help the true gems shine.

*Read more about 2022's quarter moons in the Hotspots section.

SOLAR ECLIPSES

Lights out! Solar eclipses take place during a new moon, when the Sun and moon converge at the same degree and zodiac sign on the ecliptic. As the moon passes over the Sun, it darkens the daytime sky, even changing the appearance of shadows. Equal parts eerie and magical, solar eclipses remind us that all that glitters ain't gold. Look in a new direction during a solar eclipse, because that's where opportunity lies. This can feel scary, since letting go of control will be necessary. Eclipses can also stir up buried desires, forcing us to acknowledge what we really want. Remember that change is inevitable! And it can be a beautiful thing once we finally surrender. These momentous new moons push us off the starting block and into new waters. But we have to move fast, since just like an eclipse, the manifestation period is both rare and brief.

In 2022, there are two partial solar eclipses—meaning the Sun won't be entirely shrouded. The first is in Taurus on April 30, then six months later, a second one arrives in Scorpio on October 25. These will impact the way we "do" money. While they are bound to bring new developments in decentralized finance and cryptocurrency, there could be crackdowns and regulations to contend with. The global economy overall may experience surprising shifts as we figure out how to support world citizens during the ongoing pandemic.

LUNAR ECLIPSES

Seeing red? Lunar eclipses transpire when the full moon opposes the Sun at the same degree of zodiac sign on the ecliptic. With the Earth sandwiched between these heavenly bodies, el Sol casts a shadow that slowly bleeds across the surface of the moon. (In fact, due to its reddish tint, a total lunar eclipse has earned the nickname of "blood moon.") Lunar eclipses are prime time for doing shadow work and dealing with feelings we've ignored. Buckle up, buttercup! Situations could pivot abruptly or come to a sudden, unceremonious halt. If anything in your life is "eclipsed away," here's our advise: Stop chasing and give it some space. You'll either manifest a better option or circle back to this later—after you've processed the lesson and evolved!

There are two lunar eclipses in 2022, and both are total lunar "blood moon" eclipses. The first one simmers in Scorpio on May 16, followed by the Taurus full moon on November 8. Power struggles can be explosive (and fascinating) near these days! Nefarious details may come to light, exposing hidden agendas, crimes and scandalous underground activity. Will it be shocking? Absolutely. Picking up the pieces could take a while, but with no-nonsense fixed sign energy (Taurus and Scorpio) helming the operative, these eclipses force us to deal with the facts and devise solutions that may require rebuilding from ground zero.

Eclipse DATES & VISIBILITY

APR 30
4:28PM

Partial Solar Eclipse in Taurus (10°28)
> *Visible in:*
> South/West South America,
> Pacific, Atlantic, Antarctica

MAY 16
12:14AM

Total Lunar Eclipse in Scorpio (25°18)
> *Visible in:*
> South/West Europe, South/West
> Asia, Africa, much of North America,
> South America, Pacific, Atlantic, Indian
> Ocean, Antarctica

OCT 25
6:49AM

Partial Solar Eclipse in Scorpio (2°00)
> *Visible in:*
> Europe, South/West Asia,
> North/East Africa, Atlantic

NOV 8
6:02AM

Total Lunar Eclipse in Taurus (16°01)
> *Visible in:*
> North/East Europe, Asia,
> Australia, North America, much of
> South America, Pacific, Atlantic,
> Indian Ocean, Arctic, Antarctica

times listed are Eastern US Time Zone

MERCURY

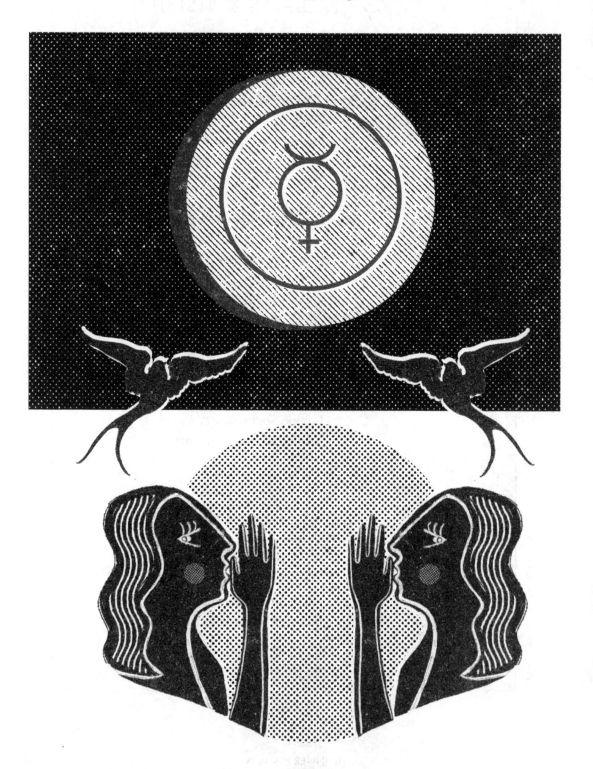

MERCURY IN ASTROLOGY

Messenger Mercury is the ruler of information, communication and our intellectual processes. The closest planet to the Sun, Mercury orbits through each zodiac sign for approximately three weeks. These cycles shape our cultural interests. From the topics we're buzzing about to the ways we communicate, whatever sign Mercury is occupying plays a role. Each year, Mercury turns retrograde for three cycles, appearing to travel backward through the zodiac. During these reverse commutes, it lingers in one or two signs for approximately ten weeks. While the scrambled signals can be agonizing, we have a chance to dive into deeper discourse. People from the past may reappear, like old friends, estranged relatives and exes with unfinished business.

MERCURY IN 2022

Mercury begins and ends the year in Capricorn, the eldest earth sign and ruler of time-honored wisdom. In a year chock full of ethereal magic and interstellar developments, the messenger planet reminds us to keep Earth (our home planet) at at the forefront of our thoughts. What impact will our new ideas have on the environment? Issues of sustainability and eco-responsibility remain top priority. With Mercury's localized focus, changing systems at the neighborhood and community level can have a major worldwide impact.

Planning WITH MERCURY

Active Mercury loves to help us map our daily schedules and routines. What will you be in the mood for at any given time during the year? If you want to spark up a bold conversation or try an adventurous activity, opt for cycles when Mercury is in a fire sign (Aries, Leo, Sagittarius). Need to hunker down to budget, research or tackle a household repair project? You're most likely to have patience for such mundane things while Mercury is in an earth sign (Taurus, Virgo, Capricorn). There's no better time for networking, hive-minding or collaborating than when Mercury is in a social air sign (Gemini, Libra, Aquarius). Creative brainstorming, processing heavy emotions and connecting to your inner circle of family and friends are best done while Mercury's in a water sign (Cancer, Scorpio, Pisces).

When Mercury turns retrograde three to four times each year, there's no need to panic! But pace yourself during these data-skewing, three-week cycles. Focus on all things with the prefix "re," such as revising, reviewing, redesigning and reconsidering. Pay closer attention to your inner world and get in touch with your thoughts, which signal all your feelings. Is it time to update certain beliefs? Mercury retrograde can help!

SEEING MERCURY *in the sky*

Get a glimpse of winged messenger
Mercury in the morning, low in the east
before sunrise, on these dates:

JAN 29 - MAR 24

MAY 31 - JUL 9

SEP 30 - OCT 26

Evening Mercury is visible low in the west
after sunset on these dates:

JAN 1-17

APR 11 - MAY 12

JUL 25 - SEP 17

NOV 25 - DEC 31

Because Mercury travels in such close connection to the Sun,
your natal Mercury sign will never be farther than one sign
away from your natal Sun sign. Find out what sign Mercury
was in when you were born with our cosmic calculator. Want
to learn more? Discover how the speedy planet shapes your
thought processes, systems and communication style with our
pocket course, The Mercury Code!

ASTROSTYLE.COM/MERCURY

MERCURY RETROGRADE IN 2022

Mercury has three full retrograde cycles in 2022. Each begins in an air sign and backs into an earth sign. Our social interactions and collaborative ventures may hit a sudden roadblock in these moments, sending us back to the drawing board to review plans. Don't be deterred by these forced pauses. When Mercury flips into reverse, it blesses us with an important timeout to review, revise, revamp (and all the other "re" words). While reversing through air signs, Mercury retrograde tightens up regulations around people and messaging. Is everyone pulling their weight? Are you all on the same page and using up-to-date technology? Have you properly stored and protected your data? When Mercury backs up into earth signs for the second half of each retrograde, put on a project manager's hat. Review budgets, timelines and environmental impact. Create guidelines so everyone knows where their limits lie.

Sidenote: In 2021, all the Mercury retrogrades took place in air signs, which rule the travel of ideas, information and cultural conversations. We're pointing to this signal-scrambling signature for the disinformation that continues to swirl around everything from vaccine facts to election results and beyond!

MERCURY *Retrogrades*

AQUARIUS &
CAPRICORN
JAN 14 - FEB 3

GEMINI &
TAURUS
MAY 10 - JUN 3

LIBRA &
VIRGO
SEP 9 - OCT 2

CAPRICORN
DEC 29 - JAN 20, 2023

Mercury THROUGH THE SIGNS IN 2022

CAPRICORN
DEC 13, 2021

AQUARIUS
JAN 2 (2:10AM) -JAN 14

AQUARIUS Rx
JAN 14 (6:41AM) - JAN 25

CAPRICORN Rx
JAN 25 (10:05PM) - FEB 3

CAPRICORN D
FEB 3 (11:13PM) - FEB 14

AQUARIUS
FEB 14 (4:54PM) - MAR 9

PISCES
MAR 9 (8:32PM) - MAR 27

ARIES
MAR 27 (3:44AM) - APR 10

TAURUS
APR 10 (10:09PM) - APR 29

GEMINI
APR 29 (6:23PM) - MAY 10

GEMINI Rx
MAY 10 (7:47AM) - MAY 22

TAURUS Rx
MAY 22 (9:15PM) - JUN 3

TAURUS D (26°09')
JUN 3 (4:00AM) - JUN 13

GEMINI
JUN 13 (11:27AM) - JUL 5

CANCER
JUL 5 (2:25AM) - JUL 19

LEO
JUL 19 (8:35AM) - AUG 4

VIRGO
AUG 4 (2:58AM) - AUG 25

LIBRA
AUG 25 (9:03PM) - SEP 9

LIBRA Rx
SEP 9 (11:38PM) - SEP 23

VIRGO Rx
SEP 23 (8:04AM) - OCT 2

VIRGO D
OCT 2 (5:07AM) - OCT 10

LIBRA
OCT 10 (7:51PM) - OCT 29

SCORPIO
OCT 29 (3:22PM) - NOV 17

SAGITTARIUS
NOV 17 (3:42AM) - DEC 6

CAPRICORN
DEC 6 (5:08PM) - DEC 29

CAPRICORN Rx
DEC 29 (4:32AM) - JAN 20

Rx = retrograde phase
D = resumes direct motion

All other dates
indicate direct motion

Times listed are when
Mercury transit begins,
Eastern US Time Zone

VENUS

VENUS IN ASTROLOGY

Venus is the planet of love, beauty and luxury, lending its decadent energy to every zodiac sign for three to five weeks each year. Who will we fall for...and how? Venus sets the global vibe, determining whether we'll pull tarot cards for each other in bed (Pisces) or conduct a relationship entirely by TikTok (Gemini). To wit, lions Jennifer Lopez and Ben Affleck revived their PDA-fueled "Bennifer 2.0" portmanteau when Venus visited exhibitionistic, unbridled Leo in 2021!

Every 18 months, Venus turns retrograde, which happens this time 'round from December 19, 2021, to January 29, 2022. During this cycle, Venus is changing its "on-screen" time from evening to morning. In the middle of the retrograde, Venus disappears from view as it makes an inferior conjunction to the Sun. This year, the rebirth of Venus happens on January 8, which might bring a major perspective shift around love!

Approximately two weeks later, Venus reappears, glittering in the sky at early dawn. The ancients thought Venus was two separate planets and thus has two Greek names: Phosphorus, "the bringer of light" for her morning star cycle, and Hesperos, "the star of the evening," for her evening phase.

Venus retrogrades are not always easy. They can exhume ghosts of relationships past...or provoke sudden ghostings just when connections are heating up. Ultimately, these cycles help us recalibrate our settings so that we can make better choices in the future. Better make that your New Year's resolution ASAP!

VENUS IN 2022

Just like Mercury, Venus bookends the year in the sign of
Capricorn, setting a serious tone for love in 2022. Are you sick of
playing around? Longing for a partner who can go the distance?
Tired of having that same old argument? That's great, but first,
how about a little introspection? Venus is retrograde as 2022 kicks
off—a cycle that begins on December 19, 2021, and lasts until
January 29, 2022. Backspinning Venus holds up the mirror. You
attract what you put out there. Your relationships are a reflection
of your own inner world. If you want to turn the tide, the change
starts with you...not them.

That's not to say you're stuck doing all the work! Overfunctioning
is another shadow expression of Venus retrograde in Capricorn.
That exhausting behavior tends to make others retreat and become
even lazier! The "givers" of the world may need to rein it in and
stop enabling their underfunctioning partners.

Fortunately, tenacious Venus in Capricorn loves a challenge.
You may feel incentivized to put in the effort and hopefully your
partner does, too. January could bring some uncomfortable
(or downright agonizing) tests for couples. But if you are both
committed and willing to push through, you can create a lasting
sense of security. Even if everything's copacetic on the surface,
check in: Are your life goals aligned? If not, how can you change
the structure of your relationship to support one another's
objectives? Maybe one of you takes on a second job while the
other goes to school for a semester or you pool resources to buy
land. You might hit the last wall and decide on a trial separation.

Whatever the case, you'd be wise to get everything out on the table before January 29. It helps that Venus lingers in Capricorn until March 6, giving everyone a chance to process the retrograde's grueling lessons.

Does it feel like you're perpetually single—and not exactly loving it? Upgrade your criteria. We all have a lusty animal living inside of us, longing for bodice-ripping passion. Nothing wrong with that! But if chasing "your type" has thusfar led to more heartache than heat, expand your palate. Add more sustainable "Capricorn" qualities to the 2022 menu such as reliability and financial security. Few people can maintain peak excitement levels 24/7. And those who boast this superpower are probably living unbalanced lives. Crash! Rather than giving in to bouts of romance addiction, try this: Commit yourself to a passion project in early 2022. Throw the same devotion you had for a Tinder thirst trap into making art, raising funds for a community-based organization or helping your sister plan her 40th birthday party. When you keep yourself busy and happy, the idea of coming home to a loving, consistent mate could suddenly become very appealing.

Do you have a "one that got away"? You may get a second chance with someone who drifted out of your life—or meet someone who has your old flame's hottest (and coldest) traits. Venus retrogrades can make you behave quite out of character. You might even act out a hidden fantasy, one that may (or may not) have been better left to the imagination. Do your best to keep a clear sense of boundaries because "going there" during Venus retrograde can wreak havoc on relationships.

P.S.: Venus was last retrograde from June 13 to July 25, 2020, in Gemini. Couples were separated by the pandemic (spawning the term "isolationship") or forced into a new form of exposure therapy by spending 24/7 together. Dating became a literal health risk. It was the scariest kind of spring fever imaginable.

But Venus' full circuit through Gemini (from April 3 to August 7, 2020) brought hidden blessings. This sapiosexual cycle favored intellectual stimulation and thought-provoking conversation—basically what flirting looked like in 2020. Gemini also rules mobile devices and written communication. During the months when texting and videosexting were the safest path to erotic fulfillment, it certainly helped to have Venus logged in to this digital domain. For couples, Venus retrograde in Gemini pushed difficult dialogues to the surface. Many fractured bonds hit the breaking point, which freed the lovelorn to find more fulfilling alliances. For other lovebirds, a healthy new communication style emerged.

VENUS RETROGRADE'S 8-YEAR CYCLES

Venus only visits one of five points on the zodiac wheel during its full retrograde cycle of 40 years. And every eight years, the love planet retrogrades back to the same position on the zodiac wheel (minus 2-3°). If you were to trace the outline of these "hotspots" they actually make the shape of a star. It's true! Even while retrograde, Venus still dazzles us with her attention to beauty and detail.

During these eight-year occurrences, old issues with love and money may arise, or even repeat themselves through a new set of circumstances. You may feel like you're going through a familiar test—or being similarly blessed, depending on what happens! Couples may revisit an unresolved sticking point or rediscover something they loved doing together. Unexpected expenses may crop up forcing you to reassess your values and find joy in delayed gratification.

Check your calendar: What was happening from December 21, 2013 to January 31, 2014? That was the last time Venus was retrograde in Capricorn and similar cycles may emerge at the beginning of 2022.

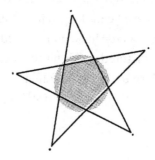

SPECIAL VENUS CONNECTIONS IN 2022

Venus meets up with her dance partner Mars twice in 2022, on February 16 in Capricorn and March 6 in Aquarius. These *paso dobles* come around every one to two years, so they aren't incredibly rare. However, the combined energy of seductive Venus and sex-god Mars cranks up the heat to legendary levels.

SEEING VENUS *in the sky*

Want to get a glimpse of the radiant love planet? Check out evening star Venus, Hesperos, before she moves too close to the Sun for us to observe.

JAN 1 - 3
DEC 3 - 31

Morning star Venus, Phosphorus, reappears before moving in sync with the Sun and disappearing from view.

JAN 15 - SEP 15

Due to Venus' proximity to the Sun, your natal Venus sign will never be farther than two signs away from your natal Sun sign. Find out what sign Venus was in when you were born with our cosmic calculator. Want to learn more? Discover how the sultry planet shapes your seductive powers, style and spending habits with our pocket course, The Venus Code!

ASTROSTYLE.COM/VENUS

Planning WITH VENUS

Know when to set the right mood—and how—with the power of Venus. Boredom is the enemy when this planet sashays through a fire sign (Aries, Leo, Sagittarius). Invite your love interest on a spontaneous adventure date, packed with surprises. Introduce yourself to someone who intrigues you. Then show that you can be equally dependable when Venus moves through responsible earth signs (Taurus, Virgo, Capricorn). Cook meals together, run errands for each other and make life more pleasant and easy all around. Give the nice ones a chance to woo you!

When Venus cruises through air signs (Gemini, Libra, Aquarius), get out for some play dates! Make plans with other couples or let friends fix you up for meet-cutes. Draw the drapes and cuddle for those intimate water sign Venus cycles (Cancer, Scorpio, Pisces), perfect for deepending your bonds.

© 2022 Astrostyle. All rights reserved.

Venus IN 2022

CAPRICORN Rx
DEC 19, 2021

CAPRICORN D
JAN 29, 3:46AM

AQUARIUS
MAR 6, 1:30AM

PISCES
APR 5, 11:18AM

ARIES
MAY 2, 12:10PM

TAURUS
MAY 28, 10:46AM

GEMINI
JUN 22, 8:34PM

CANCER
JUL 17, 9:32PM

LEO
AUG 11 2:30PM

VIRGO
SEP 5, 12:05AM

LIBRA
SEP 29, 3:49AM

SCORPIO
OCT 23, 3:52AM

SAGITTARIUS
NOV 16, 1:09AM

CAPRICORN
DEC 9, 10:54PM

Rx = retrograde phase
D = resumes direct motion

times listed are Eastern US Time Zone

THROUGH THE SIGNS

MARS

MARS IN ASTROLOGY

Mars is the last of the personal inner planets—the planets before Jupiter which are closest to the Sun. This might explain its protective, and sometimes combative, stance. Like a celestial sentry, Mars readies us to fight for what we hold dear. The red planet hangs out in a zodiac sign for approximately eight weeks, directing the global temperament and fighting style. Will we march peacefully, topple statues or sweet-talk the opposition? Tactics change depending on the sign Mars occupies. Lusty Mars is the forthright companion to seductive Venus and can bring out the "cosmic cave(wo)man" in us all. Our raw desire will be on display during certain Mars cycles, while other zodiac signs provoke a more discreet style of pursuit.

Every two years, Mars pivots retrograde, which keeps it locked in one or two signs for seven months. Mars will be retrograde in Gemini from October 30, 2022 to January 12, 2023.

MARS IN 2022

Mars begins the year in Sagittarius, making us all warriors for truth. But whose version of the story is the actual, factual one? The battle wages on as the red planet sets a zealous tone for 2022. Many of us are already exhausted by all the polarizing, disinformation and other data-skewing hype that's been raging for the past few years. Alas, don't get your hopes up: It probably won't go away any time soon. On August 20, Mars heads into dualistic, fast-talking Gemini for an extended seven-month circuit, which lasts until March 27, 2023. The reason for this protracted period? The red planet will be retrograde from October 30, 2022, to January 12, 2023. Forget about deciphering fact from fiction in the year's final quarter. The multi-ringed media circus will make heads spin with more fake news, conspiracy theories and righteous anger.

SEEING MARS *in the sky*

While the rooster crows in the barn, you can get a glimpse of the cocky red planet in the morning for most of 2022:

JAN 1 - DEC 8

Mars lights up the night like a beaming Christmas star from:

DEC 8 - 31

MARS RETROGRADE IN GEMINI

OCT 30 '22 - JAN 12 '23

When Mars flips into reverse every other year, it can turn us into unnecessary daredevils. Deprioritizing personal safety? Bad idea. This is *not* the time to take uncalculated risks. With Mars in mouthy Gemini, one nasty tweet or snarky comment can torch a bridge to the ground. Getting involved in gossip or trusting the wrong people could also wreak havoc. Distance yourself from shade throwers and nonstop complainers. Protecting your name—and your identity—is crucial during a Mars retrograde in Gemini. And since this zodiac sign rules mobile gadgets, be careful of where you log on using your phone, laptop or tablet! Strong passwords are not enough to save you from hackers. Check your location settings and delete any questionable apps.

Firebrand Mars retrograde can cause tempers to flare, so fights may erupt over the pettiest things. We all have bad days. Try to be extra compassionate when Gemini-ruled peers (friends, coworkers, neighbors, siblings) are not acting like their highest selves. As a rule of thumb, don't take their off-putting behavior personally! What can you do to de-escalate the battle rather than pouring gasoline on the fire?

Mental health challenges (ruled by Gemini) may flare up for people as a result of the pressures of day-to-day life. Talk therapy can be extremely helpful for processing the

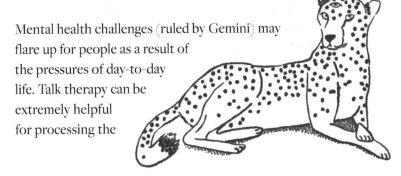

bottled-up thoughts that create anger, anxiety and insomnia. Any mindfulness and mentally soothing practices such as journaling and meditation can cool the fires of Mars retrograde in Gemini. Mars is independent, but Gemini is people-focused. Don't try to push through hard times alone! This backspin may force you to speak up and get the right support for your struggles.

Physically, you may experience a few energy slumps during the retrograde, and motivation to exercise can fall by the wayside. To stay fit, adopt Gemini's favorite life hack: the buddy system. There's never been a better time to invest in a personal trainer or enlist your workout-obsessed friend as your accountability buddy. Gemini rules neighborhood activities, so check out that hiking group or cycling club for motivation. Try a new eating schedule to see how it impacts your energy levels, whether you're giving intermittent fasting a go or making a pledge to stop skipping breakfast.

Mars can be lusty, but Gemini is the sign of platonic relationships. During the judgment-skewing retrograde, it might seem "harmless" to turn a friend into a booty-call or to temporarily bench your significant other in the friend zone. Reversing the terms will not be easy, so unless you're prepared to risk losing this person from your life, we don't suggest experimenting after October 30. Retrogrades bring back the past, and backspinning Mars can leave a trail of "sex with an ex" stories in its wake. A tantalizing but torturous past lover could resurface. While this may be what it takes to awaken your slumbering libido, the spark could turn into a dumpster fire before you pick out matching Christmas sweaters on Etsy.

By the same token, Mars in Gemini can inspire potent conversations about sex, erotic desire and even sex work. No shame in your game for wanting what you want. Whether you're exploring a kink, starting an Only Fans page or declaring yourself a proud, monogamous "vanilla," break free from peer pressure and claim your sexual truth.

On a more positive note, Mars' extended circuit through Gemini can give cooperative ventures wings. Put your focus on duos that are truly dynamic and get to work on any joint projects while Mars is direct in Gemini from August 20 to October 30. That way, you'll have a great buffer built up before the backspin. While Mars is in reverse, you can get tons of behind-the-scenes work done, especially anything Gemini-related such as writing, recording and researching.

Footnote: Renegade Mars was last retrograde in its home sign of Aries from September 9 to November 13, 2020. (The red planet had an extended circuit through fire sign Aries from July 27, 2020 until January 6, 2021.) With the brashness and anarchy of warrior Aries, rebellion became street theater. Civilians clashed with law enforcement throughout the entire Mars cycle. Crowds toppled statues of controversial historical figures and occupied city blocks in Seattle, then Portland. Gun-toting citizens attempted to obstruct registered voters from casting their ballots during the U.S. Presidential election and tempers generally flared. In the final hours of Mars in Aries (the tide-turning anaretic 29°), the U.S. Capitol was stormed by insurrectionists, many of whom were dressed in bizarrely flamboyant costumes.

SPECIAL MARS CONNECTIONS IN 2022

MARS SQUARES NEPTUNE
JAN 11, OCT 12, NOV 19

Three times in 2022, aggressive Mars throws blows at passive Neptune in Pisces, as the two planets form a challenging 90-degree square. It's hard to know who to trust during these suspicion-provoking aspects. Deceit may even come from a so-called ally. By the same token, try not to run away with your fears! The stories you tell yourself may be far from the truth.

Find out what sign Mars was in when you were born with our cosmic calculator. Want to learn more? Harness the red planet's fiercely ambitious and passion-stoking powers in our pocket course, The Mars Code!

ASTROSTYLE.COM/MARS

Planning WITH MARS

Where there's smoke there's fire, so why not build upon that heat? Daring, energetic Mars provides exothermic momentum throughout the year. While in fire signs (Aries, Leo, Sagittarius), Mars gives you the gumption to take a risk and initiate the action. Travel, play sports or get an entrepreneurial venture in motion. You may hit the gas too quickly, but at least stuck energy is moving! When the red planet is grounded in earth signs (Taurus, Virgo, Capricorn) get pumped about your routines. There's no better time to kick off a fitness regimen or take on an ambitious project at work. You'll stick it out and see results. While in air signs (Gemini, Libra, Aquarius), Mars makes you a networking wizard. You'll have the courage to slide into DMs and get into the VIP room. Just slow down long enough to make meaningful connections. When Mars plunges into the water signs (Cancer, Scorpio, Pisces), it brings its passion to our personal interactions. Starting a family, moving in together, getting engaged—you'll have the courage to take those "next steps." While things get a lot sultrier, the intensity levels can go nuclear. Careful not to overload yourself (or anyone else) with all those feelings!

Mars IN 2022

SAGITTARIUS
DEC 13, 2021

CAPRICORN
JAN 24 (7:35AM)

AQUARIUS
MAR 6 (1:23AM)

PISCES
APR 14 (11:06PM)

ARIES
MAY 24 (7:17PM)

TAURUS
JUL 5 (2:04AM)

GEMINI
AUG 20 (3:56AM)

GEMINI Rx
OCT 30 (9:26AM)

Rx = retrograde phase

Times listed are when Mars transit begins, Eastern US Time Zone

THROUGH THE SIGNS

THE *Outer* PLANETS

IN 2022

JUPITER
SATURN
URANUS
NEPTUNE
PLUTO

The outer planets include the gas giants—Jupiter, Saturn, Uranus and Neptune—plus icy, rocky Pluto. Due to their slower-moving orbit through the zodiac, they shape larger trends. Since outer planet lessons take more time to work through, they shift the trajectory of your life in a major way that's not always obvious at first. We've mapped out their movements in 2022 to help you plan your long-term goals.

JUPITER

JUPITER IN ASTROLOGY

Wise, wild Jupiter is the galactic gambler, the global nomad and the eternal seeker. The fastest spinning planet in the solar system, developments happen rapidly in this powerhouse's path! Jupiter's job is to push us out of our comfort zones and into uncharted territory—even if that means leaping before we look. The point is that we jump, as far as Jupiter's concerned. With each clumsy dismount we figure out how to do it better next time. It's all about failing faster and then getting up to try, try again.

Regardless of which zodiac sign Jupiter is orbiting through at any given time, there are bound to be exciting developments. Higher learning and philosophy fall under its reign. Here's where we collectively expand and elevate to the next level of human development! But how much is too much? Like a giant cosmic spotlight, Jupiter exposes flaws in the machinery and might even reveal a scandal. Issues of global importance are also spotlighted under Jupiter's watch and often dominate the news headlines when Jupiter has a moment.

JUPITER IN 2022

In 2022, the red-spotted planet splits its time between a pair of zodiac signs: dreamy, compassionate Pisces and high-octane, self-serving Aries. Talk about a surreal shift! Pisces is the final sign of the zodiac, akin to the elder state where we transition from earthbound beings to eternal souls. Aries is the first sign of the zodiac; the instinctual infant. Through the Aries lens, every experience is either a brand-new wonder or cause for a tantrum. If you feel like Benjamin Button this year, we wouldn't be surprised. Endings and beginnings will be profoundly magnified as Jupiter dances from the finish line to the starting line, then back again.

Times listed are when Jupiter transit begins, Eastern US Time Zone

PISCES
DEC 28, 2021
- MAY 10

ARIES
MAY 10 (7:22PM)
- OCT 28

PISCES
OCT 28 (1:10AM)
- DEC 20

ARIES
DEC 20 (9:32AM)
- MAY 16, 2023

JUPITER IN PISCES

Get your Zen moments in while you can! From December 28, 2021 to May 10, 2022, Jupiter floats down the mystical river of Pisces. Boundaries will be difficult to ascertain, much less uphold. Creatively and spiritually, this cycle is a renaissance, blessing you with a direct channel to the divine. Your subconscious will be active, enabling you to process deeper emotions like ancestral trauma and to metabolize any grief. Getting unblocked can happen at lightning speed, possibly with the support of a shaman, therapist or holistic healer, since Jupiter is in spiritual Pisces.

Hope or Delusion?

We experienced the bliss bubble of Jupiter transiting Pisces last summer, from May 13 to July 28, 2021. Not surprisingly, this coincided with the "golden hour" of vaccination hope. Masks came off, indoor seating resumed, we could hug again! But true to Jupiter in Pisces' illusory nature, the spell only lasted for a brief period. The Delta variant emerged, along with ramped up disinformation campaigns, skewing public perception of health initiatives.

Feelings, not facts, often determine "the truth" while Jupiter tours Pisces. Reality: What's that? People are quick to take a gamble on unsubstantiated claims and before they know it, they're caught up in a web of conspiracy theories. The concept of mass "emotional contagion" will continue to prove itself this year, as amplified feelings "go viral" through memes, urban legends and dubious narratives.

We already saw this happen in 2021. Distrust in government and the medical system spun into a perfect storm with the hysteria of Jupiter in Pisces. Politicians rallied behind anti-masking, comparing this preventative measure to the early stirrings of communism—despite the scientific evidence that masks prevent the spread of a disease that's transmitted by respiratory droplets. Hospitals (which are ruled by Pisces) filled their beds with intubated patients again, forcing hospitals to ration care and equipment.

Getting the facts straight won't be much easier this year. Until May 10, Jupiter in Pisces raises the volume on the cacophony once again. As astrologers, we're not going to dispel the notion that there are unseen forces at play in this universe. We wouldn't be writing this book otherwise! But is "the enemy" wielding a vaccine needle filled with heavy metals and a microchip meant to track your every move? Nope. (That's what the data-tracking mobile phone in your pocket is for!)

Swimming Through the Subconscious

Escapism will take many forms while Jupiter amplifies the Piscean proclivity to swim far, far away from reality. With the planet of travel in the sign that rules dreams and the subconscious, we may be inspired to journey deeper into our psyches than ever before. Whether processing past pain, ancestral trauma or anxiety from modern life, meditation, hypnotherapy and mindfulness techniques can bring new levels of serenity.

Graspng for a quick fix, like addictive prescription meds, can be a pitfall of this Jupiter phase. While pharmaceuticals are necessary for certain treatments, numbing out and avoiding facts won't make problems disappear. To tap the full potential of Jupiter in Pisces, pair the Rx with therapeutic healing. The brain has the ability to rewire itself, according to scientific studies on neuroplasticity. Traveling, playing video games and making music and art have all been shown to help people "rewrite" neural scripts—and are all activities that fall right into Jupiter in Pisces' wheelhouse.

That said, this year may bring profound developments in psychological healing via the use of psychedelics. Ketamine is approved in the United States as a treatment for depression and PTSD. Clinics are opening around the country, providing therapeutic infusions. Plant medicine ceremonies, which once required travel to South America, have been quietly happening in major cities around the world for years. With promises of healing past trauma, we expect more people to "sit in circle," journeying into other dimensions with ayahuasca, mushrooms, kambo or DMT. But will these ceremonies be led responsibly and in tune with the sacred, indigenous practices? With brash Jupiter helming the operative, be on the lookout for faux healers who are more "sham" than "shaman." Choose your guides carefully!

Art as Medicine

Cathartic creativity will be another effective "treatment" for depression, anxiety and isolation. When it gets too crazy out there, we can always rely on the power of our imaginations during these Jupiter cycles. With people isolated indoors due to the virus, reality-simulating digital experiences will be more in-demand than ever. Where will machine learning take VR and AI technologies in 2022? These markets could get even hotter with venturesome Jupiter in the mix.

Epic developments in art and music have often dovetailed with Jupiter's journeys through imaginative Pisces. In December 2009 (weeks before Jupiter cycled into Pisces), James Cameron's blockbuster *Avatar* brought groundbreaking advances in 3D technology to the screens. The movie *Titanic*, which treated us to the iceberg-melting on-screen romance between Leonardo DiCaprio and Kate Winslet, won the Oscar for Best Picture days after Jupiter flowed into Pisces in 1998.

Fantasy crept into our modern-day bedrooms that very same year with the premiere of Candace Bushnell's *Sex and the City* on HBO. Flash forward, and the message of female empowerment is right on time for 2022, as women's reproductive rights hang in the balance at this writing. Carrie, Charlotte and Miranda's 2021 return to the screen for *And Just Like That* may serve as a loud wakeup call that resounds into 2022. (Foot-ruling Pisces' fetish for shoes may also bring iconic Manolos back into fashion after two years of "quarantine chic." Hello, revenge dressing?)

Compassionate programming could rise exponentially in this era of amplified anxiety. Previous Jupiter in Pisces cycles brought us the first national broadcast of *The Oprah Winfrey Show* (1986) and the long-running soap opera *General Hospital* (1963).

Poetry slams first began near Jupiter's 1986 tour of Pisces and regained popularity on the indie circuit when the mighty planet circled back in 1998. To date, the hashtag #PoetsOfInstagram has over 3 million followers, fueled by talented writers like Rupi Kaur, who self-published her first book *Milk and Honey* and shared works on her feed. Live-out-loud Jupiter could bring the movement back to the microphone—hosted, perhaps, by Pisces inaugural poet Amanda Gorman.

Tide-Turning Breakthroughs?

Climate change deniers can no longer refute science. Polar ice caps are melting, sea levels are rising, weather patterns are shifting. Record floods and droughts have hit cities that had never formerly experienced such extremes. Will rapid-moving Jupiter amplify this trend while in Pisces, bringing clock-slowing breakthroughs...or both?

As galactic gambler Jupiter rolls the dice on the zodiac's Fish, we may become more enterprising about H2O. Currently, investors are looking to water as a viable commodity, much like oil or gold. It's a matter of supply and demand. Although 70% of the Earth is covered in water, 97% of it is saltwater, which cannot be utilized for much without treatment and processing. Pollution, rapid industrialization, the agricultural industry, the growing population—all of these contribute to an even greater scarcity of clean, fresh water. United Nations projections predict that more than half the world's population will live in highly water-stressed areas by 2030.

Enterprising Jupiter may pave the way for radical developments in desalination, the process of extracting the harmful hypersaline (super salty) brines to create safe drinking water. Current iterations of this treatment tend to be both expensive and environmentally harmful. But in the past year, researchers have been refining their processes.

Will water barons become the new Rockefellers? Blue-chip and small-cap companies alike are all getting in on these, er, liquid assets. Despite the environmental impacts of plastic waste, the bottled water industry continues to grow due to increased global demand. Water-based EFTs and mutual funds are now available, which may contain stocks from water utility companies, treatment plants and more.

JUPITER IN ARIES

Jupiter's shift from Pisces to Aries can be jolting, like waking from a deep meditation to the jarring blare of a fire truck's siren. As the veil of illusion (and delusion) lifts on May 10, your vision will sharpen like a hawk's. Whatever you've been ignoring will suddenly feel like a code red emergency that must be handled, stat! When Jupiter last cycled from Pisces into Aries in 2011, tragic tsunamis struck Japan, sweeping away 20,000 lives and triggering explosions at the Fukushima nuclear plant. We pray to never witness a tragedy like that again. Yet, you may feel on high-alert mid-year as the red-spotted planet keeps everyone on edge.

But, whoa! Although first instincts can be reliable guides, they don't provide the entire road map. Use them like wakeup calls, then take time to strategize. Controlling reactive urges won't be easy, as hotter heads prevail while Jupiter's in Aries—and may lead people to lash out in regrettable ways. Take your time before going into warp speed.

Feeling the Friction

Jupiter in Aries periods are often marked by friction, both in our personal lives and across international borders. Aries is the sign of the warrior and Jupiter amplifies whatever energy it touches. During the 1917 Jupiter in Aries cycle, the United States joined then-allied Britain, France and Russia to fight World War I. The start of World War II happened in 1939, during this same transit.

Sadly, violence may escalate while zealous Jupiter runs its midyear combat mission. Everyone will have an opinion, yet no one will be eager to back down. During this transit, fighting for our beliefs can feel like a "do or die" proposition. Dystopian frustration may evolve into a full-scale uprising, as was the case during the Arab Spring of 2010, which dovetailed with a Jupiter-in-Pisces-to-Aries transit.

Considering the easy access to automatic weapons and "ghost guns" (untraceable, Lego-like assembly weapons), safety concerns may mount. With militant factions forming around the world, ideological and religious disagreements are already escalating into rogue violence. In the U.S., armed civilians have been playing vigilante in alarming ways in recent years, attempting to intimidate voters at polling sites and storming the U.S. Capitol on January 6, 2021. Gun laws and 2nd Amendment rights will be hot ballot items for the 2022 Midterm Elections. In September of 2021, Texas passed a law allowing most citizens to openly carry guns without obtaining a permit or training. (This despite the statistic that shootings increased 14 percent the same year.) During the 1999 Jupiter in Aries cycle, the tragic Columbine High School massacre took place.

We aren't trying to scare you here! But we'd be remiss if we didn't add a precautionary measure for the middle of 2022. Sometimes, it's necessary to fight the good fight by being forewarned, especially when justice is being infringed upon. As principled Jupiter in Aries sounds the clarion call for personal power, "going to battle" may seem like the only option. And sometimes, it's essential, especially if human rights are in jeopardy. This year, make sure the cause you're fighting for is grounded in fact-based evidence. In some cases, what looks like a revolution might simply be a distraction that leads you further away from your power. Angry, disenfranchised masses may be easily manipulated by narcissistic extremists who are preying on their emotions. Practice self-defense, an Aries protective measure, by always thinking for yourself.

Holding Space for Peace

While it may be a study in contrast, Jupiter in Aries can underscore the need for peace. The first worldwide meditation occurred on August 16-17, 1987, during the Harmonic Convergence. As seven planets (in fire signs, including Jupiter at 29° Aries) assembled into a harmonious Grand Trine, people gathered at energy centers from Mount Shasta to the pyramids of Egypt to send up a collective "Om!"

Anything that soothes the psyche and helps you get centered is worth trying when Jupiter's blazing a fiery trail through Aries. Transcendental Meditation, which originated in India in the mid-1950s with Maharishi Mahesh Yogi, gained mass popularity while Jupiter was in Aries in 1975-76. Devotees of TM conducted a study in Washington D.C. in 1993. The goal was to see if collective meditation could reduce violent crime in the city. Although hard to prove directly, crime statistics did indeed drop during the time of this experiment. Practices like these may become more prevalent as Jupiter in Aries ratchets up fear and anxiety.

If there's friction in your household or among the people you gather with regularly, do your part to deescalate the drama. Prevention is even smarter: How can you dial down stress in your environment? Little things, like moving out clutter, plugging in an aromatherapy diffuser and playing calming music can make a world of difference. Or it might be time to bring in the big guns—and we do mean metaphorically, not literally. Skilled mediators and counselors can help restore peace when no one is willing to declare a ceasefire.

So if you must be a warrior, how about being a "warrior for love" or a "freedom fighter" who doesn't need to take up arms, unless you're (safely) encircling someone in a hug? While Jupiter blazed in Aries in

1987, Britain's Order of the Garter—the most exclusive and prestigious level of knighthood—opened to women for the first time in history. That's more reason to aim for the honorable side of Aries instead of the hot-headed one. Batman made his first appearance in D.C. Comics with Jupiter here in 1939.

Breaking into a New Beat

Blaze your trail! Expansive Jupiter in innovative Aries is a time for bold possibilities. Take those "wouldn't it be crazy if..." ideas for a test run. Let things get messy. That's how great discoveries are made, like penicillin, which was revealed to destroy staphylococcus cultures in researcher Alexander Fleming's petri dishes when Jupiter was in Aries in 1928.

Although the Jazz Age wasn't going full throttle until the 1920s, the style began evolving out of ragtime in 1916-17, while Jupiter was in Aries. The swinging, rhythmic Down Home Rag was recorded twice during that period, once by the instrumental quartet the Versatile Four, and again by the original composer Wilbur Sweatman.

Whatever your medium, tap the originating powers of Jupiter in Aries for a creative breakthrough. The trick? Letting yourself experiment wildly and make "mistakes" instead of diving in with an outcome in mind. When Jupiter cycled through Aries in 1975, DJ Grand Wizzard Theodore invented the record scratch by sheer accident. As the story goes, he tried to hold a spinning record in place so he could hear his mom talking—a happy "slip-up" that brought an essential element to the art of deejaying. ✱

SPECIAL JUPITER CONNECTIONS IN 2022

JUPITER-NEPTUNE CONJUNCTION
APR 12

Ascension, enlightenment, interdimensional travel! Profound spiritual experiences skyrocket us into elevated spaces on April 12. That day, barrier-breaking Jupiter syncs up with boundless Neptune, an event that only happens every 13 years. The sky knows no limits when these two freedom-lovers get in cahoots. And for the first time since March 17, 1856, their ecstatic dance takes place in idealistic Pisces (at 23°58'), the zodiac sign that is co-ruled by both Jupiter and Neptune!

Yes, this is a very big deal. It's one that's bound to shift the cultural landscape, as well as our internal terrain. As this cosmic duo goes to work on our Pisces-ruled subconscious, we can break free from self-imposed barriers. Bye, limiting beliefs, preconceived notions and debilitating fears. Hello, expanding compassion, near-psychic empathy and lucid dreams!

There couldn't be a better moment for launching into a meditation practice, doctor-approved cleanse, hydrotherapy treatment or psychotherapy. Anything that gets you "in the flow" is (liquid) gold. When Jupiter and Neptune last met in Pisces, the spiritualist movement was in its heyday. With Pisces ruling the afterlife and spirit realm, it's little surprise that hosting a seance was the "meditation circle" of the times. Nowadays, we read books that were channeled by the authors. Owning at least one divination card deck is de rigueur. Will we make contact with those beings aboard the Pentagon-disclosed UFO sightings? Thin the veil between life and death realities? The Jupiter-Neptune conjunction will have us deeply pondering the journey of our souls.

But get ready for some major duality! Pisces is symbolized by two fish swimming in opposing directions, and we'll feel that paradoxical power near April 12. Hospitals, institutions and jails (places we want to escape from) are as much under this sign's domain as retreat centers and sound baths. The #FreeBritney movement may resonate on far-reaching levels in 2022, as we push back against restrictive forces and seek enlightened new ways to support loved ones dealing with Pisces-ruled mental health challenges. Prisoners' rights may gain greater visibility in the media.

Tide-turning developments in the arts have occurred during Jupiter-Neptune transits. Pisces, which rules dance, film and music, is sure to conduct some fascinating orchestrations in 2022. The last cycle, in 1856, dovetailed with the Romantic era in classical music. Meanwhile, along the Mississippi Delta, (vastly unrecorded) blues music provided an outlet of expression for the enslaved African diaspora. The Jazz Age developed in full force in 1919-20, when Jupiter met Neptune in passionate Leo.

Invisible elements have the power to move us and we'll feel that profoundly near April 12. Near the 1856 conjunction, germ scientist (and skilled painter!) Louis Pasteur invented the process of pasteurization which affects the treatment of the Neptune-in-Pisces-ruled liquids we drink to this day.

Boron was "discovered" in California's Death Valley that same year. A crystal that dissolves in liquid, boron is a fundamental ingredient in everything from cleaning products to photo chemicals to pesticides. A lightweight boron steel-alloy has been used to build spaceships and diamond-tough cutting tools. Of course, many of these products are fingered as environmentally hazardous. Will this full-circle of Jupiter-Neptune conjunctions help us undo that damage while maintaining the technical strides from which we've benefitted? Scientists are hard at work on carbon-capture technologies that pull the "invisible" gases from the atmosphere. The limitless power of this transit supports groundbreaking discoveries, so we'll keep our fingers crossed. ✸

JUPITER RETROGRADE IN 2022

JUL 28 - NOV 23

Jupiter turns retrograde annually, napping in low-power mode for four months. This year, the backspin takes place from July 28 to November 23, starting in Aries, then backing into Pisces on October 28. As exciting as Jupiter's developments are, they can also be exhausting! The retrograde timeouts may come as a blessed relief, giving us a window to integrate all the rapid changes the red-spotted planet has us striving to achieve.

Let's be honest: Some of our gambling instincts do need to be tamed. While in reverse, Jupiter slows our rapid expansion before the sprawl becomes too stressful. This is a great time to go back to the drawing board to review goals, reconfigure plans, refine our efforts and make sure we are set up with all the right resources before we go back to the "build site."

Review your plans while Jupiter backspins through Aries from July 28 to October 28. Are you aligning with the right forces? Are your tactics getting results? You might just wave the white flag—or extend an olive branch—when the mighty planet retreats into forgiving Pisces on November 23. This kumbaya cycle offers a brief window for healing and dealing before Jupiter launches its second offensive in Aries starting December 20.

SEEING JUPITER *in the sky*

MORNING	MAR 19 - SEP 26
EVENING	JAN 1 - FEB 20; SEP 26 - DEC 31

ARE YOU HAVING A JUPITER RETURN?

People born with Jupiter at any degree of Pisces or Aries (0° – 8°03') will have an exact Jupiter Return this year—as the red-spotted planet transits back through the same sign (and degree) it was in when you were born. These year-long phases, which happen every 12-13 years, are marked by abundance, expansion and game-changing growth! Wanderlust may strike, leading you on a peripatetic quest to another corner of the world. Cross-cultural relations may give your life new dimension. Discovering your faith and doing spiritual work can inform an entrepreneurial or media venture. Follow this scholarly planet's prompting and enroll in schooling or an experiential self-development program. No matter the direction you choose, it's time to expand!

To find your natal Jupiter sign, cast a free birth chart at
ASTROSTYLE.COM/BIRTHCHART

Want to learn more? Discover how to unlock growth, good fortune and abundance in your chart with our pocket course, The Jupiter Code!

ASTROSTYLE.COM/JUPITER

SATURN

SATURN IN ASTROLOGY

Where have we become excessive? When is enough just...enough? The whistleblowing planet of integrity reveals where we need to set better boundaries. As a slower-moving outer planet, Saturn shapes longer trends. The ringed planet lurks in a single zodiac sign for 2.5 to 3 years and orbits through the entire zodiac in 29.5 years.

Taskmaster Saturn applauds perseverance and shines a light on where you need to keep on pushing! This is the planet that rules structured Capricorn, the zodiac's Sea Goat (a "WTF?!" creature if ever there was one). With its mermaid tail and two front legs, the Capricorn Goat makes an unwavering ascent to the top of the mountain for the win. Before Uranus was discovered by telescope in 1781, Saturn was also the ruler of futuristic, otherworldly Aquarius. Maybe that's why there's so much hidden magic to Saturn's process. One minute, you feel like Sisyphus rolling an interminable boulder up the hill. Then, your hustle yields a breakthrough and you're living the dream!

To find your natal Saturn sign, cast a free birth chart at
ASTROSTYLE.COM/BIRTHCHART

SATURN IN 2022

Come together, right now...but how? Structured Saturn is crossing the halfway point of its tour through Aquarius (March 21, 2020, to March 7, 2023), the sign of community, technology and activism. Society has undergone massive shifts since this cycle began nearly two years ago. And what a mindbender it's been! Saturn restricts; Aquarius seeks to connect. Can you see the fundamental conflict here? Social distancing is a solid "Saturn in Aquarius" concept. As the ringed planet orbits through the Water Bearer's realm for its final full year, we're learning to deal with the epic paradox of this transit.

Wanted: Strong Signals

Thankfully, innovative Aquarius excels at problem-solving. Over the past two years, we've maximized the power of "remote collaboration," thanks to Aquarian-ruled technology. It's hard to remember a time when Zoom wasn't an essential app on every phone and desktop, or when being "TikTok friends" wasn't a legitimate way to bond.

Videoconferencing apps kept the arts alive during quarantine, bringing concerts to our living rooms—including the very Aquarian "Celebrating America" concert of the 2021 U.S. Presidential Inauguration. This streamed event toed the line between inspirational celebration and protest art, as singers like Lady Gaga and Jennifer Lopez took indirect aim at the outgoing administration's divisive dominion.

We'll see massive digital developments this year, with Saturn logged in to tech-savvy Aquarius. The World Wide Web came to life during Saturn's 1993 transit through Aquarius, when the "www" source code was released by CERN, making the software free and available to anyone.

While many people worry that A.I. developments could make human labor obsolete, pragmatic Saturn cautions against spiraling into doomsday thinking. Nevertheless, the ringed planet wants us to hustle and bring our skills up to snuff. Train on the software, apps, social media and whatever technological advances are happening in your industry. In 2022, this won't be a luxury; it will be a necessary step in staying relevant.

Fly Me to the Moon

Cosmonaut Aquarius rules all things outer space, and this cycle has brought incredible developments in interstellar travel. When Saturn orbited through Aquarius back in 1962, *The Jetsons* premiered, ABC's first animated color TV series, about a family living in the space age. The Hanna-Barbera producers imagined an "impossible" world where people could talk to each other on video screens, food could be programmed to come from a machine and robots worked as household servants.

While we have yet to reverse-engineer Elroy Jetson's flying jetpack, this Saturn in Aquarius cycle has brought sweeping success in space travel. In 2021, Sir Richard Branson flew into suborbital space on the Virgin Galactic, then treated fellow oligarch Jeff Bezos to a ride. Their billionaire buddy Elon Musk brought some "power to the people" Aquarian vibes to the game, sending the first civilian-crewed rocket into space in September 2021! These journeys burst beyond the gravitational field of possibilities, setting a Saturnian foundation in place for future intergalactic expeditions.

#Popular

Saturn in communal Aquarius has spawned a new kind of popularity contest, one based more on algorithms than natural rhythms. Technology that was designed to bring people together has also polarized us. On sites like Instagram and TikTok, the race is on to be featured in the "Explore" or "For You" section—a surefire way to be seen by millions of new potential fans. However, getting there requires strategy, such as using popular hashtags like #KylieJenner or #featureme. While original content can break through, the lion's share of rewards goes to those who play the popularity game.

For content creators, this trend can be discouraging; and in some cases, insidious. Since Saturn entered Aquarius in 2020, astrology (which is ruled by the Water Bearer) has become popular clickbait. Sites that never cared about the craft before are churning out articles on full moon rituals and Saturn Returns, in a neverending effort to nail Google's keyword search game.

With ever-changing algorithms, social media has become increasingly complex. One day, Instagram Lives are favored by the app, the next the spoils go to anyone clever enough to make a 15-second impact on Reels. Boosting posts and buying ads is always rewarded with more views. This can be a disheartening experience for people who suddenly see a drop in engagement (and have zero inclination to ever learn TikTok's viral "Berries and Cream" dance!).

Divide and Cancel: Digital Segregation

Saturn's suppressive force has brought another conundrum for Aquarian revolutionaries. Cancel culture, while insidious, has been a powerful tool for activism. Massive entities have changed their policies as a result of a Twitter takedown. For example, after a viral groundswell of outrage on social media, Quaker finally removed the racially offensive imagery of Aunt Jemima and Uncle Ben from their staple products in 2020.

In other instances, it can be argued that the fear of getting cancelled has become a censoring force. Groupthink, which is the shadow of Saturn in Aquarius, might create public consensus—but it can also snuff out important dialogues. Trump's Twitter drags became so impactful that, to this day, politicians opt to stay on his good side—perhaps at their constituents' expense.

Machine learning has proven to be a double-edged sword since Saturn hit Aquarius. Bots study our online behaviors, recommending music, clothing and friends we "might also like." On the plus side, it speeds searches and connects us to like-minded people. Convenient? Sure, but there are Saturnian limitations to being delivered targeted data. For one thing, you may only see a limited range of opinions, products or worldviews, which can get really myopic. (If you're wondering how that rumor about vaccines containing microchips got started, well...now you know.)

Is it time to splinter off? Many people have already decamped to the "gated communities" of apps like Signal and Telegram that use end-to-end encryption. These apps may be the last bastion of digital privacy available in 2022. But are these virtual "secret societies" turning us into modern-day Masons? As people silo themselves off, they also drown out anyone who questions their ideologies. Until boundary-obsessed Saturn moves on to Pisces on March 7, 2023, people may continue to separate in cultish communities that are centered around a singular point of view.

Embracing Analog

But seriously Siri...does everything need to be upgraded to 5G? For some, the crush of apps, social media and rapidly developing technology has spurred a move in the extreme opposite direction. The CottageCore movement is one of many analog uprisings enjoying popularity while earthy Saturn puts the kibosh on airy, tech-obsessed Aquarius.

With a love for simplicity, home-baked, hand-sewn, woodsy wonderland everything, the CottageCore lifestyle bears the markings of a world prior to the Internet. It's a bit like living in a 1970s dollhouse. Or make that a tiny house...or a Scamp trailer with gingham curtains parked on a patch of land. High tea on the lawn replaces the high anxiety of modern life—a lovely escape.

Ironically, social media is largely responsible for the spread of this movement. Both Instagram and TikTok offer a rabbit hole of #CottageCore videos with upcycling projects, mushroom foraging tips, decorating with salvage and much, much more...trust us.

Going Nuclear?

The nuclear family is no longer considered the ideal option for many. According to Greek mythology, the Water Bearer (the symbol for Aquarius) was a young man named Ganymede who was the object of Zeus' affections. He served cups of H2O to the gods in exchange for eternal youth. While adulting is never overrated when wise, maturing Saturn's in town, communal living could extend the dorm-life vibes into old age—especially as ongoing COVID safety concerns group people into tight "pods" and "bubbles."

Pause for a Cause

The Great Pause of quarantined life began when Saturn entered Aquarius in March 2020. Time in close quarters, coupled with fears of the unknown, brought a radical mindset shift. As people re-evaluated their (Saturn-ruled) time, some restructured their entire lifestyles. A record number of city dwellers fled to the greener pastures of bedroom communities, creating the current housing bubble in suburban America.

This transit has been a consciousness-raising exercise for many. When Saturn first moved into Aquarius from March 21 to July 1, 2020, activism became the prime purpose for gatherings. Global demonstrations for Black Lives Matter and Brooklyn's historic Black Trans Lives Matter march brought people out of quarantine to participate in the worldwide protest against racial injustice and brutality at the hands of police Conversations about privilege have brought eye-opening talks into the public dialogue, popularizing books like, *Me and White Supremacy* by Layla Saad and *So You Want To Talk About Race* By Ijeoma Oluo.

Last year, three Saturn-Uranus squares intensified the clash between old-world values and an urgent call for change. Progressives and conservatives clashed and polarized in shocking ways, such as the January 6 insurrection at the U.S. Capitol, the spate of anti-abortion legislation and the Taliban's return to harsh rule in Afghanistan.

As Aquarius Bob Marley crooned, "Get up, stand up/Stand up for your rights." Optimistically, this could be achieved with the Water Bearer's high-minded ideals. But the battle for human rights could just as easily grow more violent in 2022, especially while Jupiter runs a combat mission through Aries, the sign of the warrior, from May 10 to October 28.

New Waves of Social Justice

Saturn in Aquarius has been historically tied to social justice movements. While Black Lives Matter has been in existence since 2013, the global groundswell of support began during Saturn's return to this sign in 2020 after the murder of George Floyd by Minneapolis police officer Derek Chauvin. "I Can't Breathe" became the rallying cry of the movement, words uttered as an excruciating plea for mercy, not only by Floyd, but also Elijah McClain and Eric Garner, African American men who died at the hands (and knees) of police. With suppressive Saturn in air sign Aquarius, this utterance takes on a chilling resonance, both in the death of Floyd and the suffocating effects of the coronavirus.

On March 6, 1991, one month after Saturn's move into Aquarius, four police officers were caught on video beating Rodney King, an African American resident of Los Angeles who was pulled over for speeding. Despite the visible evidence, a jury acquitted the officers. Following the trial, six days of riots broke out in L.A. in April and May of 1992. A month later, Rodney King gave an impromptu media conference and coined the ubiquitous (and very Saturn in Aquarian) phrase, "...can we all get along?"

On August 28, 1963, Dr. Martin Luther King Jr. delivered his "I Have a Dream" speech during the March on Washington for Jobs and Freedom at the Lincoln Memorial in Washington, D.C. Subsequently, the Civil Rights and Voting Rights acts were signed into law, passing after an 83-day filibuster in the U.S. Senate. When Saturn returned to Aquarius 29.5 years later, the Martin Luther King, Jr. Day federal holiday was observed in all 50 of the United States for the first time, on January 18, 1993.

In South Africa, a similar social justice pattern is traceable through Saturn's cycles in Aquarius. In June 1963, anti-apartheid revolutionary Nelson Mandela was sentenced to life in prison in South Africa. Thirty years later, during Saturn in Aquarius' 1993 tenure, Mandela was awarded the Nobel Peace Prize for laying the foundation which brought an end to apartheid and the birth of a new Democratic South Africa.

Will the activists' appeal bring justice in 2022? If history repeats itself, perhaps. But Saturn in Aquarius can be challenging for civil rights activism. Certainly following Saturn's demand for structure and a clear mission can make a difference.

Gender Rights Make Headlines

Saturn in Aquarius has historically brought developments for gender rights, too. During a prior cycle in 1993, Justice Ruth Bader Ginsburg took her oath of office as the second woman to serve in the U.S. Supreme Court. During her 27 years on the bench, she earned her title as The Great Dissenter for her fierce stance—not just for women's rights, but also for the rights of the LGBTQ+ community, undocumented immigrants and voters.

The Notorious RBG, as she was dubbed in recent years, lived through the first 2020 pass of Saturn in Aquarius. Justice Ginsburg's "most fervent" dying wish was that she would "not be replaced until a new president is installed." Despite this, hearings began within the week of her death for conservative-endorsed Justice Amy Coney Barrett, provoking since-legitimized fears about women's reproductive rights being threatened. And not without reason! During 2021's Saturn-Uranus squares, states like Texas and Mississippi took direct legislative action to overturn *Roe v. Wade* and take away women's constitutional rights to an abortion in the United States.

When Saturn was in Aquarius in 1963, President John F. Kennedy signed the U.S. Equal Pay Act into law to "prohibit discrimination on account of sex in the payment of wages by employers." Carol Moseley Braun, the first African American woman to be elected to the U.S. Senate, claimed her seat in November of 1993 when Saturn cycled back to Aquarius.

Gender rights activism continues to expand beyond the binary with Saturn in Aquarius. In June of 2020, a historic decision by the U.S. Supreme Court ruled 6-3 that the 1964 Civil Rights Act would hereby protect lesbian, gay and transgender employees from discrimination based on sex. Two conservative judges, including Justice Neil Gorsuch, who was appointed by Trump, joined the four liberal justices in this landmark decision.

In 2021, the Senate confirmed Dr. Rachel Levine as assistant secretary for health in the Department of Health and Human Services. Levine is the first openly transgender federal official to be confirmed by the Senate, making this a historic vote.

Keeping Hope Alive

Aquarius is the sign of hopes and dreams, but with dour Saturn dashing everything, it's been harder to visualize a future where anything is possible. Not only has the pandemic cast a long shadow, but the inconvenient truth of climate change (and the rapidly-shifting weather patterns) has thrown everything into a state of uncertainty.
Without a bright future to dream about, we deprive ourselves of one of the major drivers of human survival: the neurochemical dopamine. For the Gen Z crowd, this dream-crushing moment is a particularly heart-wrenching entry into adulthood. This generation has already inherited a climate crisis and, in many countries, massive national debts. It's little wonder that studies are showing an ongoing increase in opioid use, drugs which flood the brain's reward circuit with (you guessed it) dopamine.

Clearly, we need our hits of dopamine, which, along with fueling our decadent urges, play a vital role in optimal mental function, movement and focus. Thankfully, there are ways to nourish dopamine that don't require a fentanyl prescription. Brain-boosting nootropics have become the latest, er, buzz, in performance enhancement, some of which amplify dopamine production. There's been an upward trend in the "natural" versions of these, like the amino acid L-theanine that's found in green tea and reishi mushrooms. Legal shrooms, like chaga, reishi and ashwagandha are also making headlines for their adaptogenic (psychologically stabilizing) properties. ✺

SPECIAL SATURN CONNECTIONS IN 2022

MARS TRINE SATURN
SEP 28, NOV 28

One foot on the gas, the other on the brakes? That's usually a recipe for a wreck, but not in the final quarter of 2022. As accelerator Mars in Gemini trines take-it-slow Saturn in scientific Aquarius, you could find the perfect pace for developments, then hit cruise control. But don't fall asleep at the wheel! While it's great to have systems in place, Mars will be retrograde during the second trine, on November 28. Pull over and check your GPS. Did you speed past an important stop? Back up and handle your business. This "minor oversight" could snowball into a huge delay if ignored. Tick off all of Saturn's boxes, getting paperwork signed, permits authorized, budgets approved. You'll be off to the races again when these planets click for their third and final trine on March 30, 2023!

SEEING SATURN *in the sky*

MORNING	FEB 22 - AUG 14
EVENING	JAN 1 - 19; AUG 14-DEC 31

SATURN RETROGRADE IN 2022

JUN 4 - OCT 23

Saturn turns retrograde annually for approximately four and a half months. These backspins may stall progress and shuttle you back to the drawing board to ensure that you're developing plans on a stable foundation—and with proper levels of integrity. While Saturn's in reverse, relying on empirical data is more important than ever. Knowing where boundaries lie is equally essential, and you could learn some tough lessons by dropping your guard during a retrograde. Read the directions and don the safety gear—before you make a move.

Lessons around time management and authority tend to arise during Saturn's backspin. These forced timeouts can be a hidden blessing, provided you're willing to take the medicine. Sign up for a management training class, learn how to use project management software, whip your calendar into shape. With Saturn in sci-fi Aquarius in 2022, you could go back to the metaphoric lab for more experimenting before drawing a final hypothesis. No, this isn't the sexiest stuff, but think of it this way: When your obligations are in order, you free up time to play!

Want to learn more? Discover where you'll gain leadership, status and long-term success with our pocket course, The Saturn Code!

ASTROSTYLE.COM/SATURN

ARE YOU IN YOUR SATURN RETURN?

Every 29.5 years comes the Saturn return, a maturing rite of passage marking Saturn's homecoming to the sign it was in when you were born. The first return can happen between ages 27-30, depending on Saturn's degree in your chart. The planet's heavy-hitting energy will make itself known, bringing opportunities to quickly grow up and even take on powerful roles of authority.

Everyone born with Saturn in Aquarius will feel the impact of this cosmic rite of passage this year. In 2022, Saturn will travel between 11°54' and 25°14' Aquarius. Those with natal Saturn falling between those degrees will have their exact Saturn return at some time in 2022, which may feel like its peak intensity. Get ready for some eye-opening lessons in adulting. You may be called to play a more active role in shaping your community— or building one online—this year. Expect to hit some speedbumps around personal identity. Redefining yourself may feel like an act of rebellion and liberation rolled into one. Either way, a newer, truer you is emerging. Status-conscious Saturn can bring up "what will the neighbors think?" worries while also helping you build a stronger backbone when it comes to sticking up for your values.

People born in 1962, 1963 and parts of 1964 are having their second Saturn return this year. Those born in 1991, 1992 and parts of 1993 are having their inaugural Saturn return. Use our cosmic calculator to find out if you're experiencing this game-changing transit:

ASTROSTYLE.COM/COSMIC-CALCULATORS/SATURN-RETURN

URANUS

URANUS IN ASTROLOGY

Uranus takes 84 years to cycle through the zodiac, visiting each sign for approximately seven years. Because of its longer span, it's considered a generational planet, shaping the mindset of an entire age group. Since Uranus governs society and collective consciousness, its transits shape mass culture.

Technology and scientific developments are directed by Uranus, and its zodiac sign placement reveals where we'll see great innovations. As the planet of societal interactions, it directs everything from cultural trends to humanitarian efforts. The ruler of communal, innovative Aquarius, this side-spinning planet wants us to "get weird" in the most delightful ways! On the flipside, its disruptive influence can lead to dystopian thinking. Either way, it's here to help us embrace change—the only true constant in life.

To find your natal Uranus sign, cast a free birth chart at
ASTROSTYLE.COM/BIRTHCHART

URANUS IN 2022

On May 15, 2018, innovative Uranus, the planet of revolution, technology and rebellion, moved from firebrand Aries into conservative Taurus, entering the Bull's pen for the first time since 1942. Unconventional Uranus pushes for radical evolution and progress, while nostalgic Taurus upholds time-tested traditions, resisting change at every turn. This cycle, which lasts until April 26, 2026, has proven polarizing already.

Uranus only visits each zodiac sign every 84 years, electrifying the airwaves for about eight years and disrupting the status quo. Given the planet's abrupt nature, Uranus transits often announce themselves with a major event. The day Uranus transited into terrestrial Taurus, an asteroid the size of a city block nearly clipped our planet when it passed between the Earth and the moon. Luckily, it missed us!

In 2022, we reach the halfway point of Uranus' journey through Taurus, an ideal time to give ourselves a report card and correct course where needed.

Taurus' astrological rulership includes money, work, material objects, security, farming, the food supply, the arts and music. From cryptocurrency to sustainable living to 3D printouts from ultrasound scans, Uranus is giving this realm an extreme makeover. Since 2018, we've seen major shakeups in Taurus-ruled areas, which we'll continue to witness for another five years.

While a revolution in many of these systems is long overdue, a Uranus in Taurus transit is never comfortable. According to the principle of "essential dignities" in astrology, Uranus is in "fall" in Taurus—a weakened position since the energies are an awkward pairing. It's a simple energetic mismatch: Uranus governs the future while Taurus clings to the past.

Until 2026, we are tasked with resolving this planetary paradox: Can we create much-needed progress without erasing timeless traditions that still hold value and utility?

Take, for example, the statues of historical figures that were toppled and names removed from public spaces (parks, schools, buildings) in 2020-21. Many of these commemorated men owned slaves or committed acts that would be considered heinous human rights crimes today. The storming of the U.S. Capitol and the insurrection of January 6, 2021, was another vivid example, amplified by the impending square (90-degree angle of tension) between Uranus and Saturn (in progress-driven Aquarius). The explosive Saturn-Uranus showdown will be felt through March 2022.

Is It "My Way or the Highway"?

Can we find a middle ground while Uranus is in Taurus? Will we make room for critical thinking and "media literacy," or narrow the scope of information under the unconscious belief that ignorance is bliss? Unfortunately, much of the nuance that fosters connection and compassion across the aisle gets lost during this cycle. Combining Uranus' rebelliousness and the Taurus tendency to be "right" at all costs—is it any wonder the world is so polarized and divided?

Such is the exquisite grappling match between Uranus and Taurus. We're reminded not to throw the baby out with the bathwater, as the saying goes. Yet, we also have to acknowledge painful history, both in the context of its era and in step with where humanity has evolved today. The past and the future are all thrown together in a simmering stew, and that can be confusing at best. Since Uranus entered Taurus, people have dug in their heels. Revolts have taken on a bullish temperament, often one-sided and indignant.

Economic Makeovers Afoot

Taurus rules the economy, and the term "Bull Market" has been getting quite the Uranian makeover. Brexit, which was underway at the start of this cycle, has been a prelude to shakeups of Wall Street, banking and monetary systems around the world. The U.S. spent the entire last Uranus in Taurus transit climbing out of the Great Depression, which ended in 1941, right as Uranus departed from Taurus. President Roosevelt also signed the U.S. Social Security act, providing unemployment compensation and pensions for elderly citizens.

This time around, emergency government relief was needed to prevent a total economic meltdown during 2020's global shut-downs. Households under a certain income bracket received stimulus checks of $600 per person in two cycles. Businesses needing to cover operating and payroll costs were offered PPP (Paycheck Protection Program) loans, many of which were entirely forgiven. Stimulus checks and unemployment allocations of $600 per week found some folks earning more than they had from their former jobs. Meantime, cost-of-living data assembled by a team at MIT found that even a $15 minimum wage would not be enough for an average U.S. family of four to afford their basic expenses in 2021.

Interestingly, the Boston Tea Party took place during a previous Uranus in Taurus cycle, when demonstrators protested "taxation without representation." In 2021, Representative Alexandria Ocasio Cortez brought demonstration fashion to the Met Gala, wearing a white dress emblazoned with "Tax the Rich" in red letters and carrying a handbag bearing the same slogan. Whether or not this is the answer, we can expect more protests and upheaval around the Taurus topic of daily income and wages.

At this writing, a movement to bring Universal Basic Income (UBI) to the United States is gaining momentum and "platform economy" workers (from your DoorDash delivery person to Twitch streamers to rideshare drivers) are organizing in algorithm-age labor movements to protest unfair penalties and policies from their app-based incomes, which can be destroyed by a single bad review or developer update. This collective activism, coined Decentralized Collective Action (DCA) by the Harvard Business Review, is giving rise to worker-led coalitions that spread awareness of their mistreatment through social media, online forums and even through their competitors.

From Cashless Transactions to Cryptocurrency

Taurus rules money, and since technological Uranus landed here in 2018, dollars have gone digital. Not only has there been a coin shortage since 2020, but cashless technology has made it easy to pay with the tap of a smartphone or the scan of a QR code. Mobile apps like PayPal and Venmo now allow transactions to take place in cryptocurrency.

Speaking of crypto...though the first (genesis) block of Bitcoin was mined back on January 3, 2009, it took over a decade (along with Uranus entering Taurus and Jupiter's return to Capricorn on December 2, 2019) before any kind of mainstream mass adoption seemed conceivable.

As Bitcoin reached its all-time high of around $65,000 in 2021, it became evident that the technology of money would be disrupted by the innovation of cryptocurrency and blockchains. Stories of surprise Bitcoin millionaires stormed the Interwebs. And just as surprisingly, many institutional investors joined the blockchain revolution—some enthusiastically and others with grudging reluctance.

At this writing, Blackrock, the world's largest asset manager, has invested nearly $400 million in Bitcoin mining companies. As of February 2021, MicroStrategy has invested $2.171 billion, adding 90,000 Bitcoins to the company's balance sheet under CEO Michael Saylor's direction. In August 2021, JP Morgan CEO Jamie Dimon, a one-time Bitcoin skeptic who called the digital currency a fraud in 2017, quietly backpedaled and gave wealth management clients access to six newly created cryptocurrency funds. PayPal soon followed in November of 2020, allowing customers to buy, sell and hold crypto, including Bitcoin and Ethereum.

It's not just companies who are going all-in on Bitcoin. Countries are beginning to purchase for their treasuries, too. In 2021, El Salvador became the first nation in the world to buy Bitcoin and make the digital currency legal tender, doubtless initiating a domino effect of Bitcoin acquisition by other countries.

Unlike banks, which issue physical currency from a central authority, Bitcoin is entirely a virtual currency that operates on an observable, decentralized network, accessible to anyone with an internet connection. There is no central bank—or head banker—controlling Bitcoin with opaque accounting and questionable monetary policies. Transactions take place on a public database called a distributed ledger, which greatly reduces—or eliminates—the burden of a fee-charging middleman (in this case, the banks) to process, validate and authenticate transactions.

Because cryptocurrencies like Bitcoin have been created with limited and/or controlled supply capped by mathematical algorithms, they are more resistant to manipulation that erodes their purchasing power. Regardless of your risk appetite, technology has now reached an inarguable point of no return, disrupting, even toppling, our most deeply entrenched institutions of banking and "money."

Profits to the People

The peer-to-peer economy is thriving with equal-opportunity Uranus in down-to-earth Taurus. Companies centered on this model have helped keep people afloat during the instability of the past couple years. In February 2021, Airbnb reported that Hosts earned an impressive $1 billion during the pandemic. Etsy also thrived, bringing new business to makers and collectors while brick-and-mortar stores were shut down.

There are countless brokering apps like Airbnb now, which provide a safety net to individual sellers and consumers. If WFH has become a permanent way of life, you can turn your parked commuter vehicle into an income-generator by renting it out on an app like Turo. Road-trippers can test out #VanLife with Outdoorsy.com, which offers a fleet of RVs and kitted-out vans for vacationers who aren't ready to plunk down $80K for a Mercedes Sprinter (or devote every second of their spare time to installing a mini-kitchen and loft bed).

Automation has changed the in-store customer experience, too. With contactless checkout, former cashiers are now the IT department, fixing the register when technical difficulties arise—or checking I.D.s when an adult beverage is scanned. Interestingly, the last time Uranus visited Taurus it brought the invention of the first ATM machine and the physical shopping cart!

Gig Workers and Digital Nomads

Death to the cubicle? With indie-spirited Uranus in hardworking Taurus, the gig economy has grown and flourished. After 2020's work-from-home mandates, 11 million U.S. workers quit their jobs between April and June 2021, a trend now called The Great Resignation. Burnout and unhappiness were cited as key reasons for people leaving their corporate gigs. In the wake of this, companies are unrolling a flexible, hybrid workforce model, building teams comprised of both in-office and remote workers.

As A.I. replaces human labor, our relationship with money could also go through a massive shift. Out of necessity, people may adopt the barter system, or take up the "gift economy" that's practiced at festivals like Burning Man. In this model, no cash changes hands, and goods or services are offered from a spirit of generosity. Wanna start a commune, anyone?

The Rise of Populism and Dictatorship

The worst manifestations of Uranus in Taurus can be bigotry, stubbornness and warmongering. Adolf Hitler, a Taurus, seized power just as Uranus was ending its last transit of Aries, and retained his dictatorial grip through the 1930s, while Uranus was in Taurus. Mussolini also came into power during the last Uranus in Taurus transit, spreading fascism.

Extreme right-wing candidates have been on the rise again, spinning propaganda through social media, slanted news outlets, populist rallies and cyber hacking. In the past couple years, Uranus in Taurus has provoked violent disruptors, many using technology to mobilize and plot public acts of terrorism or to spread messages of hate. With the Taliban back in rule in Afghanistan and attacks on voter rights and women's reproductive health disrupting the United States, there's more than a little nervous energy in the air as we enter 2022.

From Virtual Reality to Mixed Reality

Uranus in sensory Taurus is busy altering the way we interact with the physical and digital worlds. Think your VR goggles are all that? Olfactory engineering is developing ways to include smell, touch and taste from afar. This Uranus phase is taking the IoT ("internet of things") beyond the "smart" house or driverless car. Perhaps we'll trade swiping and scrolling for computerless computing, as our digital devices become one with everyday household objects.

With Taurus ruling the throat, voice-activated devices will continue to make our lives easier, with a caveat. Siri, Alexa and Google Assistant are engaging you in a two-way conversation, recording every command you speak into the microphone. Since they know what music you listen to and what you put on your shopping lists, they can serve "suggestions" that many people find more creepy than convenient.

In September 2021, Tesla let owners request its Full Self-Driving software, which drew concern and criticism around the reliability of its safety features. Still, by the time Uranus finishes its transit through Taurus in April 2026, we anticipate roadways filled with automated vehicles—and who knows? Human drivers may be busy getting their pilot licenses so they can operate jetpacks and flying crafts!

Crypto-Art, NFTs & Music Rights: A Digital Revolution

With Uranus in aesthetic Taurus, art, literature and dance meet community activism and digital media (Uranus' domain). To wit: The streaming music business has exploded in the past few years, with paid subscriptions and on-demand services growing to a $5.9 billion market in the first half of 2021. TikTok has turned dancing into a mass cultural phenomenon, with the 15-second uploads to prove it.

Nowhere are Uranus' biometric fingerprints more evident than in the new genre of NFTs, which stands for Non-Fungible Tokens, a phenomenon disrupting the art-collection world. NFT technology allows a person to use their digital currency (at this writing, mostly Ethereum) to purchase ownership of a collectible digital asset, such as art, music or an audio file.

The craze for NFT art, also known as "crypto art," took hold in early 2021, when Christie's auction house sold a digital collage by artist Mike Winkelmann (AKA Beeple) for a jaw-dropping $69 million! The 41-year-old Wisconsin illustrator sparked an accidental frenzy when his piece, "Everydays: The First 5,000 Days," became the third-most expensive work ever sold by a living artist at an auction, carving out a $400 million-plus market by the end of 2021's first quarter.

So what makes these pieces, many of which are hackneyed and amateurish, so valuable? Digital rights. While most of these works can all be right-clicked and downloaded right to your desktop, an NFT purchase confers verified ownership of the piece. Essentially, it's like the difference between owning an original Van Gogh versus an Ikea print of "Starry Night." And because the buyer's ownership rights are recorded on the blockchain, the lucky NFT investor might resell a digital artwork for an exorbitant price, cashing in on the virtual gold rush of this new phenomenon.

While skeptics predict that the NFT bubble will burst, the craze may be just warming up. Crypto art can be purchased on sites like Rarible and Nifty Gateway, a site owned by the Winklevoss Twins (of Facebook fame and creators of the crypto exchange platform Gemini), where you can buy, sell and store digital assets, from art to collectibles to games such as CryptoKitties, where players can collect, "breed" and trade virtual kittens. With tech-savvy Uranus in "It's mine!" Taurus, the price of possession, whether virtual or real, has taken on a life of its own.

Farming & Food Technology

Taurus is an earth sign that governs sustenance and self-sufficiency. Farming and the food supply are already going through mega transitions with disruptive Uranus here. Can we implement solutions to global hunger—ones that don't involve factory farms and genetically modified seeds? At this writing, scientists are developing 3D and 4D "printed" food that's actually edible. Microloans and training programs in rural areas are helping small family farms succeed.

There are reasons to be hopeful. A movement has been evolving in recent years called *Drawdown,* which focuses on reversing climate change instead of mitigating the impacts. Emphasized in the plans are solutions like permaculture and regenerative agriculture, both which aim to heal land that's been damaged by things like monocropping and deforestation. Other strategies include reducing food waste and education and family planning which empowers women to make their own choices regarding childbearing.

Certain curveballs are tough to hack, however. Increasingly unpredictable weather patterns—droughts, fires, storms and flood-level rainfall—affect everything from crops to livestock. After COVID threw the farming industry into chaos, changing import/export capabilities shifted the laws of supply and demand. Economists are now debating the possibility of a "commodities supercycle," a decades-long stretch where commodities may trade above their former value.

Food growers are also turning to AgTech (agricultural technology) as an essential strategy. Drones now "walk the fields" to scout, map and survey the acreage. Their advanced cameras are equipped with sensors that can detect everything from moisture content to the health of plants. On the ground, internet-based sensors can provide data about soil quality, report on pest control and monitor the health and whereabouts of farm animals.

Farmers in India waged a nationwide strike on September 27, 2021, drawing support from Rihanna and climate activist Greta Thunberg. The reason for protest? Legislations were introduced a year prior that deregulated the agriculture sector and allowed growers to sell goods to independent markets. Protesters insist that the new policies will strip India's growers of the guaranteed minimum price for their goods, formerly determined by the regulated wholesale markets. The government claims that these new practices will modernize farming in India. Can the Taurean stand for workers' rights and the Uranian quest for modernization find a middle ground? Updating entrenched practices without decimating the workers is a challenge many industries will continue to face in 2022.

Keeping It Green

Meanwhile, countries around the world are pledging a 50% cut to carbon emissions by the year 2030—and aiming for Net Zero Carbon in 2050. It's a lofty goal, but an essential one if we are to keep the ocean temperatures from rising past the detrimental point of no return—a mere 1.5°C.

Replacing fossil fuels with renewable energies like wind and solar continues to be at the forefront of mitigating the climate crisis, but sadly, this won't be enough. Sequestering carbon emissions and capturing them from the atmosphere are also of dire importance. Solutions exist! Here's hoping Uranus in Taurus can unify us to take the action required to reverse the impact of climate change before it's too late.

SPECIAL URANUS CONNECTIONS IN 2022

URANUS CONJUNCT NORTH NODE IN TAURUS
JULY 26

If Mother Earth has a message for us, it's coming through with gale force on July 26. (Call it Hurricane Destiny, if you will.) Disruptive Uranus will make a rare connection to the lunar North Node at 18°40' Taurus. This chaotic connection could make the earth move under our feet—perhaps in the form of a literal earthquake. We hope that's not the case, but regardless, get ready for some tectonic shifts. What was stable may suddenly seem insecure. On a personal level, this conjunction wakes you up to places in your life that require a stronger foundation and savvier structure. Don't put off these core corrections. Thinking fast is a must!

The global economy could go through a sudden restructuring as a result of whatever happens near this day. (Could we see another black swan event like the one we predicted in our *2020 Horoscope* edition? It's possible.) "Power to the people" Uranus in Taurus demands better treatment for workers while the karmic North Node draws us toward innovative solutions. The supply chain, food sources and other basic Taurus-ruled sustenance may be affected in surprising ways. Some could be historically groundbreaking and a reason to celebrate. Progress is in the air, even if it comes with a measure of destruction or disruption near July 26.

URANUS RETROGRADE IN 2022

AUG 19, 2021 - JAN 18
AUG 24 - JAN 23, 2023

Like all of the outer planets, Uranus has an annual retrograde cycle that lasts for approximately five months each year. During these spells, progress can slow to a grinding halt. Technology, which is ruled by Uranus, can be the source of trouble. Devices break down and classified information stored online can be subject to security breaches. The best way to deal? Strengthen your passwords, then step back to reconnect to the analog world. With the metaphysical planet snoozing, developing mindfulness practices can help you stay alert and aware. Slow down and get conscious about your every move—and your impact! Your interest in community work and activism may blossom as you do. ✸

Want to learn more? Find out where you need freedom, innovation and adventure with our pocket course, The Uranus Code!

ASTROSTYLE.COM/URANUS

NEPTUNE

NEPTUNE IN ASTROLOGY

Because of its distance from the Sun, Neptune has a huge orbit to make. It takes 165 years to circle el Sol, spending an average of 15 years in each one of the zodiac signs. Every Neptune cycle shapes a generation, directing the music that moves us, the spiritual ideologies that resonate with mass culture and, the way we live out our dreams.

As the planet of unconditional love (and unconditional everything!), Neptune suspends logic. It allows us to truly dream as if anything were possible. Sometimes the visions are pure bliss; other times, they descend into nightmares. Limitlessness is the name of Neptune's game.

If romance requires a level of illusion, Neptune is the rose-tinted, soft-filter lens that lets us view the world in this way. As the ruler of watery, mutable Pisces, this planet pulls us under the sea where everything looks blurry and dark. A tumble down the rabbit hole might seem like a trip to Wonderland, but easy does it! Following Neptune's cues can spiral us into delusion and denial, as well as some dangerous addictions.

Through its trials, Neptune teaches us how to set boundaries. But first, it dissolves them, creating lessons in compassion and codependence alike. Does it all sound like a head trip? Yep, that's fantasy-agent Neptune. Try to enjoy the pretty colors while you spin this cosmic kaleidoscope.

To find your natal Neptune sign, cast a free birth chart at
ASTROSTYLE.COM/BIRTHCHART

NEPTUNE IN 2022

Let the spiritual awakening commence...or shall we say, continue. Neptune spends its twelfth of fifteen years in its home sign of Pisces, an epic cycle that spans from February 3, 2011 until January 27, 2026. This transit only occurs every 165 years, a banner time for art, spirituality and the emergence of esoteric information. Pisces is ruled by two fish swimming in opposite directions. With limitless Neptune sailing through these waters, we're ascending to new heights and achieving depth records. The highs and lows have been dizzying at times, bringing out the best and worst of humanity.

Spiritual or Religious?

During Neptune's previous transit through Pisces (1847-62), the Spiritualist movement was thriving in the United States and Europe. Centered in a belief that the departed could communicate with the living, seances and "sittings" brought mediumship into the mainstream. (Hello, spirit guides?) Connecting to ancestors has been a longtime practice for indigenous cultures around the world. But the Spiritualist Movement marked Western society's first open encounter with the esoteric realm since the Salem Witch trials—which, incidentally, occurred while Neptune was in Pisces from 1692-93. Metaphysical practices became a new sort of religion for many people who were disenfranchised by the iron grip of the church. Spiritualists were also active in the abolitionist and suffragist movements, true to the conscious, compassionate nature of Neptune in Pisces.

These cycles have brought a mix of both religious and spiritual developments. Buddhism was introduced to China during the Neptune in Pisces transit of 47 to 61AD, expanding into Japan when Neptune cycled back to home base from 538 to 552AD. Neptune's re-entry into Pisces in 2011 dovetailed with the end of a 5,126-year cycle of the Mayan calendar. Despite widespread Armageddon hype, the world didn't end on December 21, 2012. But the date did mark a symbolic "end of the world as we know it." Intuitive practices, like tarot, channeling and other divinations have been on the rise ever since. A 2017 Pew study found that 44% of Americans identified as "SBNR" (Spiritual but Not Religious).

Astrology may very well be the "neo-Spiritualism" of Neptune's 2011-26 cycle. The groundswell of interest has grown into a global obsession that reporters have compared to a modern-day religion. (Trust us, we've been interviewed for these articles!) Apps like Co-Star and Snapchat give readers easy access to their full charts, bringing talk of moon signs and Mars conjunctions into everyday conversations.

In Cuba, Santeria—which evolved from the African Yoruba religion—is flourishing after the ban on the practice was lifted in 1993. Modern devotees make ritual offerings (often flowers and cake) to the ancestors and orishas (deities). Witchcraft is also making a comeback. People around the world have reclaimed the title which was once ascribed to any woman who dared to be self-authorized or practice earth-based healing rather than cleave to oppressive, 17th-century rules. New moon circles, sound baths, channeling sessions and other intuitive practices are embraced on every social media platform and among people of all gender identities in 2022.

CGI seance, anyone? With this Neptune in Pisces cycle happening against the backdrop of technology, artificial intelligence is currently being developed that allows people to have simulated conversations with departed loved ones. Through machine learning, a bot captures mannerisms, personality traits and voice inflections by "studying" photos, recorded messages and videos of the "revived" person. And who can forget the surprise visit from the late (Pisces) Robert Kardashian, who appeared as a hologram at Kim's 40th birthday, a gift from then-husband Kanye West.

Altered States

Reality? We'd rather escape its harshness while Neptune cycles through Pisces. It's little surprise that psychedelic healing has been gaining popularity since 2011. In 2021, a six-week clinical study revealed that psilocybin, which is found in magic mushrooms, was a faster treatment for depression than the serotonin reuptake inhibitor, escitalopram, which is marketed as Lexapro.

Ayahuasca ceremonies, while still held as underground events, have gained notable popularity in recent years. The plant-based psychedelic is administered by shamans in a retreat-like setting (or sometimes a Brooklyn apartment). These guided, hours-long journeys can yield deep trances, prophetic visions, out-of-body experiences and profound illumination—grounded by Indigenous drumming and melodies. Sadly, Neptune in Pisces also brought the opioid crisis, a shadow of the healthcare industry, which is ruled in part by this planet. The deadliest drug crisis in U.S. history has been attributed to misinformation from pharmaceutical companies who assured the medical community that use of prescription oxycontin, fentanyl and other potent pain relievers would not lead to addiction. This is an example of the illusory, deceptive nature of Neptune in Pisces. Declared a public health crisis in 2017, opioid use continues to destroy lives around the world. CDC data shows that drug overdose deaths reached a record high in 2020, with 93,331 people perishing from their use.

Grappling with Grief and Trauma

Neptune in Pisces forces us to confront our pain, but it expands our ability to process subconscious triggers and ancient emotional blocks. This watery, compassionate cycle has opened up dialogues about empathy, highly sensitive people and fluidity in every arena.

The concept of "trauma-bonding" arose during this cycle. This attachment style confuses pain and passion for true love, making it hard for victims to leave their abusers. Given that Neptune is known for blurring boundaries and also rules imprisonment (including the psychological kind), it's no surprise that we're recognizing these subconscious traps.

Collectively, the pandemic has forced us to look mortality squarely in the eye. Neptune and Pisces are both associated with the dreamlike passage from life to death. Fear and panic of this "great unknown" are perhaps driving the bizarre behaviors that have been on bolder display since 2020. Coronavirus, which has proven to spread through respiratory droplets, is a watery Neptune-in-Pisces disease. And with this transit provoking fears of the invisible "boogeyman," paranoia and fear around vaccines (and masks) are equally in line with this cosmic phenomenon.

Water Is Life

Neptune is the god of the seas, and we've been doing damage to ours for years. Denial ain't "just a river" anymore; it's an increasingly polluted ocean system. In eerie synchronicity, the Tōhoku earthquake and tsunami, which devastated areas of Japan and set off explosions in the Fukushima nuclear plant, happened March 11, 2011, just one month after the watery planet moved into Pisces for the first time in 165 years.

"Water is life" became the rallying cry for activists of the Standing Rock Sioux tribe and the "Water Protectors" who joined the demonstrations to block the construction of the Dakota Access Pipeline in 2016-17. Native American groups say the planned route would desecrate sacred sites and could permanently pollute the reservation's drinking water supply from the Missouri River. In 2021, a federal judge allowed the $3.78 billion DAPL to continue building, despite an appeals court ruling that the pipeline is an "unlawful encroachment on federal land."

The distribution of fresh, clean water to places that don't have easy access to wells has become a prominent human rights topic. At the time of this writing, 1 billion people around the globe lack access to clean, potable water. Climate change has brought hurricanes and floods to some regions and extreme heat and drought to others. Meanwhile, polar ice caps continue to melt and rising temperatures are turning Antarctica green.

As greenhouse gas emissions make ocean waters warmer and more acidic, many marine species die off, unable to build their protective skeletons. Over the past 30 years, over 50% of the world's coral reefs have been destroyed, threatening a domino effect of disaster to the underwater food chain. Warming waters are already creating alarming coastal flooding and land loss. Plastic waste is washing up on shores after being ingested by fish. The environmental violations of our modern-day systems are more than enough to drown in.

Yet, the shadow expression of Neptune in Pisces has brought out climate change deniers, many who are well-funded enough to manipulate public perspectives. Sadly, with so many politicians funded by fossil-fuel companies and other environmentally damaging corporations, changing legislation around water pollution remains a deeply challenging goal.

Artistic Renaissance

The arts are blessed by this Neptune transit, which has brought fascinating developments in the Pisces-ruled areas of dance, film and music. Legendary Pisces masters include Michelangelo, Nina Simone and Alexander McQueen, all exemplifying the imaginative energy of both planet and sign.

Got goosebumps? This subconscious-activating Neptune in Pisces cycle brought us a bizarre new art-form, ASMR (Autonomous Sensory Meridian Response). Sounds like whispering, blowing into a microphone and crinkling paper are meant to bring a low-grade euphoria, stimulating a tingling sensation that travels from the scalp to the spine and across the skin.

The point of this exercise is to create relaxation—a nod to the meditative mojo of Neptune in Pisces. ASMR videos are their own genre of performance art. Nod off to sleep with an endorphin-and oxytocin-releasing YouTube of a simulated massage, or the "Dark & Relaxing Tapping & Scratching" video which has over 16 million views to date!

Dance falls under this cosmic realm, and choreographed moves are having a heyday! Apps like Dubsmasher and TikTok have given talented dancers (many still teens) a space to share their routines. In 2019, TikTok's top dancers-turned-influencers moved into The Hype House, an L.A. mansion-slash-dancer-dorm. There, they had free rein to goof off, film routines (often in the perfectly lit bathroom) and collect sponsorship deals, spawning a global dance culture.

Keara "Keke" Wilson, a 19-year-old from Ohio, ignited the Savage Challenge, inviting followers to mimic and record her choreographed routine. With people cooped up during the pandemic, the dance went viral, providing cathartic entertainment during quarantines. Celebrities from Jennifer Lopez to the "Savage" recording artist Megan Thee Stallion herself posted videos of themselves after mastering Wilson's moves.

What is your divine gift? Now is the time to let it emerge. With Neptune in Pisces until January 2027, creativity and compassion are forces that can heal the world.

SPECIAL NEPTUNE CONNECTIONS IN 2022

NEPTUNE-MARS SQUARES
JAN 11, OCT 12, NOV 19

The god of the seas goes to battle with the god of war three times in 2022, as the planets lock into challenging, 90-degree squares. If you've drifted too far from shore, Mars will send up an S.O.S. But with both planets in mutable signs, our compasses will point in five different directions. So much for consensus! Battles may erupt over religious and political ideologies, further dividing the public. As righteous anger takes the helm, people will attempt to drown each other out. These could be some of the most befuddling and mind-bending moments of the year!

On a positive note, the Mars-Neptune squares can soften hardcore stances. Coldhearted warmongering could yield to the spirit of humane compassion. Simultaneously, the "softies" out there may be forced to strengthen their backbones. Can we be tough and tender at once? This trio of squares can bring the best of both worlds into our consciousness.

JUPITER-NEPTUNE CONJUNCTION
APR 12
See page 63 "Special Jupiter Connections"

NEPTUNE RETROGRADE IN 2022

JUNE 28 - DECEMBER 3

Like the other outer planets, Neptune goes retrograde annually for about five months. These periods can be deeply introspective times—but ones that require extra reality checks! You may feel like retreating or escaping from the world, which can be a healing process or one that lures you back to a destructive habit. "Just this once" can become famous last words when Neptune's in reverse. Set up support systems so you don't give in to toxic temptations. With Neptune intensifying its boundary-dissolving effect in its home sign of Pisces, that advice goes double! ✹

Want to learn more? Invite fantasy, creativity and divine support into your life with our pocket course, The Neptune Code!

ASTROSTYLE.COM/NEPTUNE

PLUTO

PLUTO IN ASTROLOGY

What skeletons are rattling in our closets? Where do we go "unconscious," unable to see our role in a crisis? As the cosmic ruler of the underworld, Pluto's impulse is to conceal. Projection is one of this planet's favorite defense mechanisms. Whenever and wherever you're pointing the finger, Pluto is probably at play.

Because of its chaotic and unpredictable orbit, Pluto will hover in a single sign for between 12-20 years. As a result, it is one of the planets that shapes generational trends. Pluto can be a destroyer, tearing down what is begging to evolve, forcing us to rebuild from the ashes. As a result, great innovations have been born during these cycles. But they are generally accompanied by grief, crisis and loss as we release the outmoded past.

Pluto's extended cycles often begin with a massive, headline-generating event, but end with breakthroughs that transform an entire industry. Wealth may change hands as a result, resonant with Pluto's penchant for power plays.

To find your natal Pluto sign, cast a free birth chart at
ASTROSTYLE.COM/BIRTHCHART

PLUTO IN 2022

On November 27, 2008, Pluto, the (dwarf) planet of alchemical transformation, shifted into Capricorn, the ruler of governments, corporations, the economy and all things "patriarchal." Pluto only visits every zodiac sign once every 248 years, and it comes in like a wrecking ball. In mythology, Pluto rules the underworld, so there can also be a shadowy aspect to its dealings. It can bring out perverse or hidden scandals, showing us the shadow side of whatever it affects. But in the wake of all that, space is created for something new and improved to be born—like a phoenix rising from the ashes.

As Pluto winds down its tour of Capricorn, the backdoor dealings of the last 12 years are becoming very visible. In fact, 2022 is the final full year that this esoteric planet hovers in the Sea Goat's sphere, since it will dart into Aquarius from March 24 to June 11, 2023, giving us a brief preview of its forthcoming 20-year stint.

Another highly significant event is happening for the dwarf planet in 2022: The United States is having its Pluto return. When the "land of the free, home of the brave" was born—or declared independent—on July 4, 1776, Pluto was parked at 27°33' Capricorn. For the first time since then, Pluto will hit that exact same degree of Capricorn on February 21, 2022.

Pluto's mission? To destroy what's become outmoded and rebuild from the resilient remains. Talk about an extreme makeover! During the tiny powerhouse's last visit to Capricorn in the 1770s, America's Revolutionary War began and the U.S. Declaration of Independence was signed. Two and a half centuries later, global power structures have been rocked by the pandemic, leading many to question whether the end of the American empire (at least as we know it) is nigh. We will wait to hear Pluto's proclamation in early 2022.

Economic Crashes and Recoveries

There's no question about it: Capricorn-ruled arenas have been hit hard over the past decade-plus. When powermonger Pluto entered Capricorn back in 2008, the largest ever single-day stock market crash followed suit. After a slew of financial bailouts and mortgage lending mishaps, the demise of the Lehman Brothers, Fannie Mae and Freddie Mac ensued, and fiscal giant Merrill Lynch imploded. And lest we forget, there was also the low point of Bernie Madoff's arrest in December 2008 after his financially devastating Ponzi scheme was uncovered.

Soon after the 2008 market crash, the first non-Caucasian male U.S. President, Barack Obama, was inaugurated and a new economic stimulus plan was born. Markets slowly began to re-stabilize and the first block of Bitcoin, an innovative digital currency, debuted. In the years that followed, credit cards became chipped instead of magnetically stripped, while apps allowed for purchases through fingerprints and face recognition (stealthy Pluto's presence evident once again).

But nefarious Pluto doesn't free anyone from its grips without a fight. Pluto is the planet of extremes, and since entering Capricorn, the gap between the "haves" and "have nots" continues to widen. During the now famous Occupy Wall Street movement of 2011, demonstrators created an encampment in New York City's Zuccotti Park to protest social and economic inequality. Their slogan "We are the 99%" pointed to the deep divisions between the wealthiest one percent and the rest of the U.S. population.

This issue has hardly been mitigated since. A 2020 Oxfam report found that the world's 2,153 billionaires had more wealth than 4.6 billion people combined. The report also found that women are most impacted by the still-growing pay gap. According to this study, the 22 richest men in the world have more money than all of the women in Africa. Jeff Bezos, who was born with his Sun in the sign of the Sea Goat, amassed the bulk of his dizzying Amazon fortune during this transit. Currently, he is the richest person in the world, with Cancerian Elon Musk hot on his heels.

As with all prior Pluto cycles, any changes will be profound and far-reaching, leaving an indelible imprint. Pluto's next move—into Aquarius, the sign that rules society and groups—is sure to restructure our communities and networks. With structured Saturn in Aquarius from December 2020 to March 2023, prepare to see signs of what's to come.

A Rise in Authoritarian Rulership

In 2016—the halfway point of Pluto's transit through Capricorn—the U.S. almost broke the patriarchal spell by electing Hillary Clinton to be the first female president. Instead, a shocking turn of events vaulted Donald Trump into the role of Commander-in-Chief. His vitriolic manner, past scandals and elusive tax returns had the hallmarks of secretive Pluto in Capricorn written all over them.

The Plutonian deception continued after Joe Biden won the U.S. presidency in 2020 and Trump asserted that the election had been "stolen," demanding recounts and making personal calls to governors, while whipping up supporters around his Stop the Steal campaign. (This prompted Twitter and Facebook to take the unprecedented action of banning his account activity on their social media platforms.) Even while out of office, he holds powerful sway over the Republican party to date, as many chase his endorsement by subjugating facts and sworn civic duties in an effort to curry his favor, believing he has the capacity to make or break their careers.

Around the world, autocrats have unleashed a Plutonian wrath on their citizens. North Korea's dictator, Capricorn Kim Jong-un, has a long report card of human rights violations, considered among the worst in the world by watchdog organizations like Amnesty International. Famous for his military parades, he traded Twitter insults with Trump (remember "Little Rocket Man" and "dotard"?) then met Trump for a summit to discuss denuclearization, which appeared to be a bizarre lovefest. The art of the deal quickly fell apart during their second summit, however, which ended abruptly as Trump stormed off and Jong-un returned to North Korea empty-handed.

Syrian president Bashar al-Assad has committed atrocious war crimes during the ongoing civil war, which began in 2011. Allegations include gassing citizens and bombing hospitals and schools. In Hong Kong and Taiwan, pro-democracy governments are under increasing attack from mainland China's Communist Leader Xi Jinping (Gemini) whose authoritarian policies are a direct contradiction to the freedoms citizens have enjoyed.

Venezuela is currently under human rights watch due to the ruthless reign of Sagittarius Nicolas Maduro, who came into power in 2013. A bus driver turned trade-union leader who ran for President under the United Socialist Party of Venezuela, Maduro is now widely considered a dictator. Inheriting an economy plagued by hyperinflation and a legacy of profits and losses from the country's crude oil supply (a Pluto in Capricorn underground natural resource), Maduro has rigged elections and used lethal force against opposition to stay in power. All this while 5.4 million citizens have fled the country and hundreds of thousands are starving and without medical care.

Pluto's ruthless reform will be underway for the next two years, a call for the phoenix to rise among leadership before more scary regimes, like the recently empowered Taliban in Afghanistan, destroy the welfare and human rights of their people.

Tracking Past Pluto Cycles

We can track the alchemy of a full Pluto cycle by looking back to its transit through Sagittarius (1995-2008), the sign that rules publishing and global connections. At the onset of this cycle, magazines and newspapers were the most popular forms of journalism. (We eagerly awaited the monthly arrival of our *Sassy* and *TV Guide* subscriptions.)

But during this cycle, a little thing called the Internet was born, which completely metamorphosized the publishing industry. Free speech became accessible to anyone with a modem, and the world of blogging exploded. When swipe and tablet technologies were released to the consumer market a couple years later, Kindle readers and popular websites made many print titles obsolete—sad for publishers but happy news for the environment.

The dot-com bubble of 1998 to 2001 burst a few years into Pluto's transit through Sagittarius. Investors, thrilled at the prospect of this emerging industry, poured money into start-ups. It seemed like every day a fresh innovator was raking in cash from an IPO. Unfortunately, Internet speeds could not keep pace with the ideas, and many of these sites never launched. Soon, painfully slow dial-up technology upgraded to broadband and fiber optic cables, giving the Interwebs a second shot at success.

By the time Pluto moved on to Capricorn in 2008, the entire media industry was made over. We could talk in real time to anyone around the globe who had a cell phone and stable Wi-Fi. Self-publishing software allowed authors to thrive and the ubiquitous camera phone lifted the veil of mystery between cultures.

Is the COVID pandemic the Capricorn equivalent of the "dot-com crash" that happened midway through Pluto in Sagittarius? After all, Pluto is symbolized by a cycle of destroying, rebuilding and rising from the smoke and ashes.

Cryptocurrency, UBI and the Great Resignation: The Internet of the Economy

Since Pluto first entered Capricorn, we've predicted a total makeover of money, asking ourselves, "What will the Internet of the economy be?" As Pluto spends its last full year in the Sea Goat's sphere, it's revealed itself in the forms of cryptocurrency, the gig economy and the mass adoption of remote office work by corporate behemoths.

Pluto in Sagittarius birthed the Information Age, shaking up the media and travel industries while giving rise to the World Wide Web. Countries and cultures, formerly separated by distance, were suddenly connected through plutonic "invisible" forces, from dial-up internet to Skype to satellites that freed us from a tangle of telephone wires and exorbitant long-distance phone rates. By the time it departed, Pluto in international Sagittarius had birthed the new global citizen.

Now during Pluto's current transit of Capricorn, the mysterious novel coronavirus has plunged the world into a new kind of economic crisis, rocking all things ruled by this zodiac sign, from high-rise office buildings emptied by remote-work mandates to the birth of blockchain-based digital currencies. AI and robotic technology have also spurred a rise in automation—human labor replaced by machines, a trend that's certain to spike when Pluto moves into Aquarius from 2024-44.

In 2021, Bitcoin soared past the $65,000 mark, a fleet of vaccines was released and The Great Resignation was declared as one in four U.S. workers decided not to return to their office jobs in the fall of 2021. The year also brought government upheaval so out of control that the U.S. Capitol building was stormed by civilians on January 6, 2021. This insurrection drew comparisons to pre-Revolutionary War events that occurred during the prior Pluto in Capricorn transit, including the Boston Massacre. In both instances, five people were killed in the melees.

During Pluto's last spin through Capricorn in the 1700s, the American colonists created their first paper currency, the Continental, issuing it as a means to fight the tyranny of the British, who responded by counterfeiting the paper currency, thwarting the colonists' attempts to create an independent financial system. The ensuing chaos paved the road for the U.S. dollar to be minted in 1793, establishing our primary form of currency to date.

Some 250 years later, during Pluto's return to Capricorn, the meteoric rise of cryptocurrency is threatening that very monetary system established as a result of Pluto's last transit here. Governments are once again actively seeking ways to bring currency (this time, in digital form) back from the wild to be restored under their regulation.

Will Pluto in Capricorn end with some sort of new, standardized financial system? With stimulus checks and unemployment issued en masse during the pandemic, many Americans are getting behind a movement for Universal Basic Income, a government program that would issue a set amount of money to every U.S. citizen on a regular basis, eliminating the need for cumbersome social programs. Controversial and idealistic though it may seem for a nation as large (and divided) as the United States, UBI looms as a real possibility for the end of Pluto in Capricorn.

The disruption of the global supply chain and manufacturing (which we predicted in our *2020 Horoscope* would accompany the "black swan" event of Pluto's historic square to Saturn), continues to disrupt the economy, backing up container shipments, derailing industries and leading to "panic buying" of essentials like toilet paper and other staples.

At this writing in fall 2021, the bombshell disclosure of questionable offshore financial data dubbed "The Pandora Papers" has revealed the identities of more than 100 billionaires, 30 world leaders and 300 public officials who've been linked to an estimated $11.3 trillion held in hidden offshore corporate bank accounts in Vietnam, Belize, Seychelles, Singapore, Bahamas, Dubai, Panama, Switzerland and the Cayman Islands.

Major politicians, some of whom have called for transparency and the end of corruption, must now explain the likely malfeasance to burdened taxpayers and ordinary citizens in the midst of a global pandemic.

The trillions in repatriated offshore wealth could, for example, be used by national treasuries to help countries recover from Covid's catastrophic impact.

As Pluto completes its epic 248-year voyage through Capricorn, the impact of this financial disclosure will resound for years to come with trenchant calls for the swift removal of public figures and stricter international financial regulations.

We can't underestimate Pluto's pursuit of reformation at the deepest level, leaving no stone unturned in its quest. ✳

Want to learn more? Discover how Pluto can help you transform your deepest wounds and unlock alchemical powers with our pocket course, The Pluto Code!

ASTROSTYLE.COM/PLUTO

PLUTO RETROGRADE IN 2022

APR 29 - OCT 8

Like the other outer planets, Pluto spends approximately five months of each year retrograde. During these times, we will often feel relief from the planet's intensity. Retrogrades are times for introspection, and deep-diving Pluto's backspin can bring penetrating insights. While in Capricorn from 2008-2024, we are reconciling issues of financial disparity, developing new monetary systems and grappling with the impact of industry on the environment.

Transformational progress may be put on hold as we pause to process everything from pain to grief to revenge fantasies—without (thankfully) reacting to every emotion. While it may seem like nothing is changing on the surface during these retrogrades, when Pluto corrects course and flows forward for seven months, we can incorporate any necessary changes. Of course, this high-key planet doesn't do anything by half-measure. What flips after a Pluto retrograde can play out like "Extreme Makeover: Inner Self Edition." But when we emerge for the big reveal, strong and rejuvenated, we'll thank the god of the underworld for making us so damn irresistible and magnetic.

THE
LUNAR
NODES

THE LUNAR NODES IN ASTROLOGY

What's the next step in the evolution of the human race? What patterns must we break to collectively heal? The lunar nodes hold the keys to our destiny and ultimate life lessons. In astrology, life purpose is encoded in the North Node and South Node of the moon. The North Node represents our karmic paths and the lessons we came here to learn—or the "language" we are learning to speak. The South Node reveals the challenges and gifts we bring in from previous lifetimes.

Sitting directly opposite each other in the chart, the lunar nodes aren't planets, but rather mathematical points that fall in two opposite zodiac signs. They're determined by the points where the moon's orbit crosses the ecliptic—the apparent path the Sun makes around the earth. (We say "apparent" because, in reality, the earth is revolving around the Sun...but from our vantage point on the planet, it appears that the Sun is moving.) Generally, they fall in the same signs that the eclipses are in when you're born.

The nodes change signs every 18 to 19 months. Unlike the planets, they move backward through the zodiac, underscoring the idea that transformation is as much about reflecting and "unlearning" as it is about chasing new discoveries. People born within your same lunar node set (in the same or opposite configuration) are part of a shared soul group. You incarnated with them to learn the same lessons and might be each other's greatest allies and teachers in this lifetime.

THE LUNAR NODES IN 2022

NORTH NODE IN GEMINI & SOUTH NODE IN SAGITTARIUS
MAY 5, 2020 - JANUARY 18, 2022

NORTH NODE IN TAURUS & SOUTH NODE IN SCORPIO
JAN 18, 2022 - JUL 17, 2023

Karma directs us toward a new destiny starting this January 18, as the lunar nodes spin into a fresh pair of signs. After shaking up the Gemini-Sagittarius axis of (dis)information since May 5, 2020, the nodes back into Taurus (North) and Scorpio (South). Money, power and sex will be the focus of this next cycle, which wages on 'til July 17, 2023. How do we traverse our inner landscapes while also handling material world concerns? We may swing between the extremes of controlled stoicism and unbridled hedonism.

There's a popular saying that we are "spiritual beings having a human experience." As the earthbound Taurus North Node plays tug-o'-war with the mystical Scorpio South Node, we'll find ourselves seeking the elusive balance between "physical" and "metaphysical."

Warning: This paradox can be as mind-bending as the last nodal cycle, when the dualistic Gemini North Node questioned every truth that the Sagittarius South Node lobbed its way. Cold, hard facts (caught on video!) were often not enough evidence to shut down unfounded lies. As the karmic South Node slips back into secretive Scorpio, hackers, spies and other hidden forces could continue their attempts to manipulate the masses. The old-fashioned Taurus North Node could make a strong case for embracing analog living. Who wants to start an off-the-grid collective farm?

Truth Becomes Self-Evident Again

Truth? We're certain you can handle it...but can you recognize it? As 2022 begins, the lunar nodes wrap up a mind-bending tour across the Gemini-Sagittarius axis of information and communication. Since May 2020, this "powered by gaslighting" cycle pushed logic to its outer bounds. Facts became a flexible concept in a vicious arena of smear campaigns and schoolyard bullies. We have personally wondered aloud, "Has humanity reached a new low?"

Across the wheel, the contrarian Gemini North Node pointed out the paradox in everything. But in the process, it sowed the seeds of doubt to fracturing degrees. Coupled with pandemic-fueled fear, many people were thrown into a state of "hysterical blindness." Glaring scientific evidence took a backseat to disinformation campaigns, many funded by private-interest billionaires. Conspiracy theories made people doubt the very things they could observe.

After January 18, the media circus may die down. Gemini and Sagittarius rule communication, broadcasting and publishing—all industries that have gone through the karmic ringer since May 2020. From disputed election results to tamping down a global pandemic, "fake news" battled facts and obstructed progress. Simultaneously, attacks on journalists rose by 800% (from 50 to 443) in 2020 and continued to exceed prior norms by more than 200% in 2021.

With the nodes moving on to no-nonsense fixed signs, Taurus and Scorpio, people may be a little less obsessed with the 24/7 news cycle—and hopefully a lot savvier about where they source their information. (An astrologer can dream...) Still, we expect to see more private-interest funding pour into media platforms, perhaps incorporating social media in a more systematic way.

And while there's zero credibility to most of the conspiracy theories that cropped up during the Gemini-Sagittarius nodal cycle, some truths genuinely did stretch beyond prior bounds. In 2021, the Pentagon released a UFO report. Billionaires Richard Branson and Jeff Bezos flew into suborbital space. And thus, we must still remember to be curious, inquisitive and open to new possibilities—the true gift of the Gemini North Node.

A New Era in Globalism

When the South Node visits Sagittarius every 18.5 years, we must reckon with our impact on the not-so-lonely planet. Planes were grounded at the beginning of this nodal cycle when airlines limited flights due to the pandemic. COVID variants continue to rage worldwide, shuttering borders and impacting the supply chain. The tourism industry lost an estimated $4 trillion in 2020 and 2021.

In a spiritual sense, the South Node reveals our collective shadow. Behind every traveler's treasure trail across international marketplaces and mountaintops lies an inconvenient truth (Sagittarius buzzword) about the impact of tourism on cultures, ecosystems and climate change. Enlightenment-seekers' treks to remote areas have polluted water supplies and taxed waste systems, leaving locals to deal with the impact.

During the prior South Node in Sagittarius cycle, from October 2001 to April 2003, airports around the world adjusted regulations in the wake of the September 11 attacks. Twenty years later, we still remove our shoes at TSA checkpoints. In a frightening resonance, the Taliban once again mobilized during the Gemini-Sagittarius nodal cycle, turning back the clock on 20 years of human rights.

As the nodes move on to Taurus and Scorpio, a true "ego death" probably won't require a pilgrimage or a medicine ceremony. But will we swallow the bitter pill that our current model of consumption has had on the world at large? Can we reconcile our modern economic structure, which depends upon cheap, disposable plastics and customers returning to scoop the next limited-edition drop?

Hard to say, given that the fashion industry has proven to be one of the top environmental polluters along with energy and agriculture. Toxic textile dyes dumped into waterways destroy the drinking supply and poison marine life. Unsold collections that aren't dumped into landfills are incinerated each season, filling the air with greenhouse gases. Massive amounts of water are used for producing cotton, while viscose and rayon are major causes of deforestation.

Movements for "sustainable fashion" and "ethical production" could become en vogue in 2022, as more shoppers reach for products that are manufactured (or upcycled) in ways that respect both the environment and the workers. Sounds great, right? But to date, these options have been priced inaccessibly for people on modest incomes.

Another ethical challenge: Slower production will have an adverse impact on global communities that rely on the (often, fast) fashion industry for the meager wages that feed their families. Shifting this system will help the planet, but like many of the transformations that the Earth is begging for, will come with a high price for poor communities around the world.

Money Gets Funny

Will this nodal cycle bring a new cashless currency? Survival may depend on it. Earthy, practical Taurus covers our earned income—the type we collect after a hard day's work and budget for covering our living costs. Scorpio rules the "out of sight, out of mind" savings and investments that (hopefully) grow over time, such as stocks, real estate and cryptocurrency. What we earn and burn will be of critical importance in 2022. Beyond that, bartering and time banks (where hours of time are worked in exchange for goods) could create a new economic system.

But start saving up! Events of 2022 may necessitate some critical belt-tightening. The Great Depression began when the North Node moved into Taurus in 1929. The 1967 transit brought us the first ATM machine, which made it easier to access (and spend!) hard-earned cash. In 1983, a breathtaking seventy U.S. banks closed during this nodal transit.

Central banks have controlled the financial system for centuries, but during the globally disruptive Gemini-Sagittarius nodal cycle, cryptocurrency gave them a run for their fiat money. Everyday people, rather than a tiny elite, gained access to the possibility of creating generational wealth. Stories of surprise Bitcoin millionaires stormed the Interwebs. Though the first (genesis) block of Bitcoin was mined back on January 3, 2009, it took over a decade (along with Uranus entering Taurus and Jupiter's return to Capricorn) before any kind of mainstream mass adoption seemed conceivable.

Will this Taurus/Scorpio node cycle be the final run of digital currency's decentralization? Things could get interesting, especially in August

2022, when both tech-savvy revolutionizer Uranus and the North Node make an exact conjunction at 18° Taurus. Physically mined assets like silver and gold—which are ruled by rooted, earthy Taurus—could also become investment essentials over the next two years, since they tend to appreciate in value when stocks are in flux or falling.

So what makes cryptocurrency unique? Technology has now reached a point of development that can disrupt, even topple, the most deeply entrenched institution: Money. Unlike banks, which issue physical money from a central authority, crypto is virtual currency that operates on a decentralized network. Transactions take place on a database called a distributed ledger, which eliminates the need for a middleman (in this case, the banks) to process, validate and authenticate transactions.

Because most cryptocurrencies have a limited supply capped by mathematical algorithms, governments and central banks can't use inflation (e.g., the endless printing of money) to devalue its worth. However, this is where things can get tricky, particularly if governments and the wealthy simply buy up the supply.

As the 2020s wage on, it's clear the financial revolution can't be stopped, and the Taurus/Scorpio nodes will play a hand in this extreme makeover. At the very least, learning about cryptocurrency and how to invest in it is a savvy move in 2022.

Workers' Rights or Bye-Bye Little Guy?

During the Gemini-Sagittarius nodal cycle, nine-to-fivers got an unexpected taste of freedom due to work-from-home mandates. Flexible hours, no more commutes, no boss breathing down your neck 24/7? Remote work proved to be so appealing that 11.5 million people quit their jobs between April and June 2021, according to the U.S. Department of Labor; a wave that's now known as The Great Resignation.

This turnover has caused panic among companies, putting workers in a stronger position for negotiating favorable employment terms. With the North Node in hardworking Taurus, labor rights are certain to become a hotter topic in 2022. Will there finally be fair pay for the vastly undervalued workforce? If not, this could bring a wave of strikes, perhaps among underpaid school employees and overtaxed health care workers. Green industries may provide new jobs, but without proper compensation packages, benefits and hours, there is bound to be a glitch in the hiring system.

In New York City, bike delivery workers have been mobilizing after suffering a wave of violent robberies on the unlit Willis Avenue Bridge connecting Manhattan and The Bronx. These attacks were largely ignored by police and the companies they ride for, leaving them without the $2,000-plus e-bikes that they purchased independently in order to keep up with the crush of fast-moving orders (some for a single slice of cake) from apps like UberEATS and Door Dash. A grassroots network of delivery workers started setting up group rides across the bridge for protection. Within months, this evolved into Facebook pages and precinct rallies. A worker's rights group has formed, Los Deliveristas Unidos, and is now meeting with police and city officials to protect delivery workers and demand fair wages and treatment from the apps, such as the right to use the bathrooms of the restaurants where they are picking up orders. Other groups remain skeptical of police and politicians, and are organizing independently via Facebook, Telegram and WhatsApp.

There's a Catch-22 to everything, of course. To cover increased wages, mom-and-pop shops—which provide unique character to neighborhoods—may be forced to raise prices or cut back on employees. As customers seek bargains at big box stores, corporate goliaths may gobble up the market share—at least with offline, brick and mortar businesses. There's a ray of hope, however: Curated, one-of-a-kind treasures hold strong appeal during this nodal cycle. People may prefer shopping local and independent, which gets the Taurus North Node's full seal of approval.

Farming and Food Security

Developments in farming can evolve at a rapid pace with the North Node in earthy Taurus. Yet food distribution and security may remain a major global challenge in the wake of the pandemic and the travel challenges of the Gemini-Sagittarius nodal cycle. The 1987 Taurus-Scorpio nodes brought the tragic Ethiopian famine which claimed over a million lives. With droughts sweeping through the Western U.S. along with raging wildfires, wheat and corn crops dwindled, raising costs an estimated 11-12% in 2021.

Ample food is produced to feed the global population, but according to statistics, more than 811 million people still go hungry. Action Against Hunger reported that from 2019 to 2020, "The number of undernourished people (grew) by as many as 161 million, a crisis driven largely by conflict, climate change and the COVID-19 pandemic."

Precision agriculture, which uses high-tech sensors to locate ideal planting sites and improve crop yields, may be one of many tools supporting farmers as the Taurus North Node plows ahead. Meanwhile, the Scorpio South Node will underscore the need for water technologies like desalination and irrigation methods that don't drain the world's fresh water supply.

Local Politics Demand Attention

Local efforts can make a huge global impact when the North Node transits through Gemini. With the pandemic demanding community cooperation, neighbors had little choice but to work together for survival's sake. Nonetheless, social distancing was not (and is not) an easy concept for many people to swallow—particularly under the interactive influence of the Gemini North Node. Sadly, many celebratory gatherings turned into superspreader events.

New dialogues about racial and economic justice entered the global conversation in the wake of George Floyd's death, which occurred three weeks after the North Node moved into Gemini. Some communities banded together with food banks and Black Lives Matter marches. Others drew battle lines over racial differences, mask-wearing policies, vaccination status, voting rights...the list goes on.

There's no denying that local action shifted history over the past year-plus. In Georgia, gubernatorial candidate Stacy Abrams (who was born with Gemini-Sagittarius nodes) spearheaded a voter registration drive in late 2020. Her efforts served up a win for Joe Biden, the first Democratic presidential candidate to take the state since 1992 (which, incidentally, also took place when nodes were in Gemini-Sagittarius).

A year later in Afghanistan, the Taliban seized power by toppling one local government after another at lightning-fast speed. Chaos, fear and tragic deaths ensued at the (Sagittarius-ruled) Kabul airport as the U.S. attempted to evacuate troops and terrified Afghans clung to the sides of planes in an effort to flee from the country.

Grassroots efforts will continue to shift the political landscape as the boots-on-the-ground Bull charges to the helm. With the pivotal U.S. midterm elections happening in 2022, we expect to see ramped-up local campaigning on both sides of the aisle. As states push through restrictive voting bills (such as ending mail-in-ballots or early voting), access to the polls will require carpools, paid work leave and other unprecedented permissions.

With the South Node in sneaky Scorpio, the battle for power may sink to new underhanded lows. Apartheid began in South Africa during this transit in 1948. Yet, the disparate distribution of power may catalyze disenfranchised groups to mobilize and fight for transformation. The Black Panther Party for Self-Defense was founded by college students Bobby Seale and Huey P. Newton while the North Node was in Taurus in 1966.

Shaky Ground

As the first of the three earth signs, Taurus connects us to the ground under our feet. However, when the far-reaching North Node occupies this sign, maintaining stability can literally be an issue. During the last such cycle in 2004, the strongest earthquake in 40 years struck the coast of Sumatra, Indonesia. The 9.1 magnitude quake caused the floor of the Indian Ocean to rise suddenly, triggering 100-foot waves and killing over 100,000 people. Successive tsunamis caused death and devastation in Thailand, India, Sri Lanka and South Africa, taking 230,000 lives in their work. During this same 1985 nodal cycle, 9,000 people perished from an earthquake in Mexico City.

We pray that the Earth's tectonic plates remain unshifted during this transit. However, an ounce of prevention is always worth a pound of cure. Those who live on a fault line would be wise to get their earthquake preparedness up to snuff. Sites like ready.gov spell out instructions such as fastening bookcases to the floor and gathering supplies for an emergency kit. "Drop, cover and hold on!" are three lifesaving instructions to burn into your memory.

O, Give Me a Home

With home buying outpacing home building at this writing, we could enter the new year in a housing bubble. Real estate, which falls under investment-minded Scorpio's domain, will still be a hot commodity in 2022 as people seek both physical and fiscal security.

A similar housing shortage took place during the Taurus-Scorpio nodal cycle of 1948. Cheap, prefab post-war housing was built, tailored for young couples wishing to start a family. (Hello, Baby Boom.) With more people opting out of childbearing in 2022, we're unlikely to have another population spike. However, we may see more communal land sharing and collective housing in the year ahead—an ideal that sprang to life with the Israeli kibbutzim ("communal settlements") during this nodal cycle from 1909-10.

While fortune is bestowed upon lucky homeowners whose property values are on the rise, it's hardly good news to people already struggling to cover housing costs in the wake of the pandemic. More people may be unsheltered as a result of low supply and rising prices—but that's just the tip of the iceberg. While the South Node was in Sagittarius in 2021, the

U.S. Supreme Court rejected the moratorium on evictions. As of August 2021, hundreds of thousands of tenants were at risk of homelessness, exacerbating an already mounting issue nationwide and globally. These gut-wrenching economic disparities may finally force a global reckoning when the Nodes move into Taurus and Scorpio.

A Pause in the Space Race?

Rockets may be better left sitting on their launch pads once the North Node grounds itself in earthbound Taurus. Prior cycles have been a mixed bag for space travel. In 2003, the Space Shuttle Columbia disintegrated upon reentry, killing all seven astronauts on board. In 1966, Neil Armstrong and David Scott had to abort the Gemini 8 mission when their craft began to violently shake and tumble. The Surveyor 4 exploded just before landing on the moon one year later.

This is unlikely to slow billionaires Elon Musk and Richard Branson from their galactic quests. Both launched successful extraterrestrial excursions in 2021. Musk's Space X Crew Dragon made history on September 18, 2021, as the first-ever flight by (non-astronaut) tourists. Helmets off to those brave souls!

Grappling with Death

In Western culture, death is still largely a taboo topic, or one most people would rather avoid unless it's 100% necessary to discuss. Yet our mortality has loomed large since the pandemic began—and with apocalyptic warnings of a climate crisis, it's an ever-present guest in the collective psyche.

Enter the Scorpio South Node. When the karmic point traverses the sign of death, rebirth and transformation, we may find spiritual solace in facing this undeniable inevitability head on. Books on reincarnation may regain popularity. (Among our favorites are *Between Death and Life* by Dolores Cannon and *Many Lives, Many Masters* by Scorpio Brian Weiss.) Soul retrievals, channeling and past life regressions can help us make peace with the eternal aspects of our being.

During the last Scorpio South Node cycle in 2003, the world was dealing with the impact of the September 11 attacks, with increased fear of terrorism worldwide. That same year, a SARS outbreak affected 9,000 people in 15 countries, leading to 800 deaths. While it shared similar properties to the COVID-19 SARS strain, it was contained by prompt isolation and quarantine. (Thank you, orderly Taurus North Node, we could have used you in 2020...) As the North Node crossed from Gemini into Taurus in 1984, Dr. Robert Gallo and a team at the National Cancer Institute identified the retrovirus that caused AIDS and developed a diagnostic blood test to check for infection. Here's hoping that Scorpio South Node research uncovers a cure for the current strains of COVID before more variants emerge.

Even if we make peace with our eventual passage, the obsession with anti-aging is sure to swell—particularly with beauty-fixated Taurus crewing the North Node. Red light therapy is the latest rage, with claims to strengthen mitochondria, the energy creators within our cells. While clinical research is still underway, some evidence shows that RLT relieves inflammation and joint pain, promotes wound healing and smooths skin. (Sex isn't the only "red light district" we'll benefit from when Scorpio's in town for 2022!) The first cryogenically preserved man, Dr. James H. Bedford, was frozen during the 1967 Scorpio-Taurus nodal phase. He remains in his "cryocapsule" bath of liquid nitrogen to date!

Let's Talk About Sex, Sexuality & Reproduction

Sex is back on the menu in 2022! Good news for people still stuck in FODA (Fear of Dating Again) since the pandemic. In 2003, Beyoncé released her *Dangerously in Love* album, a fitting tribute to the Scorpio South Node if ever there were. Is it love, obsession or a mysteriously undefinable liaison? Figuring that out could be a fool's errand in 2022, but that won't stop you from spending hours dissecting every flashing gaze and emoji-laden text.

The free-spirited Summer of Love went down during this nodal transit in 1967, which also brought then-controversial miniskirts into fashion. Bikinis gained popularity during the prior Scorpio South Node in 1947. (So daring!) While we may still be wearing masks, skin is in for 2022. So is freedom. The Gay Rights Bill was signed into effect by NYC Mayor Ed Koch in 2004, the year that heralded the United States' first same-sex marriage. Relationship anarchy, a term used by ethical non-monogamists for years, could continue to shape the fluid landscape of sexual preferences and commitment configurations in 2022.

Protecting the rights of sex workers will continue to make headlines this year, echoing 2021's controversy around the website OnlyFans. A popular revenue stream for adult performers, the site announced that it would ban explicit sexual content in August of 2021—then reversed the decision after a massive backlash from users ensued.

Scorpio rules the reproductive system and the karmic South Node's position here will turn up the heat on the already-inflamed fight to protect a woman's right to choose. In the wake of Texas banning most abortions after six weeks—and placing a $10,000 bounty on the head of anyone "assisting" a woman seeking one—we expect massive movement around this issue in 2022. Just before the New Year, the U.S. Supreme Court will hear a case concerning Mississippi abortion law. This December 1, 2021, event (which has yet to happen at time of writing) is directly threatening to overturn *Roe v. Wade,* the historic ruling which protects a woman's constitutional right to control her reproductive rights.

The 1987 Scorpio South Node brought us ACT-UP, the AIDS Coalition to Unleash Power. This international, grassroots political group was established to "improve the lives of people with AIDS through direct action, medical research, treatment and advocacy" along with changing legislation and public policies. In the same vein, pro-choice citizens may team up to protect women's reproductive rights and access to safe abortions. (A global sex strike or vasectomy mandate, perhaps?)

Spies Are Us

Secrets, scandals and spyware—oh my! Investigative Scorpio nodal transits take us into deep cover, like the one in 1947 which dovetailed with the establishment of the CIA. In 1984, genetic fingerprinting was developed and has been in wide use by forensic scientists gathering criminal evidence ever since.

Jaw-dropping scandals collide with the Scorpio South Node as the rich and famous get busted for their nefarious behavior. In 2003, domestic doyenne Martha Stewart earned her mug shot and was jailed for insider trading. The notorious Iran-Contra Affair was exposed in a prior cycle, in 1984.

With the South Node lurking in Scorpio, privacy will be highly desired and hard to come by. Or should we say *harder* to come by. Home devices and cell phones are already tracking our every move via location settings and purchase records. Facebook, a known data-mining offender, was founded by Taurus Mark Zuckerberg during the 2004 Scorpio South Node transit.

And here's something that is truly #ScorpioProblems: Lifelike sex robots, which are gaining popularity on the unregulated market, are posing security concerns. Erotic preferences may not be the only data they're tracking. Hacked robots could be trained to choke or otherwise harm the customer. Yes, it really has come to this! ✸

2022

|

ARIES

WHAT'S IN THE STARS FOR

ARIES

THE ASTROTWINS

LOVE

This year marks a turning point you'll find both bittersweet and exhilarating. As you shed something you've outgrown—a limiting belief, an unhealthy dynamic or a relationship that's no longer a fit—you're creating space for a brand-new chapter in amour. Clarify your #LoveGoals while Venus is retrograde until January 29, then get into action. If you're making too many sacrifices or holding on to a fantasy, something's gotta give. Compromising your vision of love won't be an option when Jupiter swings into Aries and your autonomous first house from May 10 to October 28. Wipe the slate clean or engage your love interest in the fresh start you're aching for. Keep the rules a little flexible though! Lusty Mars (your ruler) takes a seven-month tour through variety-loving Gemini starting August 20, calling for more freedom and playtime. Free-spirited Rams could juggle multiple mates in the second half of the year.

CAREER & MONEY

New ventures, new techniques—Rams are breaking out of the box in 2022. Money moves could point you in unprecedented directions once the lunar nodes shift into Taurus and Scorpio (your financial axis) on January 18. With eclipses hitting these signs all year, stay on your toes and be ready to pivot at a moment's notice. Enterprising Jupiter makes its first visit to Aries since 2010-11! Raise your public profile by developing your passions while the horizon-broadening planet is in your sign from May 10 to October 28. Blaze trails and you could shape your industry, especially if you harness the power of community and technology to make your mark.

WELLNESS

Detox time! Tackle a bad habit right away. Quit smoking, clean up your diet, replace the endless coffee refills with hydrating beverages like green tea and aloe vera juice. Vibrant Jupiter returns to your sign on May 10, giving you a galactic glow-up. Raise your fitness game with adventure sports or a competitive challenge! With the South Node slinking into Scorpio on January 18, you can bring on the sexual healing! Balancing hormones may be the key to managing anxiety or sleep disruptions, so consider having your levels tested. Chiron, the "wounded healer" comet, spends its fifth of nine years in Aries (2018-27). This is a powerful cycle for discovering your own gifts as a healer. Simultaneously, you may be processing family trauma along with anger and grief you never fully metabolized. Pull back from triggering situations as needed. This is a great time to do the deep work with professional practitioners, both traditional and mystical.

FRIENDS & FAMILY

Serious Saturn is parked in mindful Aquarius and your communal eleventh house all year. Socialize with a purpose, whether you're expanding your consciousness or mobilizing for a cause. Copious amounts of "me time" are a must, as Jupiter drifts between Pisces and your solitary twelfth house and Aries, your self-focused first. Plan nostalgic reunions during the pensive Pisces cycle, which lasts until May 10 and picks up from October 28 to December 20. Connect to mentors, meaningful relatives and friends who can see straight into your soul. When Jupiter zips through Aries from May 10 to October 28, your lightning-fast mojo returns. Get with fast-paced friends who are pursuing big dreams! It won't be hard to identify them once your galactic guardian Mars zips into Gemini on August 20, supercharging your communicative, cooperative third house until March 25, 2023.

JUPITER IN PISCES

Clear the Decks

Jupiter in Pisces

December 28, 2021
to May 10, 2022

October 28 to
December 20, 2022

Lean back, Aries. Philosophical Jupiter spends the first five months of this year in Pisces and your twelfth house of rest, endings and healing—then closes it out again from October 28 to December 20. It's a dreamy, introspective cycle that comes around approximately every 12 years, and calls for a slower, more meditative pace. The fine art of surrender will be a practice to develop in 2022. Which would be lovely, except "surrender" is pretty much counterintuitive to your take-charge, fiery nature.

Nevertheless, get ready to tap into a mellower side of your nature. During these two Jupiter in Pisces circuits, you may feel out of sync with society, wondering, "What's the point of this madness?" Conversely, you might do what's typical during this Jupiter phase: try to swim upstream and force an outcome...until you realize that it's futile. The universe has a bigger plan, but you won't understand it unless you let go of your fixed vision about the way things should go.

Here's the silver lining, Ram. Once you stop fighting the current and opt to go with the flow, a sense of ease will wash over you. As our Aries friend (and author of the must-read *Boundary Boss*) Terri Cole advises, "When you feel like you're drowning, flip over and float." The path of least resistance is the one to take now!

True, this will feel abnormal for your high-octane, Type A sign. On-the-go Aries loves to keep multiple fires burning, with irons in each one of them. You don't wait for the opportunity to find you; you pull it out of thin air, with an awe-inspiring snap of your fingers. You already got a small taste of this in 2021, when Jupiter paddled through Pisces from May 13 to July 28. What were you ruminating on then? Was a relationship or situation in transition? If you didn't fully let go, you may in 2022.

> *With Jupiter in your sleepy twelfth house, you could feel more tired than usual. Honor your body's need for rest— and your mind's, too!*

"

Stillness is not the Aries forte, but with a little practice, it can be learned. No, you probably won't go meditate on a mountaintop. (Even if you tried, you'd wind up starting a wilderness school or foraging local medicinal plants to brew into a small batch holistic tincture for your future Etsy apothecary.) Spending more time in nature—especially near water—can be deeply healing in 2022.

Since no one ever earned a merit badge for busy work, stop and question your habitual actions. Are you moving with intention or just filling time to avoid boredom or anxiety? The universe has a gift-wrapped package of wisdom and insight to deliver in 2022. If you're rushing around, you won't be able to receive these offerings. View any speed bump as an opportunity, rather than an impediment. Until May 10 (and after October 28), embrace the Taoist practice of *wei wu wei*—which translates to "doing by not doing." This philosophy of non-action will prevent you from filling the space with noise and nonsense. Silence will allow something deeper to emerge.

With Jupiter in your sleepy twelfth house, you could feel more tired than usual. Honor your body's need for rest—and your mind's, too! Jupiter was last in Pisces from January 17 to June 6, 2010, and again from September 9, 2010 until January 22, 2011. Look back if you are able: Were you closing down one chapter of your life in preparation for another? You may see a recurring theme of transitions or letting go. For maximum benefits, treat 2022's two transitional Jupiter cycles like a celestial sabbatical. Even if you can't retreat from your life, guard your off-time like a hawk. Your need for solitude could ruffle feathers, but you can only explain so many times. Jupiter is the zodiac's voyager, but in sacrificial Pisces, guilt trips could derail you from deeper spiritual journeys that your soul is yearning for. Set clear boundaries, like, I'm not going to have the same conversation for the third time. Fight against fixing other people's feelings when they're upset with your choices. This is your life to live, Aries, not theirs!

Bottom line: You come first. And you'll probably need to be reminded of that, as codependent chords show up everywhere now. With eye-opening Jupiter in this martyr-prone zone, you'll soon see who's on Team Aries and who's just in it for what you can do for them. Sayonara, energy vampires! You may do some house cleaning of your inner circle in early 2022.

Rams are famous thought leaders, but this year, you could find that you have more questions than answers. Transform yourself into an open channel. Your inner guidance system is dialed up with Jupiter in your zone of spirituality and the subconscious. Sanctify your sleeping space, because dreams will be colorful and prophetic. Keep a journal on the nightstand to record any nocturnal symbols or messages.

Jupiter rules education and travel, and some Aries will study a healing modality or join a spiritual center. There's no better year for a wellness retreat, preferably near water—maybe with the addition of a service trip where you provide support to a community in need. For artists and healers, Jupiter in Pisces can inspire a creative or spiritual renaissance. Think of yourself as being "in the studio" or a teacher training. Invite the muse to hang out. Summon your guides. Ask those guardian angels for help and their handiwork will appear.

With the twelfth house's emphasis on healing and forgiveness, Jupiter in Pisces allows you to process lingering baggage. It's sad to release the memories or the hope you've invested. But there are "moths" in those garments: grudges, resentments, anger you've held onto for too long. Call it divine decluttering; because soon enough, you won't want any of your old stuff back. Clear out the cobwebs and make room for new experiences to flow your way.

Some part of your life may come to an end, and if you need space to mourn, take it now. Even if it involved a tough decision that was ultimately for the best, you still need to release any bottled-up emotions. Let yourself have a healthy outlet so you don't turn to vices and self-sabotaging habits. Traditional talk therapy is always helpful for Aries, but you may dabble in alternative treatments now. Past-life regression, plant medicine, energy work, hypnosis—all things "woo" can be incredible tools for resetting the deeper realms of your mind.

Got a bad habit to break? We all have addictions—if not to alcohol, food and cigarettes, then certainly to the demands of modern life. Jupiter in Pisces could be a fruitful time for recovery, or to change habits that don't feed your soul. Spending time in nature, especially near water, may be rejuvenating this year.

As for your love life? This pair of Jupiter in Pisces cycles could bring a soulmate—or at least, someone who appears to have that potential. Don't rush to label things, though. Jupiter in your illusion-spinning twelfth house might find you donning rose-colored glasses or falling for a charming lovebomber.

For some Rams, Jupiter in the twelfth house of endings could bring a long-overdue breakup, which will clear the way for a much better connection. But there's no skipping the healing process, which involves self-reflection and inner work. The point here is to break a toxic pattern, not to blindly repeat it with the next available candidate. (Romantic) history is doomed to repeat itself until you unearth the core issues.

Career-wise you could be plenty busy, but this is a time to dip out of the public eye and perfect your formula behind the scenes. Develop your vision "in the lab," then plan a splashy launch when Jupiter enters your sign for five and a half months on May 10. Until then, hang out in the chrysalis and let the caterpillar have time to develop into the butterfly you'll become.

As a rule, don't force anything, Aries! There will be moments when Jupiter in Pisces tests your patience and even brings you to your knees. You'll have to keep reminding yourself that it's temporary and transitional. It could be hard to keep the faith, but clarity is ahead. Sure, you may have a few dark nights of the soul as you wonder if you'll feel hopelessly lost forever. But some of your richest spiritual and emotional development can happen during this time. Allow others to support you, from friends and family to departed ancestors and your "guides." Maybe, just maybe, somebody else has a better plan for once. Invite their contributions. You don't have to do this all alone!

JUPITER MEETS NEPTUNE IN PISCES

Let It Flow

> **Jupiter meets Neptune in Pisces**
>
> April 12, 2022

A huge dose of healing could come near April 12. In a rare alignment, Jupiter will make an exact conjunction to sacred Neptune at 23°58' Pisces, opening up every one of your chakras—along with your emotional floodgates. You could heal your bond with a relative by being vulnerable and leaning on each other for support. Or, since the twelfth house rules endings, you may close a chapter for good. Try to do so with forgiveness in your heart. We're not suggesting you go into denial or invite an offender back into your universe. No! But can you see the painful lessons they "sponsored" as fodder for your spiritual growth? As tough as it may be to find gratitude for the situation, perhaps you'll discover a silver lining by acknowledging your own inner strength.

It may help to think of this transit as a cosmic cord-cutting ceremony. Release the past on every level! That includes letting go of your own guilt if you're the one who outgrew this situation. Whatever the case, buoyant Jupiter helps you move on to dreamier pastures—which could be anywhere thanks to Neptune's boundless influence. Beliefs that guided you may suddenly dissolve. Disorienting? Quite possibly. Be gentle with the process because integrating whatever arises near April 12 could take a few weeks...or possibly until the end of the year.

JUPITER IN ARIES

Reinvent Your Life

> **Jupiter in Aries**
>
> May 10 to
> October 28,2022
>
> December 20, 2022
> to May 16, 2023

And...you're back! On May 10, Jupiter will make its long-awaited homecoming to Aries, staying all the way until October 28 and then revisiting again from December 20 until May 16, 2023. This kicks off a brand-new 12-year chapter of your life—one that's filled with fresh experiences and reinventions. At first, Jupiter's entry into your sign feels disorienting. It's like stepping out of a dark cave and letting the sunlight hit your eyes. The brightness is dazzling, but you can't make out any shapes. You just know that a new day has dawned.

And so it has, Aries! If the first half of 2022 feels like an uphill climb—or just a lot of "hurry up and wait"—that changes on May 10. While Jupiter in Pisces was about allowing and surrendering, Jupiter in Aries does an empowered 180° turnabout. Switch back to make-it-happen mode—which is what Rams are all about—and leave your troubles in the rearview. You're the zodiac's accelerator, so it won't take long for you to make up any "lost time" from early 2022.

One Ram we know left a job in tech to pursue a love of photography during the last Jupiter in Pisces to Aries cycle. Another broke a spell of codependent relationships by working with a hypnotherapist while Jupiter was in Pisces. When Jupiter moved on to Aries, she met her lifelong plus-one, a Sagittarius who shared her love of travel and desire to keep separate residences in the name of romance. Since, her Instagram feed has been filled with artfully shot black-and-whites of their trips to Japan, Argentina and stateside road trips.

If you weathered tough times, it may be hard to trust that things are really changing for the better. They are, Ram. We know that Jupiter in Pisces may have pulled you into a scary undertow, but there were important lessons to learn. The sooner you can shake off a "victim" mindset, the better. We're not recommending you ignore your emotions because Jupiter is in your sign, of course. Instead, try reframing them as empowering mantras. For example, if Jupiter in Pisces had you waving the white flag and admitting, "I feel stuck," Jupiter in Aries helps you turn that into, "I'm ready to manifest the help I need."

The time you spent nurturing this from seed to fruit was well worth it. With your action-oriented first house alight, you could feel flooded with hope and optimism. And it won't take long before you're hatching big plans for the next major chapter of your life.

Fasten your seatbelt for this ride! As Jupiter barrels through your first house of fresh starts, risk-taking and initiative, all that stored-up energy transforms from potential to kinetic. Soon enough, the sacrifices and struggles you weathered make sense. They also pay off handsomely. If you've been hatching a grand plan behind the scenes, Jupiter in Aries is the perfect time for a buzzworthy launch or a big reveal. The cloak of invisibility you wore in early 2022 suddenly transforms into a technicolor dreamcoat. Welcome back! You're used to the glaring spotlight tracking your every move, so life may feel normal again.

The middle of 2022 is peak season for Aries performers and presenters. Whether you're shooting a music video or making six figures leading an online masterclass, bountiful Jupiter opens a treasure trove to Aries who brave the public eye between May 10 and October 28. "Healthy, wealthy and wise," are Jupiter's favorite words. If you've figured out a formula for achieving any (or all) of this trio of #goals, "edutainer" Jupiter could inspire you to create a patented formula—one that helps others and puts money in the bank. That's a win-win any Aries can get behind.

> **"**
>
> *If you've been hatching a grand plan behind the scenes, Jupiter in Aries is the perfect time for a buzzworthy launch or a big reveal.*
>
> **"**

Not sure what's next? Allow yourself to experiment with novel ideas and fresh opportunities, even if you don't fully hit the gas until Jupiter's second visit to Aries from December 20, 2022, to May 16, 2023. Don't pressure yourself to figure it all out. As J.R.R. Tolkien wrote, "Not all who wander are lost." Turn to a fresh page and set some bigger-than-ever intentions. Or make a resolution to start crossing big items off your bucket list. Then, give yourself a blessed couple months to metabolize these initiatives as Jupiter sinks back into Pisces for a final hurrah from October 28 to December 20.

VENUS RETROGRADE

Revise Your Love Goals

Venus in Capricorn

November 5, 2021
to March 6, 2022

**Venus Retrograde
in Capricorn**

December 19, 2021
to January 29, 2022

While you're famous for your independence and individualism, something few realize about you, Ram, is how deeply you value your close relationships. Whether friendships or romantic unions, you cherish the company of the people you connect with on a heart level and who share your deepest values. It's those bonds that mean the world to you. So what happens to those relationships when you start to drift apart in your beliefs and principles?

That question might become top of mind as 2022 begins. The planet of all relationships and values is retrograde in Capricorn and the most visible part of your chart from December 19, 2021, until January 29, 2022. Once upon a time you could just go with the flow and let your connections unfold organically. But, as they say, that was then and this is now.

With Venus hitting reverse gear in such a palpable chart section, you can't just let the relationship chips fall where they may. Not only is Venus on an extra-long sojourn through "kingmaker" Capricorn, but it's also in your tenth house of future planning and reputation. It's one thing to say you don't care what people think about your relationship choices, but if you're seeing someone who doesn't reflect well on you—from their style to their political views—you may have to walk back your public proclamation.

What's coming down the passion pike for you during this retrograde cycle could take many forms, and it certainly doesn't portend anything irreparable. Venus turns retrograde for six weeks every 18 months. While it can disrupt forward progress or delay fresh starts, this "reverse commute" has unique advantages. For one thing, you can tie up loose ends from the past and examine any issues (attachment-related or otherwise) that seem to crop up every time you get close to bonding on an intimate level.

Does this scenario sound familiar: Every time a dating prospect—or your S.O. or a business partner—get closer, you get claustrophobic and want to pull a disappearing act? Or anxiety flares up when you catch so much as a whiff of someone's dissatisfaction or "neglect"? The thing to remember is that this is normal human behavior—and there are ways to navigate it besides running for the nearest exit. That instinct is self-protective, but it comes from old wounding and (probably) not your current actual mindset. Learning how to respond to it in a positive, proactive way rather than reactively lashing out is what leads to greater emotional intelligence.

And whether it's retrograde or blasting full steam ahead, Venus in Capricorn and your future-oriented tenth house is a potent period for manifesting some of your greatest romantic dreams. When it's in forward motion, you can take action more easily. And during its rare reversals, you get a chance to refine (and change) what you want. So during this backspin, bravely challenge some long-standing notions about what will make you happy for the long run. Then, when Venus straightens out and powers forward in Capricorn until March 6, you can hit the gas with clarity and begin to align your life with what will bring you happiness.

Whatever your dream—from leading retreats to becoming a digital nomad—this annual Venus transit can intensify the desire to share that vision with your partner or potential love interests. In Capricorn, the love planet can lose a little of its quixotic romanticism and bring a stiff dose of reality to talks about the future. If you're mostly on the same page and just have a few details to hash out, this will help you with commitment. But should you be 180 degrees apart—on where to live or whether to have children—then Venus retrograde in this no-nonsense sector could be the deal breaker. What's essential now is that you stop kidding yourself and face the facts like a grownup. Venus is the diplomat of the

66

Venus in Capricorn and your future-oriented tenth house is a potent period for manifesting some of your greatest romantic dreams.

99

zodiac, so if there's any way in Hades to negotiate a compromise, it's the one to bring it.

Another advantage: In professional Capricorn, Venus helps you harmonize your career goals with your soulful ones. But rather than childishly insist you need to "have it all," see where you might be clinging unrealistically to an unviable ideal. Sometimes work is so demanding that you simply don't have time to pursue a new interest despite what you pay lip service to. On the other side of the equation, when you're in the throes of "new relationship energy" and trying to juggle the duties of daily life, you could drop a few balls. Should that threaten to become a problem, head it off at the pass and hire a coach or tap an accountability buddy.

Couples should anticipate any "wobbling" before it occurs over this month and a half. Get more dates on the weekly schedule, including one or two nights that are reserved for just the two of you—i.e., no work or family interruptions! And should you discover that your professional objectives are veering in opposite (or even less simpatico) directions or your schedules aren't aligning, don't just assume you've come to the end of the line. Book a few couple's counseling sessions to address this as well as other, perhaps unexpressed, issues. Moving past these roadblocks together can strengthen your bond more than you could have imagined.

Since retrogrades stir up the past, 2022 could start off especially nostalgic. Single? You might hear from—or reach out to—"the one that got away." If it was truly just a case of inopportune timing, Venus' backspin could offer the do-over you've prayed for. But take it slow and don't glamorize the past. Instead, talk through how things fell apart the last time around, owning your roles and discussing how you believe you've changed. And when Venus straightens out, you may just get the answer that's eluded you for so long.

LUNAR NODES IN TAURUS AND SCORPIO

Making Money Moves

> **Lunar Nodes in Taurus and Scorpio**
>
> January 18, 2022 to July 17, 2023

Passion is the primary driver for most of your decisions, Aries, but check in: What does your wallet have to say about that? Money does matter in the modern world. Even if your inner idealist dissents, personal economics will be a key decision driver for Rams in 2022.

The reason for this? On January 18, the lunar nodes are shifting into your money zones. Until July 17, 2023, the destiny-driven North Node will lumber through security-minded Taurus and your second house of fiscal foundations. Simultaneously, the karmic South Node will stir the pot in strategic Scorpio and your eighth house of merged resources and long-term wealth.

Material concerns will matter this year, in ways that perhaps they haven't for a while. Maybe you're planning for a baby, starting a business or your significant other is applying for grad school. As a result, the onus to provide shifts to you. Step up to the plate, Aries!

Steady work is solid work while the North Node is in Taurus. A day job can bring relief, settling your nerves about food, housing and college loans. Don't overthink it! Positions like these don't have to be your permanent future. But the grounded North Node in Taurus gives you a taste of stability that you possibly haven't had for a while. True, there may be some grunt work to deal with until your ship comes in, but if you can ride these winds of change, you might actually come out earning—and saving—more than before.

If you've sworn off the employee route, there are other options. Lock in steady clients if you're a business owner. Sign them up for 6-month contracts, for example. That way, you can plan ahead a little (a new muscle for some Aries to build) instead of constantly worrying about where the next check is coming from.

Bartering is another favorite for your innovative sign. Skills you've honed could be exchanged for housing or office access. One Aries we know used his savings to rent a multi-family home in Brooklyn, which he promptly turned into cooperative housing. Sharing the monthly bills isn't the only way this group saves money. Each roommate is in charge of a specific household duty, from kitchen management to IT. Unlike a lot of Aries, he was okay with communal space. But his clever idea can serve as inspiration for creative financing.

Or maybe, like March 23-born-Aries Edgar Kahn, you'll invent (or embrace) an alternative currency. A legal professor with a dedication to social equity, Kahn created Time Banks, a system based on service exchanges. Hierarchies do not exist in a time bank. One hour of work—no matter the job—equals one Time Bank credit. Value lies in the energy expenditure, whether physical labor or technical work, acknowledging that everyone has something to offer. Idealistic as this sounds, Time Banks have been established in over 30 countries with sophisticated tracking software for groups utilizing this system.

Now for the other side of the equation—the lunar South Node in subterranean Scorpio. While you're busy clocking hours, deep dive into

2022 HOROSCOPE GUIDE   153

your money narratives. What stories have you inherited from your family, culture and community that shape your outlook on finances? Unpacking these is the real key to wealth while the karmic South Node is submerged in Scorpio.

Before you can make the great strides that this nodal cycle portends, you have to turn inward. Get real, Ram: What's your relationship to wealth? Do you worry about losing your creative edge if you were to have financial security?

Rebellious Rams may read any association with "the system" as selling out. Trouble is, this mindset can trap you in poverty consciousness, whereby you glamorize the struggle of going without. While there's certainly merit in being self-made, you may be stuck in a holding pattern. Truth of the matter? Your suffering doesn't mitigate anyone else's. (Nor does caring about your cashflow make you an evil capitalist, greedy materialist or any other negative association you've cast onto "the rich.")

Scorpio and the eighth house govern shared resources. Joining forces with the right people can create an epic transformation for you between January 18, 2022, and July 17, 2023. We're not talking about a 50/50 split here, however. Aries may be shopping for investors, taking out a loan, or using money from an inheritance or settlement to fund a venture.

Warning: Gambling on the latest start-up is ill-advised during this security-minded cycle. Put your money into resources that hold the promise of increasing their value over time, like real estate, cryptocurrency, or ETF (exchange traded funds) in growing markets. Raise your financial IQ if this all sounds like gibberish. Money might not be a subject taught in school, but it's one you can literally master over the next 18 months!

Fixating on your balance sheet is the other side of the coin. As one of the three passionate fire signs, you can burn up funds like a lit match in dry sagebrush. Salary increases may lead to greater spending, which in turn, leaves you perpetually behind the 8-ball. Talk about a recipe for terminal stress!

The good news is, that with the nodes in Taurus and Scorpio, you'll see a path to getting off whatever treadmill you're on. Our own financial manager Tabor, a savvy Scorpio, reminds all her clients that money is neutral. Simply put, it doesn't carry a charge. Stories we tell ourselves about our finances are what determine where we fall on the continuum from "money is the root of all evil" to "money gives us access to healing the world."

This can be a sexy process, too! With the South Node in erotically charged Scorpio and the North Node in tactile Taurus, let desire be another driver. Ask any expert on the planet: Relaxing is fundamental foreplay. Yes, Aries, life could be a whole lot more sensual if you gave up adrenaline as your primary fuel source. Whether you're merging bank accounts, tucking more into your retirement account, or adjusting your income-to-expense ratio, not constantly worrying about cash means more headspace for fantasizing about seductive pleasures...some of which won't cost a thing!

The last time the North Node visited Taurus was between April 14, 2003, and December 26, 2004. Recurring themes may arise, specifically in your financial life. Investments made then could pay off handsomely or you may return to a field similar to one you worked in nearly two decades ago.

ECLIPSES IN TAURUS AND SCORPIO

Money Makeovers & Financial Fluency

**Partial Solar
Eclipse in Taurus**

April 30 at 4:27pm

**Total Lunar
Eclipse in Scorpio**

May 16 at 12:14am

**Partial Solar Eclipse
in Scorpio new moon**

October 25 at 6:48am

**Total Lunar Eclipse
in Taurus full moon**

November 8 at 6:02am

times in eastern time

Money burns a hole in some Aries' pockets. Other Rams are experts at using creative financing to cover expenses in lieu of bills. No matter where you fall on the cash continuum, your relationship to finances gets a makeover in 2022. For this, you can thank a game-changing eclipse series which is activating the Taurus/Scorpio axis from November 2021 to October 2023. In 2022, four of these lunar lifts will be shifting the way you spend, earn, save and invest.

On April 30 and November 8, eclipses sweep through Taurus and your second house of daily income. This could bring a job change, a promotion or an out-of-left-field money making opportunity. During the partial solar (new moon) eclipse on April 30, expect to feel a burst of motivation. This change may be born of necessity as much as desire. Perhaps your company is downsizing, inspiring you to upgrade your skill set (or contact a recruiter!) in the name of job security.

Forgotten bills may come due, kicking your earning superpowers back into gear. Nothing can stop a motivated Ram. It's finding something worthy of action that's the hard part. You'll probably look back and bless any "emergencies" that arise near April 30.

A total lunar eclipse arrives with the Taurus full moon on November 8. Near then, you might make a sudden lifestyle change that allows you to build a nest egg or enjoy more quality of life. Some Aries could have a "what is it all for, anyway?" moment, when you realize that you'd rather work to live, not live to work. You might even consider moving or downsizing.

Big-picture finances take the spotlight on May 16 and again on October 25, when eclipses land in Scorpio and your eighth house of investing, property and large lump sums. The eighth house rules merging on all levels: marriage, divorce, pregnancy or joint venture. In some way, you're being propelled into more permanent terrain.

Shaky relationships that can't go the distance will be swept away if you don't do the work. You could hit a watershed moment under May's total lunar eclipse which arrives in tandem with the "all or nothing" Scorpio full moon. The good news? This eclipse could be clearing a path (albeit abruptly) for serious contenders to move in.

A sudden windfall, such as a bonus, settlement, inheritance or venture capital, gets your feet on stable ground near the solar (new moon) eclipse of October 25. Another unplanned expense—such as legal fees for contract negotiations or closing costs on a house—may prompt you to get savvier about money management. This is a good year to pay down debt or buy real estate, and these eclipses bring surprising windows of opportunity.

MARS IN GEMINI

Negotiating Conflict

Mars in Gemini
August 20, 2022 to
March 25, 2023

**Mars Retrograde
in Gemini**
October 30, 2022
to January 12, 2023

It's not like you often hold back on much, but you'll have strong cosmic support to get things out in the open starting August 20! If you've been hesitant to speak candidly with friends, a sibling or neighbors, you'll find the inspiration (or maybe just guts) to put it all out there once passionate Mars, your cosmic custodian, blasts into articulate Gemini and your third house of communication for an extra-long visit. The red-hot planetary provocateur won't have visited this realm for almost two years, and this tour will be longer than usual because of a ten-week retrograde mid-cycle.

Between August 20, 2022, and March 25, 2023, you'll speak your mind and enjoy a more lively social life—and you won't have to travel far to get your cultural fix. With your third house activated, action is sure to heat up on the local scene. You could discover new friends, activities and favorite hangouts right in your zip code. Bring on the unbeatable trivia team, wine and book clubs and gourmet potluck dinner parties.

Just one tiny asterisk in that animated timetable. From October 30 to January 12, 2023, Mars will be retrograde, which can stall initiatives and cause tensions to rise, reminding you of what Robert Frost said about good fences making good neighbors. Friction bordering on hostility may be a hallmark of these next two and a half months, causing you to question whether you're actually on the same page—and if you can get back in sync. A friend, neighbor or colleague might become an annoyance, especially if they insist on rehashing an issue you thought was long since resolved. (Hello, retrograde in your communication center!) Do yourself a favor and privately assess whether you even want to continue with this relationship.

But while you're doing that self-inquiry, be brutally honest and see to what degree you might be fanning these flames. You're not exactly long on patience (are you, Ram?), and that legendary short fuse could be smaller than ever during this reversal of your ruling planet. On the other hand, if you're not expressing what you're feeling and just stuff it down, internal pressure might build until it erupts like a volcano. Up to you how to let this out, but you don't want to keep sitting on it. Find a neutral but savvy third party who's happy to listen while you vent.

But choose the right sounding board! Offloading to the wrong person could earn you a reputation for being impossible to please, demanding or even a gossip. (Hence the "neutral" third party!) Spilling tea to anyone smacking of a vested interest—or a mutual friend of the person in question—is never a good idea. Ditto shared coworkers. But while rash Mars is reverse in chatty Gemini, it can be hard to not let your feelings gush out, especially when you're being mistreated or compromised. In some cases, it will be appropriate to defend yourself. Just watch your words and your tone since Mars in this position can make you come across as severe and combative.

That said, there is a "sweet spot" between taking a stand and suppressing. Ignoring an offense or diluting your reaction with insincere humor won't help. Maybe count to more than ten (or if necessary, sleep on it) before you say, send or post anything. Getting something off your chest isn't worth destroying an important bond.

Do what you can in the moment, knowing that more palatable ways of compromising will emerge after January 12, 2023. This could entail some drawn-out negotiations, but in the process, you'll learn to bite your tongue and be amenable. Watch for a tendency to sound like a know-it-all. Use Mars' backspin to examine any self-righteousness and to increase tolerance for people with life views that are different from yours. You might need to issue a temporary peace treaty by agreeing to disagree—then, taking the subject off the table until next January! ✳

2022

TAURUS

TAURUS

LOVE

Karmic connections crop up in 2022 as the moon's South Node shifts into Scorpio, energizing your relationship house from January 18, 2022, to July 17, 2023. You could meet a meant-to-be mate or finish up some past-life business through a game-changing "situationship." Pay attention to who pops up near two partnership-powered eclipses on May 16 and October 25. Rather than searching for a twin flame, embrace the growth opportunities each connection brings. For the first time since 2003, the lunar North Node is in Taurus, granting you 18 months of self-discovery that can lead you into the arms of true love—or deeply enhance the bond you've already established. Romantic restlessness may find you roaming for greener pastures while your ruler Venus is retrograde in your exploratory ninth house until January 29. Some Bulls may reignite a spark with a long-distance lover or someone you met while traveling. Already locked into a relationship? This is the year to share adventures, from bucket-list vacations to couples' workshops that deepen communication and spark erotic engagement.

CAREER & MONEY

Career goals continue to be a huge priority as Saturn passes the halfway point of its journey through Aquarius and your success-driven tenth house (March 21, 2020, to March 7, 2023). Keep establishing your authority as a company (or industry) leader, even if you have to put in longer hours than preferred. Once the destiny-driven North Node enters your sign on January 18, the cosmic compass may point you in a new direction. But don't throw out the baby with the bathwater. Build upon the skills you have and see what surprise opportunities the two Taurus eclipses bring on April 30 and November 8. When go-getter Mars zooms into your money house on August 20, initiate and pursue financial opportunities. Then, hunker down to develop what transpires while Mars is retrograde from October 30 to January 12, 2023.

WELLNESS

Customize your fitness plan to suit your life, Taurus; otherwise, it may fall by the wayside. With Saturn in your achievement zone, track progress with an app and consider working with a trainer or private teacher to make sure you hit your goals. The North Node in Taurus stretches you out of your comfort zone, but that daring spirit could lead to an injury if you don't warm up and learn proper postures. (More reason to enlist a guide!) Roll out the yoga mat while high-minded Jupiter moves through your soulful twelfth house from May 10 to October 28. Dive into water sports, like stand-up paddleboard yoga or sailing. Motivator Mars helps you find a sustainable and pleasurable routine after August 20.

FRIENDS & FAMILY

Popularity soars in 2022! Play superconnector while expansive Jupiter in Pisces revs your team spirit until May 10 (and again after October 28). Bring people together but don't overcommit yourself. With the lunar North Node in Taurus, you need ample time to pursue your personal hobbies and crew-hop without feeling obligated to anyone. Two eclipses in Taurus, on April 30 and November 8, shift your direction. You may cut ties with one group to create space for another—particularly if your life goals are more in sync with the new crew. However, nostalgia will sweep through from May 10 to October 28, when Jupiter dips into your sentimenal twelfth house. Reconnect to family and old friends. This is a powerful window for making amends and healing long-standing rifts.

♉

JUPITER IN PISCES

Team Up for the Win

Jupiter in Pisces

December 28, 2021
to May 10, 2022

October 28 to
December 20, 2022

Taurus on the move! You're the clear-cut winner of every popularity contest as enthusiastic Jupiter paddles through Pisces and your eleventh house of friendship, teamwork and technology. Collaborations take your ideas to new heights while the bountiful planet percolates here from December 28 to May 10, and again from October 28 through December 20.

After a driven and ambitious 2021, loosen up your collar and have some well-earned fun! If you hustled like a champ, you might even have extra funds in your entertainment budget. One Taurus we know broke into the medical field as a 3D printer after mastering the machine and software in his garage for five years. He's now designing medical and PPE equipment for an area hospital. Another was promoted to Chief of Staff, the first Asian American woman in the tech startup's C-Suite.

There's lots to be proud of, Bull. But there's also more to life than work, work and more work. As you lift your nose from the grindstone, look beyond the usual places for your social fix. With your offbeat eleventh house alight, you'll find yourself in the company of fascinating people whose brilliant ideas inspire you to think bigger. For much of 2022, your luckiest moments will come while mingling with your soul squad and soaking up the adventures life has to offer.

You already got a taste of Jupiter in Pisces last year, when the red-spotted planet plunged into this zone from May 13 to July 28. Connections you fostered then will evolve and expand in exciting ways now. With your social circle widening, pick up wine and cheese in bulk. You won't get much alone time in the first half of 2022—but you'll have an embarrassment of riches when it comes to finding great people. Whether you're starting a non-profit, joining a drumming circle (like one Bull we know) or making new friends, surprise yourself by becoming an active member of your social squads. Mayor Taurus has a lovely ring to it, right?

"Enterprising Bulls, pick your platform! This is the year to use YouTube, TikTok, or your very own website—to launch a savvy startup."

Once again, getting everyone in the same room is not required! Worldly Jupiter draws collaborators from around the globe. Upgrade your Zoom plan if necessary, because the party size can swell! That said, sensory Bulls do need IRL interactions. Communing in a shared space could look all kinds of ways, from setting up a coworking office to a co-living residence with a curated crew of friends.

As expansive Jupiter journeys through your progressive, utopian eleventh house, you're ready to set aside rigid thinking. Forget the outworn stereotype of Taureans as strictly traditional. In 2022, Eleanor Roosevelt's words could be your mantra: "Great minds discuss ideas; average minds discuss events; small minds discuss people." Jupiter in Pisces calls for a new brand of interactivity. Distance yourself from people who cling to ignorance or espouse small-minded perspectives. Or, since you're such a loyal sign, perhaps you'll "agree to disagree" and keep certain topics off-limits. If necessary, take the lead and enlighten your friend circle. Host a documentary night and invite friends from various groups to watch, discuss and mix things up. Gather your friends to stream (or go hear) a motivational speaker's lecture instead of sitting around gossiping.

Your earthy, bohemian side could take the wheel while Jupiter is in Pisces until May 10 (and again from October 28 to December 20). Maybe you'll give van life a go for a month, or champion a social justice cause. Activism could be a major part of 2022 for Tauruses. Some Bulls could start campaigning for office or take a leadership role on a team. One Taurus we know is spearheading a diversity initiative for her company, populating the formerly homogenous enterprise with more women, POC and gender nonbinary folx.

With Jupiter in this tech-savvy position, you may find your calling in the digital sphere. An online project could draw financial backers or, thanks to global Jupiter's influence, you might team up with long-distance collaborators. ("Siri, find me a developer in Buenos Aires!") Even proud Luddites shed their stubborn-Bull ways for high-tech conveniences this year. Inventors and scientists thrive under this Jupiter cycle. In Pisces, which rules the invisible realm, Jupiter could bring anything from space travel to curing infectious diseases. Or maybe you'll trademark a creation that becomes the ubiquitous "helpmate" of everyone's home. Stranger things have happened when supersizer Jupiter storms the eleventh house.

Enterprising Bulls, pick your platform! This is the year to use YouTube, TikTok, or your very own website—to launch a savvy startup. Since Jupiter rules publishing and teaching, an informational product, like a webinar or digital download, may bring bountiful returns. You might sign up for online courses to brush up your own skills. Or, take advantage of any educational credits offered by your job and get certified in a coding language, performance marketing or social media management.

The eleventh house rules casual connections, and you'll prefer a more lighthearted vibe overall. In love, this Jupiter phase trends a bit more platonic. Couples might prefer mingling with mutual friends versus escaping for one-on-one dates. With autonomous Jupiter fueling your social life, you shouldn't feel guilty pursuing your own interests. Free-thinking Bulls could test unconventional arrangements, from dating multiple people at once to trying an open relationship. Or, you'll get experimental within a monogamous bond. Time to write the script of your own erotic "toy story"? Your bedroom could be, er, buzzing with activity by the time your birthday rolls around.

Single and looking? Shift your focus to building a circle of close friends. You never know: Your next great love may come through a mutual contact or someone you meet while hanging out. The communities you join this year could certainly turn up interesting prospects. But take your time and build a solid friendship first. That person who shares your fascination for obscure literature or collecting vintage glassware might turn out to be your soulmate-in-waiting.

Jupiter was last in Pisces from January 17 to June 6, 2010, and again from September 9, 2010 until January 22, 2011, and you could see similar themes from that time recur.

JUPITER MEETS NEPTUNE IN PISCES

Wishful Thinking

> **Jupiter meets Neptune in Pisces**
>
> April 12, 2022

Toss some coins into the wishing well this April 12! As lucky Jupiter catches up to enchanted Neptune at the same degree of Pisces, they activate your visionary powers. This special connection only comes around once every thirteen years. While it loosens your grip on reality, it allows your imagination to take the wheel. That's not an opportunity that comes around every day for you, Taurus, as the zodiac's realist.

With these two idealistic planets in your iconoclastic eleventh house, you'll get a clear picture of possibilities that are far off most people's radars. (Including yours, like a week ago.) Don't dismiss these "impossible" ideas just because you have no clue how to pull them off. It may take a village, but that's not a problem! Communal support could arrive miraculously under the spell of this cosmic coupling. If you can dream it, there's at least a 50 percent chance that you can do it!

JUPITER IN ARIES

Healing and Transitions

Jupiter in Aries

May 10 to
October 28, 2022

December 20, 2022
to May 16, 2023

Fold up those social butterfly wings temporarily—or to be exact, for about five and a half months. After a whirlwind kickoff to 2022, Jupiter slips into Aries and your twelfth house of closure, healing and release. Think of this window as a chance to "rest and digest" after a flurry of socializing and dynamic experiences that no doubt pushed you out of your comfort zone.

With the red-spotted planet hunkered in your solitary twelfth house, you could pull a 180, going AWOL on the very scene you started earlier this year. Try not to leave people in the lurch, Taurus, even if you've found a greener, serener pasture somewhere off the grid. When Jupiter swings back into Pisces on October 28, people will be your *raison d'etre* again. There's no sense in burning bridges! Just be honest about the fact that you're taking a breather for personal restoration. Besides, you'll still enjoy inspiring company when Jupiter is in Aries...maybe just in smaller doses now.

Slow down, sort and process. What belongs in this next phase and what has passed its prime? Jupiter sails into your sign on May 16, 2023, which will be handing you the keys to a brand-new adventure sooner than you know it. Until then, you can slowly and gently begin clearing the decks and creating space for the new. Whether it's a relationship, a mindset or a habit, examine what no longer serves you. You may be grieving a loss or the end of a chapter, or perhaps you're just in the weird in-between space of a transition. For example, maybe you've moved to a new city where you haven't cemented your place yet, or you have a new job and you don't quite have a feel for the company culture. Lay low and observe.

It can help to think of Jupiter in the twelfth house like a sabbatical. The only footnote? With Aries ruling this realm, your resting state will be active. In other words, when you stop to meditate, don't be surprised if you receive a download of divinely inspired creative ideas. It's an excellent time for spiritual work, therapy or diving into artistic projects—anything

> *You're a channel for the divine now, which is also why great works of art, music and writing can be produced during this Jupiter phase.*

that activates your imagination or plumbs your subconscious depths. But if you try to force things to happen, you'll face harsh reality checks and obstacles.

You're a channel for the divine now, which is also why great works of art, music and writing can be produced during this Jupiter phase. Many people attract a soulmate or have a "meant-to-be" pregnancy while Jupiter is in this mystical sector. Make space for the muse through meditation, gentle exercise and time spent near water. How about a beachside retreat where you can do all three? Now that's #Goals that Jupiter here can get behind.

This is a period to practice surrender, which can be extremely difficult for an industrious Taurus to do. All humans labor under the illusion that we're in control—or that, with the right amount of grit and hustle, there's nothing we can't achieve. True as that may be, those once fail-safe strategies may leave you spinning your wheels as Jupiter plunges into these depths. The twelfth house has a divine plan, and it will gladly show you those blueprints once you stop resisting. Humbling as it can be, you'll attract miracles when you finally quit swimming upstream. (Note: Jupiter was last in Aries from June 6 to September 9, 2010, and January 22 to June 4, 2011. Similar themes may arise in your life again between May 10 and October 28 of this year.)

♉

VENUS RETROGRADE

Revise Your Love Goals

Venus in Capricorn

November 5, 2021
to March 6, 2022

**Venus Retrograde
in Capricorn**

December 19, 2021
to January 29, 2022

However frustrating a love relationship—or even a "situationship"—has been of late, Bull, please don't think about canceling Cupid! And don't blame yourself. Look instead to your ruling planet, Venus, who's going through one of its rare—yet palpable—retrograde periods from December 19, 2021, to January 29, 2022. This happens every 18 months, and when it does, it can tempt you to swear off love—or bail on your partner. But that's the last thing you should do, at least without much more consideration. As long as you can stay realistic and not slip into denial—even if you have to redo or scrap amorous initiatives during this six-week spell—you might come out clearer and stronger than before. Slipping on the blinders could cause you to miss out on the actual gifts of this transit. And yes, there are indeed benefits to this!

For one thing, Venus retrograde can offer a rare glimpse into your own inner emotional landscape. This is a perspective you don't usually rush to observe, yet when you do take an unblinking gander at your fears, resistance and any "insecure-attachment issues," it's hard to keep ignoring them. Only when you recognize—and acknowledge—them do you begin to free yourself from their clutches and move confidently in the direction of committed and fulfilling love.

Not sure if you see yourself in that example? How about this: If you and your S.O. (or a string of hopefuls) keep getting into the same argument, is that really a coincidence? What's the common denominator? With the love planet backspinning, you have a rare opportunity to dig way beneath the superficial to unearth the root of the conflict. You might be pursuing very divergent goals or trekking along different paths to get there. But is that a done-and-dusted deal breaker? Not necessarily. That's the beautiful part. Once you can finally admit it, you may realize how much you want to try to make this work and, in the process, come up with some creative or unexpected ways to support each other through any "separate but together" journeys.

Ever since Venus entered Capricorn last November 5, it's been heating up your ninth house of global gallivanting, cross-cultural connections and looser dating (or relationship) "restrictions." All well and good—as long as all parties are on the same page. But once Venus flips into reverse, all bets could be off. Suddenly one person is all about commitment while the other is enjoying the freedom of this extended Venus transit. Or an unforeseen circumstance arises that forces a new set of "rules." Whatever you do, don't hit the panic button—or flee. This is just a temporary adjustment period, and while it's intense, it too shall pass.

In a newish situationship? However "amazing" it seems now, don't rush it. With Venus in ambitious, future-oriented Capricorn, it's natural for your amorous thoughts to seek "bigger, better, faster" arrangements. And this could very well develop into that. The thing is, if you don't give it time to develop organically, you'll never know what's real, what's a reaction to undue pressure and what you're forcing with your insistence (a Taurean pitfall). While in reverse, the love planet gives you a chance to re-evaluate your attitudes and actions. Maybe it was too soon to bring your new boo home for the holidays, especially if your family isn't the most sensitive.

If the bloom is still on the rose, let it blossom organically. In other words, don't rush to fully commit by moving in together or merging financial obligations. Those are big, hard-to-walk-back decisions, and you want to be completely sure you're ready. Wait till after the retrograde and see how you both feel then. Be willing to speak candidly, to question everything and even slow things down if that seems advantageous. Avoid any major "stress tests" until after January 29, 2022, and instead, do things to strengthen communication.

Single and eager for help attracting Cupid's arrows? Before January 29, revisit a location that makes you feel sexy and magical—a perfect retrograde activity if ever there was one. Go alone or with a date, but remember that the whole point of this exercise is to connect to your power and sensuality, not fall in line with someone else's.

Venus rules our values and possessions, and in luxury-loving Capricorn, your appetite for life's finer things may increase. But keep it real. You don't have to ignore your desires, but if you can't afford to blow a paycheck on a pair of winter boots—however perfect they are—find a great pair you can afford. And mind the standard retrograde warning: Purchases made between December 19, 2021, and January 29, 2022, need to come with a solid warranty or, better yet, a lifetime guarantee!

LUNAR NODES IN TAURUS AND SCORPIO
Finding Your Path

Lunar Nodes in Taurus and Scorpio

January 18, 2022
to July 17, 2023

Destiny's calling, Taurus...so don't let it go to voicemail! On January 18, the lunar North Node returns to your sign, charging your life with momentum that you haven't experienced since April 2003. This special point in the sky is associated with your higher calling and spiritual evolution. During this fateful and fortunate cycle, which lasts until July 17, 2023, you might feel like the world is humming at YOUR vibrational frequency.

Truth is, you've basically been the universe's tuning fork since May 2018. That's when experimental Uranus arrived in Taurus for the first time in 80 years. Since then, change has been the only constant in your life. And that's not something your security-loving sign is accustomed to. But you're getting used to it—and good thing too, since Uranus won't quit you until April 2026.

In 2022, as the North Node teams up with iconoclastic Uranus in your sign, the message behind all this madness will be revealed. Chaotic though the past few years have been, the shakeup lifted some pretty heavy stagnation. Sometimes it takes a gale force to move your tenacious sign. But where is this all taking you?

That's where the moon's North Node comes in. This 18-month cycle is here to point you in a meaningful direction. It also lays the groundwork

♉

for some very you-centric new endeavors. This is your "call to action" from the universe, a time to step into your authority and lead with confidence.

We wish we could be more definitive about what lies ahead for you, Bull, but that's not how this works. The North Node, which we like to refer to as "the zone of miracles," is an undefined realm. Even when this point in the sky corresponds with your sign, you may still feel like you're trekking on foreign soil with only a temporary visa.

Make a budget for self-development. (Or heck, apply for a scholarship!) You'll get by with a little help from not just your friends, but also coaches, mastermind groups, specialized trainings and degree programs. Whatever it takes to get your meant-to-be mission in motion—and keep you on that road for eighteen months! Don't miss this crucial window for growth. The North Node only visits your sign every 18.5 to 20 years. The last go 'round was April 14, 2003 through December 26, 2004. If you're old enough to remember what was going on then, you might see some recurring themes crop up.

On the other side of your chart, the North Node's polar opposite, the lunar South Node, shifts into Scorpio and your relationship realm. All your close connections will come under the microscope between January 18, 2022, and July 17, 2023. The South Node is associated with karma, past lives and comfort zones that are perhaps a bit too cozy. If you've lost your identity in a relationship, it could come roaring back!

Easy, though. With competitive Scorpio energy afoot, your truest allies might start looking like your biggest nemeses. You know what they say about biting the hand that feeds you...not to mention the one that strokes your hair while you fall asleep at night. No, repressing bitter feelings won't make them go away. But dynamics like these are best discussed with an outside party, like a therapist or spiritual counselor. We can almost guarantee that these feelings began much earlier in life, perhaps with a superstar sibling or a critical parent who noticed everything but your shining achievements.

66

Bottom line, Bull: Relationships are the cherry on top of the sundae while the North Node is in your sign.

99

Even the most stable relationships could go through a shift during this 18-month nodal cycle. It's only natural. When you take a step in a new direction, the people you're dancing with in life must also move. To avoid throwing them off balance, try keeping them informed during your process. That way, they can track (and support!) your accelerated growth. Changes you make won't come out of left field...well, not totally. However, you are likely to require more autonomy while the North Node is in your sign. For folks who have been leaning on you, this can be unmooring. Don't leave them in the lurch by pulling a disappearing act. But don't baby them either or get stuck holding their hands. Empower them with tips and tools, trusting that they will find their flight paths, even if they struggle for a while.

Reuniting with a twin flame is another possibility—and oh, how this can shake up your world. Whether or not you're in a committed relationship, you may suddenly feel pulled into this person's orbit. Many believe that twin flame relationships seldom last long. The intensity is too explosive to sustain! In fact, that's what brings the soul-evolving lessons that you've met up (once again) to learn.

Bottom line, Bull: Relationships are the cherry on top of the sundae while the North Node is in your sign. This is going to be an interesting phase to navigate, since by nature, you're a caretaker and loyal supporter of the ones you love. Make sure you've carved out space for "me, myself and I," along with all those shared ventures. Call it your path, your purpose or a meant-to-be mission. Whatever the case, the North Node in Taurus is here to help you make your unique mark on the world.

ECLIPSES IN TAURUS AND SCORPIO
Balancing "Me" and "We"

**Partial Solar
Eclipse in Taurus**

April 30 at 4:27pm

**Total Lunar
Eclipse in Scorpio**

May 16 at 12:14am

**Partial Solar Eclipse
in Scorpio new moon**

October 25 at 6:48am

**Total Lunar Eclipse
in Taurus full moon**

November 8 at 6:02am

times in eastern time

Get ready for some epic life changes! From November 2021 to October 2023, a series of galvanizing eclipses activate the Taurus/Scorpio axis. These momentous moonbeams reshuffle both your personal identity and your closest partnerships. In 2022, four eclipses push you to renegotiate the balance between "me" and "we."

On April 30 and November 8, eclipses in Taurus shake up your first house of solo endeavors, catapulting you into the hot seat. Have you outgrown an aspect of your life? Fixed signs can be set in their ways—and Taurus is the most stubborn of them all. But digging your hooves in won't stop the inevitable changes from blowing your way. Flexibility—not rigidity—helps you flow with the new and maybe, just maybe, enjoy the process.

TAURUS

First up is the solar (new moon) eclipse in Taurus on April 30. You could be inspired to put your all into a passion project or to spearhead an initiative at work. Venus-ruled Bulls are easy on the eyes. You may become the spokesperson for a cutting-edge platform. With your first house of identity lit, this could be the birthday season that you completely revamp your appearance or rebrand a business. Bottom line: These eclipses inspire you to present a sleek new image to the world.

Last year's lunar eclipse (on November 19, 2021) fell in your sign and really set the wheels in motion. On November 8, there will be a follow up, as the 2022 Taurus full moon lunar eclipse builds on what you started at the end of 2021. Manifestation mojo is high, and you'll reap whatever you've been sowing! So move with intention in 2022. Good things come to those who are benevolent, hardworking and kind.

Your relationships get an extreme makeover on May 16 and October 25, when two eclipses in Scorpio sweep through your seventh house of partnerships. It only makes sense that, as you change, your interpersonal dynamics also fluctuate. Eclipses can bring curveballs or surprising turns of events. Near the May 16 total lunar (full moon) eclipse in Scorpio, some Bulls might dramatically exit a duo or—conversely—leap into a serious relationship. You may part ways with a longtime work collaborator or ink a major business deal.

Where are your relationships lopsided? Take inventory: Do you give too much and end up in codependent or draining dynamics? On the flip side, maybe you demand exceedingly high levels of loyalty from people, and nobody can meet those standards. You can forge a compromise near the Scorpio solar (new moon) eclipse on October 25. Prepare to renegotiate your terms and move into greater levels of mutuality as 2022 winds down.

MARS IN GEMINI

Making Bolder Money Choices

Mars in Gemini

August 20, 2022 to
March 25, 2023

**Mars Retrograde
in Gemini**

October 30, 2022
to January 12, 2023

Get ready to shake your moneymaker starting August 20—even if you have to skip a few parties or sit out a few dances to get things rolling. Impassioned Mars leaves your sign and relocates to Gemini for a way longer than usual visit, giving you plenty of opportunities to plump up your nest egg. While Mars normally spends about seven weeks in a sign on its biennial orbit around the Sun, because of a retrograde this fall, you'll be hosting the red planet in your financial sector for six months! Between August 20 and March 25, 2023, you'll be focused on your bottom line, and there's no need to apologize.

With the motivational planet activating this house, the stability you crave is within your grasp over the coming months. Mars is about speed and intensity, which can add muscle to your hustle. But your steady sign (the natural ruler of this realm) is more thoughtful and methodical. You might need to adjust to some uncertainty as part of the "growing pains" of this upward thrust.

Set your priorities: Are you looking for a better-paying gig, a whole new career or perhaps just to launch a side hustle to test the waters? With Mars marching through your second house of income for six months, these are exactly the things to ask yourself. And then this: Are you ready to devote more time and energy to these initiatives?

When you do start pulling in more cash, don't burn it as quickly as you earn it. Some belt-tightening is probably in order (especially during Mars' retrograde from October 30 to January 12, 2023). You need a savings plan, whether for a short-term, big-ticket purchase or a long-term investment strategy. If this isn't your area of expertise, now might be the time to hire a pro for advice based on your unique needs, desires and risk tolerance. While certain pals may not get to see you as frequently, as your cash flow becomes more robust, you'll know your time is being well invested. By the end of the year, you might have hit a major monetary milestone!

Knowing in advance that Mars' retrograde can bring unexpected expenses or speed bumps with a big deal, start building a buffer as early in 2022 as you can. When Mars does go retro, things could stagnate and stall, but even then, don't hit the panic button. If you're prepared, you can reframe the situation as a golden opportunity to review your plans and make sure they're built on a solid foundation.

Once Mars resumes direct motion on January 12, 2023, you can pivot or reinvent. Plus you might get a second chance at a gig you applied for earlier in 2022—or a former client or colleague could return with an offer that's better than you'd dreamed.

Something else to anticipate? Possible tension at the office or with coworkers during this six-month cycle. Mars is a provocateur, and if this drama has been brewing for a while, its presence could turn up the heat to flammable! Head off real battles at the pass by addressing them as soon as you sniff out simmering conflict. By bringing it out into the open, it's less likely to continue to fester until it erupts.

If you handle these snafus well—and let people see you in action—you may land yourself a promotion or greater leadership role in the company. When you are engaging with difficult people or navigating delicate situations, remember to listen more than you talk and to keep your comments positive—never defensive or dismissive. Use "I language" instead of the accusatory "you." For example, "I'm feeling the need for more structure with our workflow" will yield better results than, "You're always rescheduling our meetings!" ✸

2022

GEMINI

WHAT'S IN THE STARS FOR

GEMINI

LOVE

Romantically, the year begins on a reflective note and ends on a red-hot erotic one. Venus will be retrograde until January 29, a time to draw back from drama or dive deeper into the discovery of your partner's inner workings. Make sure to share your own, too! Vulnerability creates the runway for romance while Venus lingers here until March 6. Open up to boundary-pushing exploration once the North Node heads into Taurus and your twelfth house of fantasy on January 18. But first, disentangle from codependent patterns that are zapping the juice from your love life. Self-care is the key to sexiness, not overfunctioning to please your mate! Lusty Mars embarks on a long tour through Gemini from August 20 to March 25, 2023. Autonomy and agency are more essential than ever during this rare cycle. Give yourself a long leash! Flirting, dressing up and doing things that make you feel attractive are not the same as cheating. In fact, a little more freedom might save your relationship when Mars goes retrograde from October 30 to January 12, 2023.

CAREER & MONEY

Maximize the first three weeks of 2022! The destiny-driven North Node is wrapping up an 18-month journey through your sign on January 18. This cycle only comes around every 18-19 years, providing an unmatchable opportunity to push past prior limits. Bold and audacious moves could set you up handsomely for the rest of the year—and with lucky Jupiter in your success sector until May 10—and again from October 28 to December 20—you are primed to climb any ladder you choose. Step into leadership and sharpen your skills. Powerful mentor figures can help you level up all year. Surrender to their tutelage and don't resist the "wax on, wax off" part of the process. With the karmic South Node in your efficient sixth house after January 18, use apps, reminder alarms and savvy systems to work smarter, not harder.

WELLNESS

Have yoga mat, will travel? With structured Saturn in your travel zone all year, fitness goals could lead you on long-distance adventures. Bike through wine country, hike distant trails, learn to surf on a new coast. Health is a major priority once the lunar nodes shift into Taurus and Scorpio on January 18. This 18-month circuit makes healing an inside and outside job. Create a routine that fits with your everyday life and integrates with your work. Sit on a medicine ball or put a balance board by a stand-up desk. Join a gym close to the office so you can take a class between meetings. Cleanse, detox, meditate. Look for ceremonies and holistic/ therapeutic treatments that connect you to a higher power and help you access deeper parts of your subconscious. These may be especially potent near the eclipses on April 30 and November 8.

FRIENDS & FAMILY

Free time will be a precious commodity before May, so focus attention on your inner-innermost circle. Socializing one on one will be most enjoyable, allowing you to process all the transformations going on in your life. Just remember that friends are not therapists—and that a great counselor or coach can take the weight off your friendships. Jupiter's electrifying tour through Aries restores your social butterfly status from May 10 to October 28. Meaningful connections are a must, but you'll take them with a sense of humor and a solid squad of fascinating people again. You might even organize friends around active summer plans, like group hikes, long bike rides or a team fitness challenge. Explore voluntourism or join a charitable initiative near the eclipses on May 16 and October 25. People who share your values will be waiting to meet you!

JUPITER IN PISCES

Rise Through the Ranks.

∏

Jupiter in Pisces

December 28, 2021
to May 10, 2022

October 28 to
December 20, 2022

Who's ruling the roost? Looks like it's you, Gemini—the cooperative zodiac sign who believes that twinning is winning. But in 2022, your co-stars eagerly pass you the leadership mantle. Why? Because expansive Jupiter is spending more than half the year in Pisces and your tenth house of career, success and public recognition: first from December 28, 2021 to May 10, 2022, and again, rounding out the year from October 28 to December 20, 2022.

Because Jupiter only comes here every 12-or-so years, this could be your luckiest professional cycle in over a decade. The bountiful, red-spotted planet flings open doors (and windows!) of opportunity. Even better? With principled Jupiter in the picture, you don't have to sell out or become a corporate drone to achieve success. Under this enterprising spell, one of the wild ideas you cooked up in 2021 could expand into something much bigger.

Jupiter is a renegade and the tenth house rules structure, which is a paradox you'll learn to navigate. Fortunately, Geminis are no strangers to duality. In 2022, you will discover how commitment can actually set you free. Prioritize and devote your energy to one or two ideas. You can accomplish so much when you aren't scattered! Lean in to a long-term goal and crush it.

There is a catch: While in Pisces, Jupiter forms a challenging, 90-degree square to your Gemini Sun. Along with all this rapid expansion could come some growing pains and a few tough hurdles to cross. The scraped elbows and bruised knees will be worth pushing through, as long as you take the lessons and apply them swiftly.

Since Jupiter rules risk-taking and evolution, you could feel like you've outgrown your current professional path. Maybe you already began embarking on a new career course last year, when Jupiter briefly visited Pisces from May 13 to July 28. Before that, Jupiter's last trek through Pisces was from January 17, 2010, until January 22, 2011. If you look back, you may have started or ended a significant cycle of your career during those times.

Either way, new frontiers call your name in 2022. With adventurous Jupiter at the wheel, you don't have to rush to commit to an entirely new industry. (Although you might!) Twins will field shorter-term projects that help you build credibility in your field, and ultimately, scale the ladder to a higher rung. Should you make a U-turn from computer programmer to Pilates instructor, or from midwife to mechanical engineer? Well, why not? Or maybe you'll do what your sign does best and figure out how to work as a "slasher," juggling two jobs that you love with equal fervor. To wit, we know a Gemini who is an online-marketing executive by day, and a psychic medium on the weekends.

Change could just as easily flow in via your current job. New management may be installed, or the company gets bought and decides to restructure. Think on your feet if you love it there! Write up your own job description and present it to the new hiring committee. Pitch an experimental initiative. Wise, daring Jupiter in your career zone could find you three steps ahead of the game. So don't be shy about leading discussions at the office. Boldness will be rewarded in the first half of the year, and again in the last two months.

Ⅱ

> **66**
>
> *Because Jupiter only comes here every 12 years, this could be your luckiest professional cycle in over a decade.*
>
> **99**

Even if nothing's changing, embrace the opportunity to branch out, especially if the role includes more accountability. Jupiter in Pisces opens a golden window to show how competent and capable you are. For some Geminis, your best bet might be to adopt the role of "intrapreneur"— someone who takes on an entrepreneurial role within a big organization.

The tenth house sits at the top of the zodiac wheel, and visionary Jupiter at its summit has you pondering lofty topics, such as: How do I want to be seen in the world? What kind of legacy do I want to leave behind? If you've mastered a skill, "edutainer" Jupiter encourages you to build a platform to share your experience. Invest in headshots, web developers and sleek business materials to present the most polished image possible. If you're already a veteran in your field, you may be invited to speak in public. But no need to wait for any calls to come in. Set up the camera and start livestreaming. One Gemini we know committed to posting a daily inspiration video on YouTube. Within a year, her followers topped 350K and she shopped a successful book deal as a result.

Still a newbie in your industry? Working with a seasoned pro can increase your odds of success, since the tenth house rules mentors. With lucky Jupiter in this corporate corner, your career could involve work with an established business or a publicly traded company. (Negotiate stock options if you can!) With bountiful Jupiter on your side, don't be surprised if you get enough offers to start a bidding war. Caveat: The job might require you to travel or relocate, which your peripatetic sign will probably welcome. Even if you're not the "power suit" type, you may surprise yourself by considering a full-time position that offers a solid salary and benefits.

Dualistic Geminis are both die-hard renegades and uncompromising micromanagers, and these two sides of your personality regularly battle for dominance. One minute you're the fearless influencer spearheading a TikTok dance trend, the next, you're preaching to all your friends about microbiomes and gut health. In life, you'll take the most jaw-dropping risks, only to follow them with a wave of anxiety and self-doubt. (Your friends have talked you through plenty of these freakouts—and maybe held the camera for a reality TV audition on a few tipsy nights.) That dichotomy will be echoed loudly by gallant Jupiter's tour of Pisces and your rule-bound tenth house.

The way you deal with authority can also shift before May 10. Maybe you spend a lot of time on Facebook blasting "our government" and posting outrage-provoking news stories. Or you're the unabashed office gossip, always griping to coworkers about the hamstrung leadership in your company. This year, if you don't like the way something's being done, Jupiter challenges you to take action. Who knows? Maybe you'll run for public office or make an ally out of a decision-maker. Once you have their ear, present your ideas for how to do things better. Since Jupiter rules higher education, look into formal management training. Even a natural "people person" like you could benefit from acquiring new skills now.

The key to this Jupiter phase? Balancing the right amount of autonomy and responsibility. You'll crave more guarantees and long-term plans—but not so many that you feel hopelessly boxed in. Be wise with time and money management. You could end this phase on solid ground, ready to celebrate one of your most successful years yet!

JUPITER MEETS NEPTUNE IN PISCES

Rebelling Against Responsibility

Ⅱ

> **Jupiter meets Neptune in Pisces**
>
> April 12, 2022

As ambitious Jupiter pushes you to achieve, don't be surprised if your freedom-loving alter ego kicks in. Too much responsibility causes a libertine like you to revolt, especially near April 12 when boundary-dissolving Neptune meets Jupiter at 23°58' Pisces. This sync-up only happens every 13 years, bringing together philosophy and spirituality. Sounds enlightening, but there is a catch: This cosmic combo often provokes a crisis of conscience as part of the process.

Brace yourself, Twin. If you're not bucking against the weight of duty, you may face demons of insecurity. *Am I good enough? Do I deserve this? What am I getting myself into here?* Listen, Gemini, you'd be hard-pressed to find a "great" who hasn't dealt with a raging case of imposter syndrome once in their life. It can be lonely at the top, not to mention terrifying. Give yourself a chance to adjust to new altitudes by surrounding yourself with pro-level support.

Neptune is the planet of escape, but lucky for you, it attracts "earth angels" like mentors, coaches and spiritual guides. Since you can expect to have one Yeezy out the door while Jupiter and Neptune travel in tandem from March 14 to April 30, that is good news. Before April 12, load up on encouragement props like mantras, motivational audiobooks, leadership training groups and friends who believe in your vision and won't let you quit.

The tenth house is the domain of men, masculinity, fathers and authority. Jupiter in forgiving Pisces reframes your relationship to an important guy in your life—or with men overall. As trauma-healer Neptune goes to work on your subconscious, this philosophical phase helps you process any "dad issues" or brings you closer to the father figures in your life. By the time Jupiter re-enters Pisces from October 28 to December 20, you may have a totally different way of interacting with the male-identified people in your universe.

JUPITER IN ARIES

Cultivate Community.

♊

Jupiter in Aries

May 10 to
October 28,2022

December 20, 2022
to May 16, 2023

Kindred spirits unite! You could be widening the radius of your social circle starting May 10, when bountiful Jupiter buzzes into Aries, firing up your eleventh house of friendship, groups and technology until October 28. Charismatic Geminis have a knack for attracting fascinating people. During this five-and-half-month cycle, your mission is to gather your scattered squad under one umbrella. Virtual or IRL, you can take your pick. The point is to connect the fabulous people you know, then step back and let them take it from there.

Not that you have to remove yourself altogether. Teamwork truly does make the dream work with Jupiter in Aries, so spread some of that responsibility around and lighten your load. Inspiring new collaborations and cutting-edge people could enter your sphere between May 10 and October 28 and again at the year's end when Jupiter returns to Aries from December 20, 2022, to May 16, 2023. Flex your superconnector muscles and bring people together for a dynamic effort. You could be running a victory lap together before the year is through. Jupiter last visited Aries a decade ago, from June 6 to September 9, 2010, and January 22 to June 4, 2011, and you may see recurring themes arise midyear.

Simultaneously, outmoded friendships may fall by the wayside, as growth-driven Jupiter reshuffles your social circles. Don't ditch your loyal pals, of course, but be aware of who you're spending the most time with—and make sure they lift you up instead of crushing your spirit. You might get more involved in your community, perhaps even dabbling in politics or activism (that is, if you don't already).

With entrepreneurial Jupiter logged into scene-stealing Aries, you can boost your social media presence or position yourself as a thought leader who speaks at events. Got an idea for the digital or software space? While you don't want to gamble, this is a smart time to invest in reputable tech or cryptocurrency. One Gemini we know has been working in earnest to develop a social networking app—the perfect merger of this geeky Jupiter cycle and his natural unifying abilities.

Wondering when to step on the gas? The middle of 2022 is prime time to hit the accelerator because lucky Jupiter could bring a windfall! Or, if you have a finished product on hand, go hard with new marketing and promotion efforts. Don't assume people got the memo the first time around. Think of ways that you can solve a problem for them in the 2022 climate.

The summer could be one non-stop celebration this year, an opportunity to network and blow off steam. Who knows? There's a good chance you'll celebrate a career coup. Why not do it up with an artful touch, in true Gemini style? Make sure to film every moment of it because you're bound to have a year's worth of social media posts queued up. And with Jupiter returning to Aries again from December 20, 2022, to May 16, 2023, you may be ready to add "influencer" to your ever-expanding resume. (Note: Jupiter was last in Aries from June 6 to September 9, 2010, and January 22 to June 4, 2011. Similar themes may arise in your life again between May 10 and October 28 of this year.)

VENUS RETROGRADE

Love Intensifies

Ⅱ

Venus in Capricorn

November 5, 2021
to March 6, 2022

**Venus Retrograde
in Capricorn**

December 19, 2021
to January 29, 2022

Sensuality and seduction may be your keywords this winter as amorous Venus takes an extended sashay down the catwalk that is your erotic eighth house. Normally, Venus spends just three to five weeks in a sign. But every other year, it flips into a six-week retrograde, which is on tap from December 19, 2021, to January 29, 2022. And this go-round, it's lounging in earthy, sensual Capricorn for four times longer than its usual run. And after its last reversal — in your sign from April 3 to August 7, 2020—

you should know how an extra-long Venus transit can feel. And while it probably brought up many things, the bottom line is that life was likely... complicated.

This time, the frisky love planet is heating things up in the "red light district" of your chart, which should do wonders for your libido—and your romantic life! But note that when it turns retrograde, all bets are off. This could halt forward progress with a new love interest, throw a wrench into an existing union, or bring back an old flame that never got fully extinguished. In fact, you might need to consult a psychic to make sense of some of the things that'll happen over the next month and a half. With Venus backing up through Capricorn, high-octane seduction could lead you down some dark and shadowy alleys, and even your usually reliable intuition can feel like it's on fritz.

In general, retrogrades dredge up the past, and a pivot of the planet of love and values could bring back someone for whom you still have feelings. If you're single and this relationship had legit reasons for not working out (bad timing; one of you wasn't ready to commit), and you sense there's serious potential, it's worth exploring. But ironically, the retrograde energy also means you won't necessarily be able to get a clear-eyed read

66

"Sensuality and seduction may be your keywords this winter as amorous Venus takes an extended sashay down the catwalk that is your erotic eighth house."

99

on the situation—not until after January 29, 2022. However, if you're both available, there's no reason to not meet and talk. (And possibly more—if only to check the current connectivity level.)

Be brutally honest with yourself. If this person is a toxic ex, don't let your hormones cancel out your wisdom. There's a reason it ended, and it would only be painful to revive it. Instead, do a ritual to clear their energy from your field and hopefully be done with them for good.

If you've been slowly getting closer to a special someone, this Venus stint in serious-minded Capricorn won't let you be too passive or casual. If you want more intimacy, you're probably going to have to take the lead. And while getting super vulnerable isn't always your favorite thing, you can't have a deep and lasting connection if you're both harboring secrets. Be prepared to "go there," Gemini. The good news is, Venus retrograde can help you plunge into deeper waters.

Something else this transit can assist with: If you sprinted into a relationship without considering real-life practicalities, like their financial values or future plans involving where to live or whether to have a family, retrograde Venus can pull the emergency brake. Chemistry can be magical, but it's not a strong enough foundation to build a lasting union on. In reverse, it can also guide you to express something you've been afraid to articulate out of a fear of rejection. Truthful soul-baring is the only option between December 19 and January 29. Eventually, anyone you "get in bed with" (literally or metaphorically) will find out who you really are—and what your shadow is like.

Now, if you suspect that your other half has a deep, dark secret, you need to find a way to get at this without coming across as suspicious. Venus retrograde can spark childhood or old relationship traumas, and your love interest may be getting triggered. You'll need to create a safe and judgment-free space for conversation. Be prepared to hear something unsavory or painful—and to not freak out if you do. Between November 5, 2021, and March 6, 2022 when Venus moves direct in Capricorn, the work is balancing the lust with enough trust to keep this going. We're not saying it will be easy, but fortunately, forthright conversation and a willingness to negotiate are among your savvy sign's strengths!

LUNAR NODES IN TAURUS AND SCORPIO

Health is Wealth

Lunar Nodes in Taurus and Scorpio

January 18, 2022
to July 17, 2023

Destiny's been calling, Gemini—and louder than ever since the moon's North Node moved into your zodiac sign and fired up your trailblazing first house on May 5, 2020. Since then, you've likely "come into your own," however you define it. And for Twins that spans a huge range since you share a sign with both Breonna Taylor and Donald Trump. No matter where you find yourself on the cosmic continuum, we'd bet good money that your life path has taken a fascinating turn over the past 18 months. If you haven't already stepped into a new role, perhaps you've gained clarity about what life will look like once you do.

And, Gemini, we have to ask: Are you exhausted yet? Change is exhilarating, but it demands hard work. It can be scary to step into a new space, even if you begged the universe to send these manifestations your way. Meditation experts spend most of their time teaching students to sit with emotions like fear and anxiety. These invisible forces can be like internal hurricanes, especially for your finely-tuned nervous system.

Achieving Buddha-like stillness may be too lofty a goal. But you could gain serious mastery over your emotions starting January 18, 2022. For the first time in nearly two decades, the North Node backs into Taurus and your twelfth house of subconscious healing and boundless spirituality. Although this means that you're waving bye-bye to the North Node for another 18.5 years, you'll now have a chance to deeply integrate all the newness in your universe. Since Taurus rules your twelfth house of mentors, helpful people will be miraculously accessible between now and July 17, 2023. From agents to therapists to influencers who take a shine to you, it might feel like there's an angel on your shoulder, helping you dive deep into your feelings.

While you're processing things like grief, trauma and childhood pain, make sure to remain process-driven about other areas of your life. Directly across the wheel from the North Node sits its counterpart, the lunar South Node, which we call the karmic comfort zone. Anchoring yourself in this energy can help you stay grounded while you surge toward the heights the North Node maps out.

During this 18-month cycle, the South Node will be in Scorpio and your systematic sixth house. Lather, rinse, repeat? Suddenly that doesn't sound like such a bad idea. Repetition is what makes the lessons stick, after all. So don't get upset with yourself if you're not learning everything at your usual lightning speed, okay? True, we all have phones and computers to help us recall data, but there's something to be said for becoming a master of your craft. By doing, reading or practicing the same thing over and over again, you'll start discovering nuances within nuances. And that's when the epiphanies arise!

Work and wellness are two areas getting pinged by the South Node. During this cycle, you'll feel a near-psychic connection between food and mood. Most Geminis are healthy eaters, but you may go full-on raw vegan or grow your own vegetables and pick up meat from a local farm. There's energy in everything you ingest, and how your food was sourced, prepared and harvested will be something you will feel.

Stressful situations can no longer be stomached during this nodal cycle. While last year, you were fine with moving at that supersonic pace, in 2022, you desire space to just be. This might mean scaling back your hours, even taking a temporary pay cut while you outsource parts of the job. You'll catch up again, but first, you need time to develop whatever's next. Between January 18, 2022, and July 17, 2023, your most profound awakenings will come while you're in "flow state," whether you're meditating, going for a run on an outdoor trail or dancing to your favorite music. With the earthy Taurus North Node in your twelfth house of spiritual journeys, plant medicine ceremonies or any sort of work with a shaman could move stuck energy in powerful ways.

> *We all have healing gifts to offer the world, and yours will come to light during this nodal cycle.*

With the Scorpio South Node's mystical and transformational influence, add magic to the process by ritualizing your routines. How can you make the mundane feel miraculous? For example, recite a gratitude mantra before each meal. Listen to music and dance while you're prepping dinner—and fix enough to eat for lunch the next day. Hate scrubbing the tub? How about playing a podcast or catching up with your sister for a weekly call while you do. The time will fly by!

We all have healing gifts to offer the world, and yours will come to light during this nodal cycle. With your houses of service lit up, give back through a volunteer effort, monthly donation or even by starting your own support circle for people who are dealing with the same pain that you are. There's something so humbling about this, and you'll resonate with this expression: "Before enlightenment, chop wood and carry water. After enlightenment, chop wood and carry water."

ECLIPSES IN TAURUS AND SCORPIO
Healing and Dealing

Ⅱ

**Partial Solar
Eclipse in Taurus**

April 30 at 4:27pm

**Total Lunar
Eclipse in Scorpio**

May 16 at 12:14am

**Partial Solar Eclipse
in Scorpio new moon**

October 25 at 6:48am

**Total Lunar Eclipse
in Taurus full moon**

November 8 at 6:02am

times in eastern time

Ready to activate an inside-out glowup? This year's four change-making eclipses touch down in your sixth house of health (ruled by Scorpio) and your twelfth house of healing (ruled by Taurus). During this cycle, you're learning when to lean in and fix things yourself versus when to let the universe handle it. Control or surrender? Analytical thinking or imagination? Where does the balance lie? You're about to find out, Gemini. These eclipses are part of a series running from November 2021 until October 2023.

Letting go is hard to do but you're forced to wave the white flag near April 30 and November 8. Two eclipses in Taurus and your twelfth house of closure bring an unavoidable transition or moments of vulnerability. Control is an illusion, but that doesn't stop humans from pursuing it. The April 30 new moon in Taurus heralds the first solar eclipse of 2022. An unhealed wound may reopen near that date, forcing you to finally process tough emotions like anger, grief or sadness. Open your heart, Gemini. You'll be rewarded with more

♊

support than you dreamed was possible. Therapists, shamans, holistic practitioners, mentors: When the student is ready, the teacher appears. Yes, Twin, it's time to enroll in the School of Healing.

On November 8, the total lunar eclipse arrives with the full moon in Taurus. There may be a sudden ending or curveball that takes you by surprise—and as a result, you're forced to lean on people instead of pretending you've got it all together. If you've struggled with an addiction, codependence or a self-sabotaging pattern, you may finally hit rock bottom and reach out for help. Suppressed emotions could arise unexpectedly and you may mourn a loss that you've avoided facing. As the saying goes, you've got to feel it to heal it. These eclipses are teaching you how to ask for support...and receive it.

As you plunge into the emotion ocean, take caution: While it's important to acknowledge trauma, you don't want to get stuck in a hopeless mindset. The twelfth house rules the subconscious, and you might benefit from hypnotherapy, dream work and the field of "energy medicine." You could even be drawn into the realms of shamanism or plant-based healing near these mystical eclipses. We're not saying you'll be going off-grid for a plant medicine ceremony, Gemini—but we're not saying you won't, either. Whatever modality you choose, just be careful you don't fall under the spell of a guru figure, as the twelfth house rules sacrifice and illusion.

The May 16 and October 25 eclipses in Scorpio target your sixth house of health and fitness. Have you ignored the red flags telling you to reduce stress and prioritize self-care? Near the May 16 Scorpio full moon—a total lunar eclipse—you may get doctor's orders to make a lifestyle change or begin treating a nagging ache or chronic condition. Consider it a wakeup

call, reminding you that the body is the soul's earthly address, and you need to maintain your "property!"

October 25 delivers a gentler nudge with the solar (new moon) eclipse in Scorpio. Even while the weather is cooling, you may get a burst of inspiration to start an eating program or join a new fitness studio. Since the sixth house is linked to the digestive system, explore cutting-edge research on gut health and microbiomes.

The sixth house also governs daily work and service providers. Near these May and October eclipses, you could suddenly change jobs (or even careers), possibly moving into a "green" or wellness profession. Need more credentials? You might take an in-between gig while earning certification or learning new skills, such as Javascript coding or bookkeeping. If Team Twin is due for an upgrade, weed out the slackers and replace them with capable and competent new players. Good help may be shockingly easy to find as the May 16 eclipse shines a light on someone who has the very credentials you've been seeking!

MARS IN GEMINI

Passions on Fire!

Mars in Gemini

August 20, 2022 to
March 25, 2023

**Mars Retrograde
in Gemini**

October 30, 2022
to January 12, 2023

Get ready to experience a system-wide energy upgrade! On August 20, motivational Mars catapults off the launch pad and into your sign, where it will spend an extended time thanks to a mid-cycle retrograde. This prolonged phase lasts until March 25, 2023, and is sure to bring long-desired changes to your life.

If your 2022 got off to a sluggish start, sit tight. Stalled, delayed or abandoned personal projects can revive almost magically—and may take off at lightning speed once Mars enters Gemini. It'll be exciting, but make sure you're ready for this whiplash-inducing acceleration!

Lucky for you, Gem, you're the speed demon of the zodiac and actually thrive at this supersonic Martian velocity. If you had a choice, your mercurial air sign would rather be overwhelmed than bored. So plan to get plenty of sleep and eat nutritious meals because you're going to be moving at warp drive. And while there are sure to be tons of people, conditions and arrangements to coordinate and manage, you can call upon your native charm to entice people to get—and stay—on board.

♊

Normally, Mars spends about seven weeks in each sign during its two-year orbit around the Sun. But every other year it flips into retrograde, and this fall, it'll reverse-commute through Gemini from October 30, 2022, to January 12, 2023, spending a total of six action-packed months in your sign. If you've been eager to make any epic life changes, your inertia might fly out the window with intrepid and risk-taking Mars at the wheel. While you can certainly look forward to major transformations, plan ahead for possible "collateral damage." You might have to step back from a situation (or person) you had adored because it no longer fits with this new you you're becoming.

> **66**
>
> *If you've been eager to make any epic life changes, your inertia might fly out the window with intrepid and risk-taking Mars at the wheel.*
>
> **99**

No need to be completely unbridled with your behavior, however. Impulsive Mars might have you believe that it's more expedient to completely blow up a situation, walk away and start over from scratch. While that's possible, you still get to vote! Don't push people out of your life just because you "need space" or lost your enthusiasm. The best application of Martian fuel is to dole it out slowly and thoughtfully. Think: marathon rather than sprint.

Even as you're pushing ahead, be prepared for an abrupt pull on the emergency brake—or perhaps even a derailment—when Mars shifts into reverse on October 30 (until January 12, 2023). It's not like everything will come to a grinding halt, but if you're braced for delays, confusion and a temporary stop-work order, you're likely to be less frustrated by it (especially if you build in contingency plans you can bring online without missing a beat). Whatever happens, seek out the silver lining in any slowdown. Assume there's always room for improvement and consider this a rare chance to hit pause, review your progress and assess its viability. What's still left to complete and do you have the right resources, team and funding? Embrace the spirit of revision, and reach out to people who have done something similar. By the time Mars corrects course on January 12, 2023, you might actually have hit on a faster, smarter or more economical way of getting this mission accomplished.

Fierce Mars in your sign could spark a desire for a radical personal makeover, which is understandable. Just be circumspect when it's in reverse since you could have a total change of heart once Mars returns to forward motion. (Maybe hold off a little longer on that full-sleeve tattoo?) Start Pinterest boards and plan to reconsider everything after January 12, 2023. You might not see it now, but early next year, you may realize there are plenty of aspects of your "former life" that are worth keeping around, and it would be terrible to think you can never get them back. ✺

2022

CANCER

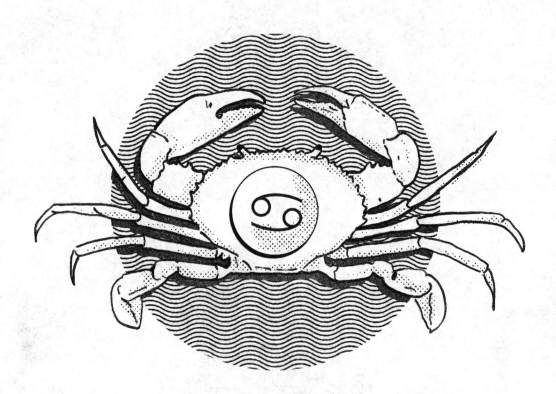

CANCER

CANCER

LOVE

Sexy is back for Cancers in 2022—and in a bold, head-turning way.
The karmic South Node simmers in Scorpio starting January 18,
greenlighting passionate PDA and erotic explorations galore. Plan
nostalgic dates while Venus is retrograde January 1 to 29, or see what
can be rekindled with "the one that got away." Whenever possible,
dress up and step out because you never know who you'll meet this
year. The eclipses on May 16 and October 25 could bring enviable
power couple fantasies to life. If babies are on the agenda this year, get
a fertility plan in place and give it a good go in the months of these
eclipses. Attached? Step out often as a pair and enjoy every photo op
you can. But don't skimp on the serious stuff. Structured Saturn is still
in Aquarius and your eighth house of joint affairs all year. Get solid
with your S.O. about your relationship status. Take that next step like
buying property or writing your wills. Free-spirited Jupiter in Pisces
brings truth, travel and transformation until May 10 and again from
October 28 to December 20. Yes, you should have the talk—and how
about having it in Portugal, Portland or Peru?

CAREER & MONEY

Can you make money while you sleep? Serious Saturn says, "Yes!" to
passive income in 2022 as it streams through your investment-savvy
eighth house. Whether you're purchasing a rental property, learning
about crypto or selling downloadable classes and products, think
beyond the nine-to-five grind. But don't rule out those corporate
connections completely. Venturesome Jupiter rises into Aries and your
professional tenth house from May 10 to October 28. You could land
a lucrative gig, either as a contractor or hired gun. Keep the suitcase
handy. You may travel for work while Jupiter is in Pisces before May 10
or from October 28 to December 20. Cancer media mavens could have
a heyday. Time to write that book or start your style blog!

WELLNESS

Good news! Vital, vibrant Jupiter is in its happy place (your ninth house) as it rolls through Pisces until May 10 and again from October 28 to December 20. Joyful movement is a must, whether you're dancing, horseback riding, or learning how to surf. Boundless Jupiter is the god of the feast and with your sign's love of epicurean delights, it's a little too easy to pack on the pounds. Follow the 80/20 rule: Stick to healthy, clean eating for the majority of meals and indulge as a regular treat! With Saturn anchored in your eighth house for one last full year, reproductive health is in the spotlight. Regulating cycles and hormone levels can lead to a more enjoyable sex life this year. When agitating Mars zooms into Gemini on August 20, you may be ready for a detox or cleanse. This seven-month cycle is ideal for deep inner work, perhaps with a shaman or craniosacral therapist.

FRIENDS & FAMILY

Who are the people far outside your neighborhood? Reconnect to far-flung friends and long-distance relatives in the early part of the year. You could cook up a visit or a collaborative project—both good reasons to get back in touch. Consider yourself the "crew glue" once the North Node heads into Taurus from January 18, 2022, to July 17, 2023. Find the right format for bringing some of the wonderful people you know together: book clubs, activist meetups, yoga in the park. Leave room for new recruits, who could arrive near the eclipses on April 30 and November 8. Mars heads into Gemini and your twelfth house of forgiveness for eight long months, starting August 20. With dedicated effort, you can move through a painful passage with a loved one.

JUPITER IN PISCES

Accelerated Growth

Jupiter in Pisces

December 28, 2021
to May 10, 2022

October 28 to
December 20, 2022

Ready, set, expand! The first half of 2022 will bring a major growth cycle, as accelerating Jupiter sails through Pisces and your ninth house of risk-taking, travel, higher learning and entrepreneurship. After an intense and internal start to 2021, Jupiter now hosts two coming-out parties for Cancers—from December 28, 2021 to May 10, 2022, and again from October 28 to December 20.

During these cycles, you'll be eager to cast a wider net and engage with people around the world. Whether virtually or IRL, cross-cultural connections will ignite. You already got a taste of this in 2021, when the peripatetic planet powered up Pisces from May 13 to July 28. Jovial Jupiter is happy to play concierge once again, introducing you to new people and ideas from a wide swath of backgrounds. Maybe you'll set up shop in another zip code (or country code) or try working from RV as you tour national parks and vortexes. For other Crabs, journeys will be those of the mind. Got more to learn? Apply to grad school or dive into a fascinating course of study. If you've mastered a topic, document your unique methodology. This could be a year you write a how-to guide, film an online course or build a program to spread your wisdom.

Jupiter is the natural ruler of the ninth house, so you're getting a double shot of this horizon-broadening energy, which only comes around every 12 years. The red-spotted planet briefly visited Pisces in 2021, from May

13 to July 28. Before that, Jupiter's last run through Pisces was from January 17, 2010, to January 22, 2011. Scroll back in your timeline, if you can, to recall your mindset at that time. Did you feel free to take more risks? Maybe you befriended someone who, on paper, was different from you in every way. Yet, you found common ground and established a long friendship. You might see similar themes repeating.

> 66
>
> *This vitality-boosting transit unleashes a torrential downpour of passion. Expect to feel friskier and more flamboyant than you have in years!*
>
> 99

Even more fortuitous? In Pisces, Jupiter forms a flowing 120° trine to your Sun in Cancer. This vitality-boosting transit unleashes a torrential downpour of passion. Expect to feel friskier and more flamboyant than you have in years!

Not sure what's next on your path? The saying "know thyself" might be your guiding mantra, as philosophical Jupiter in Pisces instructs you to look deeper. Be a free-range Crab while Jupiter is in Pisces. For best results, commune with open-minded people from diverse backgrounds. A job with flexible hours could leave time for personal growth work and self-development, which is rich terrain in 2022. Even if you have a steady and structured job, the odds are good you'll approach your work from a fresh perspective.

Any sort of physical movement is favored now, and Jupiter in the ninth house can boost your vitality big time. Your appetite may also expand, so be sure to fill your plate with plant-based dishes and low-caloric density eats (read: foods with lots of water in them, like fresh produce). That way, you lessen the likelihood of nonstop snacking. Sports you enjoyed as a kid or ones you've always wanted to try could be the perfect social outlet. Even the gentlest Crabs out there may be ready for more high-intensity workouts, or since Pisces rules all things aquatic, lap swims, sailing or stand-up paddle-boarding.

If you have an idea for a savvy startup, Jupiter in this enterprising zone encourages you to roll the dice. It's fine to begin this as a side hustle, but get ready, Cancer. Your visionary ideas can go big time in 2022. There's no need to pigeonhole yourself if you're still in an exploratory phase. Jupiter in Pisces is all about following the flow until you find your bliss. When Jupiter visits Aries from May 10 to October 28, it activates your goal-driven tenth house. That's when you can start mapping your big ideas to a firm structure and plan. Until then, soak it all in! Attend conferences and events where you can connect with other seekers. Take in the stories of entrepreneurs who did it their own way, rather than following the traditional scripts. You could cultivate an international audience if you branch out!

JUPITER MEETS NEPTUNE IN PISCES
Breaking Past Boundaries

Jupiter meets Neptune in Pisces

April 12, 2022

On April 12, Jupiter syncs up with another boundary-blurring planet, hazy and numinous Neptune. This transit, which only comes 'round once every 13 years, will double down its kaleidoscopic effect in Pisces. Don't expect to see anything clearly near this date, but know that the truth may indeed be stranger than fiction...possibly in a *Grimm's Fairy Tale* kind of way.

Abundant Jupiter in the excessive ninth house can be overwhelming at times. Add Neptune to the mix—especially as they travel in close connection from March 14 to April 30—and it can provoke a crisis of conscience. You may find yourself with "too much of a good thing," which, admittedly, is a problem most people would love to have. But even an embarrassment of riches can be a lot to integrate into your sensitive system.

Near these dates, you may need to slow down and synthesize all the new experiences and knowledge. If you've been on the road a lot, spend more time at home. And while you are on your journeys, bring "home" on the road with travel-sized versions of all your favorite creature comforts.

Can you upgrade your voyage from "basic travel" to "spiritual pilgrimage"? Both Jupiter and Neptune are masters of navigating the highs and lows. We recommend staying high vibe near April 12. Otherwise, you risk getting sucked into a vortex of hedonistic escape, which is not going to end well for anyone. If you've struggled with addictive substances, toxic relationships or any of the deadly sins, you're more vulnerable to relapses near the Jupiter-Neptune conjunction. Buffer yourself against peer pressure by having a zero-tolerance policy. "Just this once" are famous last words you don't want to utter.

JUPITER IN ARIES

Elevate Your Status

Jupiter in Aries

May 10 to
October 28, 2022

December 20, 2022
to May 16, 2023

Victory! After Jupiter's eclectic sojourn through Pisces, you're ready to make some power plays. And right on cue, the stars align. Your luckiest professional year in over a decade begins from May 10 to October 28, as Jupiter embarks on the first of two laps through Aries and your ambitious tenth house. Yoga pants and hoodies could be replaced by elevated blazers and tailored jeans—or whatever the "uniform" of your industry happens to be.

The tenth house is the domain of structure, authority and recognition. It sits at the very summit of the chart like a planetary penthouse—and with Jupiter in Aries, you've got an express elevator to this top-tier terrace. Don't be surprised to find yourself in the winner's circle, accompanied by influential VIPs. With candid Jupiter here, you have a golden opportunity to pitch your grand ideas, perhaps at a holiday party. A mentor or seasoned industry veteran could open doors before 2022 is through. And since Jupiter returns to this realm from December 20, 2022, to May 16, 2023, whatever you build now will continue mounting in 2023.

Here's a paradox you'll need to reconcile between May 10 and October 28: Jupiter is a rule-breaker and the tenth house rules structure. Explore ways that commitment can actually set you free. For example, if you have a secure job at an established company, you may take on a role in their "new ventures" department or a position that includes a bit of travel or flexible hours. This Jupiter cycle is ideal for "intrapreneurship"—being entrepreneurial within an existing company. If you own a business, you may spend the middle of 2022 at leadership summits, workshops and thought-provoking conferences where you can network and hone your executive skills.

> **66**
>
> *Prioritizing also means saying "no" to some opportunities that tug on your heartstrings, but the payoff will be well worth it.*
>
> **99**

With lucky Jupiter in this structured part of your chart, you might get an offer that convinces you to trade some independence for set hours in the executive suites. You could be handed a leadership post with a fancy title and high levels of responsibility—plus a salary and benefits to match. Travel or relocation may be part of the package. If you're established in your field, you may receive public honors or long-overdue recognition.

There is a small catch: While in Aries, Jupiter forms a challenging, 90-degree square to your Cancer Sun. Along with all this rapid expansion could come growing pains and a few tough hurdles to cross. The scraped elbows and bruised knees will be worth pushing through, as long as you take the lessons and apply them swiftly.

While we don't like to genderize astrology, the tenth house has been traditionally associated with fathers and men. You might interpret this as the parent who had the most authority in your family, or role models who lead by example without heavy-handed nurturing. Your relationship with a figure like this could go through an evolution, perhaps even a few growing pains. If you've been locked into an unequal parent-child dynamic that no longer fits, philosophical Jupiter helps you transition to a more mutual relationship.

This is for certain: Your biggest goals will get a supersized boost while Jupiter is in Aries midyear. You'll need to prioritize—not always easy for the emotionally driven Cancer—in order to accomplish these dreams. That will mean saying "no" to some things so you can say "yes" to what matters most to you. In addition to a demanding work schedule, you'll want to carve out time for personal happiness, healthy living and your loved ones. Anything else is secondary.

Prioritizing also means saying "no" to some opportunities that tug on your heartstrings, but the payoff will be well worth it. By not scattering your energy, you'll make serious headway on your dreams. Soon, you'll be too busy to notice the FOMO. Stay focused on your primary aims. Jupiter hasn't visited Aries since January 2011, and you don't want to squander this opportunity!

VENUS RETROGRADE

Pairing is Caring

Venus in Capricorn

November 5, 2021
to March 6, 2022

**Venus Retrograde
in Capricorn**

December 19, 2021
to January 29, 2022

Co-creation time! The first quarter of 2022 is packed with potential for partnerships of every stripe! Sensual, savvy Venus is parked in Capricorn and your relationship house for an extra-long visit—from November 5, 2021, to March 6, 2022. Normally, the planet of love, beauty and seduction spends just three to five weeks in a sign, but every other year, it flips into retrograde for six weeks, and this go-round, you will be treated to Venus' good vibrations for a total of four months!

With the cosmic coquette on such a long trek through this zone, every conversation will feel tinged with mesmerizing allure. And you'll be able to segue from the professional to the very personal without missing a beat. There's Cancer: reviewing a client pitch one minute, subtly flirting with a not-off-limits colleague the next. With the love goddess in your court, you may not even need the shelter of that legendary protective shell. Instead, you're all about collaborating and co-creating with people who can inspire you to break through previous creative or romantic blocks.

But in the middle of this long, slow transit comes a six-week backflip—one that started on December 19, 2021, and lasts until January 29, 2022—which can throw the smoothest-sailing relationship for a loop. This reversal happens every 584 days, meaning it's part of a predictable cycle. There's no need to jump ship, Crab, or mindlessly continue on a guaranteed collision course. Yet as you know all too well, forewarned is forearmed—integral for your security-minded water sign, which likes (needs!) to be prepared.

> **If you find yourself ruminating on 'the one that got away,' think about what qualities that person has that you're really missing.**

Look at each situation as a unique set of circumstances that requires its own response. If, for example, you clearly were the one who overreacted, it's on you to make amends. But only if you're sincerely remorseful, not out of guilt. And maybe you've pulled back for whatever reason. If you care about your love interest, you owe it to both of you to carve out quality time for a vulnerable heart-to-heart that could be the first step toward not only reconciliation but creating the best situation you've ever been in together. Perhaps the work is simply tapping into everything you appreciate about your life and relationship and spending some time refilling your "gratitude tanks." Pro tip: Do this before your reserves run dry and there's nothing you can do to fix the damage.

As it happens, Venus retrograde is the perfect time to get to the root of longstanding problems that have prevented one or both of you from fully trusting, letting your guard down or showing your true feelings in the union. Even in reverse, tactful Venus seeks to keep the peace and sidestep direct confrontation. But don't put off any relationship repair work until a crisis hits and you're both too frustrated or angry to deal. Recognize the warning signs—bickering more, less interest in intimacy—and pick some course of action to avoid going into freefall.

Venus retrograde can also bring back someone from your past. If you find yourself ruminating on "the one that got away," think about what qualities that person has that you're really missing. It's possible it's not actually them you're longing for but, rather, what they brought into your life and how they made you feel. And that's something you can probably recreate on your own or with your partner. One exception to that would be for truly unattached Crabs who've never gotten over this person. Should that be the case, then non-obsessively check out their social media pages. If their feeds state or strongly suggest they're single, and things didn't end on a volcanic note, then this backstroke of the love planet might be just the nudge you've been looking for. But keep your expectations reasonable—and other options open!

Whatever comes of your outreach, be slow to get involved until after Venus straightens out on January 29. You may think you're seeing a situation clearly, yet there's probably at least a rose-colored film over your viewing lens. While in the throes of fantasy (i.e., Venus retrograde), you could get pulled out to sea by a strong undercurrent. It's easy to project a new persona onto an old flame, but unless you see concrete evidence of them having transformed whatever was unacceptable in the past, assume nothing has changed! While it is important to forgive, that doesn't mean you should forget. On the contrary: Bygones may be bygones, but unless you've both done significant inner work, expect these old patterns to rear their heads once the tsunami of "new love energy" subsides and they're back to being the same old...them.

The good news is, with Venus in mature, stabilizing Capricorn until March 6, you have access to the wisdom and patience to work through any relationship rifts. No one's saying it's a cake walk, but with shared intentions and the willingness to do what's indicated, this persistent Capricorn energy will keep things moving forward. Now, if you're truly not sure you want this to continue, it's up to you to gain the necessary clarity to decide one way or the other. Fence-sitting isn't good for either of you, so it's truly worth "forcing yourself," if necessary, to choose one path or the other. This way, by the time Venus moves into Aquarius and your house of intimacy and eroticism on March 6, you'll know who you want to share your sexy magic with.

LUNAR NODES IN TAURUS AND SCORPIO

Time to Go Public

Lunar Nodes in Taurus and Scorpio

January 18, 2022
to July 17, 2023

You're not always comfortable basking in the spotlight, Cancer. But when a serious mission has an absence of leadership, no one has to ask you twice to step up! Ready or not, you're going to get plenty of chances to play Boss Crab starting this January 18. That day, the karmic South Node switches signs, embarking on an 18-month voyage through Scorpio and your fifth house of fame, self-expression and leadership.

Relax, Cancer: You don't have to torment yourself with ego-crushing auditions, panel reviews or any other "pick me, please!" processes. The South Node reveals achievements that come naturally and comfortably. Between now and July 17, 2023, scouts will be hunting for *you*. That's not to say you should sit there and do nothing. Astrology throws open windows of opportunity, but it's up to you to meet the stars halfway. So get to work on sprucing up your image. Resume a regular workout routine and eat in a way that gives you an inside-out glowup. Polish up your public profiles—and let that be an excuse to find clothes that fit your 2022 body in a flattering way. (Instead of punishing yourself for not fitting into clothes that you had to starve yourself to squeeze into in the first place—no thank you!)

If you're a brand owner, rework your logo or make sure all your front-facing materials, from livestreaming backdrops to social media tiles, have a consistent look and feel. Work with a public speaking or media coach if you aren't comfortable talking in public (much less recording yourself doing so). Performance skills can be learned—and more easily than many Cancers realize.

> *With your teamwork and technology sector stoked by the North Node, use your organizational gifts not to reign with a heavy hand but to inspire and support community.*

Romantically, there's a fated quality to events that happen under the Scorpio South Node. Moments of intensity are sure to arise during this transformational zodiac spell. Crabs could reconnect to "the one that got away" or finally be able to say that the person who was the best sex of your life has reached an emotional maturity level that makes them dateable.

Coupled Cancerians could bring a long-held dream to life, like building a home from the studs or getting pregnant. Waiting for the right moment to tie the knot? Wedding plans accelerate for marriage-minded Crabs now. Yet, if you've reached the end of your shared journey, this 18-month cycle will be tide turning. You just can't fake it where the South Node is concerned. Working with a sex therapist is another possibility, especially with Scorpio energy underscoring the importance of an intimate life. There's nothing light and fluffy about erotic encounters now! Unless you feel a soul-deep connection, you can't get off on a skin-deep one either.

But can you still be friends after a divorce or a business breakup—or some other irreconcilable difference? In 2022, the stars say yes. The reason? Directly across the zodiac wheel, the lunar North Node will be camped out in loyal, stable Taurus. This transit activates your idealistic, experimental eleventh house, making it easier than ever to remake traditional rules so that they suit your unique situation. No, you can't keep it "all love" with everyone. Some people live to push your buttons or gaslight you to offset responsibility. Dealing with them should be kept to the barest minimum (if at all).

Then there are folks with whom the initial magic has run its course, but you still like leaning on each other for support. There's good reason, like children or co-ownership of a thriving company, to keep things as harmonious as you can. The concept of "relationship anarchy" applies broadly for Cancers in 2022. Buck against convention and roll your eyes at "what the neighbors have to say." Deep down, they're just jealous. And, you never know: As you proudly live life by your own design, they might follow suit.

With your teamwork and technology sector stoked by the North Node, use your organizational gifts not to reign with a heavy hand but to inspire and support community. If you work with a group, this could be your chance to show people what you're capable of; namely, being a wise, fair and kind authority figure. And maybe a "mad scientist," too!

Unleash your creativity, but also reflect on how you can use your gifts to motivate others. The more authentically playful you can be with the nodes in Taurus and Scorpio, the more likely others will be to fall in love with whatever you're making, doing or offering. That's the kind of leadership the world needs now!

ECLIPSES IN TAURUS AND SCORPIO
Bold, Bright Connections

**Partial Solar
Eclipse in Taurus**

April 30 at 4:27pm

**Total Lunar
Eclipse in Scorpio**

May 16 at 12:14am

**Partial Solar Eclipse
in Scorpio new moon**

October 25 at 6:48am

**Total Lunar Eclipse
in Taurus full moon**

November 8 at 6:02am

times in eastern time

Drama or detachment? This year's four eclipses land on the Taurus/Scorpio axis, helping you clarify whether to lean in or lean back. Taurus rules your eleventh house of collaborations while Scorpio governs your fifth house of self-expression. Knowing when to play "support staff" and when to claim superstar status can be an awkward dance for sensitive Cancers. In 2022, you'll know which role is appropriate in any situation. Get ready to stretch! You'll be developing skills on both ends of the spectrum, from the #BTS magic-maker to the scene-stealing lead.

Eclipses can spark unexpected changes, and you might see these sweep through your friendships and love life in 2022. Anyone who brings drama or chaos to your world could get "eclipsed" away. This two-year cycle, which runs from November 2021 to October 2023, leads you to your soul circle...and true love, too!

CANCER

The April 30 and November 8 eclipses land in Taurus, charging up your eleventh house of group activity. The first, on April 30, is a partial solar eclipse, accelerating social developments. You might be invited to collaborate on a cutting-edge team project, perhaps one with a humanitarian twist. Be patient with the process! Learning the culture of this crew could take a little longer than expected. Friendships may go through a shakeup or a moment of bracing honesty.

During the November 8 total lunar eclipse, which arrives with the Taurus full moon, developments come fast and furious. Have you been on the fence about an affiliation? Even if everything's been "fine," you could suddenly depart from one circle and join a far more enriching crew.

The eleventh house rules technology, and the digital world might catapult you into influencer status on April 30 and November 8. This is one of those moments we warned you about, where you feel more like the backup dancer than the lead singer. But here's the thing, Crab: By helping others rise, you'll solidify your reputation as an indispensable member of this posse. Let's hear it for some lunar-powered #SquadGoals!

Your star turn will come, Cancer—not to give the shy Crabs among you anxiety! On May 16 and October 25, eclipses in Scorpio ignite your fifth house of passion and self-expression. Shuck off any stage fright and claim the spotlight. These eclipses may bring a surprise start (or end) of a love affair and, in some cases, an unplanned pregnancy. Charged up with Scorpio-level seduction, romantic developments will be intense, passionate and unforgettable.

The May 16 total lunar eclipse is especially potent since it arrives with a full moon. Plan (or protect!) accordingly. Taken less literally, you may birth a creative work that puts your name on the map—or suddenly become a viral sensation for your courageous, soul-stirring art.

On October 25, the solar (new moon) eclipse delivers a burst of motivation to go after your dreams. Burning desires spur you to take bold action. Before you know it, you might be auditioning for an on-camera role, picking up work as an influencer or completely revamping your style. Love may take a dramatic and exciting turn with you initiating the change! Forget about keeping developments under wraps. Whatever ignites near this eclipse will be far too big and bold to hide from the world. The good news is, you have nearly eleven months to get ready for that close-up!

MARS IN GEMINI

Pursue Your Dreams

Mars in Gemini

August 20, 2022 to
March 25, 2023

**Mars Retrograde
in Gemini**

October 30, 2022
to January 12, 2023

So-called real life may feel rather dreamlike starting August 20, when driven Mars downshifts into cerebral Gemini and your twelfth house of introspection, mystical musings and fantasy. The red-blooded planet typically spends seven weeks moving through each sign during its two-year orbit around the Sun. But because of a rare retrograde cycle (every other year), Mars will enjoy an extended sabbatical here for six months—until March 25, 2023. During this time, expect to be more internally focused than usual, possibly more sensitive and reactive... but also more tuned in to higher dimensions. Any healing, forgiveness or transformation you're praying for could come through under this transit.

The whole six months is a rich time for working with your intuition and dreams, but when Mars shifts into reverse from October 30 to January 12, 2023, you may have to resist becoming a full-on hermit. (Yes, it's possible.) If you find yourself inventing excuses to sit out social engagements you'd normally enjoy, check in with yourself—and take off the self-protective kid gloves. While it's great to get quality time reading, listening to podcasts, intensifying your meditation or spiritual practice—being with others can also be a positive, life-affirming activity! This is also a perfect opportunity to add soothing touches to your Crab "shell," which will make your home feel even more like a sacred space. But balance is still important, so make a point of occasionally going out for yoga or other movement classes, group healing sessions, sound baths and just pleasant nights with close friends.

Because Mars is an activator and provocateur in equal measure, you could find yourself raising your sword against some personal demons while it's stirring things up in your twelfth house of the psyche. Thought those issues had been laid to rest? If they're rearing their fire-breathing heads again, you may need one last battle to finally cut that cord. This is also an ideal time to process old hurts and especially grief. If pain or tremendous sadness do come up, don't lash out or vent to "innocent bystanders." In fact, ranting—to anyone—seldom accomplishes what you want.

Under the intensified energy of Mars' retrograde in this sensitive and mystical sector, you'll have access to the deepest levels of healing.

Under the intensified energy of Mars' retrograde in this sensitive and mystical sector, you'll have access to the deepest levels of healing. Almost any kind of therapeutic work can be extra effective from August 20 on. If you've been waiting for a "sign from the universe" to find a new healer or dabble in a new modality, this is it. You'll be more receptive, and with go-getter Mars in this esoteric realm, you might have unprecedented results with hypnotherapy, shamanic or energetic healing work.

But the opposite can also be true: If you've been working in those areas but still feel stuck, this might be the time to take a break—or go a more traditional route, perhaps with cognitive-behavioral therapy (since Gemini is the communicator and mentalist of the zodiac). And give yourself plenty of time and space to make art or get immersed in nature, which can be the greatest balm of all!

Your own healing gifts come to light with Mars here, and during this protracted cycle, they'll develop at an accelerated pace. Pay attention to signs and serendipities, especially where metaphysical matters are concerned. If you keep hearing about the same spiritual book or reader multiple times, follow the thread and see where it leads you.

Artistic Cancers will be prolific during this time, provided you drop the judgment and self-criticism and create for creativity's sake. Divine downloads could come to you while you sleep—and then keep you up half the night bringing them to form. Relax your mind and be an open vessel. You'll amaze yourself with your own capabilities! ✸

2022

LEO

LEO

LOVE

Security check! Saturn weighs anchor in Aquarius, spending its final full year in your relationship house. While you long for certainty, you may feel equally reluctant to go "all in." Circumstances (or distance) may prevent you and your amour from taking things to the next level. The good news is your sex life is not bound to suffer. Liberated Jupiter gets frisky in Pisces and your erotic eighth house until May 10 (and again from October 28 to December 20). You're ready to experiment, with or without a partner. And when the red-spotted planet grooves into fellow fire sign Aries from May 10 to October 28, it might be you who is asking for space. Either way, this mid-year cycle brings out your wild side. Long-distance love affairs, cross-cultural connections and baecations? Bring 'em on!

CAREER & MONEY

Destiny calling! Major career developments are in the stars beginning January 18, as the karmic North Node leaps into Taurus and your tenth house of success. If you're doing what you love, this 18-month cycle adds polish and panache to your dreams. You may rise to new heights of leadership or establish yourself as an expert or influencer. Bound to a bad business model? Breaking free is your cosmic duty this year—especially when indie-spirited Jupiter zips into Aries and your entrepreneurial ninth house from May 10 to October 28. Ever dreamed of being a digital nomad or traveling for work? You could go "pro on the road" mid-year. Investments may pay off handsomely before May 10 (and again after October 28). Explore real estate, crypto and other passive income streams. When go-getter Mars logs into Gemini on August 20, get your tech skills up to speed before the year is through.

WELLNESS

Wellness resolutions top your 2022 priority list—which may start with undoing a few bad habits while Venus is retrograde until January 29. Beyond those unhealthy indulgences, has stress crept in? Calming exercises, like swimming and gentle yoga, can help you stay centered when the lunar South Node dips into Scorpio and your rooted fourth house. Dietary changes can also support serenity. Dial down the stimulants like sugar and caffeine and explore adaptogens like ashwagandha that can reduce anxiety and energize you. It might be worth it to get your adrenals tested. More than anything, "tending and befriending" can boost oxytocin levels. Get a support group in motion—literally—by combining cathartic conversations with a walk or hike!

FRIENDS & FAMILY

Home is where the heart is—but sometimes you need a breather from the people you love most. With the karmic South Node in Scorpio, you may feel restricted by obligations to a parent, child or another person who is pulling on you for caretaking energy. Stop trying to be a superhero and mobilize support. This is the year to connect to people who are at a similar stage in life. Buying or selling a home may be part of your domestic plan. Popularity soars when Mars powers into Gemini on August 20 and you could find yourself at the center of a buzzing crew. Missing your people? Get the band back together when the red planet turns retrograde from October 30 to January 12, 2023.

JUPITER IN PISCES

Transformation Time

Jupiter in Pisces

December 28, 2021
to May 10, 2022

October 28 to
December 20, 2022

Bring on the bonding! Expansive Jupiter spends the first five months of this year in Pisces and your intimate eighth house—and again from October 28 to December 20. This cycle, which you experienced briefly last year (from May 13 to July 28, 2021), is where the rubber meets the road around your closest commitments.

For most of last year, Jupiter trekked through Aquarius and your partnership house, giving you license to experiment. A business alliance may have brought rapid success—or it could have fizzled out due to Jupiter's over-optimism. When the red-spotted planet is in charge, enthusiasm isn't always matched with follow-through. With 2021's emphasis on coupling, some Leos decided to get serious with one special person. Others may have outgrown a relationship and parted ways—hopefully on amicable terms. Stagnant relationships went through growing pains, forcing you to evolve as an individual. Leos in long-term relationships may have rekindled a shared sense of discovery by taking on a big passion project together.

In 2022, Jupiter's two Pisces cycles will present the kind of bonds that are tough to back out of, like marriage, joint business ventures, legal contracts, even a pregnancy. The eighth house is the realm where two become one in a certified, official way. Your sense of separateness dissolves into oneness, which can be equal parts titillating and terrifying for your individualistic sign. For Leos, who tend to cherish freedom and autonomy, this will require an adjustment. You may be a hopeless romantic, but once you're beholden to, say, a brand-new baby, a pet, a mortgage payment or an investor, you're on their clock. Say what?! Embrace this like some kind of Zen riddle: How can you feel free inside the confines of a binding commitment?

Sex falls under the eighth house's domain, and 2022 elevates your erotic adventures. Explore Tantra or other modalities that bring a spiritual dimension to pleasures of the flesh. Instead of just hopping in the sack, how about creating a scene? Delay the gratification so you can extend it even longer, and do it with all the pageantry that Leos are famous for. Jupiter in the eighth house can inspire you to play with power dynamics in bed, perhaps with a little BDSM or fetishwear. (Yay, costumes!)

With no-limits Jupiter in the mix, some Lions may toy with the idea of an open relationship. Tread carefully with outside experimentation, however. In this jealous and secretive zone, Jupiter will bring up the full spectrum of feelings if you go there. You might find insight through the work of modern love expert Esther Perel or sexuality coach and educator Pamela Madsen, who teaches how to "live the life you lust after without ditching everyone and everything you cherish." That pretty much sums up the way many Leos feel in committed relationships: Your body and spirit yearn for freedom, while your heart and soul crave security. This year's Jupiter quest asks: How can you have it all?

In a relationship? Joining forces without sacrificing autonomy is #LoveGoals for 2022. While in Pisces, Jupiter will present new ways to merge your superpowers for mutual gain. Maybe you'll take a big next step—moving in or buying property together, getting married or launching a joint business. But while galactic gambler Jupiter says, "You've got this!" the eighth house demands a certain level of trust and intimacy before you act. Choose your dance partners with the utmost discernment, because there's no such thing as "casual" until May 10 and again from October 28 to December 20.

> ❝
>
> *Your sense of separateness dissolves into oneness, which can be equal parts titillating and terrifying for your individualistic sign.*
>
> ❞

Extroverted Leos may find yourselves tightening up the radius of your social circles. Jupiter in the private eighth house puts you in a quiet and reflective headspace. Rather than have a million surface-level acquaintances, you'll prefer the company of a few sharp people who can go deep with you. With Jupiter in this powerhouse zone, you could befriend some influential and well-connected folks. Don't just look for favors and quick hookups. This is about supporting each other's growth.

Throughout these two cycles, deep feelings will surface. While traditionally you've leaned on friends, some things might best be processed with an experienced therapist or healer now. If you're still hurting from a loss, such as a breakup or a death, Jupiter helps you grieve and heal. The eighth house rules the psyche, and some of your most fascinating explorations in 2022 will be of your own mind, heart and soul.

If you embrace the focused energy of this cycle, you'll end it richer in every way. And yes, you can take that literally! The eighth house rules large piles of money such as settlements, royalties, commissions and other earnings that come in bulk. Better still? Bountiful Jupiter here wants to make it rain. Also governed by the eighth house are assets and property, as well as "other people's money"—which covers a wide swath: inheritances, investment capital, loans, grants, tax refunds, credit cards and debt. The eighth house rules passive income, and with lucky Jupiter here, you might roll the dice on an investment or property sale. Hire a lawyer to negotiate contracts or to protect your intellectual property. Get better insurance if you own property. The details matter, and this is the year to bring in the specialists!

Knowledge-seeking Jupiter inspires you to become more financially savvy. Now's the time to work with seasoned money coaches and certified planners. Enroll in workshops focusing on wealth building. This could be the year to try financial investments, such as stocks and real estate, or to partner on a promising joint venture. You may partner on one that multiplies your profits or delivers a high return rate.

Just don't bet the farm on a single hopeful endeavor. Jupiter is the cosmic risk-taker, always ready to leap without looking. Getting starry-eyed over a network marketing scheme that promises overnight millions? Not so fast. Conduct your due diligence before you join forces or plunk down your hard-earned capital.

JUPITER MEETS NEPTUNE IN PISCES

Casting Spells

A charmed day on the calendar will be April 12. For the first time in 13 years, bountiful Jupiter falls in step with fantasy-weaver Neptune, leveling up your charisma to peak magnetic levels. Under this spiritually abundant spell, the mystical could be part of your manifestation plan. Think: vision boards, creative visualizations and mantras.

> **Jupiter meets Neptune in Pisces**
>
> April 12, 2022

The Law of Attraction is on your side but do your part to overturn limiting beliefs. There's a difference between being gullible (which means you're tuned out and unaware or handing someone else your power) and being receptive (you're empowered but also present and open). While Neptune is the master of illusions, Jupiter is the agent of truth. Sit humbly at their feet and you'll gain emotional mastery that you can use for the rest of your life.

Just don't expect the lessons to come without effort. Neptune is known for provoking crises as part of its healing remedy, and Jupiter will amplify the effects. While you'll learn at an accelerated pace, surrender is essential. Let go of any know-it-all traits, Leo, and let yourself be guided. Jupiter and Neptune sit side by side for longer than just one day. Their combined power period lasts from March 13 to April 30, a time when your spiritual wisdom grows by leaps and bounds!

As far as relationships go, lines may be fuzzier during this conjunction. Even if you feel ready to go "all in," the universe may have a few more karmic tests to run first. Be patient with the process and willing to take a clear-eyed look instead of a rosy-hued one (which will be far more tempting). Facts can be obscured along with red flags. But once you open Pandora's box, you could wind up in over your head. That's more reason to wait and wade around before fully submerging yourself in another's life.

JUPITER IN ARIES

Your Global Launch

Jupiter in Aries

May 10 to
October 28, 2022

December 20, 2022
to May 16, 2023

Goodbye, confining cocoon! After Jupiter's intense plunge through Pisces, the abundant planet barrels into fiery, freedom-loving Aries from May 10 to October 28. You've rested your wings for the first part of 2022, now you're like a butterfly busting out of the chrysalis. Shake off the emotional shackles and rejoin the wider world. With Jupiter soaring through your global ninth house, you have five and a half months to travel, study, and take some enterprising risks, all in the name of personal expansion.

When Jupiter rises from Pisces into Aries, it's like someone switching the lights on in a dark room—one you thought was empty. But lo and behold! It's full of vibrant people from all walks of life, ready to celebrate! Caution: this shift can be disorienting. Give yourself time to adjust to the view and check out your options so you don't get scooped up by the first temptation that comes your way.

Jupiter is the natural ruler of the fortune-filled ninth house, bringing you a double dose of luck while in Aries. Suddenly, everything and anything feels possible...and truly, it is! The refrigerator magnet quote, "If you can dream it, you can do it," is now your mantra. And you don't care if it's a little corny, because with Jupiter here, you're like a walking motivational speaker, cheering people on, speaking fearlessly about your beliefs and unapologetically pursuing your lofty visions.

Cross-cultural connections can heat up mid-year as you passionately pursue alliances with people whose backgrounds are different from your own. Learn a foreign language or get involved in an equity and justice initiative in your community or at work. Maybe you'll advocate for immigrant rights or promote a historically relevant curriculum in schools. With Jupiter in trailblazing Aries, you may spearhead initiatives like these. Share your unifying message with the world through publishing and education, two of Jupiter's domains.

Jupiter is only here for the middle of 2022, but you'll feel the shift. Go "bucket-list" big with your summer vacation plans. Take a once-in-a-lifetime pilgrimage. Apply to school or record an album. Find investors for your start-up or get the shoestring version going on your own. If Jupiter in Pisces brought a big payout, why not invest some of those profits in your dreams?

Even more fortuitous? In Aries, Jupiter forms a flowing 120° trine to your Sun in Leo. This vitality-boosting transit unleashes a torrential downpour of passion. Expect to feel friskier and more flamboyant than you have in years!

VENUS RETROGRADE

Health is Wealth

Venus in Capricorn

November 5, 2021
to March 6, 2022

**Venus Retrograde
in Capricorn**

December 19, 2021
to January 29, 2022

Bump self-care to the top of the priority list! In fact, when you're cooking up New Year's resolutions for 2022, be sure to include all manner of self-nurturing and health- and healing-related pursuits— even those that tilt more toward beauty than hardcore wellness. And no guilt-tripping for putting yourself and your needs first!

Beautifying Venus is making an extra-long sweep through earthy Capricorn and your sixth house of work, service and healing from November 5, 2021, to March 6, 2022. Normally, the planet of love, beauty and sensuality spends just three to five weeks in a sign, but every other year, it flips into retrograde for six weeks. This go-round, you're treated to Venus' healing vibes for a total of four months! That's like an engraved invitation to pamper yourself with therapeutic treatments, eco-friendly products, healthy organic foods and whatever else your luxury-loving sign craves. Remember: It's not pure indulgence if it's good for you!

And with Venus retrograde from December 19, 2021, to January 29, 2022, this is actually a form of preventative medicine—the best kind! You know that cliché about putting on your own oxygen mask before assisting others? Take that a step further and book yourself an oxygenating facial, immune-boosting massage and maybe a full body scrub with thalassotherapy products.

Alluring as this sounds, it might nevertheless require a certain amount of willpower to do your part of the healthy-living upgrade, especially since Venus commenced the backspin smack in the middle of the holiday season. With Santa cookies and jugs of eggnog making the rounds—along with slinky holiday outfits—this is also the time of year when people can become a little hyper-focused on weight and body-image issues can flare. You may have to stay on guard to not become hypercritical of the appearance in the mirror or over-emphasize perceived "flaws." Avoid booking cosmetic procedures during Venus' reversal. You can't bank on hair or style changes coming out the way you're hoping. Even if they do, you might have a 180-degree change of heart when Venus straightens out at the end of January.

Even while those gym membership ads flood your feed, you're still a Leo, more interested in pleasure than pain. So rather than forcing yourself to endure a grueling boot camp or stick to a restrictive meal plan, let Venus lead you to enjoyable forms of exercise, like dancing, swimming (if you have access to an indoor pool) or snow-shoeing. Bonus points for anything that allows you to engage socially (IRL or virtually) because the communal aspect will keep you motivated.

As you research activities and programs that can yield the results you seek, steer clear of anything that sounds even slightly dangerous—or faddish, like mono-food diets or lengthy juice fasts, especially if you've never done one before. During the retrograde, pay attention to the relationship between what you put in your body and how you feel afterward. If you feel tired every time you eat, say, wheat products, or feel congested after dairy, you might be allergic or have a sensitivity. Try eating very clean for a week or two—maybe after New Year's—and see if the symptoms go away.

And since Venus is still the love planet, couples can use this extended visit, in effect until March 6, to get healthy together. Have date nights in the kitchen, preparing exquisite, nourishing meals; find workouts or yoga routines you can do together; spend more time outdoors—or indoors, behind closed doors. Bottom line: With enchantress Venus here, taking care of your health can be a pleasurable experience.

The sixth house also rules your daily work and routines, and charm magnet Venus could lead the way to some big professional wins to kick off the year. The six-week retrograde is a great time to do any behind-the-scenes projects and review/reconsider all your branded assets. Put in however much time is needed, because you want to be ready for your big reveal come January 29! Don't be surprised—and certainly don't fret—if driven Venus in Capricorn causes a redirect of your mojo from the bedroom to the boardroom (or from the sofa to the studio). We're not suggesting you leave your lover high and dry, but if you have the luxury of making your own schedule, this is an outstanding opportunity to focus on Leo, Inc. It's up to you to regulate your energy levels and not burn out. Managing your professional stress is key to reaching the finish line in the time—and condition—you want!

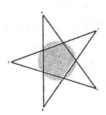

LUNAR NODES IN TAURUS AND SCORPIO

Establish Expertise, Find Support

Lunar Nodes in Taurus and Scorpio

January 18, 2022 to July 17, 2023

Leaders wanted? No one has to twist a Leo's jewel-bedazzled paw to convince you to answer the call. Taking charge comes naturally to your magnanimous sign. Good news! Opportunities to rise and shine will start showing up everywhere in 2022. On January 18, the moon's destiny-driven North Node settles into sensible Taurus and powers up your tenth house of status, career and prestige until July 17, 2023. This could bring some of the most meaningful moments for your professional life, Leo. Are you on your path? If not, you are sure to find it!

Discernment is essential during this cycle, which only comes around every 18-20 years. Sure, it's flattering to be nominated for every board chair in town. But if you spread yourself thinner than angel-hair pasta, you'll miss out on the truly life-changing opportunities that benefit you as much as the people you're serving. Our recommendation? Make a criteria checklist. If an offer doesn't tick all the boxes, either say no or negotiate a counteroffer. Here at Astrostyle HQ, we run new initiatives through the "PEEPS filter" before they pass go. That's an acronym for:

Production Time Needed
Energy Expenditure
Exposure to a Premium Audience (in other words, you!)
Profitability
Support Staff Required

Even if a project promises to be wildly profitable, we've been known to take a hard pass if the Energy Expenditure involved would negatively impact things like, say, our ability to write daily horoscopes...or this book. This is just one example of a checklist, of course, and we're sure you can invent your own. Pro tip: Keep the list short and sweet. Use an easy-to-remember acronym. You'll save yourself from the soul-sucking "scope creep" that enthusiastic fire signs fall prey to.

The last time the North Node visited Taurus was between April 14, 2003, and December 26, 2004. Whatever you were spearheading then could give clues about what's to come in 2022. No need to wait on a fateful call from a recruiter or agent. Pursue what you want with a vengeance, because luck is on your side during this success-boosting cycle.

Challenges? You'll savage them! Obstacles? You're going HAM 'til you're on the other side. But behind that fierce drive, your heart-centered style will be a constant. The reason for this? Directly across the zodiac wheel, the lunar South Node (AKA "the cosmic comfort zone") occupies Scorpio and your sentimental fourth house. During this 18-month cycle, solidifying important relationships is as crucial as producing stellar results. What's the point of making it to the top if you're utterly alone when you get there?

Warning flag: Big-hearted Lions love to hook up a friend, sculpting their raw talent like clay. That's fine, as long as you also have a baseline of support from experienced folks. (Ideally, many of whom are not a cousin, sorority sister, neighbor or your favorite barista who is brimming over with potential.) Being the expert in all matters builds a lopsided organization. Not only is that a recipe for exhaustion, but it will also make it hard to accomplish your goal.

In other words, Leo, what you devote precious time to is half the equation. How you go about producing results could also shift. Hands-on Leos will get a masterclass in letting go. It's not just about delegating and outsourcing when the North Node is in master planner Taurus. It's about cultivating the kind of team that calls people into their greatness.

A key lesson of this nodal cycle:
Learning to be supportive
without sacrificing yourself.
Yes, Leo, it is possible.

That means you can't treat your squad like helpless children to whom you spoon-feed solutions. Stop assigning the "easy" tasks away, and let the capable people take ownership of an initiative. At times you may have to keep them on track with deadline reminders or special trainings. If you've developed processes, put together an orientation manual. Better yet, how about asking your crew to document their systems? Yep, Leo, you're building a machine!

Simultaneously, the South Node in Scorpio helps you feel more anchored in home and family affairs. Lair care is increasingly essential to your serenity during this 18-month cycle. Maybe you'll renovate for an open floor plan or raise the roof and build skylight access. Other Lions may be ready to decamp to a totally different type of property or shuffle the roster of who is living under your roof. Aging parents or a child's schooling needs could also direct your GPS to a new zip code—perhaps one that's familiar from your own youth. Priceless as bonding moments will be, build in room for your own priorities. A key lesson of this nodal cycle: Learning to be supportive without sacrificing yourself. Yes, Leo, it is possible.

Financial planning could be a driving factor regarding choices. Hosting the Scorpio South node in your stabilizing fourth house drives up security issues. The rallying cry of, "location, location, location!" may shift to "saving, saving, saving!" especially if your shelter (and food!) costs have been zapping most of your earnings.

Scorpio energy is sexy. Sacred. And you'll want to feel that way wherever you live! That includes the four walls that house you and the way you feel in your own skin. Some Leos could radically transform their self-care habits, perhaps rearranging your space to leave room for dancing, yoga, juicing and joyfully cooking healthy meals. With regards to both, it's not size that matters—it's a sense of safety. Start there and you'll build the foundation of comfort that you need to roar and soar!

ECLIPSES IN TAURUS AND SCORPIO

Home and Career in the Spotlight

Partial Solar Eclipse in Taurus

April 30 at 4:27pm

Total Lunar Eclipse in Scorpio

May 16 at 12:14am

Partial Solar Eclipse in Scorpio new moon

October 25 at 6:48am

Total Lunar Eclipse in Taurus full moon

November 8 at 6:02am

times in eastern time

Work-life rebalancing? In 2022, four eclipses teeter across the Taurus/Scorpio axis, bringing noteworthy developments to your career house (ruled by Taurus) and your domestic sphere (governed by Scorpio). This eclipse series, which runs from November 2021 to October 2023, has already been shaking up these foundational zones of your chart since late last year.

On April 30 and November 8, eclipses in Taurus activate your "true north" as they charge up your tenth house of career and ambition. If your compass hasn't been pointing toward your finest gifts, get ready! Talented Leos could suddenly switch gears, moving quickly in a much more fulfilling direction.

The partial solar eclipse on April 30 arrives in tandem with the Taurus new moon, which could suddenly rocket you into a position of great responsibility. Get ready, Leo! A promotion or leadership opportunity could land in your lap or roles at the office could restructure unexpectedly. To capitalize on lucky breaks, act swiftly. Eclipses open a short window of opportunity—one that won't leave much time to deliberate. Leos will have to leap near April 30. Try to remember: without risk there can be no reward.

The November 8 full moon in Taurus is a total lunar eclipse, which is sure to bring bold developments. Leos could change jobs, possibly due to a company restructuring or a major offer that arrives unexpectedly (and is too damn good to pass up!). Clients or roles that are no longer a good fit could be "eclipsed" away. Should this happen, trust that the stars are making room for something better. The job of an eclipse is to clear out the old and outmoded. Don't hang on with your teeth, especially to a situation that's not bringing you happiness or fulfillment.

Give your living quarters a once-over when a pair of eclipses in Scorpio transform your home and family sector. The first is a total lunar (full moon) eclipse from May 16, which could bring resolution to an ongoing domestic matter. Where you live or who you live with might suddenly shift, or you may put the kibosh on home expansion plans and vow to pursue a simpler lifestyle.

In late 2022, the solar (new moon) eclipse on October 25 accelerates developments. Maybe you'll knock down walls for a décor refresh or renovation. Some Leos may relocate for a job, buy a home or oust a disruptive roommate. You might suddenly find out that you have to move— for example, your landlord sells the building and gives you short notice.

The fourth and tenth houses are also the "parent zones" of your chart. The fourth house rules mothers; the tenth house, fathers. Your mom or dad could be central figures at these eclipses. which force you to confront unresolved family issues—ones that may crop up by surprise. A pregnancy is possible for some Leos near these dates. A child or a female relative could also play into events.

Whatever happens, act swiftly, if not certainly, to resolve the situation. While you'd prefer if these developments came at a slower pace, odds are, the issue's been brewing for a while. Eventually, we bless eclipses for "forcing" us to look at things we were ignoring for too long. But near these dates, hang on to your crown, Leo!

MARS IN GEMINI

Assemble Your Dream Team

Mars in Gemini

August 20, 2022 to
March 25, 2023

**Mars Retrograde
in Gemini**

October 30, 2022
to January 12, 2023

Raise those spirit fingers to the sky! You may finally understand—viscerally—that old expression about teamwork making the dream work starting August 20, 2022. The reason? Motivational Mars marches into amicable Gemini and your collaborative eleventh house of group activities for an extra-long visit.

Typically, the red-hot planet spends just seven weeks in each sign during its two-year solar orbit. But because of a rare retrograde cycle (every other year), Mars will be on a protracted sabbatical in Gemini for six months—until March 25, 2023. While this will afford many exciting opportunities, you will want to exert caution and mindfulness during its reversal from October 30 to January 12, 2023. During that time, other people's agendas and motives may not be clearly discerned, if at all.

One way to get the most out of this cooperative power surge is to pull together, train and galvanize your Leo dream team before Mars backflips. You want to jump on this because your golden window for team-building is between August 20 and October 30. This should give you plenty of time to get these luminaries on-boarded and aligned with your vision and way of working. (And if you're part of someone else's star-studded squad, make sure you're 100 percent in sync with their mission. Passion is the key to a Leo's loyalty.)

Speaking of devotion, if valuable ideas or intellectual property are involved, get people to sign nondisclosure agreements or perhaps even more detailed contacts. Allegiance is your middle name, but not everyone is operating at the same level of integrity, and you can't afford any mutineers!

Since the eleventh house is also your tech zone, independent Mars here could help you find the best and most efficient apps, devices and software. Whether you're running the programs yourself or outsourcing, you need to know what's best for you and your brand or company. Upgrades aren't cheap, but if doing so could make your work more productive—or competitive—it behooves you to do a cost-benefit analysis. You might be surprised that a little outlay of cash could turn into a very profitable investment. Are you one of those born Leo entertainers? If so, with activating Mars in articulate, creative Gemini, you might become an overnight TikTok or YouTube sensation or an Instagram influencer.

Your activist humanitarian side may get roused under this Martian spell. Use your innate gifts to mobilize people and spread the word about a political candidate or a cause that's close to your big heart. The only potential fly in the ointment is that progress on some of these initiatives could come to a grinding halt—or go sideways—during the October 30 to January 12 retrograde.

But don't lose steam—or the faith! Use this slowdown to review your efforts, allies and even your overarching vision. If it can benefit from some tweaks, dive right in! You might need to let someone go or scale back, but if you keep your focus on the high-minded goal, it won't seem like the end of the world. Should you need to confront someone, be diplomatic. Take them aside and firmly but kindly spell out exactly what needs to change—as well as the consequences of not complying. It can help to write a little "script" and read it to a friend who'll give you sincere feedback.

Since retrogrades rule the past and the eleventh house is your community zone, you might reconnect with old friends or fellow idealists who are involved with programs to improve the world. On a more personal note, with Mars retrograde, you may stick close to your true-blue crew and not make overtures to new people or groups.

If you have a digital venture you're dying to develop, work quietly behind the scenes until January 12, 2023, getting input from experienced people who want you to succeed. Sit tight through the holidays, but be ready to launch—at least a beta version—once Mars is back to full strength. The backspin is also an ideal time to update your online presence, from your business bio to your online dating photos and bio. Be ready to showcase 2023 Leo!

VIRGO

LOVE

Relationships get a major boost in 2022, thanks to lucky Jupiter's tour through Pisces and Aries—the signs ruling your 7th and 8th houses of committed partnership. Throw some of that Virgo caution to the wind and take a chance on romance. You could meet your match while traveling or by exploring a new zip code on your dating app. Cross-cultural connections could bring the missing spark this year. Coupled Virgos: don't be afraid to explore independent interests. A healthy dose of autonomy keeps the spark alive. Plan to take at least one bucket-list vacation together before the year is through. Clear the air—or the decks—while Venus is retrograde until January 29. If you're not on the same page about kids, life paths or another must-have, go your separate ways. Bonds deepen quickly while Jupiter is in Aries from May 10 to October 28—prime time for joining lives and making vows.

CAREER & MONEY

Keep on grinding, Virgo—your payoff is in sight! Taskmaster Saturn is hustling through Aquarius for its final full year. After putting you through paces since March 21, 2020, you can finally systematize, document your process and automate a few laborious tasks that you seem to repeat over and over. (Virgo heaven!) Embrace new partnerships wherever possible, as bountiful Jupiter brings favor and fortune to your collaborative efforts all year. With the lunar South Node in Scorpio and your cooperative third house after January 18, you and a kindred spirit could rake in the profits as a dynamic duo. Stability is exciting once go-getter Mars buzzes into your security zone from August 20, 2022, to March 25, 2023. Pour energy into building your nest egg: purchase real estate, funnel savings into a retirement portfolio, trim expenses. Make sure you have a cushion in place before Mars turns retrograde from October 30 to January 12, 2023.

WELLNESS

Scheduling is the key to sanity this year! In addition to work duties and a regular fitness regimen, block out time to rest and digest. With Saturn in your sixth house (AKA the Virgo house), your parasympathetic nervous system could use a break. The good news is, you can activate its calming powers with your sign's favorite pastimes: meditation, yoga, massage, walks in nature, deep breathing, spending time with kids and pets. Dial down the inflammation-producing foods like wheat and dairy and scale back the stimulants like coffee and sugar. Gut health is always key to strong immunity and this year, you may need to add more microbiomes to your diet—especially when agitating Mars hits your nutrition zone for six months on August 20.

FRIENDS & FAMILY

Spring free from that cocoon, Virgo butterfly! Your social life is set to soar as the lunar South Node anchors in Scorpio and your third house of friendship from January 18, 2022, until July 17, 2023. Forget random encounters though! This 18-month cycle is like a soul-squad reunion tour, reconnecting you to kindred spirits who you've clearly known in past lives. Get involved in your local scene: you could leave an indelible mark on your community! But don't get stuck in one place. The lunar North Node in Taurus spins your compass in a worldly direction. Connect with far-flung friends via social media and maybe an epic travel plan. Friction and home may intensify under Mars' watch after August 20—a prompt to change your living situation or learn healthier means of conflict resolution.

JUPITER IN PISCES

So Happy Together

Jupiter in Pisces

December 28, 2021
to May 10, 2022

October 28 to
December 20, 2022

Double up for the win! After an industrious 2021, you're craving meaningful companionship again, and the stars deliver. Horizon-broadening Jupiter visits your opposite sign of Pisces until May 10—and again from October 28 to December 20. There, it brings bountiful magic to your seventh house of committed partnerships. From a legendary love affair to a prosperous business alliance, roll the dice, Virgo. With your risk tolerance elevated, 2022 could be the year that you make a connection official or move on from a situationship you've outgrown.

This Jupiter cycle, which you experienced briefly in 2021 (from May 13 to July 28), continues to inspire a whole new way of relating. Relationships that began near the middle of last year get a second wind. Get ready: With Jupiter in divinely ordained Pisces, a few past characters could return to reprise their roles in your personal fairy tale. Never say never, Virgo! If you're happily hooked up, worldly Jupiter sends you on a quest for shared adventures that breathe new life into your bond. Look back to a prior Jupiter in Pisces cycle, from January 2010 to January 2011, for themes that could emerge again.

In existing partnerships, get ready for some eye-opening role reversals. If you're the talkative one, you could find yourself in the role of the active listener. Social butterfly Virgos may suddenly prefer nights at home. If you typically keep a stiff upper lip when matters get tense, outspoken Jupiter inspires you to share your feelings—yes, even the ones that might intensify conflict. Sharpen interpersonal tools with Jupiter's thinking cap on, trying everything from couples' workshops to managerial training. But no more disassociating, please. Your voice deserves to be part of the chorus, Virgo! And an open-book policy can attract fascinating friends into your sphere.

Then again, if you're like many opinionated Virgos out there, watch how readily you serve up critiques. Open-minded Jupiter encourages you to wait a beat before delivering snap judgments. Extend that pause between stimulus and response, as Holocaust survivor and psychotherapist Viktor Frankl advised. While Jupiter is the planet of candor, in your diplomatic seventh house, the truth should be wielded judiciously. Does your date really need to know that you prefer the creamier texture of the lobster bisque at the seafood restaurant down the road? Or can you try using Jupiter's optimistic powers to focus on what you do like about the evening, like the artfully plated beet salad and the to-die-for crème brulee?

If you're more the posh-and-pampered personality, you might find yourself playing benefactor instead of beneficiary—and learning so much about yourself in the process. A Virgo who plays the provider role will discover how to be vulnerable and receive. Jupiter equalizes the give-and-take with everyone, from colleagues to companions to your kin.

Marriage on your mind? This year, many Virgos will get engaged or tie the knot. Whether you plan a destination wedding (Jupiter loves travel) or host a cottagecore ritual at an organic winery, your cautious sign could be ready to jump the broom into happily-ever-after.

While in Pisces, Jupiter will directly oppose your Virgo Sun. With the red-spotted planet furthest away from el Sol on the zodiac wheel, you may be a little too keen to leap without looking. Before you take any gambles, build in a criteria checklist for safety's sake. Judgment may be skewed, or it can take a minute for you to connect to your truth while the chorus of opinions is amplified.

Single Virgos, we suggest you burn that "My Perfect Mate" list—or at least tuck it under a crystal until May 10. Expansive Jupiter could open you up to someone who was so far off your radar, you couldn't have dreamed

66

From a legendary love affair to a prosperous business alliance, roll the dice, Virgo.

99

them up. Until now, that is, because in 2022, love may come in a very different package than ever before. Soulmates may hail from a far-flung provenance or maybe they were raised in a different cultural or religious setting. Variety adds major spice during this Jupiter cycle.

And since you actually enjoy your alone time, don't pooh-pooh a long-distance relationship. When swiping the dating apps, check out prospects in different zip codes, or heck, country codes. Jupiter rules travel and won't be mad if you rack up a few frequent flyer miles or relocate for that special someone. Plus, this could be the perfect arrangement, leaving room for contemplative monk moments. And, let's be honest, Virgo, you aren't about to give up any "secret single behaviors" that involve plucking, squeezing and deep cleansing—or (gasp) trot them out in front of your boo.

Been together forever? Jupiter in Pisces lends a fresh focus to longtime duos. Under the enterprising planet's influence, you might launch a joint venture or team up on a business idea. Learning and growing together is the key, so craft your shared bucket list and start crossing things off. Venture beyond your usual spots and try new restaurants, a night at a boutique hotel, a day trip outside city limits. Novel experiences will spike the passion factor.

Has a work or romantic relationship run its course? These Jupiter in Pisces circuits could lead to an amicable split—or one that is at least a fairly civil one. Suddenly single Virgos may be back in the dating game sooner than you think. And it won't be long until a bounty of new prospects pop up. Enjoying some casual encounters is always a great way to ease back in, but who knows? Because Jupiter in this LTR zone makes you especially attractive to serious-minded types, you may flow from one commitment right into another. Although serial monogamy suits your steady sign, don't skip Jupiter's self-discovery process. Rushing into cohabitation or speeding to the altar could get messy down the line, even if you're "sure" this person is The One.

This same warning label applies to any business partnerships. With venturesome Jupiter in your house of contracts, you might rush to sign on the dotted line. Indeed, some promising joint projects could be worth rolling the dice on in 2022. Jupiter is the cosmic gambler, however, and you may be tempted to ignore little crimson flags in the rush to seal a deal. Conduct your due diligence and don't be overzealous. Hire an attorney for a couple hours of legal work to make sure your rights are protected. If everything checks out, great! You'll have peace in your heart knowing you did this with integrity.

JUPITER MEETS NEPTUNE IN PISCES

Soulmate Patrol

> **Jupiter meets Neptune in Pisces**
>
> April 12, 2022

April 12 is a crucial date to mark on the calendar. For the first time in 13 years, Jupiter syncs up with its spiritual soulmate Neptune, pulling you deeper into Pisces' fantasy-fueled Wonderland. Relationships could hit a milestone moment, but here's the question: Will you be swept away or pulled into the riptide?

The current of attraction will be super strong on this day, but like a magnet, it can repel with equal force. In fact, you'll experience this dueling charge many times as Jupiter and Neptune swim in close connection through these waters from March 14 to April 30.

What you don't want to do (if you can help yourself, so try!) is make a binding decision in the storm of an emotional moment. Jupiter is impulsive while Neptune is the master of illusions. Since people's motives will be obscured, you need to take your time and really negotiate every point of your agreements. No matter how forthright people are being, their shortcomings may be in their own "blind spots." Take your time and look at every side of the coin, not just the shiny one that's dazzling you in the moment.

JUPITER IN ARIES

Getting Intimate

Jupiter in Aries

May 10 to
October 28,2022

December 20, 2022
to May 16, 2023

From May 10 to October 28, Jupiter plunges into Aries and your intimate eighth house. The emphasis is on merging now, and the urge will be strong! From emotional bonds to babymaking to joint financial ventures, you're moving past the point of no return. Forget about doing anything halfway: It's all or nothing now! While Jupiter only spends five and a half months in Aries this year, whatever gets churned up will have a second act from December 20, 2022, to May 16, 2023, when the red-spotted planet charges the Ram's realm again.

Now for the spicy part. With Jupiter in your erotic eighth house, a sexual awakening could be in store. You might explore your desires with a partner who opens you up to new aspects of your erotic nature. Since Jupiter rules learning, try workshops on tantra or explore sensual movement like belly dancing and tango.

But this is no light and fluffy affair! If Jupiter in the seventh house was the wedding, Jupiter in the eighth house is the post-honeymoon phase. The cake and champagne have been enjoyed, the honeymoon bags are unpacked and the gifts are all unwrapped. Mmmkay, so now what? That's what you'll be exploring over the next five and a half months. And P.S. Virgo, if you're in any sort of partnership, this is not a solo exploration!

With that in mind, couples could cement their bond by co-signing a lease, getting engaged or buying real estate. Baby talks may be on the table if you've been pondering a pregnancy. Some Virgos may go the other direction, splitting up with a partner (romantic or business) and dividing shared assets. If this involves a courtroom battle, know that Jupiter is on your side. Most Virgos should have a favorable outcome around alimony, custody or asset division. Don't back down without knowing your worth!

> **66**
>
> *With Jupiter in your erotic eighth house, a sexual awakening could be in store.*
>
> **99**

♍

Life can take a quieter turn with Jupiter in this introspective zone. During this vulnerable cycle, feelings may be raw. Anger or pain that you stuffed down could resurface, but this philosophical Jupiter cycle is an ideal time for transformational healing. Get ready to do some intense behind-the-scenes work or deep emotional processing. Talk therapy is always great for your analytical sign, but you can release stuck pain through energy healing or somatic work that helps you uncover trauma that you're storing in your body.

In business, Jupiter in Aries helps you attract an investor or ink an exciting joint venture. This could be a time of wealth planning and windfalls—one of your most prosperous cycles in a long time. You might buy or sell real estate, so if you're considering a move, lucky Jupiter will soon be in your corner.

Metaphysical mysteries draw you in, allowing you to suspend logic and go places that were formerly off limits. Your esoteric explorations could pay off in the material world, as you become well-rounded and "richer" in every sense, not just in your bank account.

If friends send out an APB, don't be surprised. You might fly under the radar once this reflective Jupiter cycle begins. Whether you're consumed with a passion project that demands extreme concentration or bawling on your hypnotherapist's couch after a mind-blowing past-life regression, your attention is decidedly internal. Stay on the journey, knowing that you'll emerge from the chrysalis as a beautiful butterfly by October 28. Shed those layers and transform.

VENUS RETROGRADE

Romantic Revisions

Venus in Capricorn

November 5, 2021
to March 6, 2022

Venus Retrograde
in Capricorn

December 19, 2021
to January 29, 2022

If the highlight of your winter plans revolved around deep rest and a long hibernation, you might want to head back to the drawing board right after New Year's Day. While the thought of going off the grid is appealing, the planets have something else in mind for you, Virgo, starting with making up for lost lockdown time. And there will be no shortage of willing conspirators.

So before you attempt to pull off any such disappearing acts, have a peek at who's hovering in your field and blipping across your romantic radar screen. Already hooked up? You might start seeing them through one of those sparkly smart-phone photo filters. Why's that, you ask? Venus—AKA the planet of love, beauty and sensuality—normally spends just three to five weeks in a sign, but every other year, it shifts into retrograde for six weeks (December 19, 2021, until January 29, 2022), and this go-round, that's happening in your fifth house of glamour and romance. That means you'll be hearing (or maybe humming) Venus' seductive siren song for a total of four months!

Since November 5, 2021, Venus has been catwalking through Capricorn and that minxy fifth house of yours, rousing up your inner vixen and filling your head with all kinds of steamy—and creative!—notions. Let's just say you won't be able to fade into the background during this visibility-boosting transit, which lasts in total until March 6, 2022. With your flamboyant fame zone activated, prepare to garner more attention than you're used to, and are possibly comfortable with. To you, any "glory" should be directed to what you do and produce rather than to you-per-se. It might help to make this into a bit of a game—challenging yourself to relish the kudos and feel appreciated. Also, focus on how you can leverage this popularity spike to do even more good in the world!

> *Get ready to do some intense behind-the-scenes work or deep emotional processing.*

Of course, we are talking about the planet d'amour and your fifth house of passion here, Virgo. If you're single, you almost couldn't ask for a more auspicious placement! If you're actively seeking a relationship, you may have four months of lucky opportunities, or at least before and after the six-week retrograde (December 19, 2021, to January 29, 2022). Under that spell, your mistletoe moments could have been, uh, misleading. And since planets in reverse can bring back the past, be mindful of how much sway you give to your memories and how much you indulge those sentimental feelings.

Should you get the "brilliant" (not!) idea to text an ex in that hazy period from December 19 to January 29, stop yourself in your tracks and ping a friend instead. Ask them to be brutally candid and remind you of every unsavory secret you shared about this person in question. And try to listen without becoming defensive. If those hurts still sting, summon the self-discipline to resist. However, if there are things you never shared, such as this person's tenderness and sincere desire to improve, well, maybe, cautiously, with exceedingly low expectations, send a message. But then immediately distract yourself with useful and engaging activities so you don't check your phone every three minutes (or seconds).

The fifth house is also the cauldron out of which drama arises. With Venus in reverse as 2022 opens, even "keep it cool" Virgos could get sucked into some hysterics before January 29. Try to see it for what it is (a time- and energy-suck) and cut yourself some slack. If you're in an LTR, don't take your partner's bait. Try to quell strong emotions (yours or theirs) and get to what's really bugging them—or you!

When the peacekeeping planet is retrograde, tempers can spark fast, so if you've been waiting for some unfinished business to resurface, you might get a chance to get closure. Set an intention for the outcome you'd like, and should tension start to approach pressure-cooker level, step away, take a few chillout breaths and redirect the conversation back to the peaceful resolution you seek. Even if you need to leave the house—or sleep on the sofa—it's better to let things settle down than succumb to the heat of the moment and risk saying or doing something that could leave a permanent dent in the union.

If you're part of a very long-running couple and yesterday's "flame of passion" has died down to barely-burning embers, Venus in reverse could leave you vulnerable to "out-of-bounds" attractions. Even if you don't cross any physical lines, you need to stay cognizant of what's happening—being brutally honest with yourself. If you find yourself sharing more intimacies, including sexual fantasies, with this "platonic" person, Google the definition of "emotional affair." What starts off safe and innocent can quickly escalate into something complicated and messy. When you're connecting on this level, attraction and desire is almost inevitable. Despite your best intentions of keeping your distance, expectations are sure to arise, leading to hurt feelings, jealousy and possibly worse.

For those who truly want to give the relationship a fighting chance, step up to the Venus-retrograde challenge and shutter out temptation and dive deeper into your union. Initiate those "terrifying" conversations and talk through what's strong and what's wobbly in the dynamic. Is there a power imbalance? Does one of you give too much (financially, emotionally); do you both feel adored and appreciated? Sometimes just being really heard can begin the healing process. Get out of town and do something outside your mutual comfort zones. Participating in a new adventure together will release dopamine and oxytocin, chemicals that promote feelings of closeness. So maybe instead of a raucous NYE, consider a pair-bonding road trip in a part of the country you've always talked about touring.

The fifth house is also your fertility sector, making these four months ripe, so to speak, for babymaking and other "creative" pursuits. So if starting or expanding a family is on the agenda, plan accordingly. Parents can revive favorite old childhood activities, like sledding or skating, or maybe perfecting your hot chocolate recipe. If pregnancy is a touchy subject—you want kids, your partner doesn't, or you're having trouble conceiving—Venus retrograde (December 19 to January 29) is perfect for having tricky conversations and researching fertility specialists, including "alternative" techniques for conceiving.

LUNAR NODES IN TAURUS AND SCORPIO

Expand Your Horizons

Lunar Nodes in Taurus and Scorpio

January 18, 2022
to July 17, 2023

Virgo ahoy! Distant ports are calling in 2022, tempting you far from your familiar turf. On January 18, the lunar North Node shifts into Taurus. As it points its compass in your ninth house of global expansion until July 17, 2023, anywhere but "the usual place" is where you'll find the most enriching opportunities for growth.

Don't squander this cycle by trying to create the perfect itinerary. This destiny-driven placement only comes around once every two decades. Exploring is the purpose here, Virgo! You don't have to justify a two-week backpacking trip by coordinating it with a work conference, for example. In fact, unplugging from all duties will open up your spiritual channels, even if you only go for a weekend getaway.

Nor should you read 1,000 Yelp reviews before arriving at your destination. We realize that no self-respecting Virgo would travel without some sort of map and a well-curated itinerary. Just keep your agenda fairly flexible when you set off on a voyage. Buy tickets for a show, make a couple of dinner reservations, book a treatment at a high-end spa. And sure, rent Vespas or jet skis. But leave lots of whitespace for spontaneous discoveries. Wandering off the beaten path is where the magic lies. Before you know it, you could be taking a weaving class taught by an indigenous elder, joining a plant medicine ceremony or learning dance moves from the locals at a tucked-away club.

Across your chart, the equally karmic South Node beams into Scorpio and your communication and local activity HQ. Virgos could become quite a fixture on the neighborhood scene during this 18-month cycle. With transformational Scorpio energy guiding your moves, get involved in initiatives to make your neck of the woods a happier, safer and hipper place to be.

Don't love where you live? The Scorpio South Node could make it unbearable for you to be somewhere that doesn't sing to your soul. During this nomadic cycle, try short-term rentals in different neighborhoods to see what suits 2022 you. One Virgo friend became a professional pet-sitter to help cover the costs of this exploration. Certified by a reputable website, she's had a taste of life from New York City to the islands of Washington State. Prior to the quarantine, she planned to live in Portugal for three months, and hopes to bring that dream to life this year. With the North Node in her ninth house, we can already taste the salt cod and Port wine in her future.

The Taurus-Scorpio nodes awaken your enterprising streak. Who knows? Maybe you'll open a raw-vegan food truck, a hair salon that offers tarot readings, or become a major online workshop leader. Any sort of writing, media-making or teaching is favored under this cycle. Consulting work could pay you handsomely. If you've been itching to escape the nine-to-five grind, now's your opportunity.

What's safe to say is that from now until July 17, 2023, your horizons will expand, even if you never leave your time zone. You can widen your metaphorical viewfinder with ongoing study and spiritual pursuits, as well as developing an idea for your own business. When you can articulate your soul's mission statement, reach out to like-minded folks and see where you can take it!

Partnerships could be quite profitable with the Scorpio South Node in this position. Where you've been stuck in solo mode, turn it into a tag team effort. The third house rules peers, like siblings and close friends, as well as neighbors and coworkers. Dynamic duos may be formed with people in these categories. Even if a verbal agreement would suffice, don't leave the relationship in fate's hands. Ambiguity has been known to breed contempt, even between people who pinky-promised to always be BFFs. Drafting a formal agreement might feel awkward, but present it in a more powerful light—because you never want anything to get in the way of the affinity you share.

Casting a wide net will also bring luck, thanks to the Taurus North Node. This may be more of a door-opener than a deal-closer in 2022, so be patient with the process! The North Node points us to new terrain; places where we have yet to gain experience. Fumbling around in the dark is normal when you're learning something new. Remind yourself of this when you get frustrated by "mistakes." Practice will make perfect eventually, but first, give yourself permission to experiment—and bless every mess!

ECLIPSES IN TAURUS AND SCORPIO
Engaging in Dialogues

**Partial Solar
Eclipse in Taurus**

April 30 at 4:27pm

**Total Lunar
Eclipse in Scorpio**

May 16 at 12:14am

**Partial Solar Eclipse
in Scorpio new moon**

October 25 at 6:48am

**Total Lunar Eclipse
in Taurus full moon**

November 8 at 6:02am

times in eastern time

Speak up, Virgo! Not that your opinionated sign needs too much encouragement to voice your truth. This year's four eclipses ignite your communication sectors, fueling you with ideas, inspiration and even a motivating message for the world. These game-changing eclipses are part of a series that's falling on the Taurus/Scorpio axis from November 2021 to October 2023. Get ready! These momentous moonbeams will shift everything from your mindset to the way you present your ideas. All year long, you'll be hungrier than ever for information and insight, and eager to share what you learn. Your voice could be a vital addition to the dialogue in 2022, both locally and globally. As one of the zodiac's two Mercury-ruled communicator signs, you could see your name in print or your byline in pixels.

On April 30 and November 8, eclipses in Taurus sweep through your ninth house of travel, entrepreneurship and higher learning. The first, a solar (new moon) eclipse on April 30, sparks new initiatives. You could suddenly return to school, start a business venture or connect with a kindred spirit across cultures or geography. Diversity and equity become a critical lens for your work or part of your mission.

The November 8 full moon in Taurus will be a total lunar eclipse. Near then, you could lock in a long-distance client or fulfill a lifelong travel wish. But since eclipses bring surprise events, plans might be spontaneous and swift. For example, maybe you score a last-minute fare to your dream destination that's too good to pass up. Don't overthink it—just go! (Luckily, mutable Virgos don't need much arm-twisting to be convinced of these things.)

The Scorpio eclipses of May 16 and October 25 touch your third house of local activity, communication and kindred spirits, bringing powerful conversations that could turn the tides. Writing, teaching, social media and marketing—the eclipses energize all the outlets you can use to spread a message.

Tough talks may change your trajectory near the total lunar (full moon) eclipse on May 16. Buried feelings surface unexpectedly, or you get wind of someone's hidden agenda. Either way, you'll have no choice but to discuss matters since the eclipses put the truth on blast. The question is: Whose truth is the real truth? There are three sides to every story, as the saying goes. Negotiations could be healing if you're willing to hang in there. Or, you might suddenly split from a longtime collaborator and go your separate ways.

Learning is emphasized near the gentler solar eclipse during the October 25 Scorpio new moon. If you're falling behind, catch up quickly by enrolling in a specialized training workshop or webinar. A relationship with a sibling, cousin or neighbor could be part of events now. You might make a dynamic duo official by teaming up on a project. Test the waters with a short-term mission to see where your synergies lie.

MARS IN GEMINI

Professional Pursuits Take Off

Mars in Gemini

August 20, 2022 to
March 25, 2023

**Mars Retrograde
in Gemini**

October 30, 2022
to January 12, 2023

The second half of 2022 is your prime time for setting new goals, taking action steps toward them...and then hitting the bullseye! Starting on August 20, when driven Mars marches into Gemini and your tenth house of professional ambition, you may feel like someone lit a fire under you. Typically, the red-hot planet transits through a sign for seven weeks, but thanks to its biennial retrograde—from October 30 to January 12, 2023—you've got six months to tap into this premium-grade rocket fuel.

Part of the secret to your success, of course, will be creating new intentions and keeping your laser focus aimed high. But beyond that, you may need to prop yourself up when you're not feeling 100 percent and even push yourself to reach a little past what you believe is your limit. Luckily, with intrepid Mars in your career corner until March 25, 2023, you may tap into reserve tanks of confidence you didn't realize you had access to. The fired-up and fiery planet only visits Gemini every other year, so it behooves you to meet the fierce provocateur halfway and accept any challenge fast-balled to you. This is not the time to play small or even modest. Picture yourself living one of your wilder dreams, like a gap year in South America or running retreats on a private island, and let that motivate you!

Whether your idea of "making it" professionally means your own office in the company C-suite, making baller bank with great perks and tons of vacation or running Virgo, Inc., this is the year you can take huge strides towards that dream scenario. But build in plenty of wiggle room—time when your forward progress may be slowed down, taken on a detour or halted altogether (albeit temporarily).

That's because energizer Mars shifts into reverse from October 30 until January 12, 2023. You're hardly one to slack off on the job or even give less than 150 percent, but with the planet of motivation off-course for two and a half months, you'd be wise to expect, well, the unexpected. This could come in the form of associates or service providers bailing on you, important paperwork going MIA, or green lights and permits being delayed due to circumstances beyond your control.

But there is a silver lining. During this unwelcome time out, you might get a chance you otherwise wouldn't have to review everything you've accomplished to date. If things could benefit from some tweaking—or out-and-out revision—now's the time to go back to the drawing board instead of continuing down the wrong avenue.

If you could benefit from some high-level business coaching, ask within your own social network for a recommendation of someone who helped a friend make quantifiable progress. Or perhaps you can offer your services and expertise to an industry pro who can become a mentor. Sometimes there's no substitute for hands-on experience. Adjusting your speed to fit the circumstances is actually one of your secret weapons, Virgo!

In fact, this ten-week retrograde is a great time to check in with all your professional relationships and give them the TLC they need (and might have been missing out on). As your savvy sign knows, it's vital to strengthen the bonds that bind with colleagues and decision makers, and when a choice comes down to you and some "random" competitor, your solid connection can make all the difference in the world. ✹

2022

LIBRA

WHAT'S IN THE STARS FOR

LIBRA

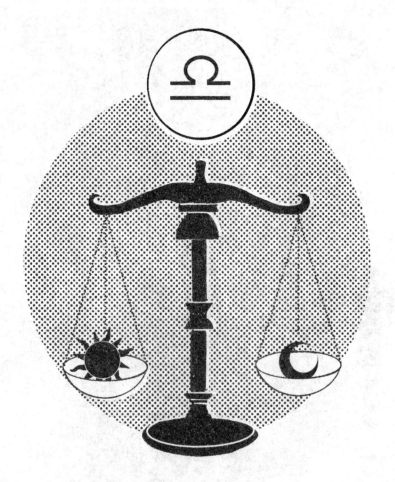

LOVE

Love takes a turn for the serious—and the seriously sexy in 2022. On January 18, the lunar North Node shifts into sensual Taurus, lighting a bonfire in your eighth house of seduction and intimacy. Erotic connection is a spiritual experience during this cycle, which lasts until July 17, 2023. But are you willing to let go and explore the depths of pleasure? With masterful Saturn in your romance zone, approach love and sex like a study. There's always more to unlock and having some tools and techniques under your (garter) belt wouldn't hurt a bit. When liberating, exploratory Jupiter soars into Aries and your partnership house, oh, the places you will go. But how will that insatiable curiosity affect the rest of your life? Daring to live by your own rules may require some negotiation before you go exploring. People may be more willing to play along than you expect, provided you include them in your plan.

CAREER & MONEY

Money moves could bring a bountiful harvest in 2022, as the lunar nodes redirect their energy to your financial axis (Taurus-Scorpio) starting January 18. The karmic South Node in Scorpio demands budgeting and planning. Restore integrity by settling debts and raising your rates if you're underearning. The Taurus North Node points you toward passive-income generators. This could be the year that you invest in your dream pad, crush it with crypto or get funding for your start-up. With serious Saturn in your fifth house of fame, focus on mastering your craft. Already a pro? You could get paid as an influencer, expert or motivational speaker.

WELLNESS

Go with your gut, Libra! Vitality-boosting Jupiter swims two laps through Pisces and your sixth house of digestion: until May 10 and again from October 28 to December 20. Hydration is the first essential step. Start your mornings with a cleansing shot of aloe vera juice and put an activating pinch of sea salt in your water bottle every time you refill it. Fermented foods that introduce health-improving microbiomes (like yogurt and kimchi) may become regular staples of your diet. Don't forget the power of sexual healing! Self- and partner-pleasuring, erotic massage and other titillating touch can be the best anti-depressant out there. If energy and moods are fluctuating, have your thyroid checked. With the lunar North Node in your second house (which rules the throat area), have your thyroid checked, especially if moods, metabolism and energy level are fluctuating. You may need to shift your diet, stress levels or supplement plan for optimal functioning.

FRIENDS & FAMILY

Family: can't live with 'em, can't live without 'em. Transformational Pluto is in the final phase of its 2008-24 tour through Capricorn and your fourth house of kin. The highs and lows are starting to smooth out as you carve out your unique role within your innermost circle. But with your ruler, accommodating Venus, retrograde in Capricorn until January 29, keep healthy boundaries in place. Couchsurfing relatives have to pull their weight; and make sure you aren't taking advantage of anyone's kindness. (Grandparents aren't "free babysitting services" every day...) Serious Saturn could bring some heavy obligations for Libra parents or stall conception. Stay committed and get scientific: a savvy system can change everything for the better. If long-distance friends ping you on WhatsApp after August 20, take orders from adventure-junkie Mars and find a way to visit each other ASAP!

JUPITER IN PISCES

Healthy, Wealthy & Wise

Jupiter in Pisces

December 28, 2021
to May 10, 2022

October 28 to
December 20, 2022

The "healthy, wealthy and wise" trinity is your recipe for success as vibrant Jupiter grapevines through Pisces and your orderly, fitness-focused sixth house for two circuits. The first, from December 28, 2021, until May 10, 2022, puts wellness resolutions front and center. And you'll hop back on the wagon again from October 28 to December 20, 2022.

Jupiter in Pisces, which you briefly experienced from May 13 to July 28, 2021, may not be the sexiest time of your life, but it will certainly be grounding. Philosophical Jupiter helps you find the adventure in the little things—which is actually a beautiful way to live. While you might sweat the small stuff (there will be a lot of it!), you'll also appreciate the subtleties and enjoy life's simpler pleasures. Jupiter was last in Pisces from January 17–June 6, 2010, and again from September 9, 2010 until January 22, 2011. Look back to that time, if you can remember it, for clues of what could resurface.

Real talk: After an indulgent and dramatic 2021, streamlining and simplifying are damn good ideas. Hand your analytical side the wheel and shift your focus to practical matters. Set up systems and processes that help life run like a well-oiled machine. Call in the cleanup crews and book sessions with health coaches and personal trainers. Learn how to read a Feng Shui bagua map and clear out your entryway—or go full Marie Kondo and get rid of things that "don't spark joy." Less is more!

While Jupiter paddles through your wellbeing zone, health becomes a priority. Get serious about clean eating, regular exercise and a toxin-free lifestyle. Hydration is always essential, and even more so when Jupiter turns on the tap in aquatic Pisces. Turn self-care into an adventure. Try water sports like stand-up paddle boarding, kayaking or lap swimming. Dance-based workouts, also ruled by the Fish, could bring the fun to your fitness regime. Adopting a pet is bound to bring happiness this year, and a dog is a great motivator to get out for daily walks.

Bear in mind, however, that Jupiter is the god of the feast. So even if you're eating clean, your appetite (and by association, your waistline) can expand during this indulgent Jupiter cycle. You may go up a size or two but have perfect health at your checkups—and if so, just embrace the new curves or cushioning. Dive into curious Jupiter's love of learning, and research nutrition and healthy living. Read up on foods that are a low caloric density. These hydrated foods, like fresh fruits and veggies, boiled eggs and oatmeal, create a sense of satiety—and much more so than fistfuls of dried nuts and seeds. It's all about balance, of course, as every Libra knows.

The sixth house rules the digestive system. Which foods agree with yours, Libra? You may benefit from anything that improves your "gut health," like taking a daily probiotic, eating more fiber or trying colon hydrotherapy. If eating organic seems too pricey, you could join a CSA (community-supported agriculture) co-op that gives an affordable weekly bundle of local produce. Do you need more vitamins or supplements? Get a full panel of tests done to learn. While you're reading labels, check the ones in your medicine cabinet. Clean, natural and fragrance-free beauty products could enhance your glow.

While you're on this make-better mission, try on the concept of wabi sabi, a Japanese worldview based on embracing imperfections. Without some checks and balances, Libra, you may veer into obsessive territory. Books are meant to be read, not stiffly arranged into a color-coded #shelfie formation. Patterns can clash and still look stylish (or not), and some days, you may be too darn tired to stream your ritual yoga class. While you do want to be a bit stricter with yourself this year, building a discipline takes practice. Be patient with your process...without making excuses to let yourself off the hook.

Jupiter in Pisces may reveal a health diagnosis for some Libras, necessitating a lifestyle change. This could be a blessing in disguise, especially if it leads to early detection. Stress has been linked to many diseases, so even the fittest of Libras should dial it down however possible. If you work at a computer, get up and move every hour or try a standing desk.

Since the sixth house rules helpful people, Jupiter in Pisces could bring the service providers of your dreams. From babysitters to virtual assistants, look for capable people who can lighten your load. Given Jupiter's optimism, it's wise to be more rigorous with your screening. People who seem like a perfect fit could be laying it on thick during the interview process. Check their references thoroughly and do a trial period before making anything permanent.

Life can get chaotic for even the most balanced Libra—especially after 2021's rush of creative experiences. Where could you implement more efficient systems that will keep your life humming along? And, more importantly, how can you make them colorful, aesthetically pleasing and chic? Your Venus-ruled sign could have a field day incorporating your filing systems into your décor scheme. Maybe those color-coded bookshelves (and closets) have a place in 2022 after all.

Hit a plateau with your job? Jupiter could send you on the hunt for a new gig. Don't rush into anything permanent if you're still feeling things out. With free-spirited Jupiter in your administrative sixth house, you could take a "bridge job"—something easy and temporary that doesn't drain your vital energy. When you clock out, engage in training courses that build your knowledge base.

Some Libras may be drawn to the service industry or a "green" sector, like environmental justice or community solar, which creates a central solar power plant that can be shared by neighbors. Or you could explore booming areas in wellness, beauty—or a hybrid of both! Creative work, perhaps for a world-bettering cause, could be part of this year's cosmic lineup. No matter where you land, you'll go farther by adopting an attitude of humble service, rather than trying to elbow your way to the top or "make" things happen. Cutting corners and forcing an agenda will flop. With outspoken Jupiter in your nature-loving sixth house, you could become an advocate for climate change prevention, wildlife preservation or even housing and relocation for people—and animals—displaced by the pandemic.

Since Jupiter rules higher education, this is the year to polish your skills, complete certifications, or develop new levels of mastery. The barter system can pay off—for example, you learn web design by designing a bestie's website, or you apprentice for an executive to get an insider's look at their expertise. Even if no pay is involved, sitting at the feet of a master is priceless training while Jupiter is in Pisces, which favors experience-based learning. (Note: Jupiter was last in Pisces from January 2010 to January 2011. Review your timeline from that period, if you can. Similar themes may emerge, specifically surrounding wellness and work.)

JUPITER MEETS NEPTUNE IN PISCES

Mind Your Wallet

> **Jupiter meets Neptune in Pisces**
>
> April 12, 2022

A pinnacle day on the 2022 calendar is April 12, when Jupiter catches up to soul-friend Neptune at 23°58' Pisces. These planets only hold a summit like this every 13 years. And when they do, the effect can be spellbinding. Epiphanies erupt, dreams actualize, miracles manifest.

But is it the real deal...or is it just fantasy? With truth-agent Jupiter snared in numinous Neptune's net, the effect can be like a magician's sleight of hand. What you think you're seeing may be far from the truth. Be especially circumspect between March 14 and April 30 as the two escape artists copilot in close connection through Pisces.

With your sixth house of work and wellness activated, read through business agreements with a fine-toothed comb. Lawyer up where money and rights are concerned. Even if it seems extra, hammering out that tiny clause about intellectual property could mean the difference between future profits or money down the drain while you sit in arbitration for months.

If you're undergoing medical treatments, become an expert in every facet of the procedure. Knowledge is power when Jupiter's in the frame, but while Neptune blurs the ink, you will have to read everything at least twice.

JUPITER IN ARIES

Dynamic Duos Abound

> **Jupiter in Aries**
>
> May 10 to
> October 28, 2022
>
> December 20, 2022
> to May 16, 2023

Set the table for two starting May 10. For the first time in over a decade, Jupiter zooms into Aries and your seventh house of partnership. This cycle, which lasts until October 28, is the first in a pair that blesses you with rapid relationship growth. (The second is from December 20, 2022, to May 16, 2023.) Talk about balm for your soul! As the zodiac's Most Romantic, Libras bliss out when you have a loving plus-one by your side. Or should we make that a plus-two, three and four? Expansive Jupiter could bring a bumper crop of compatible people into your sphere, from a long-term romantic partner to an inspiring business collaborator.

One person doesn't have to be your everything while Jupiter is in Aries mid-year. In fact, there's a paradox at play. Although your partnership house will be enlivened, Jupiter in Aries cycles make everyone insanely independent. You'll need a long leash, Libra, if not a chance to go "free range." Relationships need to happen by choice, not obligation now (and forever).

While in Aries, globetrotting Jupiter might spark synergy with someone from another culture or background. You may meet this person while traveling or interface through a virtual introduction. A long-distance romance could get serious, or you may launch an entrepreneurial project with a collaborator who lives in another zip code. Risk-taker Jupiter inspires you to cast a wide net!

One catch: While in Aries, Jupiter will directly oppose your Libra Sun. With the red-spotted planet furthest away from el Sol on the zodiac wheel, you may be a little too keen to leap without looking. Before you take any gambles, build in a criteria checklist for safety's sake. Judgment may be askew or it can take a minute for you to connect to your truth when the chorus of opinions around you is amplified.

66

> *You'll need a long leash, Libra, if not a chance to go "free range." Relationships need to happen by choice, not obligation now (and forever).*

99

Already half of a dynamic duo? Your existing commitments could shift in fascinating ways between May 10 and October 28. As you adjust the levels of give-and-take, you'll create more harmony and equality. Longtime couples could renew their vows, travel together or shift into different roles. For example, if you've been the breadwinner for a while, your mate might suddenly become the household high earner. If you're always the star, prepare to play Best Supporting Castmate. With free-spirited Jupiter here, you might loosen some "restrictions," perhaps pursuing more autonomous extracurriculars—or in some cases, exploring what an open relationship feels like. Jupiter is the galactic gambler, and while in Aries, you're more willing to play with the proverbial fire. But don't be glib about this, Libra! Read the wisdom of people who have been down this path so you go in with eyes open.

Has a relationship run its course? If life is leading you in different directions, philosophical Jupiter could find you parting ways amicably. Don't plan on flying solo for long, though! Jupiter in Aries calls in promising contenders who balance you out beautifully. Caveat: These passionate people may be consumed by their paths, leaving limited time for the two of you. But with adventurous Jupiter steering the ship, you'll quickly see the benefits of trading time in the couple bubble for the pleasure of inspiring companionship. Besides, a little less interactivity means more time to develop your own gifts!

VENUS RETROGRADE

Sweet Sentimentality

Venus in Capricorn

November 5, 2021
to March 6, 2022

**Venus Retrograde
in Capricorn**

December 19, 2021
to January 29, 2022

Libras in the northern hemisphere can look forward to an especially warm and enriching hygge season as the calendar turns to 2022. You can send your cosmic thank-you note to your own galactic guardian, gracious Venus, who will be lounging in Capricorn and your cozy fourth house for a prolonged visit—which began on November 5, 2021, and lasts until March 6, 2022. But make no mistake: You won't be settling in for any long winter naps. With the social and beautifying planet nestled in here, you'll have a full plate of hosting guests, redecorating and renovation projects and, uh, serving very full plates. Entrepreneurial types might clear off that dining room table and launch a home-based business.

During this four-month cycle, romantic Venus will bring out your affectionate and devoted nature. In Capricorn, Venus appreciates physicality and sensuality, nudging you to focus not just on the joys of the moment but on building a sustainable sense of emotional security. You have to do your part to call in the right partner (if you're single) or create the kind of relationship you seek with your S.O. It's not just about "you scratch my back and I'll scratch yours." Work the Law of Attraction by holding the bar high and leading with your emotional intelligence. And plan to talk through any minor issues before they become molehills—that's how relationships not only survive but thrive.

But don't expect to get all of your desires met without doing plenty for the sake of the relationship. You need to check in on yourself and work through any selfish reactions. The key is continuously raising your own vibration—especially when Venus flips into retrograde from December 19, 2021, to January 29, 2022. Normally, the cosmic interior decorator (and matchmaker) spends just three to five weeks in a sign, but every other year, it shifts into reverse for six weeks, and this time, you'll be treated to Venus' affectionate vibrations for a total of four months! Thanks to this "bonus time," there's no need to rush into anything. In fact, this is a perfect opportunity to hit pause and review whatever is up for renewal, whether your living room or love life.

This backspin could easily bring a few speed bumps or drive up animosity, but if you tap Venus' legendary powers of diplomacy, you can probably avoid an out-and-out meltdown. Even if everything is peachy—at least in your mind—be proactive and check in with your partner. It's easy to assume you're in perfect alignment regarding a shared future when one of you has never actually mentioned that you don't want a family or simply must spend a year of your life living on a houseboat. This is where honest communication and a willingness to compromise become essential.

Also likely to surge during this Venus retrograde cycle: nostalgia and the need to reconnect to old friends and lovers. With your domestic fourth house activated like this, it'll be hard to stay 100 percent focused on the here and now. Share favorite memories and inside jokes with your closest peeps. The holidays and especially NYE could be an epic affair, whether you're celebrating with DNA family or your chosen one. If you're the host, don't plan to do this on a wing and a prayer. You'll be grateful for all advance preparations, from the menu and shopping to creating crowd-pleasing playlists to planning a few fun activities to keep things lively—and create more great memories. Surround yourself with positive, loving people and give the downers and haters a wide berth. If you find yourself pining for someone from your past, inspect those feelings. Is this coming from an unrealistic longing or a fantasy, perhaps as a smokescreen for an actual possibility? Venus in reverse can bring back old emotions and connections, some of which belong solidly in the past!

You might find yourself re-negotiating some household rules or putting new boundaries in place as 2022 dawns. As a Libra, you can get obsessed with the concept of fairness, and when you look around your home, you may be shocked at the imbalances you see. For instance, is common space being shared equitably or is someone hogging the square footage? (And, um, might that someone be you?) Does everyone have enough privacy and room for creative projects—or just rolling out a yoga mat? If not, you need a more appropriate floor plan—stat! If you have the means and work for yourself, it could be worthwhile to invest in an outside rental, even a coworking space, if only for some peace and quiet on your timeline!

Thinking of upgrading? Venus in classy Capricorn can uplevel your aesthetic vision. You could become quite clever at sourcing your fantasies, from a statement chandelier to an oversized gothic bed. Affordable improvements make sense, but with the planet of style and values off-course through January 29, hold off on any substantial overhauls until March 6. Before then, scratch that decorator itch by creating gorgeous Pinterest boards and getting multiple recommendations and bids. You may think you're in a hurry, but at the end of the day, you're still a Libra and need to thoroughly consider every option on the table (or screen).

If there are any long-running friend feuds, this lengthy Venus cycle is a great time to extend an olive branch and make overtures to bury the hatchet. But when the diplomatic planet is backflipping (December 19 to January 29), don't rush to patch things up. This is actually a great time to peer beneath the surface and find the actual unresolved issue. If you agree to meet, do so on "neutral turf." But if you still need a little time to process this, take it unapologetically and trust that time really does heal all wounds.

LUNAR NODES IN TAURUS AND SCORPIO

Financial Goals Illuminated

Lunar Nodes in Taurus and Scorpio

January 18, 2022
to July 17, 2023

Magnetic? Irresistible? Words like these won't do a Libra justice starting January 18. When the destiny-driven lunar North Node sashays into Taurus and your erotic, esoteric eighth house, your mystique could send sailors crashing into rocks! Not that you'd misuse your enchanting powers that way. But get ready: This potent period, which lasts until July 17, 2023, will dish up some karmically-tinged interactions and serious spiritual pursuits.

Simultaneously, the karmic South Node stokes the fires of Scorpio, building a slow-burning heat in your stabilizing second house. The kind of bonding you crave requires vulnerability, especially in the case of sexual relationships, or ones that involve a merging of finances. Trust is key. If you're not sure about your chosen person, test the potential with a few soulful revelations. Little by little, you could (both) gain the confidence to drop your guard and embrace the kind of intimacy that leads to sultry AND spiritual interactions.

How comfortable are you with your sexual identity? Wherever you fall on the continuum, the Taurus-Scorpio nodes are sure to nudge you toward greater empowerment. Libra Sheila Kelley, founder of the pole-dancing movement S-Factor, leads workshops to help people discover their "erotic creature." That's the persona that emerges when you're turned on—and not surprisingly, this "character" is often 180-degrees from the role you play in your day-to-day life. You don't have to install a stripper pole in your bedroom, of course. But if you want to live a more integrated life, get more acquainted with your raw desire. In other words...own it, Libra!

The power of your pull is undeniable during this 18-month cycle, so be careful what you wish for! Words manifest into reality at an accelerated pace—which would be fine if you could take them back. But Taurus and Scorpio are committed signs, meaning you won't wriggle out of obligations easily during this nodal cycle. As a rule, only make promises if you're willing to follow through to the finish line. Otherwise, you could wind up paying a hefty fee for your liberation.

Back in the 1970s, bikers had an expression, "Gas, grass or a$$...no one rides for free." Crass as that may be, this sums up the Taurus-Scorpio lunar nodes for Libras. If you're overly dependent on someone's resources, be hardcore about weaning off their supply chain. You'll never know what you're capable of (which is so much more) if you don't take a calculated risk.

Pick off any freeloaders who have been draining your precious resources, too. Peace holds a high value in your world, but at what price? Taurus and the second house are both associated with self-esteem. Here's a wakeup call to value yourself more. Slackers might not appreciate "2022 Libra," and that is 100% their problem. Same for anyone who is abusing power, gaslighting you into believing you deserve less or manipulating your emotions.

The Taurus North Node makes you "strong like bull" when it comes to standing up for yourself. Confronting inequities is never easy, but circumstances may force your hand. You may have to fire someone or report them to HR. A bad roommate could be kicked out of the Libra Palace temporarily—or permanently! We hope circumstances don't reach such extremes. But if you've issued ultimatums—yet see zero change—you have no choice but to protect yourself with a firm limit. Since many Libras struggle to put a hard stop to anything, bolster yourself with emotional support from friends or a literal support group. Take a read of our friend, therapist Terri Cole's book *Boundary Boss* to learn the language of saying no. You can do this!

Financially, this nodal cycle gets you thinking long-term. With the North Node touring industrious Taurus, you'll have muscle for the hustle. And with your eighth house of big money activated, funds could arrive in a lump sum such as royalties or dividends. Inheritances, legal settlements and tax returns could also fill the coffers between January 18, 2022, and July 17, 2023.

Got debt to pay off? Luck is on your side for settling it—and you may finally clear up your credit or put an end to ongoing litigation. Rather than waiting for an ominous letter to arrive in your mailbox, contact anyone who you're indebted to and set up a payment plan. Integrity sets you up favorably when it comes to negotiation.

If you have extra cash left over after the bills, invest it wisely. No one loves a couture house quite like a Libra, but those front-row seats at Fashion Week aren't going to put food on the table. We're not suggesting you turn your back on Balmain or close the door on Dior! Just remember these two magic words: compounding interest. Now's the time to learn everything you can about investing, from real estate to the stock market to cryptocurrency. It takes money to make money, Libra. Tuck your funds into assets that are likely to grow in value over time and you'll be sitting pretty (in Paris, NYC, Milan...wherever!) for years to come!

ECLIPSES IN TAURUS AND SCORPIO

Hustle & (Financial) Flow

**Partial Solar
Eclipse in Taurus**

April 30 at 4:27pm

**Total Lunar
Eclipse in Scorpio**

May 16 at 12:14am

**Partial Solar Eclipse
in Scorpio new moon**

October 25 at 6:48am

**Total Lunar Eclipse
in Taurus full moon**

November 8 at 6:02am

times in eastern time

Sick of the daily grind? Money acting funny? You could have the last laugh—all the way to the bank—thanks to four change-making eclipses that sweep through your financial sectors in 2022. From tantalizing job opportunities to a property investment, make way for the new! As these eclipses remove what's old and outmoded, you could field some intriguing options. And since eclipses bring surprises, they might just come out of left field.

Investments that promise to yield a healthy return buzz onto your radar on April 30 and November 8, when these supercharged lunations land in Taurus and your eighth house of joint ventures and wealth. Since the first one (April 30) is a solar eclipse, it arrives with a new moon. Fresh opportunities crop up, offering a chance to pool your talents and resources for mutual gain. Contract negotiations get underway, perhaps for a business deal or the closing on a property. Get ready for a windfall near the total lunar eclipse on November 8, which could arrive in the form of an inheritance or settlement. Conversely, you may have to suddenly pay out a large lump sum to resolve a debt.

Credit cards, tax bills, college loans, a home repair...if any of that is looming overhead, these eclipses force you to deal. Avoidance, especially around money, can rob you of your power. The good news? You'll free up major psychic space for other things once you handle these obligations. And speaking of "psychic," this spiritual eighth house eclipse ramps up your intuition. The Law of Attraction is on your side near April 30 and November 8! Make sure you're operating with the utmost integrity if you negotiate a deal or pool your funds with anyone. Have an attorney draft and review contracts and make sure you're fully protected.

66

Avoidance, especially around money, can rob you of your power. The good news? You'll free up major psychic space for other things once you handle these obligations.

99

You could join forces on a personal level, as the eighth house rules merging in the emotional and sexual realms. For some Libras, the April 30 and November 8 eclipses will bring a surprise proposal, pregnancy or split. With little notice, you might find yourself on one end of the spectrum. A simmering attraction could reach full tilt or you attract a soulmate, someone you feel like you've known for lifetimes. (Maybe you have!) The eighth house rules all the big life cycles, from birth to death to other rites of passage in between. You may experience some serious serendipities near these eclipses.

On May 16 and October 25, two Scorpio eclipses ignite your second house of work and money. The total lunar (full moon) eclipse on May 16 puts the truth on the table. If you've been unhappily employed, a job change is possible. Or you could have an eye-opening realization that you need to budget, spend and save very differently. Maybe you've become imprisoned by all your "stuff" and you want to downsize. Perhaps your company restructures and eliminates your department or moves everyone into new roles. Remain flexible—and have faith. In the event that you do lose a job, you can rest assured that a much better fit will soon be on its way. Stay proactive and start hustling!

Promising progress streams in with the October 25 solar (new moon) eclipse. Put your feelers out, Libra. Even if you're happily hustling away, your social sign lives by the mantra, "It's all about who you know." Networking will turn up some great leads for your contact database, even if you don't officially team up until one day in the future.

MARS IN GEMINI

Blasting Past Boundaries

Mars in Gemini

August 20, 2022 to
March 25, 2023

**Mars Retrograde
in Gemini**

October 30, 2022
to January 12, 2023

However big your world has been for the past year, Libra, it's about to expand even further! Starting on August 20, master blaster Mars rockets into Gemini and your expansive, worldly ninth house for an extra-long visit. Typically, the red-hot planet lends its motivational gifts to each sign for seven weeks in its two-year trip around the Sun. But because of a ten-week retrograde this year (from October 30 to January 12, 2023), you will be treated to its energizing and thrill-seeking power surge in this realm for six months!

After being holed up for so long during lockdown, once Mars lights up your travel sector, you might already be packed and halfway out the door! If you can drop out for a while and play digital nomad, you might live out some long-held dreams involving new vistas and soul-quenching spiritual retreats and pilgrimages.

Don't worry if your entourage can't join you for this leg of the tour—they can always follow your meanderings on social media. (Unless you decide to unplug altogether for a while.) And if anyone can accompany you on any of these adventures, the bonds are sure to deepen and enhance both (or all) your worlds in ways you couldn't anticipate.

Can't get away for an extended spell? No worries! You can scratch the restless itch by expanding your horizons virtually. This motivating Mars cycle (until March 25, 2023) might inspire you to go to school for a degree or sign up for specialized training or certification. Yoga teacher, Reiki master, social-work degree: What has your big Libra heart been craving? Entrepreneurial Libras might finally catch enough wind in your sails to write that business plan, pitch angel investors or finally hang the shingle. Ready, steady, go!

> *Temper your words with tact. Brash Mars in your outspoken ninth house can make you honest to a fault!*

There's one catch: Beginning on October 30, Mars shifts into reverse until January 12, 2023. This isn't to say that nothing will happen during these ten weeks, but you might have to adjust your speed, scale back on some overly optimistic plans or navigate speed bumps you never saw coming. But stay the course! Mars retrograde can be a cautionary tale to not rush ahead without having all the details hammered out. Be more deliberate and thorough—and patient!—with plans, people and all your pursuits. You may never need to turn to it, but craft a "just in case" contingency plan.

During Mars' backspin, take to heart the expression, "When you fail to plan, you plan to fail." If you're looking to launch a freelance or entrepreneurial project, you might want to wait until the second half of January. In all stages of development, don't oversell yourself: If anything, lowball your projections and what you can deliver. It's better to accomplish a chunk of a project brilliantly than turn in something "complete" that's mediocre. And go easy on the risk-taking. Any offer that comes with a "can't possibly fail" boast should be considered a very bright red flag.

Your diligence will be rewarded when Mars resumes direct motion on January 12, 2023, so hang in there! Use this slowdown or stoppage time to get things polished until they have that unmistakable Libra high-pro glow.

If you're planning a getaway during Mars' reversal, it might be better to revisit a favorite destination than explore someplace new (the joy of retrogrades!). Also, with daredevil Mars in reverse, pay close attention to your surroundings and exercise more caution. Keep your "savvy traveler" pride in check and act like a novice. Ask questions and request guidance in unfamiliar places, even when (especially when) you think everything's under control.

One final piece of advice: Temper your words with tact. Brash Mars in your outspoken ninth house can make you honest to a fault! Unless you're actively seeking to burn a bridge, bite your tongue and lead with your innate Libra diplomacy. If someone has crossed a line, find a kind yet firm way of letting them know their behavior was unacceptable. It's up to you whether to give them another chance or not. ✳

2022

SCORPIO

SCORPIO

LOVE

Embrace the adventure of romantic expansion! Buoyant Jupiter gets frisky in your flamboyant fifth house (Pisces) until May 10 and again from October 28 to December 20. You need attention—and lots of it. Take charge of your erotic desires, even if that exploration takes you off the beaten path. Love and destiny collide starting January 18, as the fateful lunar North Node heads into Taurus and your seventh house of relationships until July 17, 2023. This cycle, which only comes around every 18.5 years could bring a meant-to-be mate into your orbit or give you the courage to go "all in." Relationships that have are puttering along on autopilot may undergo a massive shift. Self-discovery may be the catalyst for change, since the karmic South Node will be in Scorpio and your first house of identity. Sexy intensity (a Scorpio favorite) heats up when lusty Mars hits Gemini on August 20, stoking the flames of your erotic fire until March 25, 2023! Watch for jealousy and manipulative moves while Mars is retrograde from October 30 to January 12, 2023.

CAREER & MONEY

Add more soul to your goals! The lunar South Node in Scorpio sends you on a quest for meaning this year. You could uncover something that feels aligned with your deepest truths. Already on a purpose-driven path? Get yourself camera-ready! With global Jupiter in your fame zone until May 10 (and again from October 28 to December 20), you could perform, present or be the media's darling for interviews. Don't wait to be discovered. Polish up your pitch desks and promote on social media. Money management will be a midyear priority while abundant Jupiter settles into Aries and your practical magic zone from May 10 to October 28. You may travel for work then or pay some dues assisting a bigger name in your field. Systematize processes and free yourself from the grind. Investment opportunities heat up when Mars hits your joint resources zone (Gemini) on August 20. Got a venture in the works? Shop it around before the red planet turns retrograde on October 30.

WELLNESS

Saturn is rooted in your fourth house all year, and you'll feel healthiest at home. This is the summer to grow your own food, then make fresh salsa for future #TacoTuesdays. Set up a workout area for streaming yoga, choreographing dance moves and lifting weights. Get ready for a total wellness reboot when vitality-boosting Jupiter swings into Aries from May 10 to October 28. Exercise in the great outdoors or combine it with travel. (Biking through wine country, anyone?) Pay attention to your root chakra, which is located at the base of your spine, in the tailbone area. Daily squats, pelvic floor exercises, even walking barefoot in the grass can strengthen and support this energy center. This will help you feel grounded during the karmic ups and downs of the South Node's tour through your sign, which can bring a lot of fluctuating feelings.

FRIENDS & FAMILY

With serious Saturn hunkered in Aquarius and your intimate fourth house all year, you'll appreciate the company of your "chosen family" as if they were your own flesh and blood. Reunite with precious pals while Venus is retrograde in your friendship house until January 29. Saturn may create heaviness with your actual relatives. You may move or relocate to support them—or to give yourself the space you need to heal from ancestral wounds. Jupiter's time is Pisces (until May 10 and from October 28 to December 20) is ideal for making babies or bonding with the kids you already have.

JUPITER IN PISCES

Showcase Your Talents

Jupiter in Pisces

December 28, 2021
to May 10, 2022

October 28 to
December 20, 2022

Curtains up! Show pony Jupiter celebrates two acts in Pisces this year, spotlighting your fifth house of fame, flamboyant self-expression and over-the-top romance. After hovering behind the scenes for most of 2021, center stage is looking mighty good. Tadaaa! Scorpios steal the show until May 10 and again from October 28 to December 20.

This Jupiter cycle, which you briefly experienced last year from May 13 to July 28, is like a cosmic coming-out party. From your talents to your temperament, little will be hidden. And yes, that's a major departure from your secretive nature, Scorpio. Embrace your role as a fashion icon like Scorpios Anna Wintour and Willow Smith. You could debut a signature hairstyle, mix unusual pieces and set a trend or redo a space that makes décor bloggers drool. Even subtle updates draw stares when set against the backdrop of your flashing eyes, intense expressions and swaying gait.

Even more fortuitous? In Pisces, Jupiter forms a flowing 120° trine to your Sun in Scorpio. This vitality-boosting transit unleashes a torrential downpour of passion. Expect to feel friskier and more flamboyant than you have in years!

Are you a budding performer or "personality"? While Jupiter tours Pisces you could rise to the role of an influencer. Whether you accept brand sponsorships or keep it 100% organic is up to you, Scorpio. Either way, you'll gain a sizable fanbase when you put yourself out there. Heartfelt works emerge during this renaissance period, so balance time in and out of your "studio." With global Jupiter at the helm, cast a wide net to reach an international audience. This may be one of those years when you're randomly discovered on YouTube, Etsy or some other self-starter platform. Forget about polishing everything to perfection! Debuting works-in-progress and BTS videos wins you even more love, showing the world your unbeatable work ethic.

Leave space on your crowded calendar for love! Pisces rules your passionate fifth house, and while amplifier Jupiter visits, a lukewarm attraction could turn wildly exothermic! Try-anything Jupiter in this unfiltered zone will give you charisma and confidence in spades. The extra celestial swagger can attract a slew of admirers.
Single Scorpios could go on an epic dating spree or get wrapped up in a superhot, sexy romance.

Good news! For a change, your, er, particular sign won't be so worried about directing every scene. (Not that you can't produce a few that stimulate your fantasies!) With free-spirited Jupiter in your romance house, it's a relief to simply focus on pleasure some days. And if that leads to a walk down the aisle or a defined commitment, that's bound to emerge as a matter of course. In the meanwhile, let loose and expand your repertoire—an educational experience in its own right!

With global ambassador Jupiter playing Cupid, cross-cultural chemistry and baecation time will be hot! Pack a sultry little something-something in your travel bag, even if you're feeling exhausted and sun-deprived before you leave. Open your mind and heart to people wildly different than your usual type. If you normally go for the stoic surfer type, you might fall for a woo-woo wildlife enthusiast or a sexy exec devoted to bringing social responsibility to company policies. Maybe you'll meet someone who doesn't even speak the same language as you, "communicating" through non-verbal chemistry and letting your bodies do the talking.

While the fifth house rules romantic love, commitment comes under the governance of the seventh house. And with independent Jupiter here, you won't be in a hurry to lock yourself down. But even longtime couples will enjoy this libido-boosting cycle. Candid Jupiter makes it easy for you to express your desires, which could spark some unanticipated experimentation. Since the fifth house rules fertility, the stork may swoop in. (Consider yourself notified!) Although pursuing an outside attraction could get complicated, don't be alarmed if you develop a few innocent crushes or loosen up former restrictions around flirting with people you find attractive. As long as you and your partner set boundaries that are comfortable—and stick to them—you can enjoy these two Jupiter cycles with your integrity intact!

JUPITER MEETS NEPTUNE IN PISCES

Mind Your Wallet

**Jupiter meets
Neptune in Pisces**

April 12, 2022

Jupiter's expansive influence gets a spiritual boost in March and April this year, when the red-spotted planet travels in a close connection to imaginative Neptune, making an exact conjunction at 23°58' Pisces on April 12. This rare celestial sync-up only happens once every 13 years! This time, it could bring love or even fame in the most fateful, soul-nourishing way. Couples could share a fairy tale moment that brings one of your long-held fantasies to life.

With boundaries basically non-existent under this spell, you'll experience a merging that feels otherworldly. But stay aware of whose energy you're connecting with, Scorpio! Uniting during a Jupiter-Neptune meetup in Pisces is like signing a soul contract. Sharing your body, even if the experience is pure ecstasy, can bring a karmic entanglement in March and April. Even with people you plan to love for a lifetime, it's important to retain some semblance of autonomy. Not only does this keep the attraction hot, but it saves you from falling into Neptune's codependent vortex. Losing yourself may feel inevitable while this cosmic duo travels side by side from March 14 to April 30. But keep a few emotional "trail markers" (and sensible friends) nearby so you can regain your bearings after any particularly sweeping encounters.

Single? The Jupiter-Neptune conjunction encourages you to be as open as possible about your desires. You could manifest the love of your life by being specific about what you want. The universe may very well play matchmaker. There's one catch, though: You have to do it from a place of gratitude and abundance, rather than neediness. In other words, do not follow in the footsteps of fellow Scorpio Pete Davidson and start inking tribute tattoos days into the relationship.

Instead, tap into the Law of Attraction—a specialty of magnetic and mystical Neptune—and "act as if." Do a little creative visualization: Imagine that you've already met your forever love, you're blissfully happy together, and you're thanking the universe for connecting you. Feel those feelings of ecstasy and wholeness in your body. Those will radiate into the energetic field and act as a magnetic force.

No matter what you're trying to attract now, remind yourself that it may come in a surprising package, or through a series of serendipitous twists and turns. Remember: You may know what you want, but leave the universe in charge of the how, when, who and where. Focus more on the quality of how you'll feel rather than eye color, fashion statements and where you'll vacation on your one-year anniversary. Sure, those things matter, but guess what? Being too particular could block an elevated option from coming through.

The saying "a watched pot never boils" could ring true. Adopt an attitude of adventure and enjoy the journey—this year, it truly is more important (and enriching) than the destination!

JUPITER IN ARIES

Order in Your Court

Jupiter in Aries

May 10 to
October 28, 2022

December 20, 2022
to May 16, 2023

Cleanup in Aisle Scorpio! From May 10 to October 28, Jupiter shifts out of Pisces and your fantasy-fueled fifth house and lands with a bit of a thud in Aries and your sensible, service-oriented sixth house. Suddenly, your temperature shifts from wild to mild, and not a moment too soon! With your penchant for extremes, your early 2022 hedonism could make a Viking blush.

While Jupiter tours Aries for six months, the wellness wagon will be your favorite ride. No longer will an appletini pass as a "green drink," nor will a marathon hook-up be your main source of cardio. This salubrious cycle could teach you a thing or two about the power of plant-based meals and Pilates. After contemplating a status switch to "It's Complicated," the labels you'll be most concerned with are "Non-GMO" and "cruelty-free."

If you slipped into unhealthy habits, you could make an epic lifestyle change mid-year. You might even get doctor's orders to lower your blood pressure or cholesterol level. With your addictive tendencies, going extreme may be the only way—Jupiter in "go big or go home" Aries is all about it. Hewing sugar, alcohol or another "party substance" from your repertoire could save some Scorpios a stint in rehab. But no shame in your game! If you need support with breaking free, wise guides and mentors will be plentiful.

With outdoorsy Jupiter in this nature-loving zone, fresh air and sunshine put extra fuel in your tank. You could adopt a pet, giving you an incentive to get out and about. Pumping up your fitness routine is a great way to cycle out of certain obsessive habits that formed out of boredom or anxiety. Take that romantic angst to the squash court or surf beach!

66

If you slipped into unhealthy habits, you could make an epic lifestyle change mid-year.

99

Since the sixth house rules service, you could feel a deep calling to make a difference in the world with Jupiter here. You might move into a career in a "green" or wellness field, or explore booming occupations in the service industry. Some Scorpios will crave more freedom while liberated Jupiter tours this 9-5 zone. This phase may be perfect for a "bridge job," one that allows flexible hours and minimal stress. Use the additional time and energy to take skill-building classes and earn certifications, which will position you for a higher income bracket later on.

The sixth house rules helpful people, and with try-anything Jupiter here, you can finally stop micromanaging and get some assistance! Outsource to skilled specialists instead of being cheap and DIY-ing. If you've got a staff of slackers, put 'em on notice that they'll have to shape up or ship out. A new resolve for Jupiter in Aries: To stock your pond only with people who pull their weight and have your back.

If you're the typical Scorpio, there's a good chance you're also an "overfunctioner"—someone who does everyone else's emotional heavy lifting. Partially, this may be due to your need for control. It's hard for you to trust others to do the job to your exacting standards. But if you want to capitalize on abundant Jupiter's growth, you're going to have to start delegating to trainees. Few people (if any) will knock it out of the park their first time up to bat. Set a trial period and put them through an orientation process. A few weeks in, you'll be able to see if their potential actualizes into the skills you need. Since Jupiter rules publishing, how about documenting your process in a training manual? This could be as useful for you as it is for the hopefuls vying for a spot on Team Scorpio.

VENUS RETROGRADE

Variety is the Spice

Venus in Capricorn

November 5, 2021
to March 6, 2022

**Venus Retrograde
in Capricorn**

December 19, 2021
to January 29, 2022

Your seductive and private sign prefers taking action over endlessly "talking about it." But things could look and feel very different this winter, specifically from November 5, 2021, to March 6, 2022, when amorous Venus sashays through Capricorn and your articulate and expressive third house. You might have realized that you could "stand improvement" when it comes to your direct verbal communication skills. But hey, instead of teasing, tempting and dropping subtle hints, now you'll get a chance to see what happens when you straight-up ask for what you want.

You'll actually get multiple opportunities because the love planet will be activating this experimental realm for an extra-long time. Normally, Venus spends just three to five weeks in a sign, but every other year, it flips into retrograde for six weeks, and this time, you'll be treated to Venus' loving vibrations for a total of four months! No need to rush into anything because you'll have ample time to figure out where and how you'd like to (or, ahem, might need to) stretch. The only "requirement?" That you be brutally honest, at least with yourself. If your status quo is lacking in any key ways, here's your chance to consider what you can do to mix things up. Especially if your cat-and-mouse M.O. isn't delivering the relationship you want, it's time to learn some new tricks.

You can definitely examine and refine your techniques when Venus slips into retrograde from December 19, 2021, to January 29, 2022, a cycle that happens every 584 days. A little mystery and intrigue is great, but too much can frustrate someone to the point of simply giving up. Similarly, not enough transparency and vulnerability with a serious partner could blow whole relationships off-course—especially if you take too long to reveal your intentions.

> **66**
>
> *In all types of relationships, Venus retrograde will challenge—and hopefully inspire—you to improve your communication style.*
>
> **99**

Here's a good question to start with: On a day-to-day basis, how clearly do you spell out your needs? And when others are talking, do you listen intently, or do you tend to cut people off mid-sentence? Really not sure? Venus retrograde will hold up the mirror and reveal just where you fall on the communication continuum. Relationships are the best indication of how people regard us, and their candid responses and reactions will vividly reflect back what's going on inside of you.

And if you decide you do want to improve your relationships—or attract a keeper into your life—you need to accept that change is an inside job. It always starts with you! But you don't have to radically reinvent yourself, Scorpio. You can begin by making minor, manageable shifts—like pausing long enough to acknowledge someone else's opinion before you shoot it down or compare it to something in your life. This will have the bonus effect of transforming what could become an altercation into a truly productive conversation. Retract that cold shoulder and warm things up. From there, things may heat up big-time!

If you follow gracious Venus' lead and review your style of expressing your needs (and opinions, and, well, everything), you might just sail into 2022 on a note of renewed understanding. But you'll have to stay vigilant. When the typically diplomatic planet is reverse commuting, her shadow side can come to light and eclipse her tact and propriety. If you're not mindful, it'll be a little too easy to slip into a snarky smackdown with your sister or to alienate an associate with a self-righteous political rant.

Should tensions intensify between you prior to January 29, don't just march out of the room like a petulant child (no matter how much you'd love to). You do need to de-escalate the situation first. Once cooler heads prevail, this can be a great moment for frank discussions with the very folks who fall under the third-house rulership: siblings, coworkers and neighbors. Familiarity can breed contempt, as your opinioned sign is well aware of. But if you're trying to preserve important bonds, redraw boundaries to ensure that everyone has ample space, privacy and autonomy.

Seeking a solid union? Since the third house rules platonic pals, you could uncover a bevy of viable (if wildly surprising) options between November 5, 2021, and March 6, 2022. Just be aware in advance that your never-tepid emotions can run hot and cold when Venus is retrograde. That OMG twin flame might ignite then get extinguished just-like-that. Ride this out, Scorpio. It's a long transit, and you won't know how you really feel until after Venus straightens out on January 29, 2022. Another thing to be on the lookout for during the reversal: shady characters who are experts at covering their tracks. No, they won't be wearing a wedding ring if they're on the prowl, so it'll be up to you to use those well-honed Spidey senses to suss out the snakes—and turn tail when you even suspect a bad actor.

If you're in an LTR and the sizzle fades (or has been for a while), don't bail. There may be a silver lining, especially during the December 19 to January 29 retrograde. This is actually the perfect time to ease off the sexy pedal and strengthen the friendship aspect of your bond. The missing ingredient might turn out to be a feeling of connection and safety that is the bedrock of true intimacy. Create a safe space to talk about topics that might have felt too scary to bring up. Whatever the outcome, it will be a relief to have the truth finally come out, even if that requires a third party, like a couple's counselor, to facilitate.

In all types of relationships, Venus retrograde will challenge—and hopefully inspire—you to improve your communication style. If you've heard one time too many that you're intimidating, take that to heart. While it can feed your ego, that's not the same as nurturing it. Where you normally lead with intensity, ease up. Conversations don't have to be interrogations. Listen a little more and, at the same time, be willing to open up. The results may be nothing short of amazing.

LUNAR NODES IN TAURUS AND SCORPIO

Karmic Callings

Lunar Nodes in Taurus and Scorpio

January 18, 2022
to July 17, 2023

Karma is calling, Scorpio, and there's no way to send it to voicemail. For the first time in 19 years, the lunar South Node settles into your sign, charging up your first house of identity. This cycle, which lasts from January 18, 2022, to July 17, 2023, helps you "true up" with your spiritual gifts, the ones you've had for as long as you can remember. (And probably before then, too!)

We are all born with superpowers, moving people in intangible ways. Then, life happens. People misunderstand you. They tease and torment or judge you mercilessly. And you begin hiding the very things that make you special, until you forget those parts of yourself exist.

Then, every couple decades, the South Node pings your sign, snapping you out of slumber. Face to face with the real you, it's time to decide: Will you live out loud...or leave your truth buried in the vault? A transparent existence seems like the no-brainer here, but not so for secretive Scorpios. You're a highly guarded soul, even with trusted confidantes. Revealing buried parts of your identity to the world? That's a hell of a thing. But then again, so is living an inauthentic life.

So, Scorpio, who the heck do you think you are, anyway? Are you living life by your design, like inspiring signmates Willow Smith, RuPaul and

Shailene Woodley? Or have you put your real desires on hold, out of fear, guilt or shame?

Have faith! While the karmic correction of a South Node transit can be unmooring, there's a reason these tests are pushing you past the edge of reason. Stagnant energy must be broken up so you can take an honest look inside of yourself. Even if you've done twenty ayahuasca ceremonies or studied with a guru to dismantle your ego structure, there's more "unlearning" to do.

If you've outgrown certain situations, you don't have to cut anyone off— in fact, you probably shouldn't. The transformation of the Scorpio South Node is an inside job. Plus, there's another half to this equation. The lunar North Node will concurrently travel through the opposite pole of the zodiac in Taurus and your seventh house of partnerships. Until July 17, 2023, you'll have repeated opportunities to find, develop or improve on a special dynamic duo. This nodal transit can intensify your feelings, making you eager to take the plunge or give something untested a serious go. This can be your romantic interest, a writing or performing partner or a professional associate. But whoever it is, there's some weight behind the connection—that feeling of fatefulness.

While the urge to merge is powerful during this North Node transit, forget about living for other people's approval ratings. Validation-seeking is the way to stray in 2022. In fact, as you shift your focus, the people around you might be inspired to make their own long overdue changes. But this will happen as a matter of course—not because you orchestrated it on their behalf. Be warned: When the inner work feels too hard, you might want to go for your favorite fixes—firing up a steamy romance or getting wrapped up in solving other people's problems. But don't! That's just an unconscious avoidance technique. Creating drama in existing relationships is another sneaky distraction technique you'll want to avoid.

Here's the happy irony of this cycle: The more tuned in to yourself you become, the better your relationships will be! True, there may be temporary turmoil as everyone adjusts to new roles. But ultimately, there's no greater aphrodisiac than a little bit of space...yes, even when every cell in your body is screaming, "I want more!"

Starting January 18, devote yourself to discovering what makes you happy, regardless of whether or not others approve. Just remember that it's a process. Set up a sanctuary, chill space, meditation room, whatever, so you can slip off for reflective alone time. The sooner you start thinking about these quiet spells as "personal growth and development sessions," the faster you'll evolve toward your true north. Until then, keep bravely looking into the shadows—with as many coaches, healers, therapists, shamans and guides as you desire.

The last time the South Node toured Scorpio was from April 14, 2003 to December 26, 2004. Significant themes around individual growth, identity and partnership may recur this year. You might even pick up where you left off or resume a path that you thought you'd finished for good. Surprise, surprise!

ECLIPSES IN TAURUS AND SCORPIO

Balancing Relationships & Self

Partial Solar Eclipse in Taurus

April 30 at 4:27pm

Total Lunar Eclipse in Scorpio

May 16 at 12:14am

Partial Solar Eclipse in Scorpio new moon

October 25 at 6:48am

Total Lunar Eclipse in Taurus full moon

November 8 at 6:02am

times in eastern time

Relationship reset: incoming! This year's four eclipses touch down on the Taurus/Scorpio axis, sweeping through your autonomous first house (governed by Scorpio) and your committed seventh house (ruled by Taurus). As part of a two-year eclipse series happening from November 2021 to October 2023, these monumental moonbeams will retool the balance between "me" and "we." When is it time to work the tag team angle, and when should you step out like a solo star? These eclipses help you strike the right balance.

New partnerships, both business and romantic, dawn on the horizon when the year's two eclipses in Taurus sweep in on April 30 and November 8. Eclipses can serve up radical transformations. If a relationship has been idling in neutral, the April 30 solar (new moon) eclipse could jumpstart it back into fifth gear. Teaming up on a co-created project helps to set things off—but the change may just as easily begin with an epic blowout, especially if you've been holding in grievances. No need to plot revenge, Scorpio, because you'll have a chance to get all your feelings on the table and mitigate the drama before it becomes Oscar-worthy.

Bad actors may be ushered rapidly out of your life near the November 8 total lunar (full moon) eclipse. For some Scorpios, this might deliver a "make it or break it" moment. A commitment may be tested, or you'll get a sudden offer to team up with a powerful collaborator. Romantically, some couples will catapult into official territory—and rather quickly! (Dash to City Hall, anyone?) For others, these eclipses could bring a sudden split or a push off the fence if you've been sweeping an issue under the rug.

May 16 and October 25 put the spotlight directly on your individual needs and endeavors. As eclipses in Scorpio ignite your first house of self and appearances, you'll surprise the world with anything from a revamped personal style to an assertive new attitude. Whether you plan for it or not, the total lunar eclipse that comes with the May 16 Scorpio full moon could turn into a ribbon-cutting for a long-held dream. You've worked hard for this goal, so what the heck. Might as well let this lunation stage a dramatic "reveal ceremony" on your behalf. Break away from confining people and situations in May—though be aware that eclipses can make one impulsive.

During the galvanizing solar (new moon) eclipse in Scorpio on October 25, the spotlight could land on you unexpectedly. Simultaneously, a solo project might take flight. This is your star turn, so don't feel obligated to bring everyone else along for the ride now. Trust that you're "enough" on your own—and go have your moment!

MARS IN GEMINI

Transformational Twosomes

Mars in Gemini

August 20, 2022 to March 25, 2023

Mars Retrograde in Gemini

October 30, 2022 to January 12, 2023

What exactly was it they were saying about your sign being the most sexual of them all? Sure, you might be a flirt in the streets—but a freak in the sheets? That's another story, one that begins (and crescendoes) on August 20, when your co-ruler, burning-hot Mars, starts a searing voyage through Gemini and your erotic eighth house. Your seductive charms will be in rare form in the second half of 2022 as you prove exactly what it means to be the zodiac's tantric wizard.

In a normal cycle, Mars spends seven weeks in each sign during its two-year trip around the Sun. But every other year, it turns retrograde for about ten weeks, which means you'll be treated to an extra-long—and extra-steamy—visit from the heat-generating planet in this already sultry realm. So plan to take your sweet old time and savor every minute of this six-month session, which won't expire until March 25, 2023.

While this energizing and butterfly-inducing power surge is sure to include some epic sexytime, the common denominator of this prolonged transit is intensity! And because you're a Scorpio, that just so happens to be one of your own descriptors. Anything more lightweight than that won't even register on your emotional radar.

The eighth house rules intimacy, eroticism and deeply entwined interactions. But it's also the realm of shared resources, joint ventures, metaphysics, secrets—and catching the strongest of feelings. Any and all of these areas could become top of mind for the coming six months. But you'll need to manage your anxiety and jealousy (and anger and competition) because, with inflammatory Mars here, things could spiral out of control in a heartbeat. And when it's in reverse, well, all bets are off. You may need to develop stronger coping skills and line up "gatekeepers" you can turn to when your pulse starts racing.

Your seductive charms will be in rare form in the second half of 2022 as you prove exactly what it means to be the zodiac's tantric wizard.

Whatever your relationship status, it's important that you don't project your feelings or fears onto your partner—or to an innocent Bumble bystander. You're responsible for your behavior, and this biennial energy surge can test you and teach you some valuable lessons. When you start to freak out about the future (or perceived slights), you need to de-escalate things before they get out of hand. If your date or mate isn't as "all in" as you'd like, the worst thing you can do is try to force them to commit if they're not ready. By the same token, don't let anyone pressure you into anything you're not 100 percent game for.

This all goes double once the red planet shifts into reverse from October 30 to January 12, 2023. During this ten-week pivot, collaborations and partnerships that felt like they were blasting full-steam ahead may suddenly seem like they hit a standstill. If strong feelings do arise, you could easily conflate a molehill into Mt. Everest, like distracted bae not kissing you goodbye one morning. Mild disappointment could turn into anger and then combust into out-and-out paranoia. Don't go there, Scorp! Keep a list of preventative measures to tap when you start to spiral: Call a friend, book an SOS therapy session, have a calming acupuncture treatment—anything to dial it down. With the hot-blooded planet running amok in this zone, you won't be thinking clearly. You might not be thinking at all! Knowing this is possible can inspire you to get involved in activities that not only distract you, but help you get grounded.

Since retrogrades rule the past, a former flame could reignite from out of the blue. If this is "the one that got away," and you're both available, test those waters cautiously. But first, review the reasons this didn't work out the first time around. (Even if it was the best sex ever.) And if you know this is playing with fire, either block all their advances and ask that gatekeeper friend to keep you strong...or have a fire extinguisher close at hand in case this all blows up.

Of course, Scorpio, your best bet might be to block the first advance. Onwards and upwards is a motto to embrace when you feel the pull back into a toxic situationship. It's a much better bet than trying to outfox your instinctually possessive nature. With Mars in Gemini serving up new romantic options left and right, the biggest fight may be against your own false beliefs. Like the one that you'll never find anyone who loves you again? True, you may not find someone exactly like your ex, but when you open yourself to new possibilities you could discover that this is a very good thing! ✳

2022

SAGITTARIUS

SAGITTARIUS

LOVE

After two tide-turning years, relationships begin to stabilize again. Love goals may have fluctuated wildly since May 2020, when the destiny-driven North Node parked in Gemini and your committed partnerships zone. Meanwhile, the Sagittarius South Node put you in its karmic crosshairs, forcing you to deal with your own unhealthy patterns. (Have you changed your status to "relationship anarchist" yet?) That all changes on January 18 as the nodes move to Taurus and Scorpio. Slowly but surely clarity resumes, making it easier to determine next steps. This 18-month cycle demands tough, "adult" choices which may bring loss or grief. In the process, you could manifest a spiritual soulmate—or discover ways to reconnect with the one who is already in your life. Romance gets red-hot (and fun again!) when your ruler, buoyant Jupiter, soars into Aries and your passionate fifth house from May 10 to October 28. No dragging your feet once energetic Mars kicks off a six-month tour through Gemini on August 20! Make your move or you might miss out—especially if an old flame is rekindled while Mars is retrograde from October 30 to January 12, 2023.

CAREER & MONEY

You work hard for your money, but is your money working hard for you? Profitability is the keyword to focus on in 2022. Reassess spending habits while Venus is retrograde in your financial zone until January 29. If certain indulgences are zapping your security fund, tighten up your budget. Managing your workload will require clear-cut processes once the lunar North Node heads into Taurus on January 18. But with the South Node in your twelfth house of release, start letting go of time-zapping tasks that aren't bringing a healthy ROI. This "safety net" might be keeping you stuck in an underearning cycle. Get your branding and front-facing materials up to snuff! The spotlight swings your way from May 10 to October 28 when lucky Jupiter races through your fame zone (Aries) and brings widespread attention to your work.

WELLNESS

What are you digesting—literally and emotionally? If you've been stuffing down stress with food or pushing yourself past the point of exhaustion, the planets blow a loud whistle. From January 18, 2022 to July 17, 2023, the North Node points its compass towards Taurus and your sixth house of healthy routines. Commit to regular workouts—even if you have to hire someone to show you the ropes or hold you accountable. Jupiter in Pisces sounds the call for hydration and gut health until May 10 (and after October 28). Try a short-term juice cleanse; get active on the water or near it! Shedding toxic beliefs is as important as detoxing your diet, so work with a therapist who can shift your mindset in a positive direction. Speaking of detoxing, sweating is one of the best ways to release harmful substances and get blood flowing to your organs. An infrared sauna could be a life-changing splurge.

FRIENDS & FAMILY

With your ruler, free-spirited Jupiter, in your domestic zone until May 10 (and again from October 28 to December 20), you could take "home" on the road! Grant yourself greater independence from family during these cycles—without shirking obligations, obviously. Nesting Archers could score a lucky real estate deal or finally take on renovation projects that turn your house into a home. With the South Node in Scorpio, you might steep yourself in therapeutic work to break up family patterns. Learn the difference between nurturing (which empowers people) and caretaking (which zaps your energy and leaves others feeling helpless). Setting healthy boundaries is the key to creating a harmonious home.

JUPITER IN PISCES

Bless Your Nest

Jupiter in Pisces

December 28, 2021
to May 10, 2022

October 28 to
December 20, 2022

Settle down, Sagittarius, or give it the old college try. Your personal life will take a starring role in 2022. Until May 10 (and again from October 28 to December 20), expansive Jupiter floats through Pisces and your fourth house of home and family, making your nest feel blessed. The fourth house sits at the very bottom of the astrology wheel, and it represents your foundations—emotional, financial, familial. What do you need to feel secure? With your ruling planet parked here for half the year, you'll rethink what it means to put down roots.

It's quite the paradox, because nomadic Jupiter rules travel—which is pretty much the opposite of the homey, hunkered-down fourth house vibe. Have you dreamed of living abroad for a year—or even a couple months? Arrange a home swap or put your things in storage and go explore. Is van life calling your name? Rent a rig and see what it's like to take home on the road. With audacious Jupiter here, this is your time to take a bold leap! "Home" could soon be wherever you rest your head that night and whatever creature comforts you manage to squeeze into travel-sized bottles.

Back at base, Chateau Centaur could be a bustling epicenter. Maybe you'll host a rotating cast of house guests or rent out your place on Airbnb for extra income. You might explore investing in a weekend or vacation property. Caveat: Jupiter in Pisces is not great at setting boundaries. With your people-pleasing tendencies turned up, be sure to take periodic breaks from constant couch-crashers as you honor your need for personal space. It's okay to tell certain friends and relatives to get a hotel!

66

Have you been a renter or nomad for as long as you can remember? Jupiter in Pisces could make a homeowner out of you.

99

The fourth house rules motherhood and female-identified people. Some Sagittarians may expand your brood via pregnancy or adoption, IVF or a blended family situation. Your relationship to your mother, daughter or an important woman may go through a growth phase. Perhaps it's time to shift into new roles instead of viewing each other through old and outworn dynamics.

While Jupiter's in Pisces, explore your heritage and ancestry (especially on your mom's side of the family tree). Under this nostalgic influence, you could vacation to favorite childhood haunts or bring a new love home to meet the family and tour your hometown. Your soul will be soothed by spending quality time with nurturing people who adore you unconditionally. Hopefully, you're lucky enough to have a couple of those in your family tree. If not, carve out time for your "chosen family" and go visit beloved friends.

Have you been a renter or nomad for as long as you can remember? Jupiter in Pisces could make a homeowner out of you. While you love the open road, your magnanimous sign also craves grand quarters where you can host your motley crew of friends, entertain and work on your many projects. With bigger-is-better Jupiter here, you may move to a larger place, renovate or redecorate. But even if it's a 500-square-foot studio apartment, you'll find a way to put your signature stamp on it!

Thanks to Jupiter's entrepreneurial influence, 2022 is a great year to start (or expand) a home-based business. Did the pandemic's WFH mandates make it hard to imagine ever going back to the office? Well, Sagittarius, maybe you don't have to. That cottage industry you've been quietly developing might soon require its own office space. Carve out a corner— or take over a spare room—but make dedicated zones for your creativity to flourish.

During this sensitive cycle, you might take a job that involves supporting other people on an emotional level. If you've ever dreamed of becoming a coach, healer or therapist, erudite Jupiter could send you back to school. With Jupiter at its farthest point away from your tenth house of career and corporate life, you may want to lighten your schedule a bit. Not that you'll ever completely power down. That said, you'll be a lot more productive from the comfort of your couch (or your cozy corner café) than you will in a fluorescent-lit cubicle. Craft a compelling case to cut your commute, and the powers-that-be might just sign on!

Some Archers may get a long-distance job offer—and just like that, you're packing up and moving to a new zip code. Fate and fortune will be on your side in these dealings! Maybe you got a taste of this in 2021 when Jupiter briefly visited Pisces from May 13 to July 28—or in the cycle before then from January 17, 2010, to January 22, 2011. Page back for clues of what could emerge again, especially surrounding family relationships or your living spaces.

To wit, in January 2010, Ophi took a pregnancy test and found out she was positive. (Yes, a huge surprise!) Days before her daughter Cybele was born on October 3, 2010, the adjacent apartment opened up in her rent-controlled NYC building for the first time in 20 years. She leapt into that lease and connected the two units. With one as a family home and one as an office, she had a seamless flow between new motherhood and running our growing business. *Voila!*

Career-wise, a powerful woman (or female-identified she/her) could step in as a mentor and advisor—or she might become your official partner in a joint venture. You may score big with a business idea that's marketed to women (especially moms). You might also earn a nice lump sum through real estate or a home-related venture. Is it time to get your broker's license or take an interior design course? Anything's possible!

There is a small catch: While in Pisces, Jupiter forms a challenging, 90-degree square to your Sagittarius Sun. Along with all this rapid expansion could come growing pains and a few tough hurdles to jump. The struggles will be worth pushing through, as long as you take the lessons and apply them swiftly to whatever you're working on. Healing from a little hurt can make you stronger!

JUPITER MEETS NEPTUNE IN PISCES

Home on the Road

Jupiter meets
Neptune in Pisces

April 12, 2022

Deepening your bonds could plunge you into healing waters in March and April as Jupiter travels in tight formation with enchanting Neptune. On April 12, they'll make an exact conjunction at 23°58' Pisces—a meetup that only happens every 13 years. Your moods might be intense during this time, but they're also giving you near-psychic guidance. While this planetary pairing sharpens your intuition, carve out enough quiet time to tune in. Feelings can get complex and heavy, drawing you into their depths. This could be a productive time to work with a therapist, spiritual counselor or healer to process painful parts of your past including ancestral trauma that has never left your family's lineage.

With karmic Neptune joining lucky Jupiter here, you might receive an inheritance or a financial gift from a relative. Maybe your great-aunt leaves you her garden-level apartment, or a generous family member lets you know that they've written you into their will. Sagittarians with children or assets (or both) may enlist a lawyer to draft your will or take out a life-insurance policy. Not that you're planning to leave the planet anytime soon! But this added measure ensures that when your time does come, your kith and kin will be covered.

Maybe, baby? With Jupiter and Neptune blurring boundaries in your family house, unexpected pregnancies could catch Archers off guard. Even if you swore you'd never give up your independence to be a parent, you may have a gentle change of heart. Adopting a child (including a fur baby!) might bring out your nurturing side in exciting ways. Even if you don't bring in a bouncing bundle, you could make a "permanent" gesture such as getting engaged, buying a home together or moving in with a mate.

> 66
>
> *With audacious Jupiter here, this is your time to take a bold leap! "Home" could soon be wherever you rest your head that night and whatever creature comforts you manage to squeeze into travel-sized bottles.*
>
> 99

Paintbrush, please! Jupiter's alignment with divinely inspired Neptune could make you "pregnant" with creative possibilities. An art class or design workshop may provide an inspired outlet for the intense energy you'll channel during this emotional phase. Maybe you'll take up the "home arts"—macrame, gardening, cooking—to unwind. This conjunction brings out some "grandma chic," but don't knock it 'til you try it! You could find these old-fashioned pastimes surprisingly soothing.

JUPITER IN ARIES

In Pursuit of Passion

Jupiter in Aries

May 10 to
October 28, 2022

December 20, 2022
to May 16, 2023

Come out, come out! Just in time for a spring awakening, Jupiter exits your low-key fourth house and bursts into fellow fire-sign Aries, heating up your passionate and playful fifth house from May 10 to October 28. Your lust for life (and a few other things) returns with a vengeance. After beginning 2022 surfing the emotion ocean, you'll be back in your optimistic, fun-loving element. Take up the mantle as entertainment director for your entourage—and occasionally as the unhired entertainment who gets everyone to laugh, loosen up and live a little.

Lights, camera, Sagittarius! This live-out-loud Jupiter phase rouses your inner performance artist. You could attract fame or draw attention with your creative talents. Not only will you be bursting at the seams to share your brilliance, you'll attract an eager audience. Build that fanbase, Sagittarius! As one of the zodiac's lifelong pupils, you could turn some of the lessons you've learned into your own "edu-tainment"-style course offering. (Sagittarius University: Now taking applications!) Or you may literally find yourself on camera, recording livestreams, being followed by a reality TV crew or killing your lines like multihyphenate signmates Zoe Kravitz, Miley Cyrus and Janelle Monae.

Even more fortuitous? In Aries, Jupiter forms a flowing 120° trine to your Sun in Sagittarius. This vitality-boosting transit unleashes a torrential downpour of passion. Expect to feel friskier and more flamboyant than you have in years!

If you're looking to build a following, cast a wider net. With your globetrotting galactic guardian raising your profile, you could gain international appeal. Learning a new language is optional, but if you can make meaningful cultural connections wherever you explore, you'll create a platform worth telling a friend (or five) about. Entrepreneurial Archers might find a global customer base!

New romance—or rebooted passion—can add some sizzle to this six-month Jupiter in Aries circuit. But no need to make everyone live up to soulmate criteria. The fifth house is more about romantic love than actual commitment. Not that you won't attract quality prospects, but your focus will be more on enjoying the moment than nailing down a LTR or picking out forever homes. A note to the sweeties who captured your heart earlier this year: Adopt some swagger, stat! As your temperature evolves from mild to wild, you need sugar and spice to charge up your sex drive. Your tastes may do a total 180, but easy, Sagittarius! Willpower will be tested while Jupiter's in randy Aries, but you don't want to kick a good one to the curb prematurely.

For coupled Archers, this is a great time to expand your comfort zone with travel, new hobbies and learning together. Surf lessons and a trip to Costa Rica, maybe? Go big with those bucket-list items. The couple that plays together, stays together!

VENUS RETROGRADE

Renegotiating Rules

Venus in Capricorn

November 5, 2021
to March 6, 2022

**Venus Retrograde
in Capricorn**

December 19, 2021
to January 29, 2022

Financial negotiations will be front and center as 2022 dawns, thanks to the backspin of values-focused Venus in Capricorn and your second house of financial and emotional security. And since Venus is also the planet of romance and relationships, one of the "valuables" you've been focused on might be a love interest.

This backspin is part of a longer cycle that stretches from November 5, 2021, to March 6, 2022. Normally, Venus spends just three to five weeks in a sign, but every other year, it flips into retrograde for six weeks, and this go-round, you will be tuned in to Venus' vibrations for a total of four months! This should have the effect of bringing money, stability and everything you cherish and hold dear under the microscope, from how much you earn and spend to long-range goals and emotional security.

In the forward-moving part of this transit (November 5 to December 19, 2021, and January 29 to March 6, 2022), you can take action based on your goals and desires. But during the six-week reversal, you have a golden opportunity to reflect on intentions you've set, plans you've put into motion and the path you're on to get there.

This doesn't mean you'll scrap the whole shebang and start from scratch. (Though some Sagittarians may welcome that option!) It's a time to lean into Capricorn's serious and future-oriented nature and contemplate the greatest possible outcomes. Venus was last retrograde from May 13 to June 25, 2020, and because it took place in Gemini and your seventh house of relationships, it probably packed a double-strength wallop for you. In fact, you may still be dealing with some of the fallout from that cycle. Hopefully you've been able to keep the faith that whatever started to unravel—or come totally apart—needed a fix or a change.

This time around, as Venus backs up through your grounded second house, issues and challenges that come up should be more manageable— certainly less emotionally fraught. Yet all retrograde cycles invite us to look at things we conveniently sweep to the side and either outright ignore or tell ourselves we'll deal with when we "have time." When we've been putting things off a little too long, the universe has a funny way of getting our attention. So while you won't be able to prevent surprises or disruptions, the best way to handle them is by trusting that they're happening for you (not to you).

Unexpected costs, forgotten payments, accounting errors, resurfacing exes, erupting yearnings...these are part and parcel of Venus retrograde in your second house. Chapters you thought were long since closed could pop open again without much warning. A heartfelt reunion might be a wonderful thing—or it could threaten to unglue the seams of your current partnership.

When Venus first dipped into Capricorn on November 5, 2021, you might have gotten the first whiff of something being up. It was easy to do "business as usual" when it came to your finances and heart, but once it backflips into reverse gear, suddenly all bets are off. The six weeks of reverse-commuting might turn your world on its side so much that you're not even sure which way's up. Try to ride it out—and not do anything you can't undo. Once the backspin ends on January 29, 2022, you'll have another six weeks to integrate what you experienced and begin to make sense of any changes that were indicated.

If you're feeling suddenly old-fashioned and a bit traditional, there's nothing wrong with you. This is actually a sweet byproduct of Venus reversing through your conservative second house. What other urges are coming up? Lean in to all sensual and tactile temptations, from the fabrics you drape yourself and sleep in, to what you eat and drink, to how you interact with your beloved or a new prospect. Cue up some slow-jamming playlists, burn your favorite scented candle and drop the pace by about 50 percent. When you get twitchy and anxious for things to move faster, remind yourself that good things do come to those who wait.

In an LTR? Immediately shift your focus to making it your top priority for these few months. Like a garden, unions need TLC, so stop taking any aspect of it for granted. Carve out special together time to share things you haven't talked about lately; make activity and romantic dates, including unstructured cuddle-on-the-couch time. This isn't just sweet in the moment but will keep your love tanks as full as possible for when inevitable conflicts arise. For some Archers, old rejection or abandonment issues may flare during this Venus retrograde. While your reflex may be to grasp more tightly, that could come off as "clingy and needy" to your partner. A more helpful response is to recognize it for what it is and get thee to a therapist or energy healer. Then schedule some friend hangouts to keep you happily distracted and relieve any undue demands on your partner.

This is also a golden opportunity to review your finances. Your live-out-loud sign hates frugality and what you think of as pettiness.

But tightening your belt to make a big-ticket goal more reachable is neither! As much as you'd love to be wildly generous and not even look at price tags, you'll benefit from reining in these impulses and maybe even sticking to a, glug, budget. Redirect that urge to splurge into "acts of service" (whether or not that's your love language), such as cooking dinner, offering foot rubs or just driving someone to a meeting when they don't have wheels. There are plenty of ways to show affection without whipping out your wallet!

LUNAR NODES IN TAURUS AND SCORPIO

Health is Wealth

Lunar Nodes in Taurus and Scorpio

January 18, 2022
to July 17, 2023

Exhale, Sagittarius. This January 18, the moon's karmic South Node leaves your sign, ending a grueling tour of your first house of identity that began on May 5, 2020. The past 18 months have hardly been a cakewalk for Archers. At times, you felt locked in a crucible, burning up an identity that was going the way of skinny jeans. Thankfully, this trial by fire only comes around every 18.5 to 20 years. That means you won't host the South Node for another two decades. Whew.

Hindsight is 20/20, Sagittarius. Looking back, can you see the unprecedented strides that you made over the past couple years? True, you would have preferred these leaps to come without all the pain, confusion and gut-wrenching lessons. But since you're reading this now, we're pretty sure you implemented huge changes in the name of living authentically. Maybe you moved, changed jobs or left a marriage. Health troubles may have forced you to change your diet or the company you keep. Or perhaps you leaned into challenging circumstances and designed a convention-defying life. Whatever the case...congratulations! Ripping away false aspects of your life is no easy process—especially where the South Node is concerned. But like that popular Anais Nin quote says, "And the day came when the risk to remain tight in a bud was more painful than the risk it took to blossom."

Now that you're "trued up" to your genuine self, it's time to surrender!
On January 18, the lunar nodes reposition themselves across your axis
of health and healing. Until July 17, 2023, the South Node simmers in
Scorpio and the cauldron of your spiritual twelfth house. Meanwhile, the
North Node in Taurus and your sixth house of work and wellness gets
you pumped about systematizing your life. Turns out, you don't have to
sacrifice self-care in the name of success. Time to connect body and soul,
Sagittarius!

66

*If you want to break old
habits and shed limiting
beliefs, start by observing how
you think on a daily basis.*

99

Where to begin? In a word: mindfulness. These next 18 months will help
you simplify areas that have gotten overly complex or out of control.
Think in terms of getting your house—and your body, mind, spirit and
finances—in order. But you won't be successful going at it with a no-
nonsense attitude. Awareness is the key to alchemy between now and July
17, 2023. If you want to break old habits and shed limiting beliefs, start by
observing how you think on a daily basis.

Warning: The South Node in Scorpio can be triggering. Old wounds are likely to be scratched. Unprocessed grief, ancestral trauma, resentment and rage? Get ready, because it can all come rushing out. (Possibly in the middle of a yoga class or group meditation...) Consider this "good bad news," Sagittarius. Bottled up feelings lead to all kinds of unwanted things, from literal weight on your body to chronic disease. This healing nodal cycle helps you shed whatever you've been holding in. Let go and let yourself be liberated!

Reminder from the North Node in Taurus and your healthy sixth house: Your body is your soul's address here on Earth. During this cycle, you'll be pumped to eat clean and get back into a regular fitness groove. If you've been ignoring aches and pains, you'll need to address in 2022. Vitality is the goal, so don't settle for mediocre medical advice. Explore modalities of healing like functional medicine, naturopathy and holistic treatments (acupuncture, craniosacral) that focus on prevention and natural remedies.

The science of neuroplasticity is worth learning more about this year. While many neural pathways are formed during childhood, they aren't all hard-wired. Because of the brain's plasticity, new pathways can be formed, often through repetitive activities such as breathing exercises or learning a new word every day. Novel activities like traveling (a Sag favorite) and reading fiction have also proven to boost brain activity.

Or hack your body's responses with epigenetics, which studies how environment and behavior affect the expression of genes. Moving to a new area or cultivating a daily habit won't alter your DNA per se. But it can change your body's response to stimuli, for example, the way your nervous system reacts to intergenerational trauma. And with the nodes in mystical Scorpio and earthy Taurus, don't rule out the rewiring power of plant medicine, meditation and herbal remedies.

Work is bound to be busy with the North Node in Taurus, but does it speak to your soul? If not, the Scorpio South Node could direct your career compass toward a purpose-driven path. Idealistic Sagittarians are not clock punchers by nature. Before July 17, 2023, make it your mission to add more meaning to your work. Already there? Now's the time to do a health check. Have you slipped into martyr mode, working around the clock or without clear boundaries? Burning out is never a good look, Sagittarius, so let the Taurus North Node help you systematize your workflow so you have time to eat dinner with the family, hit the gym for an evening cardio class and enjoy the fruits of your labor!

The last time the nodes were in this position was from April 14, 2003 to December 26, 2004. Significant themes around health, spirituality and work could arise again between January 18, 2022 and July 17, 2023. Revisit parts of your life that fed your soul back then. Nostalgia aside, you may discover that they nourish 2022 you!

ECLIPSES IN TAURUS AND SCORPIO

Spiritual & Physical Health

**Partial Solar
Eclipse in Taurus**

April 30 at 4:27pm

**Total Lunar
Eclipse in Scorpio**

May 16 at 12:14am

**Partial Solar Eclipse
in Scorpio new moon**

October 25 at 6:48am

**Total Lunar Eclipse
in Taurus full moon**

November 8 at 6:02am

times in eastern time

Stop treating self-care as something you'll get to when you're done with all your work. For one thing, a Sagittarius never stops hustling. Secondly, 2022's four eclipses fall on your axis of health and healing, as they touch down in Taurus (your sixth house of fitness) and Scorpio (your spiritual twelfth house). These lunar lifts are part of an eclipse series running from November 2021 to October 2023, which are transforming the way you balance mind, body and soul. During this time, you're pulled between dueling themes of control and surrender. These balancing eclipses teach you when to lean in and when to lean back and accept the things you can't change.

On April 30 and November 8, eclipses will fall in Taurus and your sixth house of health, a time to focus on fitness, lifestyle changes and following any doctor's orders. The sixth house is associated with the digestive system, and near the solar (new moon) eclipse on April 30, you might explore cutting-edge research on gut health. Maybe you'll try a microbiome test, which can measure the health of your gut bacteria and potentially show your risk for certain diseases. Ask your physician about options like this—or others, such as a daily prebiotic and probiotic regimen, food allergy testing or a low-FODMAP diet. If indeed we really are what we eat, the Taurus eclipses bring a recommended change of menu—and venue. You could be extra sensitive to chemicals in your environment, not to mention those in your skincare, beauty and cleaning products. There may be an ingredient that doesn't agree with your system.

With these eclipses activating your health houses, you may get doctor's orders to change your lifestyle. As a happy-go-lucky (and sometimes hedonistic) Archer, you take a hard pass on anything that interferes with your impulsive desires. But near these eclipses—especially the total lunar (full moon) eclipse on November 8—your body could weigh in with another perspective. Discipline doesn't have to feel like deprivation, no, Sagittarius. However, exert willpower temporarily as you cut an addiction to sugar, coffee or another stimulant that's simply NOT doing your body good.

The saying "as within, so without" rings true with this eclipse series, and your emotional state can strongly influence your wellbeing. If you've been dealing with enigmatic symptoms, delving into your psyche yields additional clues. These eclipses call for a blend of both medical and metaphysical approaches.

Lessons in surrender arrive on May 16 and October 25, when eclipses in Scorpio energize your twelfth house of rest, forgiveness and release. This is a fruitful time for deep therapy and inner work that taps your subconscious. Anything from hypnosis to shamanic healing to past-life regression could shed light on stubborn blocks and help you break chronic, fear-based patterns. For artists and healers, these Scorpio eclipses may inspire a creative renaissance.

These balancing eclipses teach you when to lean in and when to lean back and accept the things you can't change.

During the total lunar (full moon) eclipse on May 16, you may be forced to wave the white flag on an issue you've been struggling with. If you're grappling with an addiction, find the courage to get help or enter recovery. Compounding emotional stress may finally cause the dam to break. Feeling is the first step in dealing, Sagittarius, and there's no hiding behind humor in moments like these. Fortunately, this lunar eclipse can illuminate incredible healers who adjust everything from your neural pathways to your chakras.

If your own journey involves working as a healer, the Scorpio new moon solar eclipse on October 25 could galvanize the action. Helpful people, like agents and coaches, will be close at hand. Even if you don't technically "need" them, they can expedite your journey from Point A to Point Z. Don't cling stubbornly to the DIY approach. Life is short, so why not work in your zone of genius instead of wearing 500 hats?

At work and in your relationships, you're also learning when to be hands-on and when to let others take the wheel. Contrary to your reputation as an indie spirit, you can be pretty large and in-charge when the situation calls for it. Do you need to be stern with people? There may be some problems this year that only you can fix, but you don't have to do it alone! With the Taurus eclipses sweeping through your sixth house of helpful people, you could hire and fire. Create savvy systems that help you stay on top of the details effectively. The two Scorpio eclipses may reveal hidden agendas or shady characters—eye-opening moments that show where you've relinquished a little too much control.

Bottom line: In 2022, you'll learn to strike a balance between micromanaging and having overly porous boundaries. Not everyone deserves a spot on the Sag Squad. Don't cling to people just because they're familiar. Should they be "eclipsed" away, trust that the universe will soon usher in someone loyal and qualified who's a much better fit!

MARS IN GEMINI

Partnerships Pick Up Speed

Mars in Gemini

August 20, 2022 to
March 25, 2023

**Mars Retrograde
in Gemini**

October 30, 2022
to January 12, 2023

Bring on the dynamic duos! Starting this August 20, all your partnerships get supercharged thanks to the biennial visit of engine-revving Mars blasting into Gemini and your seventh house of committed relationships until March 25, 2023. While you can be perfectly content on your own, one of your not-so-secret joys in life is being part of a loving union.

Red-hot Mars in this sector of commitment isn't about a wild romp of a romantic adventure, exciting as that can be. When you're done having mere "fun," you can clear the decks for a lasting, loving, connected relationship. The best part is: If you're single, you've got plenty of time to manifest this. Mars is making an extended journey through this realm thanks to a ten-week retrograde smack in the middle of it (October 30 to January 12, 2023). The hot-blooded planet normally spends seven weeks in each sign during its two-year trip around the Sun. But every other year, it turns retrograde, which means you'll be treated to an extra-long—and extra-lusty—six-month visit from the cosmic heat-generator.

Passionate Mars in quicksilver Gemini can be unpredictable, so you might want to keep a life preserver handy as you navigate sometimes-stormy seas on the Emotion Ocean during this lengthy transit. And once it flips into its two-and-a-half-month reversal on October 30, you'll definitely want to batten down the hatches. From business and creative partners to close friendships to your love life, interpersonal dynamics could hit some rough patches. You can't wish them away, Archer—or simply run away (as sorely as you might be tempted).

So what to do? For starters, acknowledge that conflict happens. Then, think about the outcome you'd like to manifest. Focus on what you might say or do to bring more harmony into the connection without putting the other person on the defensive (or stuffing down your feelings).

Luckily, self-empowered Mars gifts you extra courage; and in Gemini, it'll make you nimble enough to think on your feet, making it easier to confront problems head-on. If you sense brewing tension, address the issue before October 30, when it'll be easier to tap into your gracious nature.

Beyond the real-life interactions, this activating energy is essential for clearing out stagnant vibes and rebuilding things on rock-solid ground. Mars churns up heavy emotions and passions, but you don't get to cherry-pick them. When anger, jealousy or resentment arise, accept it for what it is but then probe beneath the surface. Where is this really coming from? You may need to work with a psycho- or hypnotherapist to get to the root of this, but it's vital to get there. Otherwise, you'll only be putting Band-Aids on surface cuts and never get to heal the core wounds. And with Mars pouring gasoline on this inner blaze, you want to make it a controlled burn and not let it conflate into a full-on wildfire.

Speaking of too hot to handle, an old flame could reignite while Mars is in reverse from October 30 to January 12. If you know for sure it could never work, make that patently clear; then, if they don't seem able to respect healthy boundaries, block them. But if you're still wondering whether it was just a matter of bad timing or circumstances—and you're both available—then set some ground rules and give it a fair shot.

While you're mulling that, devote a few brain cells to getting more clarity around why this person has you in their thrall. Mars is the planet of passion and lust, but chances are the attraction is more than that. How do they make you feel when you're together—or even just communicating? Stating the obvious: "Sexy and desirable" are great feelings, but if you know this person is trouble, you need to weigh the emotional cost against the (ego) benefit. Bottom line: Listen to indie-spirited Mars' message that you don't have to get your validation from anyone else, least of all an insincere player. ✸

2022

CAPRICORN

WHAT'S IN THE STARS FOR

CAPRICORN

LOVE

Fate is on your side as the lunar North Node spins into Taurus and your fifth house of true love this January 18. This cycle, which lasts until July 17, 2023, could bring a passionate partner into your orbit. But no playing cool! The fifth house favors full-bodied romantic expression. Drop your guard and show your feelings. Giving your all is the secret to getting it back in return. Developments accelerate during two eclipses in Taurus, on April 30 and November 8. But stay flexible! These moonbeams may direct you in an exciting (but unexpected) direction. Venus will be retrograde in Capricorn until January 29, starting the year in an introspective space. Examine unproductive patterns that keep people at a distance. Then, lean into magnetic Pluto, who's winding down a long cycle through your sign (2008-2024). Your hidden charms are ready to be revealed—and we're talking about the bedroom, not the boardroom, here. Leave work at work!

CAREER & MONEY

Your diligence is starting to pay off, Capricorn, as your ruler Saturn spends its final full year in Aquarius and your second house of cash money. Set up systems to work more efficiently and lock down bread-and-butter income. You may still be paying some dues this year, but people are taking notice of your work! Position yourself as an expert, speaker or leader however you can. Profitable opportunities could flow in near the eclipses on April 30 and November 8! Enterprising Jupiter sails through your curious, cooperative third house until May 10 (and again from October 28 to December 20). Tap into local networking opportunities and partner up on projects for the win. You may commute between several cities during this time, or work with clients around the world. Build your nest egg while Jupiter in Aries drops roots into your domestic zone from May 10 to October 28. Invest in a home or vacation property or start a kitchen-table side hustle. Work gets busier than ever starting August 20, thanks to go-getter Mars in Gemini and your sixth house of daily routines and systems. Stay organized and seek service providers who meet your standards!

WELLNESS

With the karmic South Node in Scorpio and your metaphysical eleventh house, mindfulness practices are the key to your serenity. Center yourself with meditation, yoga and breathwork. This can also activate life force energy, giving you the sexiest glow-up. Saturn's been putting you through paces since late 2017. Are you exhausted yet? Get your adrenals checked and make sure you're doing things to support their function. You'll be ready for a more vigorous fitness routine once athletic Mars barrels into Gemini on August 20. You love a challenge, but take time to stretch and learn proper posture and technique to avoid injuries. Regular bodywork like massage and acupuncture can keep you balanced all year long.

FRIENDS & FAMILY

Develop meaningful connections—then bring the gang together. The more will be the merrier this year as the Scorpio South Node activates your communal eleventh house. If there are fractures in your social circle, you can only play ambassador for so long. If people aren't willing to let go of grudges, that's on them. Jupiter in Pisces provides a huge popularity burst until May 10 (and again from October 28 to December 20). While old friends are your world, expand the radius of your circle! You could meet new pals while traveling, doing self-development work or taking a class. Looking to start or grow a family? Two fertility-boosting eclipses on April 30 and November 8 are in your corner!

JUPITER IN PISCES

Opening Up with Friends & Community

Jupiter in Pisces

December 28, 2021
to May 10, 2022

October 28 to
December 20, 2022

Mic drops: incoming! Expansive Jupiter paddles through Pisces and your third house of communication and community, mobilizing your mind and your mouth. Speak your truth liberally and play superconnector during these two socially active cycles: January 1 to May 10 and again from October 28 to December 20.

If you're not already a fixture on the social circuit, rise to the occasion. Suss out the *crème de la crème* of everything, from luxury car dealerships to bistros with amazing share plates and killer views. Rather than keep these exclusive haunts to yourself, broadcast to your community. Igniting a scene benefits you greatly while Jupiter buzzes in your zone of cooperative ventures. Not only does it make everyday life more enchanted, but you never know! A "friend of a friend" could be the not-so-random stranger who wanders into the bar and accelerates your dreams.

Most Capricorns are happy to bring great people together, like one generous Goat we know. After spearheading a legendary bar scene in Seattle, she's enjoying the fruits of her legacy with an expat friend community in Mexico. Her Instagram feed is already flooded with eye candy of the area's incredible topography, architecture (including the home she is renovating) and local fare. Mayor Capricorn, we see you!

66

Hooking people up brings you joy in 2022. That's a good reason to pay it forward whenever you can, Capricorn— without getting overly involved.

99

Are multiple pals trekking toward a common goal? Unite them on a text thread or host an introductory dinner. Years from now, they will thank you for being the "founder" of their dynamic duo. This year, your supreme social matchmaking skills could extend to local businesses, coworkers and the woman carrying an electric guitar into your favorite coffee shop. Bottom line: Hooking people up brings you joy in 2022. That's a good reason to pay it forward whenever you can, Capricorn—without getting overly involved. Once you've made the intro, step out and let folks take it from there. Then, get ready to reap your own karmic rewards as people open doors for you in return.

Stay open to fresh faces too! In 2022, you attract vibrant new friendships. With some luck, these kindred spirits may evolve into creative collaborators. Even if you're a self-proclaimed introvert, your appetite for good company and stimulating conversation will be higher than it has been in years. At the very least, upgrade to "ambivert" status—someone who is equal parts extrovert and introvert.

Find people whose skills complement yours, then sync your superpowers. For example, maybe you're a design nut with an eye for gorgeous interiors, but you're more of a business head than an artisan. Team up with a curator who knows how to source (or handcraft!) the rare items you "see" for the space. Have you developed expertise? Hire yourself out as a consultant and help people turn promising ideas into tangible productions. Once you sink your teeth into a mission, you won't stop until it comes to life. Time to monetize your tenacity and wisdom!

Although you usually play the long game with relationships, feel free to dabble and experiment with different partnerships. With untethered Jupiter in this dynamic-duo zone, test chemistry with a trial project and see how your work styles mesh. Pro tip: Do this before committing to a binding or exclusive contract. If the fit is less than ideal, graciously move on to your next project (with someone else). And if you do find a dream collaborator, you can plant strong roots by starting small and growing organically.

With info-hungry Jupiter occupying these curious quarters, learning is an adventure! Build your skills with mini courses and if it helps grow your income, get certified. But hold off on any multi-year degree programs unless you're crystal clear about the path you pursue. Have you always wanted to learn how to play drums or infuse craft cocktails? When the student is ready (and Jupiter's in the third house), the teacher will appear—and you may put together a curriculum of your own. Weave your expertise into a webinar and hang your shingle!

Got a message to spread? With outspoken Jupiter loosening your lips, take the world by storm via multiple channels—broadcasting, teaching, community action, social media. Since Jupiter rules publishing and the third house rules writing, a novel, screenplay or self-help book may find an eager audience. Start a YouTube channel or style feed. Dabble in a mix of mediums until you find your favorite outlet for expression.

With globetrotting Jupiter in your third house of local action, some Capricorns will hop between multiple cities or give bicoastal life a whirl. That's a good reason to invest in a nice weekender bag or audio system. Get creative with your commute. Invest in a great bicycle for riding to work, and if you have flexibility, rent an RV as your "remote office" for a few weeks here and there.

Thinking of relocating? Airbnb was made for this fickle Jupiter cycle since you'll want to "try before you buy." Take as many short trips as you can, staying for a few days in an appealing city or district that you're considering calling home. Get up and go through your daily routine as if you lived there: Find the coffee shop, the yoga studio, the raw vegan cafe. Embrace your nomadic side!

By the end of 2022, you may be ready to start house-hunting or to officially relocate. Research while you can! Who knows? You might end up right where you started, with a totally different mentality. Like Dorothy returning to Kansas, your time in Oz could cultivate a greater appreciation for that "sleepy small town" or "hectic, high-pressure city" you wanted to flee. Maybe you just needed time away. Or perhaps you'll move to a different neighborhood that's walkable, or greener or whatever's most important to you.

JUPITER MEETS NEPTUNE IN PISCES

Master your Messaging

> **Jupiter meets Neptune in Pisces**
>
> April 12, 2022

All that bopping around might bring a serendipitous encounter near April 12 when lucky Jupiter makes a fortuitous connection to enchanted Neptune at 23°58' Pisces. Read any room you walk into, but don't just skim the surface. People are sending out major non-verbal cues and their body language tells you as much as their words.

With Neptune adding its magic touch, a budding partnership reveals its meant-to-be purpose—and in the most poetic way! So, Capricorn, who is leaning in or moving closer in your direction? Shift your energy there and watch miracles unfold. As Jupiter and Neptune embrace, friends could become lovers. Stay open to chance but set yourself up for success by hanging out in places where there are high odds for making a solid connection. Someone with soulmate potential could emerge through social media or a dating app. Late-night text marathons could reveal a match of the minds and souls...and if you're lucky, the bodies as well.

But there is some caution tape strung up around this transit: With Neptune's fetish for secrecy and Jupiter's undying optimism, you may also project a fantasy onto the situation. Those rose-colored Neptunian goggles make everything so pretty—and optimistic Jupiter is glad to brighten the picture. An emotionally manipulative person could be saying all the right things, and you may be susceptible to falling under their spell. Make sure you really know who and what you're dealing with before you get in too deep! Keep your wits about you, even as you revel in the sentiment with an open mind and heart.

JUPITER IN ARIES

Domestic Adventures

Jupiter in Aries

May 10 to
October 28, 2022

December 20, 2022
to May 16, 2023

Home sweet home? Nesting instincts take hold from May 10 to October 28, as Jupiter starts a 13-month visit to Aries and your fourth house of home, family and foundations. After a breezy and non-committal start to 2022, you need a moment to root. Where you'll hang your fedora is anyone's guess. With global Jupiter in this domestic sector, you could relocate, take a long-distance job offer or change your living situation in a big way.

There is a small catch: While in Aries, Jupiter forms a challenging, 90-degree square to your Capricorn Sun. Along with all this rapid expansion could come growing pains and a few tough hurdles to cross. While you've never expected opportunity to be handed to you on a silver platter, May 10 to October 28 will require marathon hustle. Pro tip: Keep your ego out of the game. Embrace each setback as a learning experience rather than a failure and you'll sail through this period like a champ.

Time to convert that spare room into a nursery? Expansive Jupiter in this maternal sector could bring a new addition to your clan. For some Capricorns, this year may be time to start "baby talks"—or (surprise!) you'll find out you're unexpectedly expecting. Your mother or a female relative might play into events at the end of this year. Is your relationship due for an evolution? You may go through a few growing pains as you shift to a more balanced dynamic.

Overall, this emotional cycle will call for more nurturing and self-care. Your moods fluctuate and you might be processing heavier feelings. Solitude can give you serenity, but make sure you don't isolate yourself. Peaceful escapes into nature, especially near water, can give you the quiet reset you need. And with the year bookended by two social whirlwinds, you'll appreciate these five and a half months of hermit time. Carve out some unapologetic sacred space where you can read books, take long baths and pamper yourself without anyone demanding your attention.

VENUS RETROGRADE

Magnetic Attractions

Venus in Capricorn

November 5, 2021
to March 6, 2022

**Venus Retrograde
in Capricorn**

December 19, 2021
to January 29, 2022

All eyes on you, Cap—and not just because it's your birthday season. This year, vixen Venus is enjoying an extended romp through your sign (from November 5, 2021, to March 6, 2022), gifting you with dialed-up animal magnetism and irresistible allure. Go ahead: try to hibernate. Either the world will beat a path to your door—or you may very well be indoors a lot—but you certainly won't be alone in your cave.

Normally, Venus spends just three to five weeks in a sign, but every other year, it flips into retrograde for six weeks, and this go-round, you will be channeling Venus' charms for a total of four months! During this highly desirable cycle, you can tap into the Law of Attraction and use it to create what you desire in your existing relationships—or to call in a new one. Get clear about what you actually do want, then share that vision in the most inspirational way you can with your S.O., being sure to leave enough room for their ideas! Single? As a Capricorn, you have naturally high standards. Keep the bar high and be discerning while staying open-minded about who shows up.

When you're in alignment with your own highest values, you naturally draw in people on a similar wavelength. Yet you could be selling yourself short by focusing on things that aren't obviously fabulous. Get to know someone who may not make the best first impression. For all you know, they might be the coolest and best-suited prospect...yet are intimidated by the confidence you exude! That said, you should trust your gut about obvious deal breakers, like someone who's not emotionally available or has major insecurity around attachment in general. (A leopard can pay lip service to changing his spots, but he can't actually change them.)

> 66
>
> *Whatever your relationship status, a little alone time will go a long way this winter.*
>
> 99

It's essential that you get crystal-clear about your needs and desires while Venus goes retrograde from December 19, 2021, to January 29, 2022. This confusing transit is being staged in your first house, meaning it will affect you very personally. You might get some clues about what this may bring by reviewing major life events that occurred the last time Venus backflipped in your sign: December 21, 2013, to January 31, 2014. Look for themes involving love, pleasure and creativity, and don't be surprised if a few of them, including people from your past, make an encore appearance.

While this may be an exercise in cutting cords, it's also possible that you discover a true gold nugget among the silt and gravel. If you've been secretly pining for the "one who got away"—or who you broke up with in a moment of fear, panic or anger—the love planet's retrograde might provide a second chance to get it right. If that old flame doesn't get rekindled, you could meet someone who stokes the same embers in your heart (and elsewhere).

Attached? You may be forced to grapple with an issue that you thought was long since resolved. If one or both of you isn't quite happy about that, you've got a perfect opportunity to rehash the underlying dynamics and find other ways of moving forward. But don't dredge up the past just to keep things "interesting." There are far more productive ways to bring a little excitement to your union!

Generally, your cool and collected sign prefers stability to drama, but you still need some stimulation! While Venus reverse commutes through your sign until January 29, you might feel like an unwilling cohabitant in that couple bubble. The only way out of that mental prison is having an honest conversation about your freedom needs. You don't need to bail on this, Cap. Simply planning a getaway with your inner circle or signing up for an online course or training program can move stuck energy and rev your engines again. Aim for "healthy interdependence."

On the flip side, you might find yourself feeling a bit insecure during this retrograde, shifting from confident to clingy. If you're in an LTR, this could be the perfect moment for some couples counseling or to take a workshop together. Single? How about hiring a dating coach or signing up with an exclusive matchmaking service. And remember, underlying it all is a need for more undiluted self-love!

Whatever your relationship status, a little alone time will go a long way this winter. For starters, it'll give you more opportunities to pursue your favorite hobbies and activities, from snowboarding or cross-country skiing to crafting and reading. This extended Venus in Capricorn cycle is all about learning to value yourself, with or without a partner or any external validation.

Warning: Venus in reverse might make sketchy encounters look appealing, so investigate thoroughly with background checks and pointed questions that can be verified. At the very least, extensive Googling can put your mind at ease. If you're already committed, resist the temptation of an affair, even "just" an emotional one. While seemingly innocent, those can feel as erotically charged as physical ones. How to tell if you're getting dangerously close to crossing a line? Be brutally honest about how much you're hiding or rationalizing your interactions with this person. If you can't reveal the whole truth, you might be at risk.

Another Venus-retrograde caveat: Hold off on any radical style updates. With the beauty queen in reverse, you could be tempted to do something a bit outré; but once Venus corrects course, you may not even remotely fancy this new you. And if the tattoo was real ink or the hair dye permanent, you might be left with more regrets than feelings of liberation!

LUNAR NODES IN TAURUS AND SCORPIO
Step into the Spotlight

> **Lunar Nodes in Taurus and Scorpio**
>
> January 18, 2022
> to July 17, 2023

As a sophisticated earth sign, you love to spin the high-end classics. But over the past year, your tastes may have veered into normcore terrain. "Perish the thought!" your inner snob may protest. Relax, Sea Goat. And if you're really that upset, let yourself off the hook for "slipping." After an insanely process-driven 2021, fashion goals fell lower on your priority list. To be honest, you probably surrendered to the "leggings lifestyle" or covered tousled hair with a hat more times than you'd openly admit.

Nothing wrong with that! But here's some news you'll love: Starting this January 18, the stars are sending glamorous styles back on the runway at the Haus of Capricorn. For the first time in nearly 20 years, the lunar North Node shifts into Taurus, sparking up your fifth house of passion, creativity and romance until July 17, 2023. Now's the time to let your hair down—and boost the volume with a blowout, curl cream or a mammoth wig. During this showstopping cycle, even the most reserved Capricorns will get a thrill out of turning heads.

Sashaying down the street looking fly is one thing, but the North Node is the cosmic destiny point. Which means that you need to play a much more "high-exposure" game this year. What do you want to be known for in the world? Or in some cases, what have you already achieved? Modesty is the enemy of mastery in 2022. Take pride in your accomplishments and advocate for yourself. Agency is fully yours, Capricorn, but if you don't promote your gifts, people could literally miss out on what you have to offer. That's a far, far worse crime than only wearing pants made out of four-way-stretch elastane.

If you're lucky enough to have a daily job or steady freelance work, you won't need to abandon that. But you *are* encouraged to make time every day—or multiple times every week—to throw yourself into passion projects. Creative Capricorns may schedule regular date nights with the muse. While inspiration *can* strike at the most unexpected times, there's something to be said for getting into a routine and conditioning yourself to write, paint, make music, do crafts or even rehearse for an audition.

The camera will love you during this North Node cycle. If you're not 100% comfortable in front of the lens, do what your sign does best: practice your way to perfection. Livestreaming is a no-brainer when it comes to raising awareness about one of your endeavors. But why stop there? Industry heavyweights can share your expertise by developing motivational talks, courses, even an app. Or keep it less structured with a discussion group, meditation circle or new moon ritual club.

Passion is a must during this nodal cycle, but so is fun. News alert: You don't have to "monetize" everything that interests you. Even the most business-savvy Caps could take a break from the hustle and start having fun for fun's sake. Dancing and romancing? Remember that cheesy little rhyme, because both will be the key to your happiness. While the North Node's in Taurus, simple luxuries can be enough to bring you pleasure. Healing from trauma? Find one thing to be grateful for every day and happiness may soon become "normalized" again. We hope so, Capricorn, because joy is your birthright.

Speaking of which, your fifth house also rules fertility. Those with bambinos on the brain might get some pregnancy news between now and July 17, 2023. This destiny-dusted cycle could bring you straight to your soulmate—or into a more solid arrangement with someone you've been dating for a while. For coupled Capricorns, bringing the spark back is essential. Autonomy makes the heart grow fonder as long as you don't pull too far away. There's something to be said for the comfort of "parallel play," where you and your S.O. are both engaged side by side in your respective projects. But make sure you have enough interactivity in your relationship, too. This may require you both to break a few bad habits, like checking messages in bed or watching TV during dinner, effectively blocking out moments where intimate communication could arise.

> **"**
>
> *Modesty is the enemy of mastery in 2022. Take pride in your accomplishments & advocate for yourself.*
>
> **"**

Across the zodiac wheel, the lunar South Node will simmer in Scorpio—the opposite sign of Taurus—activating your eleventh house of teamwork and technology for this full 18-month time span. The South Node is what we call the "karmic comfort zone," stirring slumbering gifts within you.

Some take-charge Capricorns forgot the fine art of collaboration in recent years. It's no surprise! With the hustle required to keep your head above water during the pandemic, you had no time to wait for slower-moving partners to catch up. The South Node in Scorpio is sure to serve a masterclass-level reminder that teamwork makes the dream work...if you lean into Scorpio's razor-sharp discernment.

Maybe you've been giving the wrong people a chance over and over, as dating prospects, friends, service providers, employees. If so, we're certain you're frustrated. Please don't give up on the human race! Use the transformational powers of the Scorpio South Node to distill your buried hopes and wishes. Then, be merciless with yourself. How are the choices you're making out of alignment with what you say you want? Break free from the chains of obligation. You may have mistaken this for commitment, but that die-hard attitude has no place in your personal relationships as of 2022. You are allowed to graduate and find a new crew. You can spearhead an initiative to set new ethical guidelines within an organization. But don't wait for anyone to hand you an invitation. Take the initiative to add the depth you desire to your life.

ECLIPSES IN TAURUS AND SCORPIO

Lights, Camera, Capricorn!

**Partial Solar
Eclipse in Taurus**

April 30 at 4:27pm

**Total Lunar
Eclipse in Scorpio**

May 16 at 12:14am

**Partial Solar Eclipse
in Scorpio new moon**

October 25 at 6:48am

**Total Lunar Eclipse
in Taurus full moon**

November 8 at 6:02am

times in eastern time

While most Capricorns prefer to be the lead singer rather than the backup dancer, in 2022, you might play both roles. This year's four eclipses fall on the Taurus/Scorpio axis, igniting your expressive and passionate fifth house (ruled by Taurus) and your cool-headed, collaborative eleventh house (ruled by Scorpio). You'll strut on and off center stage in 2022, learning when it's best to dive into the action and when to hang back and observe.

These eclipses, which began November 2021 and end in late October 2023, are here to teach you important lessons about the spotlight, and how best to share it. This year's two Taurus eclipses, which arrive on April 30 and November 8, spotlight your talents and help you develop your platform. Fame could come calling, and you'll want to be prepared! If you're an artist, get that demo reel or portfolio ready. The solar (new moon) eclipse on April 30 is sure to bring some openings that demand responsive action.

The fifth house rules romance and fertility. Some Capricorns may get a surprise visit from either Cupid or the stork, especially near the November 8 total lunar (full moon) eclipse. This super-charged lunation accelerates developments that begin under the April 30 solar (new moon) eclipse. Romances won't be drama-free—but that's part of their appeal. Just make sure you know the difference between passion and perpetual problems. A little friction stokes the fire, but if you're relying on this to keep things exciting, you need to change your tune—and possibly your partner.

The May 16 and October 25 eclipses in Scorpio spotlight teamwork as they activate your eleventh house of networking and groups. Your friendships could go through a round of changes, especially during the ground-shaking energy of the May 16 total lunar (full moon) eclipse in Scorpio.

With a nudge from the Scorpio new moon solar eclipse on October 25, you might join a cutting-edge collaboration or search for a like-minded new soul circle. If you've got talents to showcase, this solar eclipse can lead you to the right producers, project managers and hype-makers who will take your genius ideas to the next level. If you're more the behind-the-scenes type, team up with a rising star, powering their ascent.

The eleventh house rules technology, and you could become a viral sensation during the Scorpio eclipses. Explore technology that helps you share your heartfelt message with a global audience: video, podcasting, live webinars. Digital dating brings interesting prospects in 2022. If you're single, explore connections both in-person and online.

The Taurus eclipses on April 30 and November 8 could bring a passionate face-to-face connection, while the Scorpio events on May 16 and October 25 make you an in-demand virtual vixen. Is technology preventing you from connecting with people? Couples should enforce a "no-phone zone" on date nights. Drop those distracting devices into a bucket for a few hours and go enjoy each other's company without interruption. Soon enough, your FOMO fades and you remember the (underrated) joys of being present!

MARS IN GEMINI

Green your Life

Mars in Gemini

August 20, 2022 to
March 25, 2023

**Mars Retrograde in
Gemini**

October 30, 2022 to
January 12, 2023

You can restore order to the Capricorn court in a big way starting August 20, so pull out your eco-friendly cleaning products, crafting supplies and high-speed blender. Life at Goat Central is about to get streamlined, decluttered and polished—as you get yourself into "fighting shape!"

And you've got an extra-long time to pull off your goals in these areas. Activator Mars blasts into Gemini and spends the second half of 2022 (and until March 25, 2023) in your sixth house of work and wellness. Normally, Mars spends seven weeks in each sign during its two-year trip around the Sun. But every other year, it turns retrograde for about ten weeks, which means you'll get six months to materialize the overhaul you're craving.

While Mars' usual style is fast and furious, in meticulous Gemini and your systematic sixth house, you can direct this intensity into an obsession for details and efficient routines. Get a running start so that by the time it shifts into reverse on October 30 (through January 12, 2023), you'll have things locked down and running like the kind of well-oiled machine you prefer.

Be inspired by this truism: Your stress levels are directly proportional to the clutter in your life, but one way to keep things in balance is with your fitness regimen. Get things organized with a game plan and timeline, build in regular workouts and outdoor activities, and you should be able to stay focused and grounded throughout the protracted project. Give your gym membership a workout, develop a stronger yoga practice, even hire a trainer or tap a fitness buddy to help you stay motivated. The hardest part might be simply getting off the couch or out the door. Once you're in motion, the momentum will build. You don't want to give in to inertia. Keeping your heart pumping will also help regulate your moods and energy levels.

66

While Mars' usual style is fast and furious, in meticulous Gemini and your systematic sixth house, you can direct this intensity into an obsession for details and efficient routines.

99

Don't assume everything will work itself out, however. If you start off too casual and unprepared, this ten-week retrograde can turn your orderly Capricorn universe upside down. Of course, there can be an upside to that! As they say, necessity is the mother of invention. If you do get stuck in a rut or paint yourself into a metaphorical corner, you may be forced to come at a problem from a very different perspective, which can yield surprisingly positive results. Mars' courageousness can inspire you to take a risk when there's no other obvious way forward. That's not your M.O., but when you hit a wall, you are known to become experimental. Trust your instincts—but maybe Google it first to make sure you're going about it right, whatever "it" may be.

The sixth house is the domain of all the behind-the-scenes work in your career. If there's something you've wanted to explore without showing your hand, Mars retrograde is a great time to hole up in your lab, shop or studio and try some options. With the stakes (and pressure) low, you might stretch beyond your limits and hit on a genius new idea, product or service, possibly even a new gig if you find this more to your liking.

If you're considering making any professional plays, don't ignore the devil in the details. Yours is a modest sign by nature, but it's never more important than now to be able to walk your talk and make good on all your promises. As most Capricorns were born knowing, it's far better to underpromise and overdeliver. Coming through on your word is non-negotiable, and actually surpassing expectations will amaze people.

With Mars in your realm of helpful people, you could hire (or be hired as) a service provider. But when Mars shifts into reverse, that person may suddenly become unavailable—or the gig may evaporate on you. Whatever happens, don't put undue stress on yourself! Be creative and find work-arounds, or reach out to your network and let them know what you're looking for. One good thing about retrograde cycles is that they can bring back people or opportunities from your past. Of course, it's up to you to make the most of them! ✻

AQUARIUS

LOVE

Schedule those date nights! If you don't, they might not happen. With hardworking Saturn finishing up its final full year in Aquarius, love may again take a backseat to personal developments. Nothing wrong with flying solo or "doing you." But with Jupiter in your sensual second house until May 10 (and again from October 28 to December 20), affection and companionship would sure be nice. Venus is retrograde in your twelfth house of forgiveness and healing until January 29, a powerful time for processing pain around a past relationship—or working through resentment in an existing one. Wild times are ahead though! Lusty Mars swings into Gemini and your passionate fifth house for an extended six-month tour starting August 20. If your mojo's been in slow-mo, it will come roaring back—and when the red planet turns retrograde on October 30 (until January 12), fading embers could become blazing fires again.

CAREER & MONEY

New responsibilities at work could spell money in the bank. With brave Jupiter expanding your earning potential, it's safe to take a few more risks—like requesting permanent WFH status or spearheading a new initiative. Going back to school (or taking a few classes) can position you for higher pay. Easy does it on the spending though! Expenses could balloon if you aren't careful. With the karmic South Node in Scorpio and your career zone, face down your fear of success. This 18-month cycle, which lasts from January 18, 2022, to July 17, 2023, could reveal your hidden talents to the world. Cha-ching! You might quietly work on a project that isn't ready for a public reveal. Leap on any golden opportunities that may arrive with the eclipses on May 16 and October 25!

WELLNESS

Feeling stiff, Aquarius? Blame it on stodgy Saturn who is parked in your sign for one more year. As the ruler of bones, skin and teeth, you may spend more time at the chiropractor, dermatologist or dentist this year. Get on the ball with prevention. Yes, there's a reason they told you to stand up straight and floss. With the North Node in your nutritional zone, the link between food and mood will be obvious. You may switch up your diet, opting for anti-inflammatory foods or trying something like keto or intermittent fasting. A multivitamin and other doctor-advised natural supplements can ensure that proper nourishment gets to your cells!

FRIENDS & FAMILY

While stoic Saturn may find you craving long spells of alone time, forget about being a hermit in 2022. With Jupiter zipping into Aries from May 10 to October 28, a huge popularity spike is in store. You'll feel more outgoing than you have in years—and the local scene could serve up a spate of new BFFs. When the North Node joins your ruler Uranus in Taurus on January 18, you might reconnect to an important family member or make some exciting changes to your living situation that align with your life purpose. If you aren't moving, you might be building. Can you say "project?"

JUPITER IN PISCES

New Money Opportunities

Jupiter in Pisces

December 28, 2021 to May 10, 2022

October 28 to December 20, 2022

Check that balance sheet! Your net worth and your self-worth are both on the upswing in 2022. For this you can thank bountiful Jupiter, who spends half of the year in Pisces and your second house of work, money and self-esteem. Get ready for a tsunami of confidence that you can take to the bank. Jupiter is the planet of growth and opportunity, and this cycle—which happens from December 28, 2021, to May 10, 2022, and again from October 28 to December 20, 2022—heralds an exciting career change or a profitable income stream that flows from the fountain of your goddess-given gifts.

Dice-rolling Jupiter is a bit restrained when visiting your fiscally conservative second house. Lean toward calculated risks and avoid schemes that are too much of a gamble. Delayed gratification is the name of the game. Whether you're a strict budgeter or you never check your bank balance, 2022 will remake your approach to spending and saving. If you're always swinging between feast and famine, this Jupiter cycle helps you embrace the joys of moderation. (Note: we did *not* say deprivation.)

You had some fun ideas while Jupiter visited Aquarius for most of 2021. Now, pick the "golden goose" and see if she'll lay an egg or two! And make that a nest egg, okay? Jupiter helps you start slowly and steadily saving for your future. This is a year to build, brick by brick. You already got a taste of this energy last year, when Jupiter briefly visited Pisces from May 13 to July 28, 2021. Did you abandon a mission due to time constraints? It's worth a dust-off to see if there's still anything worthwhile to build upon.

> 66
>
> *Get ready for a tsunami of confidence that you can take to the bank.*
>
> 99

Jupiter rules education, and you can raise your financial IQ by learning about everything from compounding interest to cryptocurrency or, heck, basic money management. Stash away enough cash and you'll have a little (or a lot!) left over for the experiential splurges Aquarians love. Vipassana meditation? Tantric retreat? Painting workshop in Paris? Imagine if the funds were already there when inspiration strikes next time.

A raise, promotion or even a job with relocation is possible. If you're a freelancer, maybe it's time to increase your rates? Even if you stick with your current job, Jupiter widens your financial focus and brings projects that can boost your profile. Position yourself as a savvy problem-solver and you could make yourself indispensable. Jupiter was last in Pisces from January 17 to June 6, 2010, and again from September 9, 2010, until January 22, 2011, so you may see themes from that time repeat.

The slower, grounding pace helps you prioritize every part of life—a true blessing if you're feeling scattered. The second house rules daily habits and routines. Seek ways to simplify during this "less is more" phase, whether you implement savvy lifehacks or just scale back.

From social commitments to volunteer activities, anything you feel lukewarm about needs to be shelved. Better to leave some white space in your calendar than to clutter it with halfhearted obligations you couldn't say no to. You can fill those slots with self-care (exercise, cooking, reading) or something truly meaningful.

Commit to the pillars of regular waking and bedtime, meals and movement. And if there's an app that makes this all easier, use it. This process can (and should) be simplified. For example, you attend the same three fitness classes for a month, then switch it up (or stick with them if you're still inspired). A bit of same-same repetition is better than constantly reshuffling your calendar, only to miss appointments and operate under a cloud of chaos.

The second house rules all things tangible, and you might create a product or business venture that stands the test of time. Jupiter gives you the enthusiasm to roll up your sleeves and hustle. Invest in attractive branding to use on social media and business materials to tap into the sophisticated sensibility of the second house and attract the audience you want.

Many people meet long-term partners while Jupiter traverses their second house. Often this person is someone you might have overlooked in the past or written off as boring because they weren't the flashy rebel that your wild sign can fall for (admit it!). With Jupiter grounding you in self-respect, you don't need anyone to "complete" you. Rather, you can reach a point of feeling full and content in your life—then someone comes along who can be the cherry on top. You're no stranger to this level of self-esteem, independent Aquarius, and as you know, it can be an aphrodisiac. Pump up the volume on self-love and see who flocks to your side.

Codependency alert! If you've been enabling or over-giving, Jupiter in Pisces will nip that bad habit in the bud. Unfortunately, you might discover that some friends, family and love interests preferred you as an accommodating doormat. Firm up those boundaries, even if it flies in the face of your giving nature. If the dynamics shift when you stop being at people's beck and call, so be it. They'll either start respecting your limits or they can go wipe their feet elsewhere!

If you're in a relationship, Jupiter in Pisces can bring gentle waves and placid seas. You can ease into a comfortable groove with your favorite plus-one, creating shared goals and projects together. Maybe you'll invest in a few memorable experiences on your bucket list or start investing as a couple. With worldly Jupiter in your posh second house, think "quality over quantity" when it comes to spending time together.

JUPITER MEETS NEPTUNE IN PISCES

Manifestation Magic

> **Jupiter meets Neptune in Pisces**
>
> April 12, 2022

Find the sacredness in the "small things" on April 12 when, for the first time in 13 years, Jupiter makes an exact connection to spiritual soulmate Neptune at 23°58' Pisces. You could infuse your everyday routines with spirituality—a meditation practice, rituals, restorative treatments. With global Jupiter and sea-god Neptune aligned, a yoga retreat on the beach seems written in the stars, doesn't it? Or maybe you'll tap into charitable Neptune's spirit of giving and combine springtime travel with volunteer work. Circle March 14 to April 30 if you need a date range, since Jupiter and Neptune will hover in close connection for six weeks.

*Infuse your
everyday routines
with spirituality*

Making a difference becomes tantamount when enterprising Jupiter meets compassionate Neptune in your industrious second house. If you work in the arts or a healing profession, this magnetic aspect attracts opportunities to use your talents for a world-bettering cause. If you have any kind of influencer status, alert your followers to a cause that's dear to your heart. Mystical Neptune could connect you to an incredible colleague through serendipitous events. You might also adopt a more sustainable lifestyle, switching to eco-friendly and cruelty-free product lines, reducing your carbon footprint and eating local and organic. Many Water Bearers already live in conscious connection to the Earth. If so, the Jupiter-Neptune conjunction may offer opportunities to share your knowledge or even turn these gifts into media projects or a start-up.

On the downside, a Jupiter-Neptune conjunction can provoke a crisis of conscience. If you've been feeling blue or insecure, double down on efforts to boost your self-confidence or get your finances in order. Your efforts will pay off, so don't sweep glaring issues under the rug. (A risk since Neptune can send one into denial and Jupiter can be "positive!" to a fault.)

Overall, this rare moment is here to help you clarify your values and invest your time, money and energy into what matters most to you. Maybe the things that once made you happy no longer do. Be willing to release those and explore new avenues.

JUPITER IN ARIES

Share your Ideas with the World

Jupiter in Aries

May 10 to
October 28, 2022

December 20, 2022
to May 16, 2023

Get your message to the masses, Aquarius! From May 10 to October 28, Jupiter darts into Aries for a visit to your social and communicative third house. Cast a wide net and start marketing your ideas. If you spent the first part of 2022 developing a project, now's the time to share about it on social media as you align with well-connected people who can help spread the word. Find influencers, ambassadors and word-of-mouth mavens and get them on the job!

Writing, teaching and media projects all get a favorable boost. Maybe friends keep telling you that your big ideas would make for a great book. Or if you're constantly demonstrating your technique, could you turn your skills into a monetizable online course or sponsored YouTube series? Enterprising Jupiter in this intellectual zone wants you to put more value on your "crazy" ideas. While many Aquarians are motivated by ideals before money, let's be honest, it's kind of nice to be able to treat friends to dinner sometimes or know that you can afford the lift tickets for that snowboarding excursion.

Kindred spirits show up in your own backyard while expansive Jupiter hovercrafts through your third house of neighborhood activity. Get more involved in your hometown happenings, attend building association meetings and cultural events, host a block party or volunteer for a holiday donation drive.

While Jupiter is in Aries from May 10 to October 28, you could work remotely or make short business trips. With on-the-go Jupiter in your transportation house, you could be in the market for a new set of wheels. Keep it eco-chic with a hybrid (or electric) car or invest in a great bike for your commute.

In the market for a move? You might start checking out new districts or city-hopping until you find a place to settle down. Consider waiting for Jupiter to move into Taurus on May 16, 2023, before you put down permanent roots. Use 2022 to explore your options, possibly doing Airbnb rentals in cities you're curious about before declaring one (or two) "home."

The third house rules peers, such as siblings, coworkers and neighbors. A brother or sister (real or "chosen") might become an inspiring presence. If your bond has been riddled with rivalry, this expansive Jupiter cycle could help you finally move past those traumatic dynamics. Authentic dialogue is a must, but so is active listening! With hotheaded Jupiter in Aries, it's hard not to get triggered, especially when your sib throws a dart into one of your childhood wounds. Having a third party mediate may be money well-spent, and the truest, fastest path to peace. Note: Jupiter was last in Aries from June 6 to September 9, 2010, and January 22 to June 4, 2011. You may see similar cycles arise regarding communication, peer relationships, local activity and short travel between May 10 and October 28, 2022.

VENUS RETROGRADE

A Time for Surrender

Venus in Capricorn

November 5, 2021
to March 6, 2022

**Venus Retrograde
in Capricorn**

December 19, 2021
to January 29, 2022

If you're more focused on tying up loose ends and bringing closure to a certain relationship or behavior pattern than starting anything new, the early part of 2022 will support your sincere efforts. Venus, the planet of love, romance and values, is on an extended tour through Capricorn and your twelfth house of surrender, transitions, spirituality and healing from November 5, 2021, until March 6, 2022.

Normally, Venus spends just three to five weeks in a sign, but every other year, it flips into retrograde for six weeks, and this go-round, it's lounging in Capricorn and that mystical chart sector of yours for four times as long. While you probably won't have the firmest grasp on so-called reality, you will have access to a direct line to the divine. However you choose to use it, you will have a rare and protracted opportunity to drill down to the root of an old wound or persistent emotional block.

If you've put off processing the pain of a breakup, loss or even a profoundly disappointing experience, you can begin to do that not-easy (but necessary) healing work. And if the same underlying interpersonal dynamic or insecure attachment style keeps cropping up in every relationship, that's a pretty good indication that it's time to turn inward.

Remember, Aquarius, everyone has a blind spot and Achilles heel, and they revolve around issues that are so deep they're obscured from our view. This probably began in your childhood as a form of age-appropriate protection, but now that you're an adult, it's probably not effective or suitable anymore. And when we put off facing these core wounds, we tend to project them onto other people, assuming they are to blame for our pain. Of course, in our grown-up minds we know it takes two to tango and that real change requires our full engagement. True, this kind of mature accountability can be a bitter pill to swallow, especially since some very raw and vulnerable feelings are being dredged up. But on the bright side, Venus' trek through Capricorn lends the pluck to finally face a demon that's been hounding you for years or decades. Drop the defenses and let the healing begin.

Even in stoic Capricorn, Venus lends its compassionate support, which might be more palpable because this is your tender-bellied twelfth house. If you don't pressure yourself too much, you may realize you're actually eager to review past pain and begin to process it. While yours isn't the most emo sign of the 12, be prepared for a deluge of feelings to pour in, from sorrow to anger to regret. Your head can process data like a computer, but your less-experienced heart may take a little longer, so don't try to make yourself get over it any faster than you can.

Retrogrades are great cycles for revisiting any results you're not entirely satisfied with. For instance, if you pulled the plug on a relationship out of fear or doubt and have never stopped thinking about that person, you may get a shot at a do-over after March 6. Or did you swipe left yet something is still nagging at you about this person? On an even deeper level, you could reconnect to a soulmate or the one that got away.

But don't get swept up in quixotic twelfth-house vibes. The normal gut checks are required, and you need to deeply explore whether the impulse to "kiss and make up" is coming from a healthy place or one of desperation (or fantasy). You could meet someone for the first time—in this lifetime, that is—who you are convinced you have old karma with. Be careful there, Water Bearer. The twelfth house rules illusions and denial. So even if you have been together in a past life, that doesn't mean that hooking up in this one will be a walk in the park. Could be quite the contrary!

Coupled Aquarians may face a good-news-bad-news scenario during this deep-diving Venus cycle. For one thing, you may not be able to continue sweeping that issue under the hand-loomed rug. But by finally taking off the kid gloves and discussing this like loving adults, you might be struck by some illuminating insights. If you've talked about working with a couples' or sex therapist, this could be the perfect time to book a series of sessions. Perhaps you can find a weekend workshop to help you heal issues and support one another through your self-discoveries.

If you're struggling to move on from a breakup, here's an idea: Create a mourning ritual. Even relationships that go up in flames probably started out with some sort of promise. Honor the parts of this person or experience that you still love and miss by setting up an altar with gifts they gave you or photos. Allow yourself to feel the pain of the loss fully as you sit in front of it. But plan to do a ceremonial burning of those mementos—or pack them away in storage—by January 29, 2022. If that's too triggering, ask a friend to take those objects, at least temporarily. Immerse yourself in healing books, podcasts and videos, and give your emotions space to unspool.

LUNAR NODES IN TAURUS AND SCORPIO

Give Me Shelter!

**Lunar Nodes in
Taurus and Scorpio**

January 18, 2022
to July 17, 2023

The past couple years of WFH and sheltering in place notwithstanding, you're about to get really good at making your home your sanctuary. On January 18, the kismet-kissed lunar North Node joins your ruling planet Uranus in Taurus and your fourth house of roots. Home and family will be the focus of this cycle, which hasn't happened in nearly two decades! Between now and July 17, 2023, Water Bearers have the rare opportunity to (re)invent "domestic bliss" according to your specs.

Innovative as you are, this could mean moving into a modern loft apartment with floor-to-ceiling glass...or starting a cottagecore community with a group of friends. Your ruling planet, side-spinning Uranus, has occupied this zone since May 2018, so you're already getting a taste of "intentional living," Aquarius style. In fact, two Water Bearers we know have been forging ahead on this path ever since. One friend is converting a double plot of residential property into an urban farm, with a goal of hosting classes, raising hens and selling flowers and veggies at local produce stands.

The other Aquarius pooled funds with friends to transform a woodsy property into a shared living space. This outsized mission has brought her joy and design challenges. Configuring wi-fi in the deep woods, for example, required a slower, mobile network solution to avoid a hefty, five-figure bill for running cable to their remote locale. Of course, knowing that they'll one day host retreats on the land keeps them forging ahead. Life is short, so why not make it sweet?

Yes, your "back to land" signmates are on to something, but we recognize that an earthy lifestyle's not for everyone. Whatever your dream scenario—a different (or no) roommate, to live with your love, to moving or buying a place of your own—start envisioning it as if it's already taking place. Get really clear about what this new situation looks, feels, even smells, like. The more time you spend visualizing this new reality, the closer you get to manifesting it.

> *With your sensitivities heightened, living (even working) with energy vampires affects your mental health.*

Don't wait too long to make changes, because the unspoken visual cues affect your subconscious in more ways than you realize. If you haven't redecorated post-quarantine, you may be charging up traumatic memories in your subconscious day and night. Start with switching less-expensive items, like duvet covers, framed art and paint colors. Add plants, temporary wallpaper, crystals. Reconfigure rooms, tapping into the principles of Feng Shui to harmonize your design plan and hues to best suit the elements: wood, fire, earth, metal or water. If you haven't done our Home Reset course, we're making a shameless plug for all Aquarians who want to add more "om" to your home.

Who you spend your downtime with is going to be a lot more important during this 18-month cycle. With your sensitivities heightened, living (even working) with energy vampires affects your mental health. Some people will never stop stealing your peace, leaving you no choice but to distance yourself. Don't waste your breath explaining, because they'll probably try stealing that too! Quietly craft your exit plan, then bounce.

In the case of needy friends and relatives, avoid performing the classic Aquarius magic trick of turning yourself into an iceberg. True, they may technically "deserve" the cold shoulder, but that just makes you have to work harder to ignore them. Could it be possible that you haven't spelled out your wishes clearly enough? Or maybe you've been too quick to compromise, a pitfall of being the zodiac's team player. Family roles will need to be negotiated, even in the most harmonious enclaves. Desired outcome? To make your space work for 2022 you. But first, get clear about what that is so you can communicate without misunderstandings.

Taurus rules your fourth house of sanctuary as well as the way you nurture yourself—mind, body and soul. Food and mood are indelibly entwined with the North Node here. Dietary changes can vastly improve health in any year, of course. But you'll have added motivation now to tackle things like your addiction to sweets and adult beverages or excessive coffee consumption.

On the other side of your chart, the lunar South Node is shifting into Scorpio and your career corner for the same time span, from January 18, 2022, to July 17, 2023. Slumbering gifts wake up when the South Node activates this ambitious part of your life. Charged up by alchemical Scorpio, your work could take a turn for the "woo" in 2022. One Aquarius we know is a Jungian psychologist who incorporates dreamwork and astrology into her practice. Another Water Bearer friend has been licensed to do psilocybin healings in Oregon, a state where "shrooms" were legalized for therapeutic healing in late 2020. While we're not saying you'll follow in their cutting-edge footsteps, we're not saying you won't!

How you get paid could also shift. Scorpio rules lump sums of cash, such as royalties, dividends and commissions. With the South Node here, seek new avenues for financial stability. Even if you're just exploring, you could stumble upon an awesome new possibility for a side hustle. The nine-to-five grind doesn't always suit your free-flowing persona, anyway. If you're ready to shake things up, consider a job in sales or do something very "Scorpio" like investing in real estate.

Transformation is another one of the Scorpio South Node's superpowers. Have you always had a knack for helping people improve an aspect of their lives? Yes, for your humanitarian sign, the thrill of seeing someone go from breakdown to breakthrough may be payment enough. But we still live in a world where it costs money to put food on the table. Consider getting certified as a coach, consultant or holistic healer. As that classic Confucius quote reminds, "Find a job you love and you'll never have to work a day in your life."

ECLIPSES IN TAURUS AND SCORPIO

Home & Career Get a Makeover

**Partial Solar
Eclipse in Taurus**

April 30 at 4:27pm

**Total Lunar
Eclipse in Scorpio**

May 16 at 12:14am

**Partial Solar Eclipse
in Scorpio new moon**

October 25 at 6:48am

**Total Lunar Eclipse
in Taurus full moon**

November 8 at 6:02am

times in eastern time

Time for a new work-life balance? This year's four eclipses touch down in major zones of your chart, reshuffling your personal and professional priorities. As part of a series falling on the Taurus/Scorpio axis from November 2021 until October 2023, your living situation, career path and closest ties undergo seismic shifts.

Eclipses can bring curveballs or demand quick action. And let's face it, Aquarius—sometimes it takes a huge planetary push to get your heady sign to stop overthinking! We're not saying you're stubborn, but without enough "scientific evidence," you've been known to resist change. Even if said evidence comes in the form of a message from your angelic guides, you tend to be up in your head (or crown chakra), waiting for a sign. But not in 2022! If you've been dragging your feet around an important home, family or career decision, these eclipses push you off the starting block.

> 66
>
> *If you've been dragging your feet around an important home, family or career decision, these eclipses push you off the starting block.*
>
> 99

On April 30 and November 8, two Taurus eclipses shake the roots of your domestic fourth house. That could bring a relocation, a pregnancy or a major home reset. Near the solar (new moon) eclipse on April 30, new developments accelerate. The urge to nest or move could strike suddenly. You might play interior designer, changing your décor scheme or ripping up the rugs for a gut renovation. This eclipse stirs up powerful emotions, putting you in touch with your bottom-line needs. What makes you feel secure at the most fundamental level? Add more of *that* into your life. Your mother or an important female will be in the spotlight.

Simmering situations reach a boiling point with the total lunar eclipse, which falls on the November 8 full moon in Taurus. The cast of characters living under your roof could alter dramatically, or you may transform the way you deal with a volatile relative. Have you been pondering a purchase of property or land? To score a dream deal you'll have to move swiftly, one of the clauses of fast-moving eclipse energy. Know what you're getting yourself into—at least enough to make an informed best guess. Nothing is guaranteed in the real estate game, but whether you're buying or selling, you may have to act upon more instinct than you're comfortable with in order to seal a deal.

On May 16 and October 25, eclipses in Scorpio remix your tenth house of career, long-term goals and success. Prep your professional pages and drop power suits at the dry cleaner. Near the total lunar eclipse on May 16, you could be catapulted into a prominent role that involves leadership or public recognition. Or, you might make a dramatic career change. A job shift could arise from changes outside your control, such as a corporate restructuring or buyout. Should this happen, take a deep breath and trust that a better position is headed your way.

If you're craving more creativity from your career, these eclipses help you design a fulfilling new role, possibly within your existing company. Will you go open a satellite office or get promoted to an executive title? Anything is possible when an eclipse rides through town, and the solar eclipse on October 25 sets new developments in motion. The tenth house also rules men and fathers, and these eclipses spotlight your relationship with an important guy in your life. Stay tuned!

MARS IN GEMINI

Red-Hot Romance

Mars in Gemini

August 20, 2022 to
March 25, 2023

Mars Retrograde in Gemini

October 30, 2022 to
January 12, 2023

Lights, camera, Aquarius! Starting on August 20, electrifying Mars blazes into Gemini and your fifth house of passionate romance and flamboyant self-expression. Look out world, there's a fired-up Water Bearer on the loose! And this is no mere "now they see you, now they don't" flash in the pan moment. Normally Mars spends seven weeks in each sign during its two-year trip around the Sun. But every other year, it turns retrograde for about ten weeks, which means you'll be hosting the white-hot planet in your amorous center for six months, until March 25, 2023.

More on that retrograde in a moment, but this protracted passion parade should be a game-changer, regardless of your relationship status. Newly dating? You could feel ready to commit (or cut bait) before the red planet reverses course on October 30 (until January 12, 2023). Couples may be eager to take that next big step, whether that's moving in together, officializing the union or spearheading a babymaking project.

Single? Your magnetism is reading off the charts, so if you're truly ready to let love in, a few sincere efforts in that direction should yield some worthy prospects. But give 'em a chance before you send anyone on their way. Mars can be flashy, but you might be happier for the long haul with a diamond in the rough than some over-the-top bling.

The fifth house is also your fame zone, and this lengthy Martian tour could yield some Hollywood highlights. Follow dashing Mars' lead and don't be shy about stepping into—and actually basking in— the limelight. Performers, artists and all creative types will have ready access to the muse, but when you're not downloading directly, you may have to place the call. Find the right métier to showcase your talents, whether it's a public art exhibit or streaming a live concert to an appreciative social media audience.

Whether at play or work, your brand of bold and empowered leadership will have a positive effect on other people, inspiring them to believe in themselves. Self-assured Mars in Gemini turns up the heat on your own natural talent of unapologetically being yourself, which is the best thing you can model. And knowing ahead of time that the energizing planet will flip retrograde from October 30 to January 12, 2023, can help you shore yourself up whenever you sense you might crumble a little, perhaps when having to deal with a bossy or entitled coworker.

If this retrograde does leave your ego a little fragile, watch out for low-vibe compensatory urges. Don't, for instance, go on the offense and become a bully yourself to make up for feeling threatened or insecure. Rather than fight fire with fire, anchor yourself in your values and the shared mission, which will help you rise above any petty squabbles or even power grabs. That said, should a rival try to strike you below the belt, tap the fierceness of Mars' warrior side—and Gemini's gift of gab—and let your words be mightier than whatever "sword" they brandish.

This could be the moment you've been waiting for to hire a coach or enlist a mentor who can restore your confidence by teaching you some insider tricks of the trade. And since fame could be your middle name for the second half of 2022, you want to be as authentically self-possessed and assured as humanly possible. Humble yourself enough to recognize where you might be a little lacking and find the right kind of support to seal that leak. This is how you'll become unstoppable by the time Mars straightens out on January 12. ✹

2022

PISCES

WHAT'S IN THE STARS FOR

PISCES

LOVE

Catch you if they can! Free-spirited Jupiter is bookending the year in Pisces, taking a wild ride through your adventurous first house until May 10 and again from October 28 to December 20. Pining and fantasizing are kind of your thing, but this year could find you on the receiving end of all that adoration. Flattering though it may be, don't let a good one slip away while you're reveling in the ego boost. Love should be reciprocal, Pisces, and you need mates and dates to support your interests this year. You may feel in a hurry to settle down (and maybe start a family) when energetic Mars barrels into Gemini and your domestic zone on August 20. This six-month cycle includes a retrograde, from October 30 to January 12, 2023, so careful about rushing to put down roots. In a relationship? Expand your horizons as a pair, traveling, taking workshops and connecting to your spiritual and philosophical interests.

CAREER & MONEY

How can you bring more autonomy and independence to your work? With liberated Jupiter in Pisces, then Aries and your money house (May 10 to October 28), you're highly self-motivated this year. Although you won't take kindly to a rigid boss breathing down your neck, Saturn could bring a powerful mentor your way who guides you down your life path. Travel may figure into your workflow this year, or you could work with remote clients. Study, too! With the karmic South Node in Scorpio and your ninth house of education as of January 18, this could be the year to finish a degree or get a specialized certification. A hot real estate deal could land in your lap any time after August 20. Spend the early part of the year getting finances sorted. Raise your credit score, prep paperwork and look into mortgage pre-approval. With so much luck on your side, you might as well be ready to leap!

WELLNESS

Exhale! Disciplined Saturn is on its final full year in your meditative, healing twelfth house. Since March 2020, you've been processing heavy issues—and finding all the enlightenment a Pisces lives for. This cosmic cleanse continues until March 7, 2023, so you might as well dive in. Detox your diet, sanctify your sleep and see a hypnotherapist if you're struggling to reach the far corners of your psyche. You might even train as a healing practitioner, or work closely with a therapist, shaman or holistic specialist. Vitality-boosting Jupiter will give you more energy than you've had in years. Enjoy the rush and if you're trying any daring sports, wear a helmet!

FRIENDS & FAMILY

Your 2022 paradox: How to participate in a crew without feeling pinned down. Indie-spirited Jupiter in Pisces will find you flowing more freely than you have in years! But with the destiny-driven North Node in Taurus and your friendship house, you'll fall in love with people again. Get involved in the local scene. Meeting your neighbors and connecting to area businesses will give you a sense of belonging that you'll enjoy...that is, when you're actually home. Family bonds may strain when agitating Mars hits your house of kin on August 20 for six months. But this may be the wakeup call you need to finally sort out your differences. Watch out for guilt trips and pity parties, Pisces. There are far more effective ways to express your feelings.

JUPITER IN PISCES

Starting Fresh

Jupiter in Pisces

December 28, 2021
to May 10, 2022

October 28 to
December 20, 2022

Set your GPS for "anywhere but here," Pisces. This is a year to embrace the new and uncharted as your co-ruler, auspicious Jupiter, returns to your sign for two cycles: first from December 28, 2021 to May 10 and again from October 28 to December 20. Before Neptune was discovered by telescope in 1846, Jupiter was considered your cosmic custodian. Wherever Jupiter trails, it blesses you with extra fortune. And when it comes to your sign every 12 to 13 years, you feel that tenfold!

With Jupiter submerged in Pisces, it kicks off a fresh 12-year chapter of your life. Many Fish will do a total reset in 2022. In your trailblazing first house, Jupiter's transit heralds new beginnings, novelty and experimentation. You got a brief taste of this exhilarating reboot last year when the red-spotted planet visited your sign from May 13 to July 28, 2021. Once again, you'll be shot out of your comfort zone like a cannonball. It's anyone's guess where you'll land. The journey is the adventure now. Plus, you'll be too busy defying gravity to worry about the destination.

Wondering how you'll grow? Look to your Aquarius friends, who hosted Jupiter last year. A recent example is Aquarius Harry Styles, who shed the boy band stigma for a gender-fluid style, and emerged as a noteworthy film actor. While Jupiter toured his sign in 2021, he further defied norms. After being cast in her film, *Don't Worry Darling,* Styles became smitten with and "inseparable" from 12-years-older love interest (Pisces) Olivia Wilde. Dare to be different, says Jupiter—and watch where it takes you.

Even the security-minded Pisces out there would be wise to give some slack to the line. The truth is, it would be impossible to map out your ultimate goals in early 2022, because you're just getting started. Plus, you couldn't possibly predict the from-left-field opportunities Jupiter is cooking up on your behalf. The spotted supersizer was last in your sign from January 17 to June 6, 2010, and again from September 9, 2010 until January 22, 2011. Page back to then if you can: You might see similar themes of reinvention from that time.

With Jupiter in your trailblazing first house of fresh starts and solo ventures, your personal pursuits take center stage in 2022. Whether you embark on a voyage, sign up for teacher training or start taking private lessons with a master teacher, the idea is to try, try, try without an agenda. Learning can be fun if you stop trying to ace every effort on the first go. Get your hands dirty and adopt a playful mindset.

Early this year, let yourself brainstorm, even if that means detouring off the main roads. You might opt to take a huge risk. If you do, tune out the naysayers. Follow the words of Nelson Mandela who said, "It's only impossible until it's done." When Jupiter makes its second circuit through your sign from October 28 to December 20, you may catch wind of how to monetize one of your big ideas. Or you'll just look back and see a bunch of items crossed off your bucket list. If you can review the year on December 31 and say that you prioritized joy over suffering, Jupiter's work was properly integrated.

Did you know that people form an opinion within seven seconds of meeting you? Visuals count more than ever during this Jupiter phase, because the first house rules first impressions. Invest in headshots and, if applicable, a videographer. Consider booking professional hair or makeup for your shoots. Use your gift for aesthetics and launch a sleek and well-designed website. Write in the first-person voice, so your visitors feel like they're having a conversation with you over a cup of tea, which is how you'd do it IRL anyway.

If you're a "solopreneur," this autonomous Jupiter cycle is great for building buzz through PR, social media and a message that focuses on you. What's your unique niche or "brand story"? Why are you passionate about what you do? Jupiter in your star-powered first house nudges you to make yourself stand out—or "come out"—as the heart and soul of your mission. Play up your individuality and be your edgy, mystical self. As usual, that will get people noticing...and talking! For example, maybe you're a wellness coach who needs to differentiate yourself in a crowded market. Flaunt your personality and highlight your expertise. Do you specialize in a certain type of bodywork or a teaching method? Do you have offbeat hobbies that you could weave into your practice like crystal bowl sound healings, or something that would make your bio memorable? For example, if you love to hike, maybe you'll lead treks that end with a mermaid plunge in a sparkling mountain lake.

What fires you up on an idealistic level? Intrepid Jupiter in your sign can make you something of an outlier (or an outlaw!) this year. Look to late Pisces Ruth Bader Ginsberg whose legal legacy created precedents that women are fighting to uphold today. Or, across the aisle, Senate Minority Leader Mitch McConnell, whose stronghold on his party inspires awe and ire. Love them or hate them, these lightning-rod Pisces became historical figures whose actions broke open huge, institution-changing dialogues.

Where can you take a risk in the name of something greater? Position yourself as a leader with a clear and audacious message.

In love, you're invited to take the same gutsy approach. If you're dating, lead with your quirks and humor instead of making small talk (or studying people with that silent and piercing gaze). Relationships will need to stretch and grow to accommodate your needs this year. You could be traveling, starting a new job, and devoting yourself to an all-consuming new interest. Maybe you're starting a big life phase that requires the people in your world to adapt.

> **66**
>
> *With Jupiter in your trailblazing first house of fresh starts and solo ventures, your personal pursuits take center stage in 2022*
>
> **99**

Let's be clear, Pisces: When Jupiter is in your sign, you are the lead actor, not the supporting cast. And while that's not license to act like an obnoxious celebutante, don't miss this chance to "do you." With Jupiter in your first house of appearances, you could make a bold change to your look, experimenting with an edgy new hairstyle, head-turning makeup or, as is the case with the envelope-pushers among you, a body modification.

Warning: Excessive Jupiter is the "too much is never enough" planet. Avoid impulsive decisions like, say, getting a full back tattoo at 3AM with a random drop-in appointment. While your mantra in life may be #NoRegrets, you could stretch that to its outer limits this year.

Not that anyone can change your mind. Jupiter has swagger, and it can make people a little cocky when it visits the "me"-centric first house. (Your new favorite subject: Yourself!) Watch that your antics don't tip into ego trips. It's great to feel so awesome about your accomplishments, and even to self-promote a bit. Just don't treat friends like unwitting audience members of The Pisces Show.

No-filters Jupiter can turn even the most esoteric Pisces into an unlikely blabbermouth. There's a temptation to share about every mundane moment—from a brunchtime "table read" of your text chain with a Tinder date to a long-winded recount of the entitled barista who skipped over you twice in the ordering line. Ask yourself: How does sharing this serve others? Your colorful tale could change someone's life or it could put them to sleep. It's all in what you choose to discuss.

Jupiter rules publishing, broadcasting and public speaking. Maybe your experiences could be an inspiring life lesson. What's the takeaway for your listener? Curate those personal stories and you might have the makings of a memoir or a motivational TED-style talk. Even camera shy Fish could get bitten by the performance bug in 2022. If you're truly passionate about something, you'll barely even notice when those shutters start clicking.

JUPITER MEETS NEPTUNE IN PISCES

Epiphanies Abound!

> **Jupiter meets Neptune in Pisces**
>
> April 12, 2022

Circle April 12 in neon ink! For the first time in 13 years, lucky Jupiter catches up to your other ruling star, fantasy-agent Neptune. Better yet? Your two galactic guardians are joining forces in your sign (at 23°58' to be exact), lending their soulful magic to your first house of identity. Talk about a major moment for manifestation! With the planet of good fortune in a *paso doble* with your cosmic guardian, you are more than #blessed. You have wizard-like powers to cast a spell over the world!

Use this enchanted energy to dazzle folks as you see fit. If you've been hiding your light under a bushel, that beam will be impossible to conceal. A little shock value goes a long way, but even if no one is technically surprised by your big reveal, this is a "go big or go home" moment, Pisces.

While April 12 is the most potent day of their alignment, Jupiter and Neptune travel in tight correspondence from March 14 to April 30. That means you have six weeks to tap this prodigious energy and promote yourself like a Hollywood publicist. Glamorous Neptune and supersizer Jupiter could bring fame. Your creativity and charisma are at an all-time high, so use them for good. With compassionate Neptune and global Jupiter aligned, you may be the spokesperson for a world-bettering cause—especially if you use art, music or a creative medium as your vehicle.

Just watch out for ego trips, especially at the hands of a charming flatterer. Jupiter can inflate confidence, and paired with Neptune in your sign, can lead to delusions of grandeur. Don't swing to the other extreme either! Self-deprecation is a Pisces specialty but there is zero good that can come from kicking yourself ever, much less on a day when your two ruling planets are aligned in your sign!

With your attraction quotient so high, single Pisces might meet someone who's a soulmate and a playmate in one. Chemistry will heat up fast, and you won't be shy about letting this person—and the world—know how you feel. Whether it lasts for the long haul or not, romantic connections will help you grow. This person can draw out a more open and expressive side of your personality.

Attached Pisces might need a little extra support during this Jupiter-Neptune cycle. Engage your love interest in your visionary plans. For example, you could throw an epic benefit party for disaster relief or spearhead an art installation that promotes cross-cultural dialogue in your town. Bring people together to feel great, connect from the heart and make a difference.

JUPITER IN ARIES

Creating Security

Jupiter in Aries

May 10 to
October 28, 2022

December 20, 2022
to May 16, 2023

Alright, Pisces, you've given an Academy Award-winning performance with Jupiter in your sign. And there's no question about it: You deserve applause for all the risks you've taken and the ways you've grown. What's next? From May 10 to October 28, Jupiter drifts through Aries, activating your stable second house during the middle of the year. After five months of adventure and discovery, you'll shift into a building phase. As your focus turns to work, money and security, review the wild ideas you've had, and pick out one or two winners. Could you develop them into a profitable and fulfilling new path? With Jupiter in this hardworking zone, you're eager to roll up your sleeves. Luckily, you should have plenty of opportunities to do just that!

Buh-bye, glass ceilings and wage gaps. Bountiful Jupiter wants to compensate you fairly—generously—for your work. This cycle could bring a promotion, a raise or a plum new client list. Since Jupiter rules long-distance travel, you might start racking up airline miles at your job, working with people over Zoom or even relocating for a big opportunity. Keep an open mind. An offer on the other side of the state, country or world may be too good to pass up.

If you're a little hungover from all the excitement of Jupiter in your sign, you'll welcome this chance to prioritize and follow a clear action plan. There's work to do! But first, simplify. What do you value most? Getting clear on that is vital now, as you'll want to design your life around truly meaningful things. For example, if you crave meditative alone time, living in a crowded metropolis won't cut it. Start exploring a possible lifestyle change midyear.

In love, Jupiter's tour of Aries could bring a passionate but stable partnership. If you're single, someone you might have written off as "predictable" may now seem absolutely perfect. You're drawn to the quietly supportive types rather than to flashy arm candy. Couples will enjoy just being present with each other. Jupiter in your tasteful and tactile second house encourages you to get sensual. Plan some sophisticated dates that are also "high touch." How about a couple's massage, a weekend in a winery or a hot air balloon ride?

With Jupiter in Aries, you're focused on quality over quantity. Use the middle of the year to streamline your schedule, budget and routines. After a nonstop launch into 2022, you'll savor the chance to take your time with everything. The best things come from a slow and steady approach. And when the red-spotted planet circles back to your sign from October 28 to December 20, you'll know just how much gas to give it to speed to the finish line with success.

Note that Jupiter will return to Aries for another round—from December 20, 2022 to May 16, 2023. Whatever financial initiatives begin mid-2022 will get a second wind before NYE. The point is to plant seeds and get the ball rolling even if you don't make it very far past the starting block this year.

VENUS RETROGRADE

Rethinking the Future

Venus in Capricorn

November 5, 2021
to March 6, 2022

**Venus Retrograde
in Capricorn**

December 19, 2021
to January 29, 2022

It's perfectly natural to focus—and even fret a bit—about the future, but when it comes to your love life, you might find yourself getting out-and-out obsessive in the early part of 2022. That's a natural consequence of hosting vixen Venus in Capricorn and your eleventh house of hopes and dreams for an extra-long spell (November 5, 2021, to March 6, 2022). And when it flips into retrograde from December 19 to January 29, your thoughts could race in a dozen different, and conflicting, directions.

Normally, Venus spends just three to five weeks in a sign, but every other year, it has a six-week retrograde, and this go-round, it's lounging in Capricorn four times longer than usual. This six-week signal jammer could lead you astray from your best judgment which, let's just say, isn't always the most trustworthy when it comes to affairs of the heart. And you won't be able to rely on your rich intuition to reliably inform romantic decisions. With Venus off-course, you'll be anything but logical! Ironically, this is a time to sharpen your perceptions and not let your heartstrings tug you in the wrong direction.

Retrogrades are famous for reviving past issues and bringing certain folks back into your life, especially if certain aspects of the relationship never got closure. You could reconnect with someone you dated (or flirted meaningfully with) years ago, or perhaps parted ways with during the pandemic. If it truly was a matter of bad timing, it's worth an honest exploration to see what, if anything, is still simmering. And since Capricorn rules your tech-savvy eleventh house, don't be surprised if you get a text or an email from a person you only got to know a little. It'll be tricky, but try to use your Spidey senses to see whether this has actual potential or if you're being "paper-clipped." In fact, revisiting some old missed connections or lost conversation threads on dating apps is a perfect activity while Venus is in reverse. So is joining an online community or mastermind group. The eleventh house is your communal sector, and if you're looking for *amour*, ask some savvy friends if they know anyone who might be compatible with you.

And don't rule out one of those platonic pals as a potential "person of interest." A casual connection could suddenly feel charged up with romantic intensity. If you're both unattached and feel the same sparks, it's worth checking out. But definitely proceed with caution: With Venus off-course, you may not be able to neutralize any regrettable line-crossing. You could always flirt and get to know each other better, but hold off until the love planet resumes forward motion on January 29 to "take the plunge." There are many other ways to accept Venus' invitation to invoke the pleasure principle, like renting a cool Airbnb mountain cabin—or maybe a houseboat (perfect for your watery sign)!

If you do meet someone swoon-worthy, don't let your common sense fly out the window. It's your right and obligation to run background checks on anyone you're thinking of getting involved with. Even a Google search could reveal a lot about a potential prospect (or, yikes, your current love interest). But better to dodge a bullet than stay in the "line of fire." And who knows? You could stumble on some hidden successes. That aw-shucks Tinder date might turn out to be an award-winning performer or author. Bottom line: It's better to be safe than sorry.

Coupled Pisces should talk about your shared future, especially if you've been leaving that up to wishing and hoping instead of checking in and actually discussing. If you're serious to any degree, it behooves you to find out exactly what you're dealing with. Discuss where you both want to live, whether your S.O. wants kids (and if so, approximately when) and how much they like to be involved with their family of origin. In the context of true love, almost everything is negotiable, but if you're harboring any secrets or unrealistic desires, you could trigger some unwanted and unnecessary resentment.

Open a conversation that begins with the mature acknowledgement that life trajectories don't always align perfectly. And even if you're standing at a fork in the road and eyeing different paths, there are plenty of ways to resolve seeming irreconcilable divergences. You have a choice: Fall prey to worry and distrust or reframe this "out of sync" phase as the opportunity to begin an adventurous new chapter. The most important thing is simply getting it all out into the open. Then you can evaluate whether or not you can actually play the long game together.

If you *are* on the same page, Venus' tour of your outgoing eleventh house could refresh your mutual social life. An old friend group could come back together again, the perfect plus-twos with whom to enjoy *hygge* season double dating. And since the eleventh house rules exploration and experimentation, your sex life can get a spicy level-up. This goes for singles, too. But everyone should pay attention to the number-one rule with any planet in retrograde: Err on the side of overcommunicating!

LUNAR NODES IN TAURUS AND SCORPIO

Powers of Persuasion

Lunar Nodes in Taurus and Scorpio

January 18, 2022
to July 17, 2023

Whatever you're selling, Pisces, we'll take two! This January 18, the destiny-driven North Node shifts into Taurus and your articulate third house until July 17, 2023. This 18-month cycle, which hasn't happened in your communication center since April 2003, can do wonders for how you think and express yourself.

As a passionate and poetic sign, when you get fully behind something, that thing is hard to resist. You might be elected to promote a company or important message—or even become the spokesperson for a meaningful movement. Hello, influencer! Whether this is for Brand Pisces or a larger organization, you'll have plenty of opportunities to showcase your skills and take them to the next level, either on an existing platform or something of your own, like a podcast.

The other side of the coin to the North Node is the South Node, which is touring Scorpio and your global ninth house simultaneously. This can spark karmic connections with people around the world, so cast the widest net possible. Is your ancestral homeland calling—or the childhood zip code you paddled far away from after high school? A far-flung fanbase could crop up in these familiar spaces, especially if the people and vibe there still resonate with you.

Piercing Scorpio rules your truth-telling ninth house, which does explain a few things. For one, why you can suddenly switch from compassionately soft-spoken to fiercely outspoken in the flip of a mermaid's tail. Tact isn't always part of that equation—and even the gentlest fish out there has been known to turn a subject into shark bait when the waters get rough between you. With the karmic South Node here for 18 months, you're bound to have some "come to Jesus" moments with the people in your day-to-day life.

> 66
>
> *Traveling may figure into the work you do in 2022, or you may arrange your position to be "permanently remote," allowing for global exploration without missing a paycheck.*
>
> 99

But easy now! Timing is everything, Pisces. Emotions rule you as a water sign, and when you're triggered, it's basically impossible for you to think about anything else. But the North Node in measured Taurus teaches a masterclass on communication. Rather than forcing dialogues to happen immediately, put new practices in place. The box breathing technique, where you inhale and exhale four times, for four seconds with each in and out breath is a simple game-changer. Rooted in Ayurveda and used by Navy SEALs(!), this stressbuster can help you achieve a sense of calm in, literally, a minute. If you don't already have a morning meditation practice in place, start now.

Beyond calming your sensitive temperament, the goal is to gain better control over your thoughts—and in turn, what comes out of your mouth. Words can hurt or words can heal. Simply airing your feelings to get them off your chest won't move any needles in 2022. In fact, this can do more harm than good. Learn how to craft your message with care, taking out any blaming or shaming. That's the key to achieving the kind of understanding that the North Node in your cooperative third house desires.

Speaking of which, collaborations could be insanely successful during this 18-month spell. Team up with fellow visionaries who think like you do. Someone you considered "the competition" could evolve into an incredible project partner. Ditch the grudges and form that dynamic duo! Since the third house rules peers such as siblings, friends, coworkers and neighbors, these people could be the talent pool from which you draw. But to protect the longevity of these bonds, make sure you spell everything out in writing!

Multi-city living could become the new reality for many Pisces, as you commute back and forth between locations. Traveling may figure into the work you do in 2022, or you may arrange your position to be "permanently remote," allowing for global exploration without missing a paycheck. Even if #VanLife isn't your ultimate goal, exploring new cities and neighborhoods by wheel could be an unforgettable adventure for you in 2022.

ECLIPSES IN TAURUS AND SCORPIO

Spread Your Message

**Partial Solar
Eclipse in Taurus**

April 30 at 4:27pm

**Total Lunar
Eclipse in Scorpio**

May 16 at 12:14am

**Partial Solar Eclipse
in Scorpio new moon**

October 25 at 6:48am

**Total Lunar Eclipse
in Taurus full moon**

November 8 at 6:02am

times in eastern time

Say what? You have the soul of a poet, Pisces, and this year's game-changing eclipses give your gifts a chance to shine. All four of 2022's eclipses will fall on the Taurus/Scorpio axis, igniting your third house of local action, ideas and self-expression (ruled by Taurus) and your ninth house of travel, study and entrepreneurship (powered by Scorpio).

These eclipses, which span from November 2021 until October 2023, are here to reshape the way you think, speak and present yourself. On April 30 and November 8, a pair of Taurus eclipses rock your articulate third house. Your message, no matter what the medium, could have far-reaching influence in 2022. Is there a book or a blog in you waiting to hatch? Get started on it near the galvanizing solar eclipse that arrives with the April 30 new moon. You could gain recognition as a thought leader or an influencer on social media. Opportunities to build your platform—or just spontaneously step up to the mic—may come when you least expect them. Be ready to pitch at a moment's notice!

Partnerships are also percolating—the platonic variety that can be every bit as satisfying as anything Cupid slings your way. Move over Ethel and Lucy, Eric B. and Rakim. Pisces may partner up with peers to form legendary dynamic duos. Siblings, neighbors and coworkers are third house domains, and you may discover a shared passion near April 30, then

The saying "think globally, act locally" will become your mantra this year, as the eclipses push you to take a more vocal role in your community.

blow up as overnight sensations under the light of the total lunar (full moon) eclipse on November 8. This November is also prime time to debut any writing, media projects or workshops that you've developed. The power of the Pisces pen is mighty in 2022!

The saying "think globally, act locally" will become your mantra this year, as the eclipses push you to take a more vocal role in your community. Maybe you get involved in homegrown activism or become a voice of change in your neighborhood. Teaming up with like-minded people around a shared agenda can take your plans to new heights. Keep an eye out for kindred spirits, both in-person and virtually.

While you're busy becoming a local sensation, cross-cultural and international synergies can also heat up. You might be tapped as a motivational speaker or see your work published. Thanks to two Scorpio eclipses activating your global ninth house on May 16 and October 25, you'll have a much farther reach. This could be one of those years that you become a global sensation or find success in surprising places off the beaten path.

If you've been hustling away since late 2021, an entrepreneurial venture could hit its stride near the total lunar eclipse in Scorpio on May 16. People who've pooh-poohed your words in the past could suddenly start treating you like their personal guide. Try not to let this go to your head, Pisces, even if you have every right to say, "I told you so!" Don't punish them, either. When the student is ready, the teacher appears. Near May 16, they'll be calling on you for advice.

Travel opportunities could crop up out of the blue near May 16. Be ready to leap if they do! Maybe this ties to a business opportunity or a spiritual pilgrimage. Either way, you're set to expand. Cross-cultural connections heat up again during the solar (new moon) eclipse on October 25. Prepare for an eye-opening moment of truth, Pisces, especially if you've been holding yourself back to "please" other people. No more! These liberating lunations demand independence. Take a stand for your dreams and let others follow suit if they don't want to lose you. You are worth fighting for!

MARS IN GEMINI

Build Your Base

Mars in Gemini

August 20, 2022 to
March 25, 2023

Mars Retrograde in Gemini

October 30, 2022 to
January 12, 2023

Spoiler alert: All won't be quiet on the Pisces homefront starting August 20, 2022. Not with energizer Mars marching through changeable Gemini and your domestic quarters from that day until March 25, 2023, turning up the passion—and the tension—in relations with your closest peeps.

In a normal cycle, Mars spends seven weeks in each sign during its two-year trip around the Sun. But every other year, it turns retrograde for about ten weeks, which means you'll get to experience all the ups and downs and in-betweens domestically for six whole months. Try to take the long view and not do anything rash or regrettable, since Mars can heat up tempers and make them hair-trigger. The entire time could be fraught with intensity and uncertainty, in between extreme fun and a lot of activity, but the retrograde period (from October 30 to January 12, 2023) may be altogether erratic and unpredictable.

With Gemini energy ruling your sensitive and sentimental fourth house, it might be challenging to sit still or stay focused on your days off or when you're working at home. And with activating Mars holding court, you can look forward to more interactions, less diplomacy and more blunt expressions of feelings.

Have your relationships become a bit too dull or routine? Then this Martian cycle could shake things up in desirable ways. But before you do something too radical, make sure the other people it'll affect are on board with your plan. Livening things up is one thing, but putting key partnerships in jeopardy is not the goal! Mars can be brash and self-interested, and you don't want to do anything in the name of "excitement" that will wind up causing you great remorse.

Mars in your home court can drive up the desire to redecorate, renovate—or relocate. If you are seeking a change (of home, scenery or personnel), think it through before you act. Considering a big move with your love interest? Have long, honest conversations about everything this might entail and how you both feel about all possible consequences. Unfettered Pisces could do something radical in the second half of the year, like moving to a new city, becoming a digital nomad or buying your first vacation property.

At the other end of the spectrum, some Pisces will feel more attachment to home than ever and might consider launching a cottage industry from the dining room table. This could take off like gangbusters but warning: your hopes and expectations may be unrealistic when unstoppable Mars flips into reverse gear.

The same "think it through carefully" warning label applies here. While you want to tap this free-flowing motivation, you don't want to be naive or make any rookie mistakes because you skimped on the research and due diligence. And no matter how it takes off (or doesn't), make sure work doesn't overtake your personal activities and space, both of which are necessary for your sanity and peace of mind. Just don't retreat so far into this personal rabbit hole that you become a hermit. The world still wants you to come out and play!

Another smart thing to do during this protracted Mars trek: Evaluate your financial situation, with an eye toward building your nest egg. You might not be as realistic as you think with excitable Mars driving up action and drama in this personal zone. You don't want to spend more than you can spare on home-improvement projects, even if they match your fantasy Pinterest boards. No need to compromise your vision; just find savvy and cost-conscious ways to accomplish it!

Should you need to plump your bottom line to achieve these grand intentions, energizing Mars in multifaceted Gemini can spark all kinds of ideas as well as motivation. Create an online course, accept a freelance or part-time gig, sell some clothes, vintage collectibles or crafts. The only thing limiting your earning potential now is your imagination. ✹

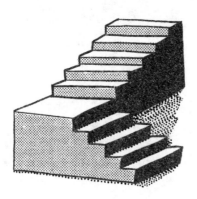

2022

HOTSPOTS

JANUARY *Moon Phases*

SUN	MON	TUE	WED	THU	FRI	SAT
						1 ♑ 6:02PM
2 ♑ New Moon 1:33PM	**3** ♒ 5:44PM	**4** ♒	**5** ♓ 7:17PM	**6** ♓	**7** ♓	**8** ♈ 12:26AM
9 ♈ 1st Quarter	**10** ♉ 9:47AM	**11** ♉	**12** ♊ 10:08PM	**13** ♊	**14** ♊	**15** ♋ 11:11AM
16 ♋	**17** ♌ 11:03PM **FM** ♋ 6:48PM	**18** ♌	**19** ♌	**20** ♍ 9:02AM	**21** ♍	**22** ♎ 5:03PM
23 ♎	**24** ♏ 10:57PM	**25** ♏ 3rd Quarter	**26** ♏	**27** ♐ 2:35AM	**28** ♐	**29** ♑ 4:09AM
30 ♑	**31** ♒ 4:43AM					

KEY: ♈ ARIES ♊ GEMINI ♌ LEO ♎ LIBRA ♐ SAGITTARIUS ♒ AQUARIUS

♉ TAURUS ♋ CANCER ♍ VIRGO ♏ SCORPIO ♑ CAPRICORN ♓ PISCES

FM FULL MOON   **NM** NEW MOON   **LE** LUNAR ECLIPSE   **SE** SOLAR ECLIPSE

SUN-URANUS TRINE

1 JAN

Raise the bar on resolutions! The year is off to an electrifying and inspirational start as the confidence-boosting Capricorn Sun gets charged by the practical magic of innovative Uranus in Taurus. There's one clear directive this NYD: Think outside the box. (Supremely daring souls might ditch the box altogether!) This visionary trine blasts away limitations, revealing what *else* is possible. If you begin a conversation with, "Wouldn't it be crazy if...?" you're on the right track!

MERCURY IN AQUARIUS

2 JAN - 27 MAR

Let the brainstorming begin! Savvy Mercury initiates its first of two trips through quirky, collaborative Aquarius, bringing out the mad scientists in us all. During this experimental transit, getting everyone on the same page could be as easy as herding cats. But as long as everyone has a clearly defined role in the "lab," team efforts will soar. With activism awakened by social Mercury in Aquarius, now's the time to connect to causes, both in person and via social media. Upgrade technology, software and apps before Mercury turns retrograde mid-month.

Supermoon!

CAPRICORN NEW MOON

<table>
<tr><td>2
JAN</td></tr>
</table>

The first new moon of 2022 plants its flag in achievement-minded Capricorn. As resolutions take root, make sure you're playing a big enough game. Could you elevate your vision? Challenge yourself to go farther? This ambitious lunar lift rewards risks, as long as they are well-calculated. And thanks to a trine from innovative Uranus, your ambitions could involve a cutting-edge methodology that you never considered in the past. Pro tip: Rather than scattering energy in multiple directions, radar in on one (or two) epic goals that you want to achieve by mid-year. Then, tap a mentor, accountability buddy or coach to help you manifest them into reality. With tech-savvy Uranus in the frame, make sure you're up-to-date on apps and best practices. By summertime, you could be toasting a massive win!

and in love...

Are you willing to go the distance in love? Today's new supermoon in tenacious Capricorn could get you excited about the idea of building something long-term. We all bring special gifts into this world and this lunar lift amplifies pride in our achievements. Rather than listing the qualities you long for in a mate, clarify your "offerings." What do *you* want to provide to a relationship (present or future)? Once you claim your superpowers, you'll naturally attract someone who appreciates what you bring to the table. When plotting out love goals, don't be afraid to write your own script. With game-changing Uranus trine the new moon, your reinvented vision of love could break the mold.

SUN-VENUS MEETUP

8
JAN

Did you let a good one slip away? Forget to celebrate an important moment with your true love? Today's meet-up of the Sun and back-spinning Venus could bring a fateful second chance. Nothing flashy required here—in fact serenades and skywriters could come across as disingenuous. With these planets in salt-of-the-earth Capricorn, it's a heartfelt commitment that will make the difference. If you could promise something "better" for the future, what would it be? Before you unleash any declarations, check in: Can you make good on the promises? With Venus in reverse until January 29, make *sure* that you're sure this time.

WAXING QUARTER MOON IN ARIES

9
JAN

Don't wait for anyone to pass you the ball. Today's waxing quarter moon in self-starter Aries rewards initiative. Nothing grandiose is required under these moderating moonbeams. Just take an action that will nudge the needle in the right direction. It may be as simple as replying to a text, making a call or asking friends to recommend a great service provider. Get proactive in relationships, too. How do you want things to go next? This quarter moon helps you speak truth to power. And once you do, it will be clear who is on the same page and where you may need to negotiate more balanced terms.

MARS-NEPTUNE SQUARE

11 JAN

It may seem fun to take a gamble today, but that's a slippery slope. Unless you have the facts in front of you, hedge your bets! With the most active planet (Mars) at loggerheads with the most passive one (Neptune), you could take yourself on a wild ride of impulsivity and skewed intuition. Go back to the drawing board and do some quality research. Don't assume that a "maybe" is a "yes" until you've 100 percent confirmed it. Moreover, don't let anyone sweet talk you into making decisions, especially if they involve a financial transaction.

MERCURY RETROGRADE IN AQUARIUS & CAPRICORN

JAN 14 - FEB 3

Even the best-laid plans require more time at the drawing board over the coming three weeks. As strategic Mercury pivots into its first retrograde of the year, it reverses through innovative Aquarius (until January 25), then mission-oriented Capricorn. Back up all electronic data and devices, which are susceptible to damage from Mercury's mayhem. Group interactions require more democracy and well-defined agreements. Is everyone clear on their marching orders? Are there unspoken resentments to air? Pause to inspect and correct. Since this retrograde can muddle your message, proof all emails and presentations before hitting send—and don't go rogue on social media! If a project hits a speed bump, use this "forced timeout" to perfect your plans. Then unveil them after the retrograde.

SUN-PLUTO MEETUP

What's stewing beneath the surface? As the revitalizing Sun shines into subterranean Pluto's vault, it could reveal everything from well-kept secrets to your own hidden superpowers. If you've been lowkey about your accomplishments, come out and let the world see what you're made of! But be warned: As egos flare and intensity runs high, there's a lot to navigate—and do so with kid gloves! With these luminaries meeting in ambitious Capricorn, it's a great day to align with an influential VIP or decision-maker. Could they lend support to a project or open doors on your behalf? If you don't ask, you don't get!

CANCER FULL MOON

Let your softer side peek through as the first full moon of 2022 arrives in nurturing Cancer. If you wake up thinking about a loved one, reach out. Emotions are close to the surface for everyone today. Even the smallest caring gesture can lift someone's spirits. With home and family in the spotlight, a security-minded personal decision may crystallize within two weeks. Ready to change something about your living situation? Whether you're changing your bedding or your address, this full moon accelerates plans. Be graceful with transitions. Since this full moon opposes prickly Pluto, people could misread your intentions and take everything personally!

and in love...

Feelings aren't just flowing, they're spilling out of every pore. If you're feeling nurtured and secure in love, this could be a wonderful day of intimacy and bonding. But if not—look out! Stormy dynamics threaten to drown out any goodwill. If you've been hiding unhappiness, this full moon cracks the shell. While it's great to get your truth out into the open, there's a risk of wounding tender hearts (and egos). As the saying goes, "Hurt people hurt people." Better to nurse any wounds with the support of friends and family than to inflict pain in an endless back and forth. On a happy note, plans involving cohabitation, meeting the parents or growing a family could become more than just lip service. Couples could get cozy and secure by working on their 2022 savings plan. Spreadsheets, anyone?

NORTH NODE IN TAURUS & SOUTH NODE IN SCORPIO

**18 JAN '22
-
17 JUL '23**

Destination: Stabilization? After 18 months of embroidering truth with fiction, the lunar nodes (karmic destiny points) end their spin-doctoring cycle through mutable Gemini and Sagittarius—the axis of communication and information. Since May 5, 2020, the world waded through conspiracy theories and misleading news. We re-examined long-held narratives around race and privilege, allying and polarizing in equal extremes. Starting today, the lunar nodes anchor across the fixed signs of Taurus (North, destiny) and Scorpio (South, karma), shifting the focus to money, power and the (mis)use of natural resources. From global supply chains to our personal possessions, the way we distribute and consume goods could shift in epic ways over the next 18 months. Simultaneously, the line between "needy" and "greedy" could grow brighter. New systems of monetization, such as cryptocurrency, explode and expand, shifting global markets in unprecedented ways.

URANUS RETROGRADE ENDS

18 JAN

Who said routines have to be boring? Revolutionary Uranus wraps up its annual five-month retrograde and powers forward in sensible-but-sensual Taurus. The planet of genius, innovation and radical shifts is pacing through the Bull's pen from May 2018 to April 2026. During this time, consider novel approaches to earning money and creating security. Practice makes perfect—and a project plan turns a cutting-edge idea into a profitable product! While Uranus rules technology, earthy Taurus is tactile and analog. So how to keep "the good old days" alive without fighting progress? As future-forward Uranus rocks Taurus' traditional structures, it can incite a wave of conservative backlash. Warning: When Uranus "stations" back to direct motion, people's behavior can be erratic and unpredictable. Give the energy a few days to settle before making any major decisions. While you may be headed for an exciting change, it's not something to embark on impulsively. To remain in balance, see what happens if you reduce screen time and increase connection with the natural world.

SUN IN AQUARIUS

JAN 19 - FEB 18

There's strength in numbers (and magic, too!) as the Sun cycles into innovative, community-loving Aquarius. For the next four weeks, make togetherness your guiding principle. Everyone has a gift to offer the world. Why not make it your mission to uncover the best in the people you meet? Roles may reshuffle on teams or you may leave one group to work with another crew whose interests and values are in line with your own. Technology can speed processes, so lean in to project management software and group messaging apps to keep everyone in sync. Aquarius governs activism and social responsibility. How can you level up your work to make this planet a better place, even if profits are not involved?

and in love...

After four weeks of family-friendly activities and Q1 career demands, we're all ready to cut loose! Experimental Aquarius takes the wheel as the Sun buzzes into this open-minded sign. While the Water Bearer is known for playing it cool, this rational four-week transit can bring *verrrry* interesting developments to the game of love. Let your mind (and fantasies) wander beyond their prior scope. Maybe you're not ready to consider things like polyamory, group playtime, or tantric retreats—or maybe you are? Aquarius rules electricity, so perhaps your toy drawer could get an update. In the sign of friendship and universal love, lines could blur between friendship and situationship. Couples can enjoy more time socializing as a pair, especially if your date nights come with a wild and edgy flair.

SUN-MERCURY MEETUP

23
JAN

Open mouth, insert performance athletic footwear? As the Sun meets retrograde Mercury for a socially awkward summit in Aquarius, watch every word that you say. One thoughtless post could get you #Canceled. Group activities are mired in complexity, but there is a silver lining. This illuminating mashup might reveal the weak link in the chain. Don't rush to vote them off the island if their behavior's not egregious—but don't allow them to sink the ship either. On a brighter note, reunions are favored today. Get the band back together, if only for one encore!

MARS IN CAPRICORN

24 JAN
- 6 MAR

How strong is your need to succeed? You're about to find out as goal-getter Mars leaps into ambitious Capricorn and brings out your desire to do, be and have the best. Mars is exalted in Capricorn, meaning it's one of its most powerful positions on the zodiac wheel. Harness the red planet's power and rise through the ranks. To grab the brass ring, you'll need to bring laser focus and serious hustle, but there's more to it than just working hard. The endorsement of prestigious people may be your golden ticket into the big leagues. Find a way to mingle with the influencers and gatekeepers in your industry—even if you have to fetch their coffee to get your foot in the door. Everyone starts somewhere, but the cream always rises to the top. Already in the VIP lounge? Make a point of supporting others who are just starting out. What goes around, comes around.

and in love...

MARS IN CAPRICORN

**24 JAN
- 6 MAR**

Could your love be so legendary that it creates...a legacy? Such lofty ideals are top of mind as hot-blooded Mars settles down on Capricorn's iron throne. After a wild romp in "anything goes" Sagittarius, it's probably time to set some standards—and maybe a few boundaries while you're at it. Be discerning, but don't raise the bar *so* high that no mere mortal can reach it. This phase is ideal for future planning and mapping out sexy #LoveGoals. Playing with power dynamics in the bedroom can be titillating, too. Tie on the blindfold and choose a safeword! (Maybe something besides "Daddy," since a few father issues could arise?) Warning: You could become so fixated on a relationship's trajectory that you apply unwarranted pressure. To combat a lover's resistance, bring fun to the present moment. This Mars cycle may be better spent discovering whether your long-range goals align and hammering out compromises where they don't.

MERCURY IN CAPRICORN

**25 JAN
- FEB 14**

Retrograde Mercury backs into Capricorn for the rest of its retreat, until February 3. After trolling techie Aquarius for two weeks and creating all kinds of digital drama, this final lap could muddle messages in the professional realm. At work, take every extra precaution to follow protocol. Get clear on the chain of command, if only to navigate power dynamics like a pro. On the hunt for opportunity? Connect to colleagues you worked with in the past. Common ground could bring you together for a sequel success once Mercury powers forward in Capricorn from February 3 to 14.

WANING QUARTER MOON IN SCORPIO

25 JAN

Is that the green-eyed monster whispering in your ear? Under today's waning quarter moon in Scorpio, a subtle undercurrent of jealousy is in the air. Is this envy justified or are you taking things a little too personally? While you don't want to dismiss your intuitive hits, this darkening moon can obscure the full truth. To distinguish facts from feelings, go deeper than casual observation. Apply this same investigative curiosity to relationships of all stripes. Instead of getting defensive, display inquisitiveness: "Can you tell me a little more about that?" Curiosity won't kill the cat today. In fact, it could deepen an intimate bond in unexpected (and sexy!) ways.

MERCURY-PLUTO MEETUP

28 JAN

Words pack a powerful punch today as Mercury connects to Pluto for the first of two exact meetups this quarter. (The second one is on February 8) Radar in on the ballers and big shots and don't waste time on people with zero ability to influence the situation at hand. Be precise with your language, if you say anything at all. Since Mercury is still retrograde, it's wise to observe before musing aloud, and doubly with cloak and dagger Pluto in the picture. If something seems off, investigate quietly and strategically. These planets unite again on February 11, when Mercury has corrected course, so it might take until then to sort through the data.

VENUS DIRECT IN CAPRICORN

Welcome back, Cupid—and not a moment too soon! Seductive Venus wraps up a terse retrograde that began on December 19, one that may have dampened loving feelings while inflaming drama. After throwing curveballs into your holiday season, the planet of love and harmony resumes forward motion, flowing in forward motion through elegant, ambitious Capricorn until March 6. Did your plans for an idyllic future veer off course? Maybe you pushed away a stable sweetheart for the "excitement" of a disruptive rebel—or a toxic ex. Use the next month to sort through any rubble and, if possible, realign about future plans. While some relationships may be too fractured to repair, don't give up too soon. With Venus now restoring the spirit of diplomacy, win-wins are in sight!

SUN-URANUS SQUARE

Them's fighting words! The ego-driven Sun throws down with rebellious Uranus, pushing everyone's buttons. With riotous spirits ignited, the adrenaline runs high today. Do everything in your power to *not* take people's bait. While renegade moves bring a temporary rush, the thrill is short-lived. Anything brazen or inflammatory could come back to haunt you—if it doesn't burn bridges on the spot. You never know: The person you flip off in traffic could be the hiring director of the company you apply to or your boss' sister. So rather than nursing a shame hangover from playing the power-tripping provocateur, rewind and be kind.

FEBRUARY *Moon Phases*

SUN	MON	TUE	WED	THU	FRI	SAT
		1 ♒︎ New Moon 12:45AM	**2** ♓︎ 6:00AM	**3** ♓︎	**4** ♈︎ 9:57AM	**5** ♈︎
6 ♉︎ 5:53PM	**7** ♉︎	**8** ♉︎ 1st Quarter	**9** ♊︎ 5:27AM	**10** ♊︎	**11** ♋︎ 6:27PM	**12** ♋︎
13 ♋︎	**14** ♌︎ 6:17AM	**15** ♌︎	**16** ♍︎ 3:43PM FM ♌ 11:56AM	**17** ♍︎	**18** ♎︎ 10:51PM	**19** ♎︎
20 ♎︎	**21** ♏︎ 4:19AM	**22** ♏︎	**23** ♐︎ 8:29AM 3rd Quarter	**24** ♐︎	**25** ♑︎ 11:28AM	**26** ♑︎
27 ♒︎ 1:36PM	**28** ♒︎					

KEY: ♈︎ ARIES ♊︎ GEMINI ♌ LEO ♎︎ LIBRA ♐︎ SAGITTARIUS ♒︎ AQUARIUS
♉︎ TAURUS ♋︎ CANCER ♍︎ VIRGO ♏︎ SCORPIO ♑︎ CAPRICORN ♓︎ PISCES

FM FULL MOON **NM** NEW MOON **LE** LUNAR ECLIPSE **SE** SOLAR ECLIPSE

AQUARIUS NEW MOON

<table>
<tr><td>1
FEB</td></tr>
</table>

The spirit of unity is in the air! The annual new moon in Aquarius fosters collaboration, drawing people together around common ideals and community missions. Inclusivity is more essential than ever during this open-minded lunar lift, but look out! Thanks to a harsh square from changemaker Uranus in Taurus, gathering people together may not turn into an instant bonding experience. Go out of your way to welcome a wide spectrum of viewpoints and personalities. You don't create a chorus with everyone singing the same note, right? This evening also ushers in the Chinese New Year, as we bid adieu to the process-driven Metal Ox and welcome the charming, courageous Water Tiger as our ruling creature until early 2023.

and in love...

If you could wave a magic wand over your love life, what would you create—and with whom? February's new moon is in Aquarius, the sign of hopes and wishes, and it's evoking romantic idealism. Why *not* visualize every possibility instead of simply settling for what's in front of you? We're all set in our ways. During this new moon, you may have to battle against your own stubbornness, thanks to a tense square from cranky Uranus in Taurus. How you choose to level up your love life is up to you, but here's a spoiler alert! Experimentation is strongly favored starting tonight as the lowkey Metal Ox hands the keys to the fierce Water Tiger for a year. Talks about the future—Aquarius' favorite f-word—arouse all kinds of offbeat ideas. Explore!

2

MERCURY DIRECT IN CAPRICORN

3 FEB

Foiled plans and stalled initiatives find their footing again as Mercury wakes up from an aggravating three-week retrograde. Focusing has not been easy since January 14, and it may take a few days to sharpen it like a laser beam again. Starting now, distill what's worthy of time and effort and what would be better shelved for a future date. Business conversations will be productive with Mercury powering forward in Capricorn until February 14. What are you hoping to build in 2022? DM the movers and shakers and get on their books!

SUN-SATURN MEETUP

4 FEB

How serious are you about that goal? Put some muscle in that hustle as the magnanimous Sun makes its once-per-year connection to masterful Saturn. Your disciplined approach draws attention, helping you project authentic confidence. But keep your ego out of all affairs. You'll catch more flies with humility than you will with swagger. If you've been tight-fisted or heavy-handed—or conversely, playing fast and loose with resources—find the middle ground. Then, get back out there—with plenty of grace.

WAXING QUARTER MOON IN TAURUS

8 FEB

Does it make sense on paper? Today's waxing quarter moon in Taurus calls for checks and balances. Tap the brakes and sift through the details with a fine-toothed comb. Do you need to streamline? Even the most well-oiled machines require periodic maintenance. This is how you keep things humming and avoid bigger, costlier breakdowns. But if plans have become too austere, lean in to the more decadent side of the Bull. Add a few sophisticated touches (think luxe, not *louche*!) and aim to hit the mark of "simple elegance."

MARS-URANUS TRINE

8 FEB

Filters come off today when brash Uranus in Taurus, aligns with disruptor Mars in Capricorn. You might not be able to hold in unprocessed thoughts, so if you do blurt, be sure you can live with the consequences of saying the first thing that comes to mind. Some ideas are truly better left unspoken—and un-emailed—so before you do provoke a controversy, try to distract yourself. With these planets in productive earth signs, you'll have considerable energy to pour into a work project. Let yourself experiment, but make sure you save a backup! Acting impulsively could destroy weeks of hard work.

MERCURY IN AQUARIUS

14 FEB - 9 MAR

Teamwork: Take Two! Social operator Mercury spins into Aquarius for its second circuit of the year. Connections you fostered between January 2 to 25—or re-engaged during the retrograde after January 14—get a second wind over the coming three weeks. Spruce up your online and social profiles now. A savvy digital presence will help you get your message beyond the echo chamber and into the zeitgeist. Take projects to new heights by teaming up with free-thinkers, technologists and the metaphysically minded. While this "more the merrier" groove might interrupt your pre-scheduled V-Day plans, who's to say you can't have fun feting Cupid as a party of nine?

VENUS-MARS MEETUP

16 FEB

How far will you go to prove your devotion? Cosmic lovebirds Venus and Mars share a flight path today, their first of two exact connections in 2022. With this duo paired up in unstoppable Capricorn, do something to demonstrate that you're committed and ready to go the distance. If you find yourself questioning a lover's interest level (or your own), take this uncertainty seriously. Discussions about a shared future will be both fiery and sweet, but it's better to lay cards on the table than labor in delusion. Happy couples: What will you build together in 2022? This is your day to start dreaming and doing.

2

LEO FULL MOON

The year's only Leo full moon evokes the spirit of courage and generosity, all with a Tony-Award-winning twist. All the world's a Broadway production under these flamboyant moonbeams, and in this crowded "marketplace," it takes something to stand out. But if you're going to be "extra," consider a couple things. First, make sure to lead with your heart (the Leo-ruled part of the body) because people will feel the genuine warmth and connection as you do. Second, only make moves that help you transform the past and move closer to your destiny. The reason? This full moon is forming a dynamic T-square (three-way tug of war) with the lunar nodes in Taurus and Scorpio. What you *don't* want to do is repeat an unhealthy cycle of power struggles or seeking validation from the wrong sources. Play your cards right, and you can launch yourself into noble leadership, opening up new paths to abundance and contribution!

and in love...
VENUS-MARS MEETUP

How far will you go to prove your devotion? Cosmic lovebirds Venus and Mars share a flight path today, their first of two exact connections in 2022. With this duo paired up in unstoppable Capricorn, do something to demonstrate that you're committed and ready to go the distance. If you find yourself questioning a lover's interest level (or your own), take this uncertainty seriously. Discussions about a shared future will be both fiery and sweet, but it's better to lay cards on the table than labor in delusion. Happy couples: What will you build together in 2022? This is your day to start dreaming *and* doing.

SUN IN PISCES

FEB 18 - MAR 20

The line between business and personal could blur over the coming four weeks as the Sun shifts into watery, compassionate Pisces. During this solar spell, soulful undertakings are the name of the game. What do you care about...deeply? Put your attention there and cultivate it. After four cool weeks in rational Aquarius, we've had enough talk about metrics, KPIs, algorithms and statistics. Empathy reigns supreme during Pisces season, a time when it's all about the personal touch. No faking it! If you've gotten a little too detached from your heart, you can make up for lost time. Check in with the people you interface with on an everyday basis. How's everyone doing...really? While it's important to keep *some* sort of boundaries in place, softening may be necessary to restore a healthy climate from your workplace to your home.

and in love...

Bring on the poetry, playlists and peak romantic experiences. Love knows no bounds as the Sun drifts into Pisces' esoteric waters. Sweet escapes from reality are what make romance so rich. Just try not to lose sight of daily duties like showing up at work and returning important messages. While we'll all rock the rose-colored glasses for the coming four weeks, don't let them screen out red flags. Seeing the best in people is a noble quality—as long as you aren't projecting imaginary traits onto people that they haven't earned. Fall in love with who they are, not just their potential.

2

WANING QUARTER MOON IN SAGITTARIUS

23 FEB

There are three sides to every story—and, technically, none of them are "the truth." But under the dimming lights of today's quarter moon in Sagittarius, it's easy to get caught up in a philosophical debate. That's also the perfect recipe for spinning your wheels. For best results, let go of the need to have everyone agree. A uniquely brilliant ability of this worldly zodiac sign is creating room for a rainbow of perspectives to coexist. So, agreeing to disagree is one answer. Another is to allow everyone's voice to be heard, recorded and considered. Pro tip: Use a talking stick and make a "no interruptions" rule.

MERCURY-URANUS SQUARE

24 FEB

Bending the rules is as good as breaking them under today's rebelliously unpredictable skies. While the renegade routine might earn you street cred, goodwill can shatter in the process. With daredevil Uranus in Taurus slamming into mouthy Mercury in Aquarius, think twice before going rogue. If ranting on Twitter doesn't get you canceled it could earn you a rep as a loose cannon. Before you rush to defend anyone, run a search: Are they as credible as you believe? If you're presenting an idea, organize your points and research statistics. While it's great to be original, you don't want to be so far from center that nobody understands your concept! Choose clarity over cleverness today.

MARCH *Moon Phases*

SUN	MON	TUE	WED	THU	FRI	SAT
		1 ♓ 3:54PM	**2** ♓ New Moon 12:34PM	**3** ♈ 7:53PM	**4** ♈	**5** ♈
6 ♉ 3:00AM	**7** ♉	**8** ♊ 1:40PM	**9** ♊	**10** ♊ 1st Quarter	**11** ♋ 2:25AM	**12** ♋
13 ♌ 3:32PM	**14** ♌	**15** ♌	**16** ♍ 12:59AM	**17** ♍	**18** ♎ 7:26AM FM ♍ 3:18AM	**19** ♎
20 ♏ 11:45AM	**21** ♏	**22** ♐ 2:59PM	**23** ♐	**24** ♑ 5:54PM	**25** ♑ 3rd Quarter	**26** ♒ 8:56PM
27 ♒	**28** ♒	**29** ♓ 12:32AM	**30** ♓	**31** ♈ 5:31AM		

KEY: ♈ ARIES ♊ GEMINI ♌ LEO ♎ LIBRA ♐ SAGITTARIUS ♒ AQUARIUS
♉ TAURUS ♋ CANCER ♍ VIRGO ♏ SCORPIO ♑ CAPRICORN ♓ PISCES

FM FULL MOON **NM** NEW MOON **LE** LUNAR ECLIPSE **SE** SOLAR ECLIPSE

PISCES NEW MOON

2 MAR

The floodgates of fantasy open today as the year's only new moon in Pisces tunes in to the imagination station. Since the veil is thin under these moonbeams, this is one of the best days of the year to download divine inspiration. Get yourself into a quiet space where you can "hear" the guidance of your inner voice. With abundant Jupiter hovering in close connection to la luna, you can expect a downpour of ideas! Try leading with a softer touch, remaining receptive to input rather than forcing yourself to be productive or give feedback. Suffering is optional!

and in love...

How much would you sacrifice in the name of love? Today's new moon in selfless Pisces brings a golden opportunity to be the supportive angel of your lover's dreams. But check in with yourself before you offer up time and energy. Is compassion veering into caretaking terrain...even codependence? "Giving" feels best when it comes wrapped in boundaries— an important reminder since no-limits Jupiter is hovering in close contact to this new moon. Measured generosity spares you future resentment, and you'll avoid putting pressure on a relationship. Harboring a secret desire? The floodgates to fantasy open today. Surrender and enjoy!

MERCURY-SATURN MEETUP

2 MAR

The glass may appear half-empty under a sobering conjunction of mental Mercury and dour Saturn. Even if resources are scant, don't fall prey to pessimism. These planets are synced up in experimental Aquarius, and that's your cue to keep on testing until you find a solution that clicks. Ditch the doomsday mentality and don't waste what could be a wildly productive day. If you can set your ego aside, you'll see that this situation isn't a "failure." It's an opportunity to step back and look honestly at what's not working here. How can you realistically improve this situation, one step at a time? Reach out to your network for resources. Someone in your circle could offer a great solution. Lean on the wisdom of their experience.

MARS-PLUTO MEETUP

3 MAR

How far will you go to achieve your goal? Today, make-it-happen Mars gets in sync with power-thirsty Pluto—in unstoppable Capricorn, no less! Power and charisma reach peak levels during this every-other-year summit. Pour your genuine best into a project and you could produce transformational results! Just be warned, with competitive vibes amplified, it's easy to cross over into cutthroat terrain. Be proactive, assertive and "take-charge," yes, but don't compromise your ethics. Winning at any cost is a hollow victory, especially if pulling into the lead involves cutting corners or doing anything remotely underhanded. It's like Gandhi said, an eye for an eye just leaves the whole world blind.

VENUS-PLUTO MEETUP

3 MAR

What happens behind closed doors should definitely stay there as secretive Pluto casts a smoldering gaze upon ardent Venus. With both planets in image-conscious Capricorn, here's the ideal recipe for amour: Be a socialite in the streets and a tiger in the sheets. Single and searching? Keep the bar raised high. Don't be afraid to demand more from your love interest. This planetary pairing could elevate you to power couple status, as long as you're both willing to bring your best to the table. Are you? The rubber meets the road under this provocative transit—and your very own feelings may surprise you!

SUN-JUPITER MEETUP

5 MAR

Boundlessness can expand in any direction today, as the life-giving Sun is buoyed by optimistic Jupiter's unflagging faith. Our recommendation? Look up... literally! Casting your eyes toward the horizon cues your brain to release dopamine, the molecule that reminds you that there's always more available. (And there is.) Plus, with this Sun-Jupiter conjunction taking place in emotionally unrestrained Pisces, it's important to direct your energy toward the positive and proactive. Negative thought spirals can plummet you into a state of despair, and it will be hard to pull yourself out of that riptide. If you need to grieve or unleash pent-up frustration, do so in a healthy way, leaning on supportive people who will lift you higher as you emote.

MARS IN AQUARIUS

6 MAR - 14 APR

Come together! Mars zips into collaborative, innovative Aquarius today—its first visit to the Water Bearer's realm since March 30, 2020. During its last go-round, Mars in Aquarius birthed concepts like social distancing, Zoom school and other "new abnormals." Starting today, we can reset the dials of human interactivity. With the energizing planet marching through this unifying zodiac sign, you can be an agent for change, getting people back on the same page. Focus on commonalities and shared goals while creating an inclusive space where everyone's voice can be heard. Sound idealistic? That's how Mars in Aquarius rolls. During this biennial cycle, you could get involved in some very exciting team projects. Social anxiety may spark up under Mars' pulse-quickening influence. In air-sign Aquarius, there's nothing more calming than four long, deep breaths!

and in love...

The line between platonic and erotic could get blurry over the next six weeks as lusty Mars treks through Aquarius, the experimental sign of friendship and intellect. It's your call whether to "dabble" or not, but if you do, you may discover the farthest reaches of your personal edge. Minds will be wide open during this boundary-pushing transit, and three, four or five could be the magic number for some. Choose a safe word before you go play, and make sure everyone's in alignment on what constitutes a "yea" or a "nay." Since Aquarius governs the digital domain, finding a love connection online might be a smarter approach than dipping into the friend pool, since you won't risk losing an important relationship. Attached? Burst out of the couple bubble! With Mars in Aquarius, autonomy makes the heart grow fonder.

VENUS IN AQUARIUS

6 MAR - 5 APR

Friendly fire? Seductive Venus spends the next four weeks in Aquarius, sparking up a round of cosmic cosplay with dance partner Mars. Save the traditional trappings for April. With these heavenly heartthrobs canoodling in the sign of casual connections and unconventional relationships, life feels much sweeter—and hotter!—when you're pushing the envelope. A mutual contact could play matchmaker, and online connections ignite. For couples, this period can spark honest dialogue about the way *you* envision a happy union. Drift as far from the standard playbook as you want. From living in separate spaces to opening up a relationship to exploring a gestational carrier, no topic is off limits. Create a safe environment where you can discuss your desires freely. Talking about them doesn't necessarily mean you'll actually pursue these things. The point is to banish fear or possessiveness, which will create breathing room for your individuality.

VENUS-MARS MEETUP

6 MAR

Old distinctions between "platonic pal," "friend with benefits" and lover could dissolve under today's recherché connection between the cosmic lovebirds, Venus and Mars, in Aquarius. While this is their second of two exact conjunctions in 2022, it's been years since they shared a moment like this in the Water Bearer's realm. As romance meets passion in an unforgettable swirl, give in to the desires that swell up inside you. If you have a partner, then all you need is some alone time—and a willingness to experiment! Singles might strike a spark with a new friend, Tinder date or a random fix-up. Cast a spell with your intellect and wit, and stay open to serendipity!

MERCURY IN PISCES

9 - 27
MAR

Subconscious triggers, secret agendas and subliminal messages, oh my! You'll gain greater awareness of "the invisible realm" starting today, as mindful Mercury plunges into dreamy, imaginative Pisces. Don't waste time rehashing every word that was spoken. During this three-week cycle, what's *not* being said contains more truth than any random musings or Twitter threads. Relax into a creative, compassionate mindset. It will certainly be a relief after Mercury's trek through brain-bending, intellectual Aquarius. Dial down the overthinking and get in touch with your emotions. Let intuition guide your decisions a bit more. Journaling, art and recording your dreams can lead to breakthrough insights.

WAXING QUARTER MOON IN GEMINI

10
MAR

Power to your partnerships! Today's waxing quarter moon in Gemini illuminates new ways to pair up with your peers. Under these moderate moonbeams, it's wise to let relationships unfold at a measured, organic pace. Start small, perhaps testing the waters with a one-off, short-term project. Since Gemini is the sign of the twins, you're most likely to click with people who have similar talents and values. But consider this: Too much sameness can lock you in an echo chamber. This may be the day you decide to branch out a little and mingle with people who challenge you to think differently.

SUN-NEPTUNE MEETUP

13 MAR

You could find yourself at a loss for words today, and that's okay! The shimmering Sun and dreamy Neptune take a savasana together as they meet at the same degree of Pisces. This day is best used for nonverbal activities like meditating, exploring, and listening to music. One thing to avoid? Pushing yourself to show up out of guilt or obligation. Not only will it be exhausting, but it may churn up serious resentment. Rather than blowing the big meeting, reschedule. Or change your tactics to something less rigid. As Neptune's "go with the flow" spontaneity gets a playful boost from the Sun, a spur-of-the-moment strategy shift could clinch the deal! Take note that under this once-per-year mashup, showing your emotions will be viewed as a sign of strength, not weakness. For artists or healers, the confident Sun inspires you to hang your shingle or share your talents with the world.

VIRGO FULL MOON

18 MAR

Need to bring some order to your court? Today's full moon in Virgo hands you the eco-friendly cleaning products and takes you to task. If you're sorting through chaos, start with a master list. Write out all the things you need to finish, clean up and execute in the coming two weeks. But don't just auto-pilot into your old, industrious methods. Neptune in Pisces opposes this full moon, underscoring the importance of opening up more flow time in your daily routines. How can you work smarter rather than harder? From apps to virtual assistants, seek out better systems for productivity and project management. Wellness is also in the Virgoan spotlight. Is it time to switch up your routines for spring? Heed Sea God Neptune's influence, upping your water intake, finding a pool for lap swims and dancing as much as you can!

3

and in love . . .

'Tis the season for simplification, and that includes your approach to love and romance. True sensuality doesn't require props or complicated narratives, which is something the zodiac's virgin teaches us. Connect to your basic senses: touch, taste, scent, sight, sound. Under today's full moon, you'll feel sexiest when you put down your devices and connect to the earthy rhythms that have guided humans through every evolutionary cycle. Open a window and let some fresh air in. Rub your palms together, play a favorite song, circle your hips. Embodiment is an aphrodisiac, even if you're simply enjoying how delicious it feels to be in your own skin. But get ready: Self-love raises your vibration, giving you quite the attractive aura. You are beautiful!

VENUS-URANUS SQUARE

19 MAR

Help...air! People's requests for time and energy sound more like demands under today's horn-locking square between Venus in Aquarius and nervous Uranus in Taurus. Have you fenced yourself in with too many commitments? Suddenly, they feel as restrictive as a way-too-snug turtleneck. Check yourself before you blow up on anyone! Fuses will be short, and no one will have the greatest perspective under this brief, but agitated, transit. Need to shake up a flat-lining relationship? Boundaries can be flexible, but don't underestimate the potential aftermath. If you've always been the sensitive type, yet suddenly feel like throwing caution to the wind, don't act in haste. Have a levelheaded conversation (with yourself, the universe, or a wise mentor) about your natural limits BEFORE you take any intimate risks.

SUN IN ARIES

MAR 20 - APR 19

Hello, equinox! Ciao, Aries season! The solar calendar starts anew as the Sun begins its annual, month-long trek through the Ram's realm. Beginning now, you can slowly and gently "un-Hygge" yourself. Replace crafting supplies with garden tools and binge-watching marathons with breezy walks in nature. The spirit of renewal is in the air, and soon enough, you'll be fired up with the Ram's daring initiative, eager to embrace the next adventure. Live-out-loud Aries season is a time to grab life by the horns and push the envelope on maximalism. Head's up: Since Aries is #1 in the zodiac, competitive vibes can get fierce. Are you living your best life? Go for the gold and don't let anyone slow you down. But once you've crushed it, remember to bring your teammates along for the ride!

and in love...

Kundalini: rising! New friendships and virtual flirtations will sprout like spring crocuses as the life-giving Sun bursts into Aries. Not only is this the spring equinox in the Northern Hemisphere, but the Sun's arrival at 0° Aries restarts the zodiac "clock." Exhilarating as this feels, don't invest too much too soon. Text trysts and late-night wooings will be hot, but many will fizzle as fast as they sizzle, thanks to the Ram's impulsive influence. And even if they don't, how much sexier is it to stay grounded in your own individuality and power? (SO much!) When out on dates or just interacting with your boo, keep your argumentative streak in check. Debates can heat up quickly with the Sun in this combative sign. What starts as an innocent dialogue about loading the dishwasher could quickly devolve into a heated, bridge-burning exchange. When tempers start flaring, call a time-out!

MERCURY-JUPITER MEETUP

21
MAR

If you've been struggling to put a soul-stirring notion into words, today could bring a white-light epiphany that helps you verbalize your vision. Savvy Mercury syncs up with candid Jupiter in poetic Pisces, turning those seeds of inspiration into a blossoming idea. Pay special attention to intuitive hits and knowing feelings. They are pointing you toward something important, be it a "next step" or an ultimate destination. Have you been hesitant to share your latest insights? With these outspoken planets spurring you on, you'll find it surprisingly easy to talk about your work. By the same token, don't share your esoteric revelations with just anyone! Protect the magic of your budding brainstorms from anyone who has historically cast a shadow of doubt over your precious strokes of genius. What you need right now is the kind of support that keeps you feeling inspired and productive!

MARS-URANUS SQUARE

22
MAR

Good luck keeping things "peace, love and harmony" today, as combative Mars crashes into a complicated square with combustible Uranus. This 90-degree mashup only happens twice every other year and can cause quite the disruption. With both planets in stubborn, fixed signs—Mars in Aquarius and Uranus in Taurus—tempers flare as egos and ideologies clash. If you've been a little *too* agreeable for your own good, the Mars-Uranus square can push you to your breaking point. Forget about sucking it up and "taking one for the team." This ain't the day to accept peace at any price! But if you're feeling too heated to hash things out diplomatically, steer clear of situations that are potential powder kegs. This might be a better moment for privately clarifying your anger...but NOT attempting to hold a summit between warring factions. If you're able to approach the matter with a cooler head, however, this transit inspires eye-opening dialogues.

MERCURY-NEPTUNE MEETUP

**23
MAR**

Is this real life, or just a fantasy? You might as well sing a Bohemian Rhapsody today as foggy Neptune clouds the clear waters of mentally incisive Mercury. With these planets meeting up in deep-diving Pisces, you're going to have to plunge below the surface to find out what's true. (And even then, your discoveries may be too esoteric to fully understand.) Be prepared for confusion and delusion to muddle your mind—and just surrender. If attempts to focus are fruitless, don't force it. Save tasks that require logic and intellect for another day. What this wildly imaginative transit *is* best for is allowing your creative, right brain to drive. If you've been guarded or stiff in your interactions, try a more heartfelt approach. Keep the tissues handy, because your squad may be moved to tears by the power and impact of your shared mission.

WANING QUARTER MOON IN CAPRICORN

**25
MAR**

Check those benchmarks! As the quarter moon wanes in Capricorn, make sure you're on track to hit your monthly milestones. You may realize that someone's been slacking on their duties—or perhaps misunderstood them altogether. It's not too late to salvage this, but you may have to burn a little midnight oil to keep your mission afloat. When was the last time you reviewed your goals? (Or set any clear-cut ones?) No need to plot out anything epic. What could you achieve before March is through? One small victory brings the confidence boost for the next one after that.

MERCURY IN ARIES

27 MAR
- 10 APR

Switch from "sweet talker" to "fast talker," as quicksilver Mercury glides into passionate, fired-up Aries. During this pulse-quickening cycle, there's no time to sleep or skip a single beat. Zone out for two seconds and you could miss the punch line or get taken for a ride by a charmer. If you're the type that hates small talk, get over it. With attention spans nearly non-existent for the next few weeks, a witty one-liner will make a stronger impact than a long and meandering tale. For maximum impact, break everything down to bullet points, acronyms and emojis.

VENUS-SATURN MEETUP

28
MAR

Love is serious business today as celestial siren Venus gets swept under Saturn's stern spell. With the two planets meeting up in Aquarius, you don't have to veer into conservative terrain. But you *do* need to get back to brass tacks about basic agreements. Spell everything out in black and white. Where do you both stand on things like managing finances, raising kids and where you ultimately want to put down roots? These no-nonsense discussions may reveal some genuine disparities. Saturn rules experts, and if you can't get past a sticking point, a coach or couple's therapist could help. If you've been caught up in a never-ending situationship or pining for a lost soul, today's mood could force you to take an unblinking look at reality. Time is precious, and you don't want to waste your life waiting for someone who "isn't ready" and may never be!

APRIL *Moon Phases*

4

SUN	MON	TUE	WED	THU	FRI	SAT
					1 ♈ New Moon 2:24AM	**2** ♉ 12:51PM
3 ♉	**4** ♊ 11:04PM	**5** ♊	**6** ♊	**7** ♋ 11:31AM	**8** ♋	**9** ♋ 1st Quarter
10 ♌ 12:00AM	**11** ♌	**12** ♍ 10:08AM	**13** ♍	**14** ♎ 4:46PM	**15** ♎	**16** ♏ 8:23PM **FM** ♎ 2:54PM
17 ♏	**18** ♐ 10:17PM	**19** ♐	**20** ♑ 11:52PM	**21** ♑	**22** ♑	**23** ♒ 2:17AM 3rd Quarter
24 ♒	**25** ♓ 6:15AM	**26** ♓	**27** ♈ 12:10PM	**28** ♈	**29** ♉ 8:19PM	**30** ♉ Solar Eclipse **NM** 4:27PM

KEY: ♈ ARIES ♊ GEMINI ♌ LEO ♎ LIBRA ♐ SAGITTARIUS ♒ AQUARIUS

♉ TAURUS ♋ CANCER ♍ VIRGO ♏ SCORPIO ♑ CAPRICORN ♓ PISCES

FM FULL MOON **NM** NEW MOON **LE** LUNAR ECLIPSE **SE** SOLAR ECLIPSE

ARIES NEW MOON

Calling all trailblazers! Today's new moon in daring, pioneering Aries—the first sign of the zodiac—feels a lot like a bonus New Year for the world. Whether you're making a fresh start or taking a bold step forward on an existing project, plans accelerate quickly under this lunar lift. How can you turn your passions into reality? Whatever you begin today could yield an unprecedented bumper crop six months from now under the light of the Aries *full* moon. Begin inquiring into next steps. Ask the experts in your field and vocalize your newly-forming vision. You never know what influential stranger might be listening!

and in love...

Relationship reset time! Whether you're single, in a situationship or committed for the long haul, today's new moon in Aries blesses your heart with a deliciously fresh start. While you might feel "so over it," ditch the defeatism. Last week's bad date or frustrating argument is this week's lesson for how to do things differently in the future. Even if you're starting from scratch, take heart. The daring new moon in Aries gives you the courage to try again. With clever Mercury at a close angle, get creative! While the apps can be surprisingly fruitful, there are other ways to connect to people who share common interests, like joining a sports team or mastermind group. Couples: bring on the day trips, staycations and interactive fun!

MARS-SATURN MEETUP

Start your engines...wait, no, hit the brakes! Speed-demon Mars collides with Sunday-driver Saturn, a befuddling mashup that can give us all a case of whiplash. As the planets tangle in futuristic Aquarius, good luck figuring out the right next step for your life. It's probably best to just pull over to the side of the road and check the GPS! If you hit a speed bump, don't curse it. This may be a blessing in disguise. Perhaps you've been racing ahead without a proper plan in place. Cautious Saturn warns us that haste makes waste—is that a message you need to heed? If you've been stalled in neutral, Mars brings the jumper cables and gets you back on the freeway of life. Try to stay cool. In a week, Mars will pull ahead of Saturn and clarity will return. In the meanwhile, see if you can stop fixating on the future and just "be here now."

VENUS IN PISCES

Let the birds chirp louder and the bees amplify their buzz. Ardent Venus leaves airy, intellectual Aquarius and plunges into the fantasy-fueled waters of Pisces. The love planet is "exalted" in the sign of the Fish, meaning its alluring powers are extra potent during this four-week phase. If you reduce your speed, this enchanting cycle can spur a romantic renaissance. Relaxing will put you in a receptive state, ideal for creating magic and enjoying heart-opening moments. Try to keep one foot in the reality zone though! Pisces is the master of illusions, which works for composing love sonnets but can be dodgy when it comes to screening Tinder dates. Run the background searches (and take your time!) to avoid falling head over red soles for someone who isn't 100 percent available or reliable. Couples may need to do some forgiveness work or process old pain that's blocking intimacy. The good news is, with Venus in Pisces, you can really go deep!

WAXING QUARTER MOON IN CANCER

9 APR

Could your space use a refresh? Today's waxing quarter moon in Cancer brings domestic dreams front and center. No need to overhaul your entire décor scheme. But how about painting (or wallpapering!) an accent wall, replacing standard pulls with decorative knobs, or setting up a closet system? If you're in the market for a move, start casually searching and setting up Zillow and Redfin alerts. Take a walk through neighborhoods you find inspiring. You could stumble upon an unexpected listing while you're meandering about.

4

MERCURY-PLUTO SQUARE

10 APR

Keep your best material under lock and key today. Although clever Mercury is shimmering brightly in attention-seeking Aries for a few final hours, it's on a collision course with controlling Pluto in Capricorn. Not only should you be more protective of your intellectual property, but also aware of audience receptivity. Even if you trot out a masterpiece, it will be hard to read the room. What looks like a lukewarm response could be a competitor taking note of your brilliant plan. (Have them sign an NDA!) Prepare to answer a lot of skeptical questions if you want to get a key player on board. The silver lining? Even if they say "no," you'll know exactly where you need to build a stronger case or do more research to make your plan absolutely bulletproof. If someone makes you an offer, do plenty of digging before you commit.

MERCURY IN TAURUS

10 - 29 APR

If your dreams are going to thrive, you need to bolster them with concrete plans. Good news! Today, savvy Mercury swings into efficient Taurus, bringing bonus support in the project management department. From budgets to timelines to human resources, how can you get your vision running like a well-oiled machine? If you've put the cart before the horse, slow your roll. Simplify anything that's become overly complex...but not at the expense of luxury! Tasteful Taurus loves life's finer things, as long as they also serve a purpose. Maybe it's time to invest in an ergonomic desk chair or live-edge wood table to style up a conference room.

JUPITER-NEPTUNE MEETUP

12 APR

Rainbows and unicorns! Magic is in the air as jovial Jupiter unites with dreamweaver Neptune, their first conjunction in 13 years. When these heavenly hedonists join forces, miracles happen! And since this meetup is happening in enchanting Pisces, it's anyone's guess what can unfold. While you certainly don't want to limit yourself, *do* keep some awareness of boundaries. The sky is the limit, as Jupiter and Neptune love to plumb the depths. Unchecked, this can easily lead to unhealthy excess. Stay off the slippery slopes and look for the kind of fun you can have on stable ground.

MARS IN PISCES

14 APR - 24 MAY

Going with the flow could be the quickest path to productivity for the next eight weeks as make-it-happen Mars floats into dreamy Pisces. Just as you sit down to focus on your daily tasks, you could get diverted to the Enchanted Forest...or onto some other random but fascinating quest. Carve out time for creativity, but *do* keep one eye on the clock. Reminder alarms are a saving grace during this cycle. Mars in Pisces is not exactly directional—but it IS quite dreamy. The next six weeks are an ideal time for plumbing the depths, exploring life's mysteries and bringing more compassion into daily interactions. Add more soul to your goals. How can your work uplift others, making them feel seen, valued and inspired?

and in love...

Life could resemble a page-turning fairy tale as lusty Mars joins Venus in Pisces. During this passionate, poetic cycle, love's fast-moving current could sweep you off to enchanted shores. But in the sign of healing and fantasy, you could get pulled into a quixotic or even clandestine attraction. Part of you will relish getting caught up in these wild feelings, but deception (including self-deception) could be at play. Attached? This transit is ideal for a couple's retreat or long-overdue healing work. In an increasingly divided world, this Mars phase can act as a soothing salve and, since Pisces rules the feet, an invitation to walk a mile in each other's shoes. It's time to shift your closest relationships—and the collective conscience—by choosing love over fear and hate.

LIBRA FULL MOON

16
APR

Solo acts could become joint ventures as the annual full moon in Libra inspires cooperation over competition. With these peaceful skies overhead, you can have a fruitful dialogue with people who, quite frankly, have been a thorn in your side. Yes, everyone's going to have to give a little here. But with patience, you can align around everything from vision to process to agenda. Pro tip: Talk less and practice active listening instead. Mirror back people's points and ask questions like, "Did I hear you correctly?" or, "Do you agree?" instead of rapid-fire responding. If your team has been adrift, call a summit. Over the next two weeks—peak manifesting time for these magnanimous moonbeams—you can get back on the same page with colleagues and business partners. Remember, splitting everything 50/50 isn't the only recipe for playing fair. In fact, trying to force that might be part of the breakdown. How can you divide up responsibilities to play to each person's needs and strengths?

and in love...

You'll get clear signs about a relationship's potential as the annual full moon in Libra opens hearts and minds. Connections that have been percolating for the past six months could reach a defining moment. Couples may decide to combine forces in a more official way or finally blast off on a co-created project that brings more pleasure and playtime to your lives. Has there been a lack of equanimity in your closest partnerships? Over the next two weeks, negotiate more harmonious ways of interacting. In some cases, this may involve bringing in a third party, like a couple's therapist—or a contractor like a bookkeeper or house cleaning service, who can do the "dirty work" that the two of you keep squabbling over.

4

MERCURY-URANUS MEETUP

<table>
<tr><td>18
APR</td></tr>
</table>

The only thing constant is change today as agile Mercury buzzes into an exact conjunction with chaotic Uranus. With these two clever "cosplayers" in pragmatic Taurus, a financial or work-related epiphany could strike. If you've been frustrated with a project's direction or struggling to figure out next steps, get in a huddle with friends who think outside the box. The solution may be a hive-mind happy hour away! Since both planets rule technology, look for apps that can help you stay on top of confusing details. Or set up a Pinterest mood board to gather inspiration. Today may be a turning point for you in an important area of your life as these two clever planets unite. Think (and seek!) beyond the obvious for new opportunities.

4

SUN-PLUTO SQUARE

<table>
<tr><td>18
APR</td></tr>
</table>

Who's the boss? Power struggles erupt under a twice-per-year standoff between the ego-ruled Sun and domineering Pluto. As intense reactions rise to the surface, it's easy to overreact or worse, lose control of your emotions. Although you have every right to be upset if you feel oppressed, a hotheaded reaction could torch an important opportunity. If you choose to stand up to a forceful person, show your strength by remaining composed. However, with both planets in unyielding cardinal signs, it will be hard to *not* push back forcefully. If things get heated, take a time-out and resolve this another day.

APR 19 - MAY 20

SUN IN TAURUS

Taurus season begins as the Sun hunkers down in the zodiac's bullpen for a month. For the past four weeks, Aries has been stoking our creativity and originality. Now the rubber meets the road: Which of these innovative Ram-fueled visions can we legit bring to life? Don the project manager's fedora and add practical magic to the recipe. No need to rush! Since Taurus is both sensible AND sensual, the next four weeks are as much about ritualizing a beautiful process as they are about yielding results. Carefully consider every detail of a plan. An elegant outcome is just as important as creating something useful.

and in love...

Bring it in! Intimate relationships are the sweetest of all for the coming four weeks as the Sun beams in traditional Taurus. Reconnect to family and close friends. Dating someone new and promising? This is the perfect time to introduce them to your crew and (hopefully!) get their stamp of approval. Not that you need it, of course. Shared values are the glue that keep people together when the Bull is ruling the skies. What matters is that you and the object of your affection see eye to eye on the important stuff, like personal ethics and lifestyle. Long-term couples should make an effort to sync your schedules—and not just for practicality's sake. Get some date nights on the calendar, and level up a few of them so that they're earthy and decadent.

WANING QUARTER MOON IN AQUARIUS

23
APR

You can't please everyone, so you might as well make yourself happy. That's an ethos to embrace under today's waning quarter moon in individualistic Aquarius. When you're true to yourself, you attract kindred spirits with whom you share an authentic connection. Test the waters, backing away from groups where you have to put on a faux personality. Simultaneously, how about connecting to a crew who seems to share your ideals? Aquarius rules technology, so your entourage might even form online. Are you a superconnector? Bring your people together around a common cause. With humanitarian Aquarius vibes in the air, bonus if it does good for the world!

MERCURY-SATURN SQUARE

24
APR

Stubbornness could derail forward momentum today as Mercury in tenacious Taurus battles authoritative Saturn in progress-driven Aquarius. Since people's resistance to new ideas will be high, wait a few days before presenting anything edgy or controversial. (Or at least, roll it out in bite sizes.) If you're the one seeing red flags, it's definitely wise to tap the brakes. Ask all the questions and do your own research. But if you're being overly skeptical out of fear, stop yourself. At a certain point, there are no guarantees. Taking a calculated risk might be the best you can do.

4

VENUS-NEPTUNE MEETUP

Two of the solar system's dreamiest co-stars—Venus and Neptune—spoon shamelessly in poetic Pisces. Reality? Take a pass on that. This cosmic connection only comes once annually, opening hearts everywhere. This heavenly heart-to-heart brings a fairy-tale quality to all romantic interactions. While it's easy to get swept away, try to keep one glass slipper planted on solid ground. The risk of this fantasy-fueled energy is that you could get sucked into a charming player's undertow. Since Pisces is the sign of forgiveness, this peacekeeping mashup supports all fence-mending activities. If you're the one extending the olive branch, why not sweeten the deal with a flower arrangement or custom playlist?

MERCURY IN GEMINI

Mic drops: incoming! Voluble Mercury throws a homecoming rager as he zooms into Gemini and pours a double shot of articulation! There's no time like the present to start working on your memoir, record a podcast episode, or stream multi-screen TikToks or Instagram Lives with guests. When Mercury is in Gemini, it's dynamic duos for the win! Wordplay could be foreplay during this cycle and intellectual repartee will be the ultimate glue for kindred spirits. But plan ahead! A retrograde begins May 10 which may cause technical difficulties and data issues. Back up all those files!

PLUTO RETROGRADE IN CAPRICORN

29 APR - 8 OCT

Veiled intentions may become even murkier starting today as Pluto slows its calculating roll and backs into its annual five-month retrograde. If you keep hitting the same wall, take a break from playing detective. This introspective cycle is ideal for flipping the lens inward and doing your own soul searching. But don't drop your guard completely. With the hypersensitive planet in snooze mode, you may be extra susceptible to people's shady schemes. It's a powerful time for inner transformation and forgiveness work, or to dive into research. When Pluto pivots back into direct motion on October 8, those mysteries may have solved themselves!

4

VENUS-JUPITER MEETUP

30 APR

Heart explosions: incoming! As supersizer Jupiter nuzzles up to seductive Venus in Pisces, we could all melt into giant puddles of mush...or morph into the sultriest sirens the world has ever seen. The Venus-Jupiter duo calls for love that is passionate, limitless, honest and true. Let fauxmances crumble and situationships implode. There are 7.6 billion people on the planet, and at least three who could be your soulmate. Keep reeling in the same sad sacks? Stop fishing in that factory-farm pond and cast your line into wider oceans where you might find someone wild and fresh. Since Jupiter is the global ambassador, diversify your dating portfolio. Need to rev things up with your amour? A change of scenery will get your blood pumping!

Partial solar eclipse!

TAURUS NEW MOON

30 APR

Stability without mobility? Not this year! Normally the new moon in Taurus stops the action and helps you get your feet on solid ground. But in 2021, this lunar lift arrives as a game-changing solar eclipse, which shifts your view to the next stage of the game. Put your mind on your money—and your material security in general—but think about it in two ways. First, if you've been burning through cash, put out those fires and wrestle your spending under control. Second, get proactive! Let these momentum-boosting moonbeams spur you toward greater earnings, even if that means doing something dramatically out of character. When opportunity knocks, don't hesitate! A speedy answer is needed to capitalize on the gifts of an eclipse.

and in love...

Sensuality is the name of the game as the year's only new moon in Taurus activates all five of your senses. But what will leave you tingling from head to toe? Since this new moon is an electrifying solar eclipse, it packs an extra charge...and challenge! How can you level up your skills in the lovemaking department? Hint: Focus on foreplay, touch and anything body based. Since Taurus rules our material possessions, couples may find themselves at odds about finances or values. This is your cue to get it all out in the open and, ideally, attempt to resolve your differences. Stay open to the creative and surprising solutions a solar eclipse can reveal!

MAY *Moon Phases*

SUN	MON	TUE	WED	THU	FRI	SAT
1 ♉	**2** ♊ 6:47AM	**3** ♊	**4** ♋ 7:05PM	**5** ♋	**6** ♋	**7** ♌ 7:50AM
8 ♌ 1st Quarter	**9** ♍ 6:53PM	**10** ♍	**11** ♍	**12** ♎ 2:34AM	**13** ♎	**14** ♏ 6:34AM
15 ♏	**16** LE ♏ 12:14AM ♐ 7:51AM	**17** ♐	**18** ♑ 8:02AM	**19** ♑	**20** ♒ 8:53AM	**21** ♒
22 ♓ 11:50AM 3rd Quarter	**23** ♓	**24** ♈ 5:40PM	**25** ♈	**26** ♈	**27** ♉ 2:23AM	**28** ♉
29 ♊ 1:23PM	**30** ♊ New Moon 7:30AM	**31** ♊				

KEY: ♈ ARIES ♊ GEMINI ♌ LEO ♎ LIBRA ♐ SAGITTARIUS ♒ AQUARIUS
♉ TAURUS ♋ CANCER ♍ VIRGO ♏ SCORPIO ♑ CAPRICORN ♓ PISCES

FM FULL MOON **NM** NEW MOON **LE** LUNAR ECLIPSE **SE** SOLAR ECLIPSE

VENUS IN ARIES

2 - 28 MAY

Get ready for a blast of blazing heat as vixen Venus vaults into Aries, igniting a passionate spring awakening! Impulse control will be scarce, but as a rule of thumb, zip and unzip judiciously. Venus is in "detriment" in Aries, a tricky placement for the cosmic seductress. Feelings run hot and cold, attractions sizzle then fizzle. Devoted partners may question their loyalty when they experience a burst of scorching chemistry...with someone else. On the plus side, Venus in adventurous Aries can break up stagnancy. (Bye-bye love drought!) Since Aries is the zodiac's warrior, it might take an explosive lovers' quarrel to reignite the sparks that lead to exothermic makeup sex.

WAXING QUARTER MOON IN LEO

8 MAY

Curtains up? As the waxing quarter moon debuts its theatrical talents in Leo, a little bit of drama goes a long way. A few glittering touches can elevate the mundane into the magical—but please, use them sparingly. With this being a moderate quarter moon, you want to keep things "elegantly understated." A week from now, you can wow the world with your epic drop under the enchanting light of the full moon. Until then, tease out the release by sharing just enough sparkle to entice the crowds.

MERCURY RETROGRADE IN GEMINI & TAURUS

10 MAY - 3 JUN

Signals scramble and systems go sideways as Mercury flips into its second retrograde of the year. Once again, the communication planet backs up through a pair of zodiac signs, bringing two distinct waves to its dramatic effects. Until May 22, we may feel a double dose of communication chaos, as Mercury retreats through its home sign of Gemini. Expect friction in peer partnerships and do your best to avoid getting roped into taking sides. Triple-check your words before posting, sending or signing anything. Since Gemini rules transportation, try to hold off on purchasing anything with wheels until early June. Got an unfinished manuscript, podcast or workshop idea? Blow off the dust: This *is* an excellent time to take a deeper look and make revisions. On May 22, the buzzy planet backs into reality-checker Taurus, throwing everyone's sense of security into a bit of a tailspin. Budgets, schedules and relationship rules will demand keenness and clarity. Assume nothing and try to stay nimble—even while everyone around you is stubbornly digging in their heels!

5

JUPITER IN ARIES

**10 MAY -
28 OCT**

What's new, innovative and never been done before? No, that's not a riddle. But it's where our collective focus shifts for the next five and a half months. As grandiose Jupiter revs its engines in Aries, it restarts its journey through the zodiac. This enterprising cycle is all about breaking barriers, developing new philosophies and candidly calling things like we see them. With everyone's gambling instincts red hot, there's a danger of leaping without looking. Leadership grabs and diva duels could leave jaws on the ground (and power structures in tatters). For best results, take the initiative in all areas of life, but play fair! It's hard to be patient with process and protocol now, but avoid rushing to the finish line. After October 28, Jupiter backs into Pisces again, then returns to Aries for another lap, starting December 20. clarity will return. In the meanwhile, see if you can stop fixating on the future and just "be here now."

Total lunar eclipse!

SCORPIO FULL MOON

16
MAY

Power mergers, shocking scandals and sudden transitions—oh my! Expect major shake-ups as a total lunar (full moon) eclipse in Scorpio lifts the veil on behind-the-scenes developments. You may learn that a key player is exiting a project or management is changing hands. This is the first eclipse in Scorpio since October 2014. If you've merged assets, the partnership might reach a pivotal turning point. Do you plan to move forward? If so, a longer, rock-solid commitment is advised. But if this duet doesn't align with your soul purpose, you may want (or need!) to bow out. Investment opportunities may appear unexpectedly, or someone may reach out with an offer to fund your work. Since eclipses always bring an X factor, harness Scorpio's investigative powers and thoroughly research anyone you're getting into bed with, literally or figuratively. On a purely positive note, this eclipse can bring a legendary burst of creative genius. And thanks to la luna's trine to Mars and Neptune in Pisces— and a sextile from Pluto in Capricorn—it's the kind of support that puts your name on the map.

5

and in love...

Intensity ignites as the year's only Scorpio full moon—a doubly potent total lunar eclipse—electrifies the ether. An erotic connection that's been bubbling since last November could explode into a bodice-ripping embrace. No more bedroom boredom! Invite more sultry fun and games into your playtime. Have you been waffling about the future state of your union? This all-or-nothing eclipse demands an answer: Are you in or are you out? Nothing short of a rock-solid commitment will do. Forget staying involved out of a sense of obligation. If you're *really, really* in, the eclipse will power up your connection with soulful sensuality. Be warned: With an eclipse rocking this mysterious sector—and connecting to Neptune and Pluto—a buried secret may be revealed. (Chill with that jealousy...) Can you let down your guard and be vulnerable? If trust has been earned, this could be the opportunity you didn't even know you were waiting for to bare your soul and cement a crucial bond!

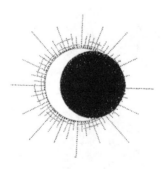

MARS-NEPTUNE MEETUP

If you catch yourself in a lucid dream, don't panic! It's just the befuddling, biennial conjunction of aggressive Mars and passive Neptune. As they meet up at the same degree of Pisces for a totally awkward dance, it's hard to tell an oasis from a mirage. That's good reason to hold off on making any binding decisions, especially if fear or FOMO kicks in. Wait a few days until the fog of Neptune burns off—no matter how impatient Mars is making you feel! What this every-other-year transit is good for? Getting in touch with the "peaceful warrior" inside yourself. Mars is a planet of action while Neptune rules compassion: How can you stand up for what you believe in while turning enemies into friends? This daunting task is worth taking on!

and in love...

Oh, sweet surrender! Your imagination is on fire as lusty Mars teams up with fantasy-fueler Neptune—their first tete-a-tete in two years. Under these soft-filtered skies, it'll be easy to get swept up in daydreams and more so, a lusty encounter. There's no telling what a kiss will lead to, but we promise you it's unlikely to stop at "just a kiss." With these planets entwined in fluid Pisces, good luck stopping the current of attraction once you break the dam! All's fair in love, true. But that doesn't mean you should let integrity fly out the window. Nefarious actions still have consequences. Run from temptation that could destroy existing commitments and choose a clear safeword if you're "experimenting." Be realistic about believing people's promises, especially if they're whispered in the heat of the moment

SUN IN GEMINI

Two is everyone's favorite number starting today as the Sun beams into Gemini until June 21. But that's not to say three, four or five is a crowd! This buzzy solar season turns us all into social butterflies, fluttering from one entourage to another. This solar cycle is known to heat up neighborhood activity. Patronize area venues and stimulate the economy by shopping local when you can. Considering bi-city living? Test the commuter waters and see how it flows. In the sign of the Twins, it's fun to have a plus-one as a companion for all favorite activities. Find a buddy for working out, going to shows or sharing services like babysitting and carpooling. (Note: You can have different "twins" for each activity!) As the cosmic communicator, Gemini gets us excited to write, broadcast, and make media. Get ideas out of your head and into the world!

and in love...

Gemini season begins with a fickle flourish, making variety the sexiest spice between now and June 21. Holding a long conversation—much less anyone's lasting attention—could be an almost comedic effort when you're in a room full of attractive people. As heads swivel and promising options intermittently ghost, just do your best to *not* react to every plot twist. If you want to keep a relationship at cruising altitude, be "a lover and a best friend." In other words, cut your boo some slack for being human. Yes, this means you can give yourself a little wiggle room too. Looking isn't the same as touching. And if it turns you both on, talk about who you each find attractive. That said, texting a random hottie at 2AM is not going to win any "get out of jail free" cards! In sapiosexual Gemini, seduction begins between the ears. Wordplay is foreplay!

WANING QUARTER MOON IN PISCES

22 MAY

Today's waning quarter moon in Pisces activates your compassion. Stop doomscrolling and start doing something about those triggering headlines. Could you donate to a fundraiser or join a volunteer group in your community? One small act of kindness can make a world of difference—do what you can! On the flip side, if you've been drowning in other people's sorrows, these balancing moonbeams bring back the boundaries. While you can empathize with other people and empower them, you can only feel your own feelings. Pump up the self-care so you have the energy to support the ones you love.

5

MERCURY RETROGRADE IN TAURUS

22 MAY - 3 JUN

The devil is in the details starting today, as retrograde Mercury slips back one zodiac sign, from buzzy Gemini into business-first Taurus. For the rest of its retreat—until June 3—we'll feel the plodding, stubborn slowdown of the Bull at play. Pro tip: If a string of green lights suddenly turns red, don't charge ahead like a tempestuous toro! Instead, see this forced timeout as a hidden blessing. Go back to the drawing board and review all your plans, from budgets to timelines. Don't make any sudden money moves! With Mercury scrambling signals, it's hard to tell a lemon from a luxury steal.

MARS IN ARIES

24 MAY – 5 JUL

Go-getter Mars hosts a seven-week homecoming party in its native sign of Aries—and it's going to be a rager! As this double-dose of warrior energy permeates the collective psyche, the feisty red planet demands that we choose a "side" and stand up for what we know is right. A word to the wise: Find a physical outlet for blowing off steam, because egos and tempers could rage out of control. On a personal level, Mars in Aries wakes you up and gets you psyched to take initiative. Embrace the competitive spirit! Just remember that the real goal is simply to be the best version of *you*.

and in love...

Swagger alert! Lusty Mars fans its feathers in Aries, peacocking through the Ram's realm for seven arousing weeks. Like the legendary opening of Studio 54, this "more is more" cycle removes any shame barriers around desire and erotic expression. Is that a good thing? Absolutely, as long as you stay alert! Between now and July 5, life-changing experiences can break open unconscious biases around sexuality and gender. Yet when Mars is in Aries, what begins as "Dionysian" can turn destructive fast. Anger is a touchstone for both this planet and sign. What begins as a basic lover's quarrel could snowball into a nuclear meltdown. Jealousy, even if well-founded, could spur irrational acts. Taking cool-down breaks will be essential to saving everyone's sanity...and reputations.

VENUS-PLUTO SQUARE

27 MAY

Vivacious Venus in Aries gets side-swiped by possessive Pluto in Capricorn as the two lock into a tense square. What one person considers "harmless banter" may churn up jealousy and a flurry of unfounded accusations. Or *not* so unfounded. This shadowy square brings the players out of the woodwork. If someone's story (or omission of details) raises red flags, trust your intuition and investigate. The married person who is "only staying together for the kids" could turn into the heart-wrenching scourge of your warm-weather fun. Does a date keep postponing? Don't send another rescheduling request—leave the ball in their court and turn your attention to other options. Couples: Avoid triggering topics today. With tempers simmering like active volcanoes, disagreements could erupt in a damaging way.

5

VENUS IN TAURUS

28 MAY - 22 JUN

If you'd rather be soul food than eye candy, here's some delicious news. Sweet, sensual Venus comes home to traditional Taurus today, bringing a deeper dimension to all romantic interactions. While attraction is essential, common values are the glue. Between now and June 22, radar in on people who share your views on all the key topics from money to spirituality to lifestyle. Venus in Taurus can make us all a touch old-fashioned, placing a high premium on comfortable, consistent companionship. Wherever you are on the romantic continuum, relationships can turn more serious under the stabilizing spell of Taurus. But don't forget to pamper yourself and spoil the ones you love. "Too much of a good thing" feels like the perfect dose of pleasure now.

MARS-JUPITER MEETUP

Kaboom! May 29 is a big deal day, as make-it-happen Mars teams up with make-it-bigger Jupiter at the same degree of Aries. Even if motivation's been lagging, you could suddenly feel like you downed a multipack of 5 Hour Energy drinks. These two accelerators connect once every two years, but they haven't teamed up in Aries since 2011. For the record, that was a year when ambitions soared so high that people started styling their hair in the "Snooki Pouf" a la the spray-tanned Jersey Shore icon. (Note to beauty editors reading this, we'd be grateful if you DON'T bring that trend back...) But as this pair of brash planets pass over the same zodiac point, there's no stopping anyone from living out loud—or living their truth! On the global stage, there could be some shocking power plays and "for the people" revolutions like the Arab Spring that was waging during the last Mars-Jupiter meetup in Aries.

5

GEMINI NEW MOON

Kindred spirits come out of the woodwork today as the year's only new moon in Gemini sparks synergies. The spirit of cooperation is in the air. And with these "twinning" vibes ignited, your perfect partner-in-crime may already be installed within your very own circle of friends. Need to upgrade your transportation? Start shopping around for your new ride, like an eco-chic electric car or bike. (Though we recommend waiting at least a week after Mercury ends its retrograde on June 3 to make any final purchases.) As the ruler of peer-to-peer relationships, the Gemini new moon may kindle a fresh chapter with a sibling, neighbor or coworker.

5

and in love...

Don't judge a book by its cover! But definitely peek at what paperback that coffeeshop cutie is reading. (Hello, opening line...) The new moon in brainy Gemini kicks up savvy repartee with plenty of witty wordplay thrown in. That's sure to make anyone swoon under the spell of this sapiosexual new moon. If you've been looking for love in all the wrong places, switch it up. Where are the thoughtful, curious and culturally aware people hanging out? Over the next two weeks, you could meet your match in an online mastermind, weekend workshop or discussion group. Or they might just be hanging out at your local pub trivia night. Conversation is key to fostering any sort of deeper connections. Coupled? Stop recycling the same "how was your day" chatter. If you don't have any new subjects to hash out, consider trying something new, exciting and worthy of post-game analysis! Novelty brings a rush of dopamine, which brings a burst of sexual energy. Oh, heyyyy there...

JUNE *Moon Phases*

SUN	MON	TUE	WED	THU	FRI	SAT
			1 ♋ 1:49AM	**2** ♋	**3** ♌ 2:38PM	**4** ♌
5 ♌	**6** ♍ 2:22AM	**7** ♍ 1st Quarter	**8** ♎ 11:23AM	**9** ♎	**10** ♏ 4:41PM	**11** ♏
12 ♐ 6:32PM	**13** ♐	**14** ♑ 6:14PM **FM** ♐ 7:51AM	**15** ♑	**16** ♒ 5:44PM	**17** ♒	**18** ♓ 7:02PM
19 ♓	**20** ♈ 11:37PM 3rd Q ♓	**21** ♈ 3rd Quarter	**22** ♈	**23** ♉ 7:58AM	**24** ♉	**25** ♊ 7:14PM
26 ♊	**27** ♊	**28** ♋ 7:52AM **NM** ♋ 10:52PM	**29** ♋	**30** ♌ 8:40PM		

KEY: ♈ ARIES ♊ GEMINI ♌ LEO ♎ LIBRA ♐ SAGITTARIUS ♒ AQUARIUS
♉ TAURUS ♋ CANCER ♍ VIRGO ♏ SCORPIO ♑ CAPRICORN ♓ PISCES

FM FULL MOON **NM** NEW MOON **LE** LUNAR ECLIPSE **SE** SOLAR ECLIPSE

6

MERCURY DIRECT IN TAURUS

3
JUN

Mercury wraps up a three-week retrograde today, pivoting forward in Taurus. Situations that have been bound up in red tape for the past few weeks could soon get the green light needed to move ahead, albeit slowly. Caution: What seemed like a glittering opportunity a few days ago may lack enough practical value to justify the investment of time and money. (Yes, those persnickety details *do* matter when Mercury is in the Bull's pen.) If you've been stuck in a stubborn deadlock since May 10, do what it takes to break that heat. Perhaps some key information surfaced over the last couple weeks. Factor it in—the changes you make may be a blessing in disguise.

SATURN RETROGRADE
IN AQUARIUS

4 JUN -
23 OCT

Come in for a landing—yes, even if you've orbited light years from base. Structured Saturn flips into its annual, five-month retrograde, a time meant for tune-ups and audits. This year, the backspin goes down in "space cadet" Aquarius, which can put the kibosh on anything wildly experimental...or mildly innovative. While you don't have to abort your mission, do send your inner mad scientist back to the lab. Run more tests before you forge ahead again. Progress can be a double-edged sword after all. With Saturn in "one love" Aquarius, take time to assess the impact your efforts are having on different communities. Have unconscious biases crept in? Are you using technology ethically and effectively? On a personal level, do you see more effective ways to collaborate with family, colleagues and neighbors? Answering questions like these can elevate all your missions once Saturn powers forward on October 23. Game-changing!

WAXING QUARTER MOON IN VIRGO

7
JUN

Better done than perfect? Those are infamous last words under the exacting beams of today's waxing quarter moon in Virgo. So if you catch yourself rushing to get 'er done, slow down immediately. Skipping integrity checks on a day like this could have costly, even detrimental, effects. This is especially true where health and safety are concerned. If you have a kernel of doubt about how to proceed, it's better to "look bad" by 'fessing up than to fake it until you (don't actually) make it. On the plus side, your attention to detail could win you the proverbial merit badge, not to mention people's undying loyalty.

6

VENUS-URANUS MEETUP

11
JUN

Change may be the only constant today as seductive Venus shares a flight path with disruptor Uranus. The fact that both planets are conjunct in steady, sensual Taurus is a silver lining. All the same, it's hard to ground yourself in the face of any unexpected romantic developments. Your love life may take a sudden detour, or an unanticipated expression of desire (on your part or someone else's) could catch you way off guard. This may feel heaven-sent. But if you're in a relationship that's been on shaky ground, these seismic shifts might topple it. Single? With love planet Venus logged in to techie Uranus' network, dating apps will be lit. Couples may feel boldly experimental, which could direct everything from bedroom play to adventure-planning. Just talking about a two-week road trip or taking a class on tantra could refresh your zest.

MERCURY IN GEMINI

Is the grass *really* greener on the other side of the fence? You won't know until you meander over and check it out for yourself. The timing is perfect for semi-random discovery missions, as curious Mercury shifts back into its home sign of Gemini for three more weeks. This is the buzzy messenger planet's second trip through Twinseltown. Look back to see what surfaced from April 29 to May 22, and moreover, whom? A friendship that kindled then dwindled could get a second act. Slide into those DMs and re-break the ice with a witty line, interesting link or some other clever conversation starter.

6

Supermoon!

SAGITTARIUS FULL MOON

14
JUN

Hitch your wagon to a vintage VW bus! (Then go and hitch THAT baby to a star.) The full Sagittarius supermoon lights up the skies, activating extreme wanderlust and a desire for limitless expansion. Work travel could take you to exciting ports over the next two weeks. Since Sagittarius rules education, sign up for a seminar in a different city...and see if the company will cover (some) costs. Got a skill to pass along? Teaching could pad your pockets, or if you need to brush up to keep up, sign up for the necessary training. (Your wallet will thank you.) The enterprising energy of this full moon is like a round of celestial start-up "funding." If you have an idea for a business—or a project that will put your name on the company leaderboard—the mission could really get in motion over the next two weeks. The only requirement? A willingness to stick your neck out for what you believe in!

and in love...

Do you need to diversify your dating portfolio? If you keep going out with the same person in a different package over and over (and over!), that would be an obvious "yes!" And that goes double for couples who have slipped into an old-marrieds groove. Yawn no more! Today's fiery and excitement-boosting full supermoon in Sagittarius activates the spirit of adventure! Expand beyond comfortable and familiar "borders." This full moon favors multicultural mingling, baecations and romantic retreats where you can learn a sultry new skill like erotic massage or tantra. How far are you willing to travel beyond your comfort zone? This full moon gives everyone the gambler's instinct. Stuck in a rut? A nakedly honest conversation can bring back the heat.

SUN-NEPTUNE SQUARE

16 JUN

Triple-check directions as the distractible Sun in Gemini squares nebulous Neptune in Pisces. Under this twice-a-year dust-up, it's too easy to get swept into the role of the rescuer, hero or "the only one who understands" a tortured soul. Sacrifices can bring a temporary high, but it's a slippery slope...and one that can lead to a bottomless pit of (co)dependency. Looking for a healer? Guard against charismatic figures who get YOU hyped up with big promises and no action plans. That said, the Sun-Neptune square *can* move a stuck needle. Thanks to this boundary-loosening mashup, you may finally work up the nerve to discuss your deepest fears and reveal your buried brilliance!

6

VENUS-SATURN SQUARE

18 JUN

Romantic reality check! Doe-eyed Venus in Taurus gets body-checked by structured, pragmatic Saturn in Aquarius. Which means, come down from Cloud 9 and deal with what's actually happening. This could be a minor issue or a major ordeal. Either way, a pragmatic approach is warranted. While it's never fun to learn things the hard way, make sure you track the teachings of this tough lesson! But don't punish yourself—that won't help heal your heart. On a creative note, the Venus-Saturn square can be beneficial for brainstorming. Pop on Venus' rose-colored glasses and borrow Saturn's project management chapeau. When you run your creative ideas through a quality-control filter, you may come up with a solution that's not only genius, but also completely doable.

WANING QUARTER MOON IN PISCES

20
JUN

Be honest: Is a once-stimulating situation feeling as dry as cold, unbuttered toast? Instead of waiting for "the universe" to make it all better, park yourself in an inspiring location like a lakeside park or a glamorous bistro. Close your eyes and let your imagination flow. If there were no barriers here (time, money, annoying people), how *would* you want things to develop? Allow the waning quarter moon in Pisces to help you weave that dream. Then tap into the Law of Attraction, focusing on your idealized picture—and maybe turning it into a vision board for further psychic stimulation. Ask your angels, guides and earthly mentors for an assist with making this so. Today, support could show up in "hidden" places.

6

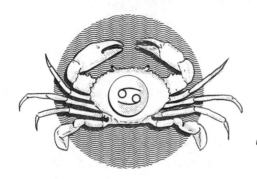

SUN IN CANCER

The Sun floats into Cancer today, arriving as it does every year with the summer solstice. For the past month, Gemini's solar flares have given us all a case of astrological ADHD. Focusing deeply on anyone's words much less remembering what events we promised we'd show up at, has been... trying. But now, the friends-and-family reunions begin. With Cancerian warmth nurturing our souls, nesting instincts are on high alert. Give your innermost circle priority on the calendar. Bonus if that involves a beach vacation or whipping up home-cooked meals together! Speaking of which, does your home feel like a haven? And how about your workspace? Take time to personalize all your square-footage with sweet and cozy touches. The longest, lightest day of the year is a powerful moment of personal illumination. (And a day of deep introspection for our friends below the equator.) Tender emotions that have been buried beneath our shells are ready to be examined—with journals, supportive friends, and maybe a great therapist. For the coming four weeks, creative bursts could give birth to transcendent works of art. Set up an inspiring "studio" and be a vessel for the muse.

and in love...

Cupid spins a sweet, old-fashioned love song for the next four weeks as the Cancer Sun casts a cozy spell over our lives. A warm heart is the ultimate accessory—and aphrodisiac—during this annual solar cycle. Don't be afraid to let your softer side show. As a water sign, Cancer inspires us to be fluid. It's anyone's guess who you'll cuddle up to between now and July 22. (Bonus if their embrace makes you feel right at home.) It's equally important to create a safe container for processing emotions, so they don't spill over into casual interactions or muddy boundaries. This "container" could be a pod of close friends who can talk you down from a tree. Or a private place to retreat to when you're feeling off center. Make room for all the feels now. Just don't confuse them with facts!

6

VENUS IN GEMINI

22 JUN - 17 JUL

Set your system to pairing mode! The search for kindred spirits is on—but not necessarily the marrying kind. Gemini governs our peers and platonic pals, but when Venus travels through this sign once every year, love may be found in the friend zone. If you feel attraction bubbling up, exploring can be fun...with a caveat. Will a night of fooling around bring drama to your social circle or break up the band? Think carefully before letting the love goggles blind you to potential collateral damages. If you are with a "happily ever after" plus-one, bring more playfulness to your time together. Take the classic advice of putting a weekly (or more often) date night on the calendar, switching off as planners and surprising each other with the agenda. Pro tip: Plan outings that spark dialogue! Conversation is an aphrodisiac while Venus hovers in this sapiosexual sign.

SUN-JUPITER SQUARE

28 JUN

Your ego is *not* your amigo, but good luck remembering that today! As the ultrasensitive Cancer Sun crashes into a square with arrogant Jupiter in Aries, pride steers the ship and people can be downright petty. Don't waste time trying to strike any deals, especially when adulting is a distant dream. Better to let everyone sulk (or fume!) in their corners. You can approach the topic again once smoke stops pouring out of your ears. While you wait for molehills to stop looking like mountains, see if you can find a common cause. While you may have very different approaches for achieving an end goal, *do* you actually want the same thing? Focusing on that may be the saving grace today—especially with someone you consider "family."

NEPTUNE RETROGRADE IN PISCES

28 JUN - 3 DEC

Life could feel like a giant reflecting pool starting today, as soothsayer Neptune dips into its annual retrograde until December 3. From 2011 to 2026, the numinous planet is paddling through its ruling sign of Pisces, doubling down on its mystical effects. This meditative five-month cycle can be a profound blessing, opening a window to heal core wounds, deal with addictions (from liquor to love to limiting beliefs) and tap into buried realms of creativity. Make sure to keep your psychic shield up, especially while in public. Like a sponge, you can absorb the mood of a room or get thrown off emotionally by a stranger's vibes. With fog-machine Neptune in the time out chair, you can cut through illusions...IF you are willing to take an unflinching audit of your life. Use this period to explore the shadows. Awareness is the key to evolution! By owning up to unhealthy patterns you can learn to break them. And get plenty of rest, because the best ideas may arrive while you're sleeping, meditating, or just staring at the clouds.

6

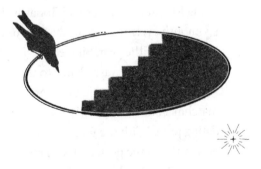

CANCER NEW MOON

"Show me the money!" Words made famous by Cancer Tom Cruise—and a mantra worth uttering under today's security-minded Cancer new moon. Having "enough to get by" is a great place to start, but what's your plan for the future? While it may take six months (peak manifesting time for this new moon) to get a decent savings plan underway, let la luna refresh your outlook on abundance. Wouldn't you sleep better at night knowing that you had something tucked away? This could be your cue to downsize or, since Cancer is blessing your nest, start a cottage industry in your very own home. Speaking of which, this new moon could bring word of a real estate opportunity. If you've been considering a home equity loan for upgrades or a refinancing, begin exploring possibilities today.

6

and in love...

Catching feelings? That's an understatement under today's new moon in soulful, sentimental Cancer. This lunar lift can act like a cosmic bonding agent for couples who are ready to get cozy. Speaking of which, is it time to exchange keys or shop around for that love nest? Or maybe get plans going for your dream home? Today is the beginning of a six-month cycle that could shape your co-living situation by the end of the year. Single? Even if you weren't looking, at least give a sideways glance to the "nice guy" types. Family and friends could do a bang-up job of playing matchmaker. Take it slowly, but dip your toe back in that dating pool. With the focus on home, roots and emotional bonds, this is the perfect day to reach out to the nurturers in your life. Whether you share DNA or they occupy the esteemed title of "chosen family," having their support reminds you that you're never alone in the world.

JULY *Moon Phases*

SUN	MON	TUE	WED	THU	FRI	SAT
					1 ♌	**2** ♌
3 ♍ 8:32AM	**4** ♍	**5** ♎ 6:25PM	**6** ♎ 1st Quarter	**7** ♎	**8** ♏ 1:15AM	**9** ♏
10 ♐ 4:34AM	**11** ♐	**12** ♑ 5:01AM	**13** ♑ Full Moon 2:38PM	**14** ♒ 4:14AM	**15** ♒	**16** ♓ 4:18AM
17 ♓	**18** ♈ 7:18AM	**19** ♈	**20** ♉ 2:23PM 3rd Qtr ♈	**21** ♉	**22** ♉	**23** ♊ 1:11AM
24 ♊	**25** ♋ 1:54PM	**26** ♋	**27** ♋	**28** ♌ 2:36AM NM ♌ 1:55PM	**29** ♌	**30** ♍ 2:11PM
31 ♍						

KEY:

♈ ARIES	♊ GEMINI	♌ LEO	♎ LIBRA	♐ SAGITTARIUS	♒ AQUARIUS
♉ TAURUS	♋ CANCER	♍ VIRGO	♏ SCORPIO	♑ CAPRICORN	♓ PISCES

FM FULL MOON   **NM** NEW MOON   **LE** LUNAR ECLIPSE   **SE** SOLAR ECLIPSE

MARS-PLUTO SQUARE

1 JUL

As in-your-face Mars in Aries clashes with volcanic Pluto in Capricorn in a fierce, 90-degree square, a cesspool of secrets could spew to the surface. Though you may feel like running for cover, good luck turning away from this hot (lava) mess. If something feels off, follow your intuition and investigate. But be as stealthy as a panther! Clumsily handled cases could give the secret keepers a chance to destroy key evidence. On a personal level, moods may be stormy. Letting rage run rampant (a Mars-in-Aries pitfall) could bring a swift rebuke from vengeful Pluto. Under this dynamic mashup, risks—if warranted—should be calculated extremely cautiously.

MERCURY-NEPTUNE SQUARE

2 JUL

Take nothing at face value today as foggy Neptune obscures any data that intellectual Mercury brings to the surface. And don't expect any straight answers either. With both planets in dualistic signs (Mercury's in Gemini and Neptune's in Pisces), people are likely to talk out of both sides of their mouths. Dodge those mixed messages by quietly observing instead of attempting to hash things out in dialogue. Your own communications may be unclear. Avoid taking sides, unless you're certain about where you stand on a matter.

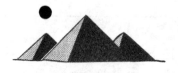

MARS IN TAURUS

Pick up the pace, but don't break the speed limit! As motivator Mars zooms into sensible Taurus, you can tackle your to-do list with a clear head on your shoulders. It's unwise to rush during this every-other-year cycle. Be like the tortoise and win the race by methodically moving through your missions, one step at a time. Seeking new opportunity? Don't rush to accept the first offer or plunk down your hard-earned cash without research. A bill may come due, and you could feel the pressure to pay it. Since Mars can ratchet up stress levels, soothe anxiety by slowing down and savoring simple pleasures like art, music, and nature. If some extra funds do land in your wallet, treat yourself to a luxurious but practical splurge. Think: investment piece.

and in love...

Lusty Mars charges into Taurus, elevating your senses and whetting everyone's appetite for affection. If you're not getting your RDA of TLC, do something to change that over the coming seven weeks. Create "slow down" rituals to get comfortable in your own body, like massaging oils into your skin, scheduling a massage and practicing gentle movement. Hop back on the apps when you're ready for some loving. Even if you have someone to cuddle with, you still have to set the mood. Create a relaxing environment with downtempo music, low lighting, and calming aromatherapy—and don't forget the food and wine! Taurus is the sign of traditional courtship gestures, but with impatient Mars hitting the gas, relationships may accelerate into serious status, fast! You may be tempted to splurge on pricey gifts and upscale dates. The downside? Combative Mars in headstrong Taurus can lead to formidable fights where nobody backs down easily. Of course, the sparks you set off with marathon makeup sex could be (almost) worth the trouble.

7

MERCURY IN CANCER

**5 - 19
JUL**

Messenger Mercury updates the global privacy policy as it wings into cozy, private Cancer for its annual retreat. Over the next few weeks, be discreet about what you share in whispered exchanges and on social media. The walls have ears! That said, all kinds of heartfelt exchanges warm up quickly with Mercury in the sign of the nurturing Crab. Make an extra effort to listen with compassion and speak gently since people will be more sensitive than usual. Get your spaces in order, from your home to your work zone. When you have any moments to spare, prioritize your inner circle. Bonding with family and close friends is the key to your work-life balance!

WAXING QUARTER MOON IN LIBRA

**6
JUL**

Peace at any price isn't actually peace at all. In fact, avoiding conflict can delay an important breakthrough. If you've been backing down from your beliefs, today's principled quarter moon in Libra helps you take a stand once again. Fortunately, Libra is the zodiac's diplomat, guiding you toward the high road as you (re) open charged discussions. Avoid personal insults and state your beliefs clearly. Back up any claims with well-researched evidence—and get ready! Digging for proof of concept could be eye-opening and you might realize that *you* are the one who needs to say, "I'm sorry." Don't stall—today's the day.

MERCURY-JUPITER SQUARE

9
JUL

What's the big idea? As mindful Mercury bangs into visionary Jupiter, it breaks our thinking out of the box. New possibilities could become tangible realities...fast! But tap the sensitivity of Mercury in Cancer and weigh it against the can-do momentum of Jupiter in Aries. It's great to blaze trails, but how will new developments affect the ecosystem of your life? If you forgot to consider feelings or ask for consent, you may need to revise plans. But that's not the same as people-pleasing! If you're hiding your truth because you don't want to make people "feel bad," play with being self-authorized and making a bold move.

VENUS-SATURN TRINE

13
JUL

Budding connections could blossom into something "seriously serious" as supportive Saturn in Aquarius locks eyes with radiant, romantic Venus in Gemini. Both planets are parked in buzzy air signs which fans Cupid's more tempestuous flames. But it's all good since this transit can light a bright fire in our hearts. Our heads too. A casual conversation may build into a legendary love affair! A word to the wise: check out mature options. Not necessarily in age, but in their ability to "adult" and be a trusty partner. If an existing relationship has been rocky, Saturn lends supportive scaffolding and Venus and helps us diplomatically discuss conflicts. Focus on solutions and try to remember that you're on the same team

7

Supermoon!

CAPRICORN FULL MOON

13 JUL

Destiny calling! Set your mid-year resolutions today, as the full supermoon in Capricorn illuminates the long, strategic view for accomplishing a mission. Bonus! The fate-fueling Taurus North Node sits at a supportive angle to the full moon, pushing you to think big-*big* picture. Whether or not you've found your life path, today is an important moment to hit pause and assess your progress. What's working and what's left you feeling like Sisyphus rolling a boulder up a hill? While tenacity is Capricorn's strong suit, so is productivity. Maybe there's a better route to the finish line, or a better team to support your vision. Also, what goals were in your crosshairs at the dawning of 2022, especially near the January 2 new supermoon? If you strayed off course, today's full moon motivates you to pick up the ball and run with it again. Did you bring this mission to fruition? Celebrate the victory of reaching your milestone!

and in love...

Take yourself on a date with destiny, as the full supermoon in Capricorn illuminates your romantic goals. Are you waiting for someone else to fulfill all your fantasies? Try a more proactive approach. See what happens if you operate by "the law of assumption" which hypothesizes that you can draw something (or someone!) to you by acting as if those circumstances already exist. For example, see what happens if you dress up and take yourself out for a fancy dinner. Sit at the bar and say hello to another solo patron. Or maybe you start house-hunting in the area you'd like to live with your someday-someone. If you're in a relationship, today could bring a perfect moment to dream together about next steps. But first, take time to appreciate the ways you've been there for each other over the last six months. An attitude of gratitude is the ultimate aphrodisiac today!

VENUS-NEPTUNE SQUARE

14 JUL

Assumptions are the enemy of intimacy! But that won't stop anyone from jumping to conclusions under today's foggy mashup of double-talking Venus in Gemini and obfuscating Neptune in Pisces. Catch yourself if you start to spiral. Are you reacting to reality or unconfirmed fears? Shield yourself from gossip or your friends' unsolicited opinions about your romantic choices. This is *your* life to live! If people are moody or running hot-and-cold, let them be. Your own disenchantment with a romantic interest may confuse you. Bottom line: These fickle skies make decision-making challenging, so hold off on issuing any decrees. Although this will take some self-restraint, accept your fluctuating feelings today without reflexively acting upon them.

VENUS IN CANCER

17 JUL - 11 AUG

Naughty by...nurture? As affectionate Venus snuggles into sentimental Cancer, summer love takes a turn for the sweeter. Slip into the couple bubble with your S.O. or make sure you have ample private time to simply enjoy each other's quiet company. Shower your love with caring gestures that prove you've been paying attention to their preferences, like streaming their favorite movies to preparing morning coffee exactly how they like it. Talks could turn to cohabitation—or make you put a spare key on your partner's ring. Just make sure you don't get too close for comfort! Time in your respective "shells" can make hearts grow fonder. Single? Give the nice ones a chance to woo you. If friends (or your mom!) want to fix you up, let them! Just be aware of how your fluctuating moods may impact a partner. If you're single, watch for neediness during this period, which can make you act too clingy, too quickly.

7

SUN-NEPTUNE TRINE

17 JUL

Feel free to hide out in your bubble today, whether that's under a beach umbrella or in a tub full of perfectly cool water. As the cozy Cancer Sun gets intimate with esoteric Neptune in Pisces, getting lost in your daydreams will be all the entertainment you need. Unless, of course, there's someone close by who wants to live out a fantasy with you. Pack a gourmet picnic (and a book of poems), and slip off to an isolated location where you can enjoy some uninterrupted bliss. With the food-obsessed Cancer Sun in the mix, this could turn into a Bacchanalian feast on a blanket.

SUN-PLUTO OPPOSITION

7

19 JUL

If you want answers, slip on the sleuthing hat and maybe throw down some tarot spreads. There will be so much going on below the surface that it will be impossible to interpret anything at face value. We're not saying you should treat perfect strangers like prime suspects. But if someone's motives seem questionable, tap Pluto's investigative powers and take a deeper look. Keep stormier feelings under wraps...and off of social media. With the Sun in emo Cancer, people are prone to taking things personally. Just don't be so esoteric that your cloak-and-dagger act arouses suspicion or makes you look like you are hiding something. Such a tricky line to walk!

MERCURY IN LEO

19 JUL - 4 AUG

Restore your roar! Communicator Mercury struts into loud, proud Leo, turning up the volume on creative expression. After a lowkey few weeks, this passionate cycle directs us back into the public eye. If you don't want to get lost in the shuffle, make a bolder statement! Use storytelling techniques and eye-popping visuals to underscore your message, whether you're pitching a business idea or posting on social media. Play with music, video, and any other effects that will get people to stop scrolling and tap on your profile. With heart-centered Leo playing communications director, there's no reason to be crisp and formal. As long as you don't blur professional lines, it's okay to share those warm-fuzzy feelings. This might be the key that unlocks team spirit!

7

WANING QUARTER MOON IN ARIES

20 JUL

Today's quarter moon in impulsive, energetic Aries brings your focus back to the present moment. Quick! Stop snapping selfies and look around. What's happening beyond the perimeter of your mobile screen? Magic can happen if you follow the suggestion of Aries Ram Dass and "be here now." Have you been placing other people's needs above your own? Refine and rediscover *your* happy place. Self-love is not an act of selfishness, it's one of self-preservation! Detach from sticky entanglements and give your personal wish list a review. Are those goals bringing deep down fulfillment or could they use a tweak? Today, you'll find that it's easy to tap the quick-fire, spontaneous vibes of this star sign and stir up excitement.

JUL 22 - AUG 22

SUN IN LEO

A long red carpet rolls out today as the Sun struts into Leo until August 22. This annual solar cycle is high season for all things glamorous, romantic and creative. Does your name belong in lights? Or maybe a history book or the hall of fame? Visualize it, then start positioning your personal "brand" for the ascent. If you're not sure where to begin, start with some competitive research analysis. What are the leaders in your (desired) industry doing? How would YOU put your own unique spin on this? If you have a finished product to promote, use this week to put a final coat of high-gloss polish on it. Then, schedule your big reveal or trot it out for a test pilot to your savviest friends.

7

and in love...

Is it time to elevate your standards? The Sun marches into regal Leo, trumpeting out a PSA: You deserve to be treated like royalty by the one you love. But hear ye, hear ye! Keep those expectations realistic, too! Most people don't have the time (or budgets!) to fawn over each other 24/7. Invest equal energy into your creative pursuits—and commit to following through! That's how to keep your love life in balance. Get ready, because you might fall head over summer sandals for your own fine self in the process. Tap into the noble traits of Leo instead of falling prey to the self-serving ones. Love *is* a two-way street, after all. How can you be a more generous lover, in and out of the bedroom?

VENUS-JUPITER SQUARE

25
JUL

People might talk a good game, but can they back up their swagger with action? Today, big-talking Jupiter in Aries locks into a tangled angle with Venus in guarded Cancer. While these benefic planets have a strict "no negative vibes" policy, their rose-tinted outlook makes everyone gullible. To avoid being a victim of this hustler's holiday, don't take people's promises at face value. Googling that Hinge hottie doesn't have to burst your bubble. Ideally, background checks will make you *more* confident about pursuing a shared future. Even solid relationships require periodic reviews. Schedule a sit-down under today's diplomatic skies to make sure you're operating from a level playing field. Leave ample time for the conversation, so you can talk through any uncomfortable truths that arise. Getting it all out into the open is always better than sweeping it under the rug.

7

MERCURY-MARS SQUARE

26
JUL

Let your word be your bond today and make sure you're prepared to back up your claims with legit credentials. Mouthy Mercury is in Leo, making everyone prone to exaggeration. Nothing wrong with adding a few colorful details! But if you're bedazzling the truth with these, er, embellishments, check yourself and correct yourself! Otherwise, you could face some backlash (and a potential #Cancel) from no-nonsense Mars in Taurus who is busy regulating every statement. On the other hand, are you flying *too* low under the radar? Stop wearing struggle like a merit badge. Support is all around you, but you have to ask for it!

MERCURY-URANUS SQUARE

28
JUL

Biting off more than you can chew? You might need to scale back on an ambitious goal today since certain key players will be impossible to rein in. Swallow your pride and adjust, fast! The last thing to do right now is forge ahead on a wing and a prayer. Under the erratic mashup of chaotic Uranus in Taurus and anxious Mercury in Leo, "improvising" is bound to go awry. To avoid ending the day feeling like it was a total loss, set one modest objective and be satisfied if you can pull that off. And if you can keep disruptive team members away from this mission, all the better!

JUPITER RETROGRADE

28 JUL -
23 NOV

Pump the brakes! Bountiful Jupiter flips into its annual, four-month retrograde today, putting a halt to fast-moving progress. The red-spotted planet has been speeding through daring Aries since May 10, inspiring everyone to dive headlong into new (ad) ventures. By now, your head may be spinning from all your discoveries! Before an exhilarating ride turns into a collision course, take a pit stop. Utilize this forced slowdown to analyze early results. Are you progressing in the right direction? Making the impact you hoped to? Ask for honest feedback (and don't get mad if people don't tell you exactly what you want to hear). Advance notice: On October 28, retrograde Jupiter backs up into Pisces, drawing a more spiritual and creative dimension into all these plans. You might even take a pilgrimage then, to learn about a lost art or to get in tune with a deeper dimension of your own imagination!

LEO NEW MOON

28
JUL

Need to restore your roar? Fierceness returns with a vengeance today, as the annual new moon in Leo plugs us into our own personal power grids. Self-expression is the order of the day, especially since this new moon forms a free-flowing trine to Jupiter (retrograde) in Aries. No more bottling up your authentic style or telling people what they want to hear at the expense of your inner truth. Go back and clue others in (lovingly, please) if they missed any of your memos. Does the "problem" lie within your presentation? If your messages keep getting lost in translation, get to work on your branding. The Leo new moon traffics in first impressions, and that begs the question: How do you want to shine in the world? Do one thing to put your talents on display or draw attention to your gifts. Permission to graciously self-promote? Granted!

and in love . . .

7

Romance rebooted! Today's new moon in Leo, the only one of 2022, opens hearts and lifts voices. If you've been suppressing your loving feelings, just wait! They could come rushing out before you can stop them—especially since candid Jupiter in Aries is in a supportive sync-up with this new moon. Ready to start (or expand) your fam? These fertile moonbeams could start the clock on babymaking, adoption or IVF efforts. Single and looking? Pump up your efforts over the next two weeks and remember: Confidence is the most attractive trait of all!

MERCURY-SATURN OPPOSITION

31
JUL

If you're hoping to win hearts and minds today, you'd better have a plan. As skeptical Saturn stares down frenetic Mercury, the last thing you want to do is come across as flighty or unprepared. Certain gates are already closed tighter than Fort Knox. If you're not ready to be grilled on how you'll execute your grandiose vision, don't even think about faking it till you make it. Let people know that you're still "in the development phase" before you launch into a starry-eyed presentation. Or, hold off on sharing with the doubters and decision-makers, and spend the day putting a master map behind your brilliant, blue-sky vision. Keep it simple but don't skim over the technical parts. Make sure that people can clearly understand how you'll execute this, phase by phase.

SUN-JUPITER TRINE

31
JUL

There's almost no such thing as "too much" today when the glowing Leo Sun gets in cahoots with bountiful Jupiter in Aries. Pull on the patterned prints and snap some sexy selfies. Under this limitless mashup, it truly does feel like anything is possible. But stop before hitting the launch button! Despite this cosmic confidence booster, certain rules still apply, like budgets, decorum...and gravity. With both planets in excessive fire signs, you could burn through resources like nobody's business. So for now, just enjoy the enthusiastic experience of kicking around creative ideas and being as playful as a kid at recess. Wherever you go, check your pride at the door! While swagger can win you points, it's equally important to be approachable when taking on challenges. Starting an ego-based rivalry could leave you with a huge mess to clean up. Don't provoke that fight!

AUGUST *Moon Phases*

SUN	MON	TUE	WED	THU	FRI	SAT
	1 ♍	**2** ♎ 12:06AM	**3** ♎	**4** ♏ 7:47AM	**5** ♏ 1st Quarter	**6** ♐ 12:39PM
7 ♐ 4:43PM	**8** ♑ 2:39PM	**9** ♑	**10** ♒ 2:45PM	**11** ♒ Full Moon 9:35PM	**12** ♓ 2:45PM	**13** ♓
14 ♈ 4:43PM	**15** ♈	**16** ♉ 10:23PM	**17** ♉	**18** ♉	**19** ♊ 8:07AM 3rd Quarter	**20** ♊
21 ♋ 8:29PM	**22** ♋	**23** ♋	**24** ♌ 9:09AM	**25** ♌	**26** ♍ 8:25PM	**27** ♍ New Moon 4:16AM
28 ♍	**29** ♎ 5:45AM	**30** ♎	**31** ♏ 1:11PM			

KEY:

♈ ARIES	♊ GEMINI	♌ LEO	♎ LIBRA	♐ SAGITTARIUS	♒ AQUARIUS
♉ TAURUS	♋ CANCER	♍ VIRGO	♏ SCORPIO	♑ CAPRICORN	♓ PISCES

FM FULL MOON   **NM** NEW MOON   **LE** LUNAR ECLIPSE   **SE** SOLAR ECLIPSE

8

MARS-URANUS MEETUP

1
AUG

Brace yourself for a combative day! As feisty Mars unites with disruptive Uranus, stubborn righteousness could send a once-peaceful mission flying off the rails! With fuses *this* short, steer away from controversial topics as best you can. And if you are going to open Pandora's box? Set some ground rules for these conversations. If everyone's willing to play nice, this *could* be an incredible day for brainstorming revolutionary approaches to age-old problems. On the bright side, community-spirited Uranus is the high-minded futurist of the solar system, while Mars in Taurus can bring the courage needed to fight for an important cause. Activist efforts spring up, perhaps in response to some unsettling power plays. Just make sure you don't run anyone over in the process. Strong intellectual and sexual attraction can blaze up fast—when you least expect it!

MERCURY IN VIRGO

4 - 25
AUG

Ready, set, systematize! Mental Mercury hosts a homecoming parade through Virgo, its native turf, giving us three weeks to whip our lives into an efficient groove. Keeping too much data in your head? That's a recipe for stress. Bring order to the chaos by syncing calendars and automating where you can. Tap into secure apps that can help you stay organized. Pre-schedule bill payments, transfers to savings and other routine monthly transactions. With the communication planet in this healthy zodiac sign, you can successfully start (and sustain) new habits by writing things down and planning ahead. But keep it simple! Steer clear of social situations that ramp up your anxiety. If a decision has left you with analysis paralysis, hit the brakes and do more research before making a move.

WAXING QUARTER
MOON IN SCORPIO

5
AUG

Dial up the intensity or keep your burning feelings under wraps? As today's moderating quarter moon turns down the heat to a steady simmer, you'll make the strongest impression simply by being warm and sincere. (As opposed to "hot and spicy" or "cool and icy.") Share information in a measured way. Mysteriousness will arouse suspicion but oversharing could breach confidentiality in regrettable ways. Find a happy medium: Reveal the story in broad strokes and save the sensitive details for later in the game—if you actually make it there! Flag any "suspicious activity" and keep an eye on it. A week from now, the full moon will reveal some missing information.

MARS-SATURN SQUARE

7
AUG

Slow your roll! Fast-paced Mars in Taurus has you climbing steadily toward your goals, but that high-flying starship could get grounded thanks to a buzzkill from skeptical Saturn in Aquarius today. It's great to dream like the sky is the limit. But it's also important to check the atmospheric pressure, cloud coverage and other weather-related concerns. You don't want to be the downer in the room, telling people, "That will never work!" But do plan to run every genius idea through a set of serious tests before passing "GO." If critics poke holes in your plan, don't dismiss their feedback. This could be a hidden blessing, motivating you to tighten up your concept or apply smarter science to your approach. Is your current team failing to live up to the dream? Perhaps their "mutiny" is frustration in disguise. Before you cut anyone loose, listen to their complaints. They may be privy to insights that you've overlooked.

8

VENUS-NEPTUNE TRINE

<table>
<tr><td>7
AUG</td></tr>
</table>

True love or just an illusion? Ardent Venus spins a web with fantasy-agent Neptune, dissolving boundaries. With Venus drifting through sensitive Cancer, feelings are tender. Meanwhile, empathic Neptune in Pisces amplifies every mood. Intimate feelings are always "real," in some sense; you wouldn't be experiencing them otherwise. But are they meant to last? Today, that's impossible to tell. If you want to enjoy the day, stop focusing on the clock. The relationship may not last forever, but the dreamy memory will!

VENUS-PLUTO OPPOSITION

<table>
<tr><td>9
AUG</td></tr>
</table>

There's a thin line between "secretive" and "self-protective," and you'll need to walk it carefully today. As delicate Venus in Cancer goes head-to-head with powermonger Pluto in Capricorn, trust issues are bound to arise. If people's motives are not transparent, you may be tempted to fire off an interrogation. Trouble is, this could set off their defense mechanisms. It may be wiser to "innocently" observe anyone who trips your emotional alarm system. Surface activity won't tell the whole story, however, so plan to dig deeper with your investigations. Do you feel like someone's gaslighting you? Don't take the bait!

SUN-URANUS SQUARE

<table>
<tr><td>11
AUG</td></tr>
</table>

Egos, tempers and tantrums...help! Narcissistic tendencies are on breathtaking display, thanks to a volatile collision between the domineering Leo Sun and disruptor Uranus in Taurus. As people dig in their heels and take cheap shots at each other, it might feel like everyone's sinking to an all-time low. Do your best to stay elevated. If you find yourself walking on eggshells, diffuse the situation by calling a timeout instead of further provoking the "opposition," or letting them scratch your raw wounds. Bottom line: Today, everyone is simply too committed to their own agenda to really hear a differing point of view. Don't waste your breath arguing!

AQUARIUS FULL MOON

11
AUG

Wishful thinking is encouraged (and then some!) as today's full moon in Aquarius shines the spotlight on our hopes for the future. What would *your* ideal world look like—and who would be there to enjoy it with you? Take time to meditate on that, and make a vision board if you feel so inspired. With this full moon squaring the lunar nodes and game-changing Uranus, whatever you arrive at could have a destined quality to it. And you may feel extra impetus to start exploring and experimenting right away! Collaborations and community ventures get a boost. Over the next two weeks, you may feel a virtual vibe or IRL click with people who share your most high-minded values. If you've already united with your soul squad in this lifetime, how can you join forces to make your corner of the planet a better place? Put your heads together and see what you come up with. If it's time to refresh your tech, start shopping around for time and energy-saving devices that bring ease to your life while lowering your footprint.

and in love...

Lighten up! The full moon in airy Aquarius brings levity back to the love game—and boy could we all use it. Free your mind. We're not advising you to be naïve or gullible. Just remember that you are the author of your own "romance novel." And if you want to break into a new genre, quirky Aquarius will be your strongest advocate. With this full moon squaring unconventional Uranus and the destiny-driven lunar nodes, you could get some strong downloads about what feels right for *you* in this realm. Tune in and get real with yourself. Forget about labels, unless you feel like trying on "relationship anarchist" for size. Even traditional types will have fun experimenting under this lunar light. But talk through risqué scenarios in advance and choose a safe word. Today you may be feeling frisky and unbound, but some fantasies are best left to the imagination—at least until you've seriously considered the pros and cons.

8

VENUS IN LEO

Can we get a meow, baby? Love goddess Venus struts onto Leo's catwalk, bringing out the spotlight-stealing siren in us all. Summer love goes from mild to wild—then up to scorching hot—when the planet of glamour and romance enters this fire circle every year. Don't sleep through invitations that connect you to beautiful, fabulous people. Baehunting could turn up prime catches, for both romantic and creative collaborations. No matter your relationship status, sincere flattery will get you far! Be generous with your praise and gracious about the accolades you receive. If you're due for a romantic reboot, this could be a "renaissance period" for amour. Wear your heart on your decorative sleeve (or your backless bandage dress, shredded tank or slinky swimsuit).

SUN-SATURN OPPOSITION

Leo Season is in full swing, putting us in hot pursuit of our passions. The spontaneous treasure hunts have been fruitful, but where are they actually leading? Today, integrity-hound Saturn faces off with the Sun, demanding structure to balance the freestyle explorations of the past few weeks. Have you strayed too far from your intended path? If so, use today to recalibrate. Although this may require some downsizing or delayed gratification, don't let disappointment take the wind out of your sails. You can celebrate a smaller victory, then build upon it, one step at a time. During this annual opposition, *how* you go about doing things matters as much as the outcome you produce. Are you being fair, inclusive, and conscientious? Examine your processes before putting yourself in the public eye, because this transit can deliver some tough ego checks. While the Leo Sun promotes showmanship, Saturn gives rewards based on merit. If you can bring the sizzle AND the steak, you will hit the right mark!

8

MARS-PLUTO TRINE

Summon your courage! Today's potent trine between take-no-prisoners Mars and investigative Pluto could bring eye-opening epiphanies. Don't be afraid to look in the shadows. That's how you'll get to the root of your stumbling blocks. Limiting beliefs may be shrouding your view of what's possible, especially if they were born out of trauma or fear. And have some self-sabotaging behaviors crept in? Get real and start making a change. Owning your issues is the way to ensure that they don't own you.

VENUS-JUPITER TRINE

As jovial Jupiter in Aries envelops amorous Venus in Leo in a passionate embrace, good luck NOT wearing your heart on your sleeve. With these planets striking such a sweet (and sexy!) chord, relationships of all manner will just click. And with both Venus and Jupiter in fire signs, the buzz of excitement will spread like flames. There's a tendency to idealize, however, or put the carriage before the horse. Instead of letting chemistry burn wildly, contain the blazes strategically. Then you can direct the heat towards your desired venture...or should we say, co-adventure!

WANING QUARTER MOON IN TAURUS

If you've been scattering your energy in a million directions, stop! Today's quarter moon in Taurus offers a blessed opportunity to get your feet back on solid ground. Under this waning light, scrutinize the details and decide which ones are worth investing in and which are just extra. Utilize the day's strong bull**** detector, a gift of the quarter moon, to trim away anything unnecessary. A simple plan works best when Taurus is in town! Just don't hack things back *so* much that you erase all creativity from the plan. Artistic touches, in the right measure, keep things elevated, not basic!

8

MARS IN GEMINI

Whatever you're selling, we'll take two! Passionate Mars blazes into persuasive Gemini, turning the world into an open marketplace. It won't take much convincing to get people on board with your wild schemes, but here's the catch: If you want to maintain their trust, make sure you can deliver the goods! The red planet is spending a rare seven *months* in the sign of the Twins—as opposed to its usual seven *weeks*. There's no wriggling out of any promises penalty free. Caution: This transit can also bring out the smooth talking salespeople. Don't rush into any dynamic duos. Be especially cautious while Mars is retrograde from October 30 to January 12. Monitor your screen time, too. With stressful Mars in this gadget-loving sign, a digital deluge of texts, alerts and electronic info could quickly devolve from "stimulating" into fraying your nerves.

and in love...

Talk might be cheap, but for the next seven months, it's undeniably hot! As lusty Mars logs into loquacious Gemini for an extended cycle, racy repartee becomes an art form. Fearless Mars favors bold expression—and during the hot-tempered retrograde cycle from October 30 to January 12, avoid any possibility of your messages being misconstrued. Variety is the spice where Gemini is concerned, so mix it up with new locations, positions, role-playing, toys, whatever! Attractions may be fast, fickle and fleeting, however. Don't start planning the wedding after the third date. If your attention span is short, don't worry. Just make sure you're not leading anyone on. Couples may argue more or treat each other with brusque impatience. Remember that respect is the foundation of any lasting relationship. If insults or contempt creep into your dynamic, stop and address the frustration behind your biting (and fighting) words. Or, save your edgy talk for the boudoir!

8

MERCURY-NEPTUNE OPPOSITION

**21
AUG**

Decisions derailed? Rational Mercury in Virgo loses normal clarity today as it plunges into the quicksand of Neptune in Pisces. During this annual opposition, thoughts are as blurry as an impressionist painting. If you're giving instructions, write them out step by step—and even then, prepare to play "support chat" when people misconstrue your guidance. While logic will be MIA, there's juicy opportunity to tap into if you "draw on the right side of the brain." This is a red-letter day for creative brainstorming, meditation or spiritual healing. You could dream so far outside the box, there isn't even a box anymore. No matter how bizarre, capture your visionary gems in a journal or Notes app before they evaporate into the ether. In a few days, you can bring them back to the drawing board and figure out which ones are worth incorporating into your plans.

AUG 22 - SEP 22

SUN IN VIRGO

After a month of neon-bright hedonism and unapologetic excess, the razzle dazzle simmers down. As the Sun downshifts into earthy Virgo for a month, minimalism reigns supreme. Start a Pinterest board of clever storage solutions and efficiency hacks. And don't forget that some of the best things in life are still free, like rides to the beach, yoga in the park—anything involving fresh air. Virgo is the sign of healthy habits, but also devotional ones! Turn your routines into rituals. How can you make your daily tasks just a little more pleasurable? For example, set up a gorgeous (and plant-filled!) environment in your workspace so you get an aesthetic rush when you look up from your computer screen. Wear clothes that are comfortable but also make you feel attractive—yes, even when dashing off to the gym or to pick up the kids from practice. Take a few extra minutes in the evening to prepare a nourishing lunch for yourself that you can bring to work the next day—you might just make a couple extra portions of your nightly dinners for this purpose. And when the moment of choice arises to either be helpful or pretend you didn't see someone struggling, stop and give 'em a hand for two seconds. The caring vibes will come back to you in the form of genuine support and connection with the people you see every day.

and in love...

With the Sun beaming into Virgo for the next four weeks, giving will feel twice as good as receiving. Ask not what your partner can do for *you* (or ask a little less). Instead, observe 'em in their natural habitat. Then, find ways to make life both easier and more pleasurable. Need more support? Ask for it simply and spell out directions clearly. Virgo is the zodiac's purist and perfectionist, but curb your inner critic. Complaining, nitpicking and fault-finding are three deadly horsemen to intimacy. While this is a fine time to improve relationships, steer conversations in a proactive direction. Sync your schedules, set up a shared calendar and reserve slots for the requisite date nights. Tap into Virgo's earthy sensuality! Snuggle up in the starlight. Lie in bed talking. Learn how to give each other mind-blowing massages. The best things in love are free!

URANUS RETROGRADE IN TAURUS

**24 AUG -
23 JAN '23**

Expect the unexpected! Game-changing Uranus does an about-face, backing up through Taurus for its annual retrograde. Progress may stall and money could get funny. You might need to pick up a side hustle or start an indie venture to keep the books balanced. On a broader level, assess this: How well are we cooperating as humans? When the side-spinning planet shifts into reverse, it can slow (or outright halt!) progress. Since Uranus began its uncomfortable eight-year trek through Taurus in May 2018, there's been a war between rapidly moving scientific developments and stubborn "old school" beliefs. Futuristic Uranus loves to push the envelope. Traditional earth sign Taurus wants things to stay the way they've always been. Can you see the contradiction here? Navigating the balance between old and new could force some deeper inspection for the rest of 2022.

8

MERCURY IN LIBRA

25 AUG - 23 SEP

Welcome to the justice league! Mercury begins its first of two passes through fair-minded Libra, highlighting any imbalances in our social interactions. Start leveling the playing field now, before the messenger planet spins retrograde on September 9. Aim for mutuality and a solution that takes all parties' needs into consideration. Even if it takes a little longer to hammer out the terms, the long-term payoff is worth it. Pro tip: Get contracts signed before the September 9 backspin—or wait until Mercury corrects course on October 2 (in Virgo). Hashing out creative compromises could spur some fascinating discussions for the next few weeks. Romantic ones, too, so let yourself be transported in a heady space whenever possible. Remember that communication is as much about listening as finding the perfect words to express your point of view. Pay extra attention to aesthetics. Visual cues are Mercury in Libra's love language!

VENUS-URANUS SQUARE

27 AUG

Desperately seeking...space? You might feel like making a break for freedom today, as liberated Uranus gets into a combustible clash with romantic Venus. Sacrificing autonomy should not be the entry fee for partnership. If your love interest's needs are cannibalizing your personal time, set clear boundaries. Maybe *you've* drifted a little too far into the couple bubble and now it's getting a tad claustrophobic in there. If you're feeling smothered, take a day or two for yourself rather than doing anything extreme. Maybe you're ready to remix a radical relationship with old-school romantic ideals. Dabble and discuss until you find the formula that works for you.

8

VIRGO NEW MOON

27 AUG

Bless this mess—then get to organizing! With the new moon in neat-freak Virgo, cleanliness is next to godliness. Those distracting piles and unchecked messages take up a lot of mental energy—even if you *think* you're ignoring them! And with stressful Mars in Gemini elbowing the new moon, you could have a meltdown trying to dig for that lost item. Rather than letting it get to that point, open up your Notes app and make a list! Over the next two weeks, start ticking off tasks one at a time. Since wellness is also in Virgo's wheelhouse, let this lunar lift reboot your fitness goals. Temperatures will soon be perfect for more outdoor activities, where earthy Virgo reigns! Could your meals be healthier, your sleep more sanctified? Feather your nest with everything you need to keep your body humming like a well-oiled machine—from a fridge full of fresh produce, snacks like raw almonds in the pantry and an essential oil diffuser on your nightstand.

and in love...

If your love language is "acts of service," you're in luck! Today's new moon in Virgo, the only one of 2022, makes giving feel so good. There are always more nuances to discover about the one you adore. But have you stopped searching for those? See what happens if you approach your favorite people with "beginner's mind." Treat them with the same curiosity as you would a stranger. If your busy life has cut into the quality time you once spent together, make some changes now. How can you align your schedules and support each other more? If you keep passing each other like ships in the night, you could both drift off to other ports. Invest energy into "together time" to fortify your connection. How can you make everyday rituals, like working out and eating breakfast, into bonding opportunities?

8

SUN-MARS SQUARE

<table>
<tr><td>27
AUG</td></tr>
</table>

Quick! Find an outlet for that simmering tension! Combative Mars challenges the competitive Sun to a duel, and what started as a friendly rivalry could explode into a heated battle! Pro tip: Don't let your simmering temper reach a boil, even if you *do* have a point to make. Table triggering topics and go work off stress in the gym, the bedroom, or the outdoor track. Taking a break is a far better idea than losing your temper on the company's all-hands Zoom! If the chemistry is on with a prospective partner, however, this provocative square could ignite a dynamic duet. Intellect, wit and a flexible mindset are great components to bring to the table today—*and* to look for in your collaborators. Carve out each person's turf to avoid stepping on each other's toes.

VENUS-SATURN OPPOSITION

<table>
<tr><td>28
AUG</td></tr>
</table>

Have your boundaries been slippery? Firm them up today before you lose your grip on a romantic situation. As soft-hearted Venus gets caught in the crosshairs of tough-loving Saturn, the universe delivers a firm reminder that "loving without limits" isn't always a good thing. Before resentment creeps in—or the one you adore thinks it's cool to creep around—put a hard stop to behaviors that aren't in alignment with self-love. Do you keep delivering ultimatums? With Venus in Leo for the past couple weeks, a strong attraction or a good heartstring tug was all it took for you to go back on your word. Put in some reinforcements (like calling a friend) to stop yourself from caving so easily. If you reward bad behavior now, you'll only create a bigger problem later. On the fence about a certain relationship? This pessimistic starmap could make you overly judgmental. Don't sweep the downsides under the rug, but sleep on it before you call the whole thing off.

8

SEPTEMBER
Moon Phases

SUN	MON	TUE	WED	THU	FRI	SAT
				1 ♏︎	**2** ♐︎ 6:40PM	**3** ♐︎ 1st Quarter
4 ♑︎ 10:03PM	**5** ♑︎	**6** ♒︎ 11:41PM	**7** ♒︎	**8** ♒︎	**9** ♓︎ 12:43AM	**10** ♓︎ Full Moon 5:59AM
11 ♈︎ 2:47AM	**12** ♈︎	**13** ♉︎ 7:40AM	**14** ♉︎	**15** ♊︎ 4:16PM	**16** ♊︎	**17** ♊︎ 3rd Quarter
18 ♋︎ 4:00AM	**19** ♋︎	**20** ♌︎ 4:38PM	**21** ♌︎	**22** ♌︎	**23** ♍︎ 3:54AM	**24** ♍︎
25 ♎︎ 12:43AM NM ♎︎ 5:55PM	**26** ♎︎	**27** ♏︎ 7:15PM	**28** ♏︎	**29** ♏︎	**30** ♐︎ 12:04AM	

KEY: ♈︎ ARIES ♊︎ GEMINI ♌︎ LEO ♎︎ LIBRA ♐︎ SAGITTARIUS ♒︎ AQUARIUS
♉︎ TAURUS ♋︎ CANCER ♍︎ VIRGO ♏︎ SCORPIO ♑︎ CAPRICORN ♓︎ PISCES

FM FULL MOON **NM** NEW MOON **LE** LUNAR ECLIPSE **SE** SOLAR ECLIPSE

9

MERCURY-JUPITER OPPOSITION

2 SEP

Opinions, opinions! Everyone's an "expert" today, but they might be preaching advice with limited information. Before you get hooked by the hype, take time to research what you've heard—and check a few credible sources. Throughout the day, it could feel like everyone is carrying on their own conversation, while not listening to what anyone else has to say. Try not to add to the cacophony. If you have to fight to be heard, then you're probably wasting your breath. Map out your vision on paper, then pitch it on a day when people are more open to input. For now, your best bet is to pop in your earbuds, turn on the white noise station (or your favorite productivity music) and drown out the drama. Is someone trying to sell *you* on a big idea? If it sounds too good to be true, this starmap practically ensures that it is.

WAXING QUARTER MOON IN SAGITTARIUS

3 SEP

Bigger, stronger, faster? Easy, tiger! Today's moderating quarter moon calls for measured, responsible growth. In our progress-obsessed modern world, "expansion" is considered one of the ultimate benchmarks for success. But at what cost? In broad-minded Sagittarius, these moonbeams shine a light on new considerations. Are you creating a truly inclusive space for your audience, patrons, and community? How will any buildouts impact your environment, your family and people in the area? Review your strategy, taking a brave and unblinking look at every aspect of your plan. If something needs to be adjusted, hop to it before the full moon, one week from now!

9

VENUS IN VIRGO

**5 - 29
SEP**

Get ready for a galactic glow-up as beautifying Venus moves into Virgo, the sign of radiant good health. This sensible cycle can be quite sensual if you slow down and appreciate the little things. And get physical—with self-care, a pleasurable exercise routine (solo or with your S.O.) and through lots of affection. While tenderness is always important, "acts of service" is the primary love language that Venus in Virgo speaks. Ask not what your lover can do for you. Instead, learn how to give a killer shoulder rub, cook your S.O.'s favorite meal and support their dreams in every way possible. Put phones away and give your undivided attention to the one you love. Listen generously, give advice only if asked and keep feedback constructive (not critical). Single and looking? Start with the intellectual connection. Long, analytical conversations can be the key to deeper connection during this intellectual Venus spell. Take a timeout from the dating apps and see who you might meet at a book club or spiritual discussion group. What begins as a meeting of the minds could evolve into much, much more!

9

MERCURY RETROGRADE

9 SEP -
2 OCT

For the next three weeks, think twice before you speak, post or press "send." With communication planet Mercury backing through discerning, fair-minded Libra and persnickety, critical Virgo (starting September 23), the margin for error will be slim. Since Libra is associated with legal matters, review contracts to make sure you're in compliance. This deep dive could save you future legal issues or set a healthier tone for your work environment. Knowledge is power—and on an emotional level, the path to feeling safe and secure! Even the best relationships could drift into choppy waters between now and October 2. Patience will be required to keep things on an even keel. Exes will be especially prone to reminiscing—consider yourself warned!

PISCES FULL MOON

10
SEP

Surrender, and let the universe reveal its wisdom. As 2022's only full moon in Pisces loosens our clutches, we get privy to the "source code" that's embedded in things like divine timing, serendipities and dreams. Reality can be tough to digest or even discern! This full moon won't help matters much, but that's kind of the point. Because esoteric Pisces is the master of illusion, it's like you're lost in a labyrinth. If you panic, you'll feel even MORE out of sorts. But stop, breathe, and listen to your intuition, and you'll reconnect to your inner guidance...as well as a few ancestors and guides! This compassionate full moon paves the way for deep, soulful healing. Unexpectedly, you may see an "enemy" in a very human light. While you don't have to accept their wrongdoings, you may find a spot of forgiveness in your heart. On the flipside, you may realize that it's time to put up boundaries with a bully. Enough's enough!

9

and in love...

The more you cling, the less in control you feel—oh, the irony! There's only one thing to do today: Let go and allow the universe to guide you. Today's full moon in limitless Pisces opens the floodgates of compassion and romance. Let down those walls! A willingness to be open-hearted can bring major life shifts. This enchanting lunar lift lends a fairy-tale quality to encounters. Over the next two weeks, how can you elevate the experience of falling (or being) in love? Ditch the cynicism but keep the common sense. Galloping off into the sunset after a few great dates is not advisable—but it's certainly okay to fantasize about it! Just know the difference between dreams and reality and you can sip this sweet celestial nectar without getting punch drunk. As the twelfth and final sign of the zodiac, the Pisces full moon helps us release what no longer serves our highest good. Farewell, toxic frenemies and energy vampires! Hello, to all that is good, true and beautiful... inside and out!

SUN-URANUS TRINE

11 SEP

Play with your processes! Under today's experimental link-up between the Virgo Sun and Uranus in Taurus, take a moment to assess your routines. Sure you've been doing things "that way" for years—and maybe you're even getting solid results. But periodic reviews can ensure that you're not only working with maximum efficiency, but also employing the latest techniques. Tech-savvy Uranus love to "appify" everything. Why not see if AI can make your job easier? That only gives you more time to be innovative! If you're already on the cutting edge, mix up your schedule. Work out before you sit down at your computer—or close all the browser tabs except for the ones you're using and see how much faster you blaze through your work.

9

SUN-NEPTUNE OPPOSITION

16 SEP

Struggling to see things clearly? Blame the annual opposition of the bright, shining Sun and lens-blurring Neptune. This once-per-year transit makes it hard to discern reality. Much like shining your headlights into thick fog, your scope of vision is limited. The trick is to concentrate on what's directly in front of you and proceed at a cautious pace. Or, better yet, pull over and wait for the metaphoric fog to lift. While you're parked, quiet your mind and tap into the "spiritual sight" that Neptune provides. Today's forced timeout can illuminate subconscious desires, gut feelings and intuitive hits. If you "listen" closely, there could be some mystical messages coming through the ether. WWYAD: What Would Your Ancestors Do? It wouldn't hurt to call upon the wisest souls in your lineage for a little "support."

VENUS-MARS SQUARE

16 SEP

Is a relationship veering off course? Today's challenging dust-up between cosmic lovebirds Venus and Mars could bring a sharp wake-up call. With Venus in pragmatic Virgo, do your level best to focus on solutions rather than pointing out your love interest's "mistakes." That will be extra challenging though! As Mars gallops in on Gemini's game-playing steed, the most basic conversation can turn into a mind-boggling debate. While this is certainly not the time to sweep issues under the rug, put the triggering ones in the parking lot until this temperamental transit passes in a couple days. Even if you DO lay all your cards on the table, you're likely to be misunderstood. Remember: Trouble in paradise doesn't have to mean the end of the fairy tale. If you've been stuck in a holding pattern, the dynamic Mars-Venus square motivates change. And it can be as simple as planning a weekend day trip instead of spending another Sunday watching movies on the couch. Single? Spark up a conversation with an intriguing stranger. With Venus and Mars in mutable signs, you'd do well to stretch yourself outside what's comfortable. This cosmic catalyst will get your heart racing again!

9

WANING QUARTER MOON IN GEMINI

17 SEP

Will they, or won't they? Should you, or should you just... not? Something in your life may be drawing to a close, brewing up a cauldron of conflicting emotions. Part of you may be terrified and sad about starting over, but you're also feeling a sense of relief and new possibility. The real question is: How can you make this transition in a powerful way? Under the dimming light of today's quarter moon in Gemini, take time to explore the non-obvious possibilities. Note: These are likely to be found in the grey area, where people push beyond societal norms of "all or nothing." Is there a healthy way to incorporate both the past and the future? Can you break away without burning bridges? As you consider your strategy, siphon off the compassionate energy from last week's Pisces full moon. Don't expect to make a final decision today. Just use this prismatic moon to consider a broader set of perspectives, including the most essential one—your own!

SUN-PLUTO TRINE

18 SEP

How much is too much? Relying on gut checks and public consensus won't be the best yardstick as the Virgo Sun dances into a mystifying formation with secretive Pluto. Better break out the measuring cups and read over those Google analytics reports. The benefit to this muddling mashup is that it allows you to powerfully tune in to the present moment. Pause from strategic planning and postpone those Zooms. Downloads could come while you retreat from the action and draw from a deep well of inspiration within your own psyche. An esoteric notion might make more sense than you think

9

MERCURY-JUPITER OPPOSITION

18 SEP

Messenger Mercury hits an opposition to candid Jupiter today, pushing the envelope of what is considered "appropriate" communication. What were you carrying on about during the first of these planetary face-offs on (or near) September 2? That topic could be a hot one again, but it comes with a heat advisory warning! Thanks to Mercury being retrograde in diplomatic Libra this time, the gloves are off. And with Jupiter in combative Aries, you might deliver a knockout punch if you make your point with forceful aggression. While that might feel like a victory, don't start pouring the champagne yet. You're going to have to face the same music on October 12 when these planets duel again. A word to the wise: Don't provoke any battles if you aren't sure you can finish the fight with dignity.

VENUS-URANUS TRINE

20 SEP

Been stuck in your comfort zone? You can shatter past those limits using today's boundary-busting trine of Venus and rabble-rouser Uranus. Keep an open mind and see where it leads you. You don't have to veer completely off the traditional path—and you probably won't since both planets are in modest earth signs. But, um, could you stray from routine...a little? (Yes!) If you're single and looking, soften your focus instead of squinting suspiciously to see the flaws. With experimental Uranus in the mix, there's a strong chance you'll swoon for someone refreshingly unlike your usual type. Longtime couples can add sizzle by trying something new together. What "wouldn't it be crazy if?" adventure can you pull off in the next few days?

9

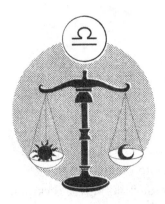

SEPTEMBER

SEP 22 - OCT 23

SUN IN LIBRA

Collaborate, cooperate, co-create! Dynamic duos hit their stride for the next four weeks, but not in the "OMG, we have *everything* in common!" kind of way. Since Libra is the sign of the scales, join forces with people who have complementary skills sets. That's what creates the perfect balance. This gracious zodiac season is ideal for networking with new folks while also fortifying existing relationships. No need to wait until the holidays to send gifts to your top clients or treat a prospective project partner to lunch. Personalized touches, no matter how big or small, will go a long way to cement loyalty. Already assembled your dream team? Use the next four weeks to align around creative concepts and maybe revamp your mission statement to incorporate shared values.

and in love...

Life could feel like a bonus Valentine's Day celebration...make that Valentine's *Month*. Today, the Sun changes costumes, shedding Virgo's white cotton oxford for Libra's body-con date night gear. Cupid will make plenty of cameos over the next four weeks, and many of his arrows are sure to hit the mark. (As long as you open your heart and provide a clear shot, of course.) If you've been flying solo, it's time to collaborate, cooperate and communicate with joy once again. And indulge! Libra season gives us all a weak spot for life's finer things: haute cuisine, beautiful fabrics, art, music and all kinds of revelry. Just watch the cashflow when following the hedonistic impulses. Luxury dates should be just that...a luxury. In between wining and dining, go out of your way to appreciate "the little things." Is it time to make a peace offering? Libra's harmonious vibes help smooth over rough patches in our most important unions. It's rarely too late to at least *try* to make amends. Thanks to the gracious diplomacy of this solar cycle, others are more willing to accept a heartfelt apology.

9

MERCURY IN VIRGO

23 SEP - 10 OCT

The devil is in the microscopic details as retrograde Mercury slips back from even-keeled Libra into keen-eyed Virgo. Review everything on the finest setting possible during the backspin, which lasts until October 2. Be an unapologetic purist when you go on any research or sourcing missions. Can you find a greener solution that not only saves you cash but is also socially and environmentally responsible? Constructive feedback is hard to suppress while Mercury's in its home sign of analytical Virgo—but check the judgmental attitude. Buffer your pro tips with a "praise sandwich," starting and ending with the positives so people feel empowered by your input. Focus on wellness, too! With the mindful planet in this healthy sign, you can successfully start (and sustain) new habits by writing things down and planning ahead. Keep it simple!

VENUS-NEPTUNE OPPOSITION

24 SEP

Hypnotic spells will be cast today, as romantic Venus in Virgo opposes enchanting Neptune in Pisces. If you're charmed and dazzled, enjoy the moment, but know that some of this energy may be a mirage. During this annual transit, it's hard to tell if someone's interested in you or just being extra friendly. Don't assume anything under these obfuscating skies. Simultaneously, check the paranoia. When red flags start waving, investigate before flinging accusations or trying to pep talk your way out of "negative" feelings. There's undoubtedly more to the situation than meets the eye. But finding it requires a thorough examination. Strap on the headlamp and have a look. Peering into the shadows could uncover a hidden gem.

LIBRA NEW MOON

<table>
<tr><td>25
SEP</td></tr>
</table>

Come together! Today's new moon in Libra activates a new six-month cycle for partnerships. Is there a missing link in your chain? Start searching for someone who can fill in those ever-important blanks. DO take your time with this process! Jupiter (retrograde) in quickfire Aries sits opposite this new moon, bringing some instant connections to people who may not have the depth or experience you are *really* searching for. A helpful idea? Outline criteria before you look around. What capabilities, specialties and know-how do you need from a collaborator? Avoid "settling," or worse, shoe horning someone into a role just because you don't want to deal with the discovery process. Haste makes waste, *but* a little extra prep will attract partners with legit staying power.

and in love...

Ready for some world-class romance—and romanticizing? The new moon in Libra, the only one this year, tickles us pink. It also drops a rose-colored filter over the lens, helping us see people in the best possible light. Nothing wrong with that as long as you keep one foot planted in the reality zone. With Jupiter retrograde in speed-demon Aries, budding relationships will accelerate based on pure animal attraction. But are you glossing over the whole picture? Everyone has a "human" side, which, of course, is why marriage vows include the "for worse" clause. So even if your hormones are firing on all cylinders, take time to learn the full spectrum of any fascinating new characters who come into your life. Need to find a better balance between "mine" and "ours"? Healthy relationships include room for autonomy, as well as togetherness. Couples may begin important conversations today around ways to better support each other's independent interests—without getting triggered or threatened!

9

VENUS-PLUTO TRINE

26 SEP

It's safe to turn on the charm as enchanting Venus makes eyes at provocateur Pluto. Just be genuine! With both planets in integrity-bound earth signs, a failure to walk your talk could bring serious recourse. If you can deliver on your promise, intensify your pitch. Let people know that you really, REALLY want an opportunity—or that you're 100 percent smitten. The only thing to look out for? This transit makes it easy to say yes to attractive offers, so careful not to be seduced by a slick sales pitch. During this sultry trine, unspoken chemistry could finally explode into something so hot that it's exothermic. And with both Venus and Pluto rolling through stable earth signs, this could be more of a long game play than "just a moment."

MERCURY RETROGRADE-VENUS MEETUP

26 SEP

They said tomato, you heard "tomorrow," but that's no reason to call the whole thing off. Be warned, however, that minor grievances can escalate into full-on battles today. As Mercury retrograde collides with Venus at the same degree of Virgo. It's hard to *not* see every "flaw" in others, much less stop yourself from pointing them out. But even the most helpful hint can feel like a low blow under these skies. If your love interest starts playing life coach, do both of you a favor and call a timeout. The urge to "fix" each other can provoke your fighting instincts. On the plus side, this is a good day for doing a deep dive into any practical matters, like balancing your shared budget, paying off bills and getting your schedules synced up.

9

MARS-SATURN TRINE

You may discover the right balance of "hit the gas" and "ride the brakes" today, when speed racer Mars in Gemini harmonizes in a dynamic duet with slow-and-steady Saturn in Aquarius. Although these two planets operate at very different paces, they are both touring breezy air signs. Still, this is not the moment to zip ahead without a solid plan in place. Saturn is the ruler of time and doesn't mind being the tortoise to impulsive Mars' hare. Use this planetary pairing to pop the hood and give those big ideas a tune-up, ensuring that everything is running like a well-oiled machine. From there it will be easy to move the needle on stalled projects without "scratching the vinyl" in haste. Make sure that anything you do has a sound strategy behind it but also leaves room for at least a little bit of spontaneity.

VENUS IN LIBRA

Elevate, luxuriate, decorate! Beauty queen Venus dons the homecoming tiara, strutting onto Libra's native soil for her annual visit. This is home base for the love planet, which means she operates at her fullest strength here. Willpower, on the other hand, may be at its weakest while Venus is in Libra. Good luck controlling yourself in the face of temptation—the one thing Libra Oscar Wilde could *not* resist. If you're in a relationship, make this your second, third—or fifteenth!—honeymoon phase. Push past resistance and stop keeping score. Romantic energy is contagious now—at least with the right people. The extra effort you make to tune in to your love interest can get stalled engines turning. Situationships may evolve into exclusive relationships over the coming few weeks. With Venus in gentle Libra, slow and steady devotion wins the race. Dial down the pressure, dial up the sweet gestures and charm.

9

OCTOBER *Moon Phases*

SUN	MON	TUE	WED	THU	FRI	SAT
						1 ♐
2 ♑ 3:38AM 1st Quarter	**3** ♑	**4** ♒ 6:21AM	**5** ♒	**6** ♓ 8:47AM	**7** ♓	**8** ♈ 11:57AM
9 ♈ Full Moon 4:55PM	**10** ♉ 5:04PM	**11** ♉	**12** ♉	**13** ♊ 1:08AM	**14** ♊	**15** ♋ 12:11PM
16 ♋	**17** ♋ 3rd Quarter	**18** ♌ 12:45AM	**19** ♌	**20** ♍ 12:26PM	**21** ♍	**22** ♎ 9:24PM
23 ♎	**24** ♎	**25** Solar Eclipse NM ♏ 6:49AM	**26** ♏	**27** ♐ 6:55AM	**28** ♐	**29** ♑ 9:22AM
30 ♑	**31** ♒ 11:43AM					

KEY:

♈ ARIES	♊ GEMINI	♌ LEO	♎ LIBRA	♐ SAGITTARIUS	♒ AQUARIUS
♉ TAURUS	♋ CANCER	♍ VIRGO	♏ SCORPIO	♑ CAPRICORN	♓ PISCES

FM FULL MOON   **NM** NEW MOON   **LE** LUNAR ECLIPSE   **SE** SOLAR ECLIPSE

VENUS-JUPITER OPPOSITION

1 OCT

Expand your romantic palette! As worldly Jupiter dances into a dynamic opposition with amorous Venus in Libra, you may have eyes for someone who is so *not* your usual type. Attractions heat up quickly, thanks to Jupiter hitting the accelerator in Aries. Since the red-spotted planet is retrograde, reach back in the time machine. Is there still promise with a former flame, or someone you met while traveling? One caveat: Venus and Jupiter are the astrological optimists, but today's feelgood vibes won't wash away unresolved issues. Existing relationships benefit from a little experimentation. But agree upon things like boundaries, comfort zones and safe words in advance. There's a thin line between "risky" and "risqué." Need some excitement? It's a great day to start planning a trip or setting up a shared vacation fund.

WAXING QUARTER MOON IN CAPRICORN

2 OCT

Go ahead, fall in love with people's potential...including your own! Today's waxing quarter moon in Capricorn keeps your eyes on the prize *and* the process. Achieving feels great, always. But *how* you ascend to the mountaintop also matters. Rushing around and cutting corners could mean cheating yourself out of essential learning—the kind that builds lasting strength and credibility. If "work-life balance" sounds more like a riddle than a reality, make some adjustments! Overexertion leads to burnout which ultimately slows productivity. Rather than pushing to do "one more thing!" see what happens if you start logging out and, say, going to yoga to recharge. Has it been slow-going for your career? These brightening moonbeams could illuminate a work opportunity that (re)builds your skillset. Picking up an extra shift or taking a webinar can get you back in the black!

10

MERCURY DIRECT IN VIRGO

<table>
<tr><td>2
OCT</td></tr>
</table>

Scrambled signals are clearing up today, as messenger Mercury ends an agitating retrograde that began on September 9. As the cosmic communicator powers forward through sanity-restoring Virgo until October 10, logic reigns supreme. What to do with this earthy, orderly energy? Get obsessed with systematizing and simplifying. Color-code your bookshelves and purge processed junk food from your fridge. Straighten out your schedule and do your level best to achieve "inbox zero." Rejig your budget and have any necessary conversations about money that you've been putting off. Since Virgo loves wellness, accessorize with your fitness tracker and create an October workout plan. Just be careful not to hop on the latest fad. That gemstone-infused, activated-charcoal healing tonic sounds divine, but uh, could you whip one up at home? Pin that recipe!

PLUTO RETROGRADE ENDS

<table>
<tr><td>8
OCT</td></tr>
</table>

Unsolved mysteries may soon be cleared up as shadowy Pluto ends its annual retrograde. This period of soul-searching, which began on April 29, may have brought some introspective insights. But brace yourself! Pluto waking up from a retrograde is like a volcano going from "dormant" to "active." Whatever's been buried under the surface could bubble up like hot lava. Money, power and sex are Pluto's domain, and some scandals might make headlines before the day is through. On a personal note, Pluto's backspin may have left you stuck with stormier thoughts. As the dwarf planet shifts into drive for the coming seven months, you'll be ready to tackle the tough stuff like processing grief, or healing from addictive tendencies and compulsive behaviors.

ARIES FULL MOON

**9
OCT**

Take a daring leap into the spotlight! The year's only full moon in passionate powerhouse Aries supplies you with drive to achieve a personal goal or to let your solo star shine. A project you've been working on for the past six months could come together. But don't wait to be noticed. Self-promotion is the name of the game. Even if you're not ready for a full-scale launch, trot it out for a beta test in the early part of the week. But don't play it too safe! Audience receptivity isn't really the point of this full moon. Just put yourself out there, unvarnished, fully authentic and 100 percent amazing—as YOU define it. Competition could get fierce, but for best results, make room onstage for others to shine rather than fighting for headliner status. As you unleash your fierceness, beware! This full moon may churn up a wave of buried anger. Hit the boxing bag, vent to a levelheaded third party, scream into a karaoke mic...just don't escalate the drama!

and in love...

Want their attention? Make it obvious! Heck, use a little shock value if you must. Capitalize on the courage that arrives courtesy of the full moon in showstopping Aries. If you're stuck in a comfortable groove, ignite magic by doing something unexpected. Surprise your sweetie with lunch, get a nail-art mani, post your creative work on social media (and @ your crush). What will get your pulse racing? Novelty releases a sexy rush of dopamine, which can wake up a stale vibe. Tandem skydiving isn't for everyone...but if it's your jam, now's your moment to jump! A partner *is* optional during the Aries full moon, which resonates at the frequency of *self*-love. That, of course, is the base ingredient for any relationship, so no matter your status, shower yourself with adoration. With decadent Venus in Libra sitting across the table from this full moon, treat yourself to something luxurious, like a special talisman from an indie jeweler or takeout from your favorite restaurant. When you're happy, everyone benefits.

10

MERCURY IN LIBRA

10 - 29 OCT

How balanced is your perspective? Mercury returns to Libra, restoring harmony to fractured bonds. Did you judge someone's idea too quickly last month, or write them off because you didn't see eye to eye? Justifiable reasons notwithstanding, reconsider your hardline perspective over the next few weeks. Fair-minded Mercury in Libra reminds you that there are two sides to every coin. Even if you agree to disagree, can you hear someone else's POV? That willingness alone can invite proactive dialogue (which Mercury in Libra lives for). From there, don't be surprised if an unexpected solution emerges. Even if negotiations are time-consuming, a patient, peaceful approach will be the most effective.

MARS-NEPTUNE SQUARE

12 OCT

Don't jump the gun! With quickfire Mars battling illusion-spinning Neptune, you could rush into a situation that sounds a lot more promising than it actually is. Details may be purposely obscured or, thanks to Mars in fast-talking Gemini, you could get lured in by a slick sales pitch. A "user-friendly" person might butter you up to get what they want, then leave you hanging. On your end, make sure you can truly deliver before you commit to anything. If an offer sounds promising, give yourself a few days to run the numbers, consider the time involvement and weigh this all against your existing obligations. It feels great to be generous, but with sacrificial Neptune in Pisces, you could get pulled underwater trying to fix someone else's problems. But the Mars-Neptune square can be healing, too. Today, you may finally gather the courage to bring up an important subject or reveal your buried brilliance! Prep yourself: Because of Mars' upcoming retrograde, there will be three squares to Neptune in the coming months. You may consider and reconsider decisions a couple more times. As a result, some truths may not reveal themselves until early 2023!

10

VENUS-SATURN TRINE

14 OCT

Is it lasting love—or just a magic moment? With cosmic charmer Venus touring Libra, feelings have ballooned to larger-than-life proportions. Maybe you became insta-BFFs with a fellow TikToker, or you're falling head over Doc Martens for a pandemic pen pal turned situationship. Nothing wrong with catching feelings! But you'll need to approach this from a more grounded perspective today. The reason? Pragmatic Saturn in Aquarius enters the picture and delivers a gentle (but unwavering) reality check to idealistic Venus. As the two dance into a cooperative trine, they'll enjoy some parallel play, meaning you don't have to chuck ALL romanticism out the window. Just slow it down a little, okay? Fun as it's been to get swept along in the Venus-fueled good vibes, Saturn's approach to emotions is full spectrum. Stop prolonging the honeymoon phase and discover the joys of truly knowing someone's ins and outs. Their quirks might just grow on ya!

SUN-MARS TRINE

17 OCT

Ready for liftoff? Today's airy trine between the Libra Sun and energizer Mars in Gemini will give you wings. But check your GPS instead of letting sponteneity be your guide. With Mars retrograde, this excitable transit could lead you on a wild goose chase—or worse, you could get lured into a complicated social situation that makes your own life messy. Enjoy a day of dabbling without making any major commitments. Move freely and don't let anyone tether your spirit. Discoveries will be inspiring and enlivening as long as you stop yourself from hitting the gas on any plans. You don't have to keep people at arm's length, but you also shouldn't hand them the unearned keys to your kingdom just because you felt instant synergy. Mantra for the day: time will tell.

10

WANING QUARTER MOON IN CANCER

17 OCT

Cozy up! Embrace the hygge season vibes as the quarter moon nestles into nurturing Cancer. Where could you bring more homey touches to your daily life? Tuck slippers under your desk and place at least one beautiful object in your line of vision, like a plant or crystal. Pause between professional duties to restock your tea selection, chitchat with coworkers or call a relative you've lost touch with. When you're back at base camp, set up your living room for movie, craft and game nights. If you're on the lookout for a new space, set up alerts from Zillow and Redfin. A lucky listing could pop up while you're organizing your office supplies or scrubbing the tub!

SUN-PLUTO SQUARE

19 OCT

Pay attention to subtle cues today. It's possible that people are being evasive or throwing shade, but don't race to conclusions. Ask clarifying questions and see if they balk. Even if you *do* have a case, quietly catalog the "evidence." That way, you can articulate the issue and back it up with proof. Competitors may be lurking; or jealous haters who can't stand to see anyone else shine. Protect your dreams like priceless artifacts. "Shield your field" and be discerning about the company you keep. Are others misreading *your* signals? Instead of assuming that your actions are "obvious," clearly state your intentions, leaving nothing up to chance. Need to hash out a problem? Pull people aside for a private chat. Confidentiality is everything today!

VENUS-PLUTO SQUARE

**20
OCT**

Love shouldn't feel like a competition or a game with a scorecard, but good luck telling people that today. As seductive Venus gets sucked into Pluto's undertow, pettiness and mean streaks are on full display. Lay low and let the storm clouds pass. Engaging with people when they're "in a mood" will only escalate the drama. Alas, your best efforts to cheer up your pouting lover might put you in their crosshairs. And if you wind up triggered, look out! Controlling, dominating or avoidant behavior will only heap fuel on the fire and deepen the divisive dynamic. You may find yourself obsessing over a (potentially toxic) heartbreaker—or grappling with a bout of jealousy based on unfounded suspicions. Hard as it is to stop your brain from fixating (and your fingers from Googling or texting), exert extreme willpower! On the plus side, the dam could burst on pent up erotic energy. Head to the bedroom and work it out!

SUN-VENUS MEETUP

**22
OCT**

If you've been overlooking the obvious—like someone's radiant spirit, say—it could hit you like a ton of bricks. With the Libra Sun giving Venus a galactic glow-up, your own attractive qualities will also shine. Yes, today will be a lovefest! No, you shouldn't hold back the compliments! The effusive mashup of the Sun and Venus is poetic, romantic and perfectly enchanting. Take time to notice people's finer points, then acknowledge them for what you see. Not only will you make their day, but you'll catch a buzz from these uplifting exchanges. And if there's more to explore, you've already broken the ice.

10

SUN IN SCORPIO

OCT 23 - NOV 22

Money, power, success! The Sun heads into Scorpio for a month, shining its high beams onto hidden financial opportunities. Instead of focusing on what you *don't* have, get resourceful. A closet dig could turn up some valuable treasures to sell on Poshmark. Maybe a neighborhood business needs a freelancer to help with social media posts. During this magnetic solar cycle, energy flows where your attention goes. Scorpio governs long-term investments and joint ventures. Learn about cryptocurrency and real estate or set up a chemistry meeting with a prospective business partner. Seeking startup capital? Scorpio season is prime time to find the right person to put dollars behind your dreams. Think beyond the 9-5 grind—and not just because Scorpio season turns us all into night owls. You could hit an idea for a passive revenue stream, like a downloadable product or rental equipment, that makes you money in your sleep. (Even if you don't hit the sack until the breaka-breaka dawn!)

and in love...

What lies beneath all those subtle come-ons? And how deep are you willing to dive in? The Sun embarks on its annual, monthlong journey through Scorpio, the sign of the legendary sex symbol. While the air is *this* charged with erotic energy, you might as well pursue intriguing leads. No need to rush the courtship process. Anything too obvious will be a bore over the coming four weeks—and the person who exercises the most willpower wins all the love. Certain relationships may arrive at a crossroads. Are you in or are you out? Unpack the attraction slowly, allowing trust to build through private, one-on-one encounters. Rocky relationships (and never-ending situationships) will arrive at a crossroads under Scorpio's "all or nothing" spell. Time to decide: Are you in or are you out? And if you are going to proceed, how can you revamp your relationship so that everyone feels safe and supported? Trust *and* lust are essential benchmarks during Scorpio season.

SATURN RETROGRADE ENDS

**23
OCT**

Reboot the revolution! Structured Saturn wakes up from its annual retrograde, correcting course in Aquarius, the sign of activism, teamwork and technology. As the planet of "adulting" turns direct, it's time to put the walk behind your idealistic talk. Since the backspin began on June 4, some of your ingenious plans may have stalled. You might need to modernize your equipment, get organized on apps and even bring in a savvy project manager to map out the game plan. If a group endeavor has been on shaky ground, you can get the band back together, but don't settle! Masterful Saturn rewards authority. Is it time to upgrade to a more experienced crew, or deal with a bad apple in your barrel? Saturn in Aquarius supports community organizing—both on the ground and virtually. Now's the time to align with people and organizations who are being the change you want to see in the world.

VENUS IN SCORPIO

**23 OCT -
16 NOV**

Venus shimmies into Scorpio, adding another dollop of sex appeal to the month. Just talking about your turn-ons could get motors revving—and if you get you-know-who behind closed doors, there's no telling what will transpire. Get in touch with your eroticism through dance, sensual movement or good old-fashioned sexytime. Secrecy and mystery are hot while Venus is here, which can be a double-edged sword. Temptations can veer toward the taboo and good sense could fly out the window in the face of a scorching-hot attraction. Find ways to get your kicks that don't require you to break any binding relationship rules. Stuck in a holding pattern? Dive deep into emotional exploration to move past any blocks. This transformative time could open the seductive floodgates! Warning: The green-eyed monster will make regular appearances during this cycle. Leaving something to the imagination? Mais oui! Riling up jealousy? Don't even THINK about going there.

10

Solar eclipse!

SCORPIO NEW MOON

<table>
<tr><td>

25 OCT

</td><td>

Looking for answers? Search beyond your usual range— and shine the light deep within your psyche. Today's new moon in mystical Scorpio is also a rare solar eclipse. As the crossing moon dims the light of the Sun, what you *don't* see may be far more telling than anything your eyes radar in on. Stay open to non-obvious insights and chance encounters. A bond that begins today could develop into a strong soul connection. Shared finances, passive income and property matters come under the microscope, especially since this new moon lands next to value-driven Venus. How can you pool funds for greater wealth? If you've been spending indiscriminately, start tucking more away for the future. No, that doesn't mean stuffing cash into a mattress or even a basic savings account that pays miniscule interest. Have a portion of your paycheck automatically streamed into your 401K (or SEP IRA if you're self-employed). Search for investments with compounding interest. Is that all Greek to you? Start learning the language of money. Read a personal finance book to educate yourself on the basics or ask savvy friends to recommend a money manager. Build a diversified portfolio, one that sets you up for a future of greater security *and* freedom.

</td></tr>
</table>

10

and in love...

Quelle surprise! It's anyone's guess what will come to light in love today. For this we can thank the solar eclipse in Scorpio, which unleashes a transformational tsunami of passion. For some people, emotions will run hot and cold—and you may have a hard time turning off the "faucet" once you let them out! Before you make any definitive declarations, *really* think through the pros and cons. What you say today could become a binding agreement, as this eclipse opens a fresh, six-month chapter for intimacy. Remember: Cutting people off doesn't stop them from living rent free in your head. So, if there's a chance you can hash out the conflict, this new moon could guide you to creative solutions. Tackling a shared mission is a great way for couples to bond. Shifting roles may be part of the equation, so be prepared to step out of your comfort zone. This is a potent day for hashing out important relationship points, like shared finances and sexual satisfaction. Have these talks in private and keep them between the two of you. It's about trust!

10

MERCURY-PLUTO SQUARE

27 OCT

Is it them or is it you? People are projecting their issues onto each other at every turn today, as expressive Mercury gets caught in combat with manipulative Pluto. Before you go pointing fingers, do some personal inventory. You may be blaming people for the very same "crime" you're committing. It takes two to tango in every interaction, so don't let anyone dump their issues on you, either. Having boundaries means being responsible for *your* actions—and not taking responsibility for anyone else's. Under this moody square, you could spend the day ruminating over a recent problem. Catch yourself if you start obsessing. Tunnel vision won't get you where you want to go.

JUPITER IN PISCES

28 OCT - 20 DEC

Woosahhhh. Philosophical Jupiter, which has been retrograde in high-octane Aries since July 28, slips back one spot on the zodiac wheel into enlightened Pisces beginning today. While the backspin wages on until November 23, you may still feel some relief. This serenity-restoring cycle can feel like a head trip at first—especially after the frenetic pace of Jupiter in Aries. But like the tornado that transported Dorothy Gale (and Diana Ross!) to Oz, you might feel like a portal opened and snatched you back into another dimension. How to navigate this yellow brick road? Surrender to divine timing and let things flow. (Call it an energy-conservation plan.) Warning: This paranoia-provoking cycle may bring confusion and delusion. Don't believe the hype! That "news" story sent by your conspiracy-theory-loving friend needs to be scoured for truth, with the instincts of a private investigator. Careful not to hop on the collective fear bandwagon during Jupiter's remaining tour through Pisces until December 20. Conversely, don't drop your guard so much that you put yourself in danger.

10

THE ASTROTWINS

MERCURY IN SCORPIO

29 OCT - 17 NOV

An air of mystery and a measure of control—there's something so powerfully seductive about those qualities. Expressive Mercury hits the mute button and slips into secretive Scorpio for three weeks. Get your point across, but don't rely on words. The pregnant pause, the flashing gaze, the heat (or chill) of body language...these all speak volumes. The next couple weeks are ideal for researching, editing and crafting your magnum opus behind the scenes. Hold off on the big pitches and press releases. Instead, perfect your presentation and make a grand debut in the middle of next month. Loyalty tests could come out of the blue. If you want to pass these "pop quizzes," show and prove your allegiance. And above all, keep confidential information locked in the vault. The toughest part of this Mercury cycle? Knowing when to be transparent and when to play cat and mouse!

MARS RETROGRADE IN GEMINI

**30 OCT -
12 JAN '23**

FOMO alert! If variety is the spice of life, then season with care over the next two and a half months. Frenetic Mars turns retrograde in Gemini, a cycle bound to churn up confusion and creative insight in equal measure. There will be a zillion great ideas forming, but which ones really make sense to pursue? Making any kind of a decision could be downright mind-boggling as there will always be another avenue to explore. Anxiety provoking, too! Buyer's remorse may kick in before you've hit "send" on that DocuSign. Choosing a "good enough" option may be better than not choosing at all. But conduct solid research first. Disinformation travels fast with the brash planet off course in signal-scrambling Gemini. Arguments with peers (coworkers, neighbors, relatives close in age) could get ugly now. Do your level best to play nice and avoid gossiping at all costs. Find a workout buddy (twinning!) who can keep you motivated to bust through stress the Mars-inspired way: through physical exertion.

and in love...

Romantic restlessness has been brewing ever since Mars entered Gemini on August 20. But as the lusty planet spins retrograde in the sign of the Twins, you may have second (third and fourth) thoughts about the future—or nature—of a relationship. Are you just friends, is it an emotional affair, are you growing apart? Argh! Lead with logic and don't let suspicions run wild. The propensity for overthinking is high now, which can cause you to freeze. If you catch yourself analyzing every text exchange (and dragging friends into the drama), you literally should get a hobby. Boredom can lead to mischief, so fill your life with engaging, interesting friends. Gemini rules the hands, making touch (with consent) a healing salve. Taking time to ask "Does this feel nice?" ocan be illuminating and titillating. And you might just learn something new about your lover in the process!

10

NOVEMBER *Moon Phases*

SUN	MON	TUE	WED	THU	FRI	SAT
		1 ♒︎ 1st Quarter	**2** ♓︎ 2:47PM	**3** ♓︎	**4** ♈︎ 7:07PM	**5** ♈︎
6 ♈︎	**7** ♉︎ 12:15AM	**8** ♉︎ Lunar Eclipse **FM** ♉︎ 6:02AM	**9** ♊︎ 8:37AM	**10** ♊︎	**11** ♋︎ 7:23PM	**12** ♋︎
13 ♋︎	**14** ♌︎ 7:48AM	**15** ♌︎	**16** ♍︎ 8:04PM 3rd Q ♌︎	**17** ♍︎	**18** ♍︎	**19** ♎︎ 5:58AM
20 ♎︎	**21** ♏︎ 12:16PM	**22** ♏︎	**23** ♐︎ 3:16PM **NM** ♐︎ 5:57PM	**24** ♐︎	**25** ♑︎ 4:18PM	**26** ♑︎
27 ♒︎ 5:07PM	**28** ♒︎	**29** ♓︎ 7:15PM	**30** ♓︎ 1st Quarter			

KEY: ♈︎ ARIES   ♊︎ GEMINI   ♌︎ LEO   ♎︎ LIBRA   ♐︎ SAGITTARIUS   ♒︎ AQUARIUS
♉︎ TAURUS   ♋︎ CANCER   ♍︎ VIRGO   ♏︎ SCORPIO   ♑︎ CAPRICORN   ♓︎ PISCES

FM FULL MOON   **NM** NEW MOON   **LE** LUNAR ECLIPSE   **SE** SOLAR ECLIPSE

WAXING QUARTER MOON IN AQUARIUS

1 NOV

Protect your tech! The quarter moon logs in to digitally savvy Aquarius, sending a friendly reminder that not every app you download or feed you follow is, well, friendly. Nowadays, it's almost too easy to pass around disinformation via meme or buy into 30-second product reviews from an "expert" whose only real credentials are TikTok editing skills. Just because you upload, post and save to the cloud, how secure *is* your data, really? And are your favorite apps tracking your every move (and geotagging them, to boot) because you kept the location accuracy "on" in the settings? It might make your head explode to think about this, and if so, you should probably hire someone with IT cred to ensure that you're not leaving yourself vulnerable. And, uh, is that your Twitter bae or a bot who's been @-ing you? Better triple check.

VENUS-URANUS OPPOSITION

5 NOV

Assume nothing today...but expect anything! Controlling Venus in Scorpio is at loggerheads with bombastic Uranus in Taurus. Strong emotions might erupt like molten lava under this explosive and unpredictable face-off. Try not to interact with someone who's behaving like a ticking time bomb. And if your love interest signals a need for space, give it to them instead of frantically texting or pushing for a talk. Feeling the urge for more freedom? You don't have to throw out the baby with the bathwater. It's totally possible to create more space in a relationship without calling the whole thing off. Rule of thumb for the day? Assume nothing. Just because you and your partner were on the same page in the past doesn't mean you're aligned for eternity. Avoid making any unilateral decisions. Check in and get consensus (and consent) before taking action.

11

VENUS-SATURN SQUARE

7 NOV

If you've been charging full steam ahead in your love life, today's cautious cosmic clash could hit the brakes. Don't dismiss any reservations or nagging gut feelings. Instead, be grateful for this rare reality check from the stars. Considering a commitment? Make sure you're both on the same page for what you want long-term. The only way you'll know is by setting your emotions aside and talking it through. For couples, it's a good day for a serious discussion about future plans or an unresolved issue. Warning: If you aren't careful, your inner critic could short-circuit the bonding process. And with Venus in Scorpio, venomous words can be poison to a relationship. Turn on Saturn's quality-control filters and adult your way through the conflic, avoiding any slings or stings.

Lunar eclipse!

TAURUS FULL MOON

8 NOV

Show them the money! Today's full moon in fiscal and security-seeking Taurus would be powerful enough on its own. But as a game-changing lunar eclipse, it brings epic opportunities to shift (and increase!) the way you save, spend and earn. Ready to do away with a longtime bad habit and start fresh? Here's where the sensible-yet-sensual Taurus moon can save the day, reminding you that true change is a marathon, not a sprint. That said, this *is* a rare total lunar eclipse. And it could serve up a promising possibility that you need to decide on...fast! Don't stall if you're excited about exploring something that shows up today (or over the next few days). This may indeed be a "once in a lifetime" gift, like a chance to travel for work or collab with a dream client who you've followed for years. Jump into research mode and see what it will take to *not* miss out. Practical magic is plentiful today, but you have to take action in order to tap into it.

11

and in love...

<table>
<tr><td>

8 NOV

</td></tr>
</table>

Sense and sensuality? Yes, the twain can meet, and today's earthy full moon in Taurus is here to prove it! Bring on the TLC, affectionate gestures and long, lingering hugs (and then some). Love doesn't have to come in like a wrecking ball, then race off like a runaway train. But if that's your story, pull into the station and check your GPS before you derail. Brace yourself. Since this full moon is also a total lunar eclipse, you might be hit with some surprising information. Like maybe that nice guy is actually a manipulative tool—and the one you pegged as a player is marriage material. Misaligned values could be cause for a breakup, or some heavy-duty couples' therapy. But then again, perhaps your love interest is more stable than you gave them credit for. (And, glug, maybe *you* were the secret commitmentphobe of the two of you?) Bottom line: When you slow down and get back to brass tacks, you may discover inconsistencies that need to be dealt with. But that's where pragmatic Taurus shines. Sort it out with logic and lots of touch, if the love isn't lost.

SUN-URANUS OPPOSITION

9 NOV

Touchy, touchy! Egos get testy today as the sensitive Scorpio Sun faces down button-pushing Uranus in Taurus. Steer clear of thin-skinned people who are always spoiling for a fight. And don't go playing devil's advocate. You can try to smooth things over by focusing on common ground, but easy does it. Attempts to break the tension with humor may go over like a lead balloon. Although you might feel anxious about a pending event, this isn't the day to demand a firm answer or make a binding decision. Plans could change without notice. If you must pivot quickly, adopt a flexible attitude instead of digging in your heels. (Tough, given that the Sun and Uranus are at loggerheads in tenacious fixed signs.) Stay nimble! A completely unexpected approach could actually lead to a breakthrough.

11

VENUS-NEPTUNE TRINE

Subtle signals say it all today, as amorous Venus in Scorpio gets in a flowing formation with enchanting Neptune in Pisces. Their dynamic dance, which generally happens twice a year, sends seductive undercurrents rippling through the ether. Cast a spell with nonverbal cues, dab on a titillating fragrance; show a little skin. A little cat-and-mouse game can be arousing in affairs de coeur. Wait a little longer to reply to a new love interest's text—but not *so* long that they think you're uninterested. Uncertainty builds anticipation...and attraction. The only risk of a Venus-Neptune trine is that it can make boundaries a little hazy. Don't lose sight of *all* propriety in the heat of the moment. There's a time and a place for everything.

SUN-SATURN SQUARE

A battle of the egos could burst out today when the strong-willed Sun in Scorpio clashes with authoritarian Saturn in Aquarius. The know-it-alls are out in full force—and no one will be quick to concede. Be on guard for bullies and don't step into their gaslighting booby traps. The minute you feel your emotions overtake you is the moment you hand them all the power. Silence may be the strongest weapon in your arsenal, so don't be quick to show your cards (or even drag them on Twitter). Practicing restraint is the way to win, but we're not saying it's going to be easy!

SUN-NEPTUNE TRINE

<table>
<tr><td>14
NOV</td></tr>
</table>

Slip behind the scenes and drift into your subconscious. Today's Sun in esoteric Scorpio gets in a flow with soothsayer Neptune in Pisces, setting the stage for profound introspection. Stepping back from the fray is important from time to time. Not only does it give you a chance to unwind, but it also helps you regain perspective. If you've hit a creative block, this mental breathing room will get past it. Since both planets are in water signs, ideas could hit you while you're in the shower or tub! Stay open to serendipities. Today's psychic celestial mashup sends your "random" thoughts into the ether, helping you manifest dreams at an accelerated speed.

VENUS-JUPITER TRINE

<table>
<tr><td>15
NOV</td></tr>
</table>

Get ready for a huge heart-opening as love planet Venus dances into a dynamic formation with supersizer Jupiter. Like a wave washing over you, a sudden realization could hit. Whoa! You have feelings—and profound ones at that—possibly for someone you haven't thought about "that way" before. Or maybe you notice something incredible about your rock-steady boo, and it makes you swoon all over again. If the coast is clear, down the truth serum and speak up. Leaving anything up to chance could mean missing your window of opportunity. Will divulging your truth get you tangled up in a complicated situation? If the object of your affections is otherwise engaged, leave this one in the fantasy zone for now.

11

WANING QUARTER MOON IN LEO

16
NOV

When does "just a little more" cross the line into "hella extra"? The answer could reveal itself during today's moderating quarter moon in Leo. Have you fallen into a rut of basic-ness? Add a few glamorous, theatrical bells and whistles to your presentations. Already creeping into "Liberace Museum" terrain? This lunar leveling wags a bejeweled finger at anything *too* ostentatious. Leo style maven Coco Chanel advised people to remove one accessory before walking out the door. Apply this principle broadly today. If stress has been rising, book a massage (Leo rules the back) or stream an upbeat dance class. Pampering yourself pays off in productivity and pleasure!

VENUS IN SAGITTARIUS

16 NOV
- 9 DEC

Ardent Venus swings into worldly Sagittarius, stirring up attractions across every aisle. Sagittarius is the zodiac's gambler and over the next few weeks, you could take a Vegas-sized chance on romance. Candid confessions come spilling out, blowing covers on lovers everywhere. But hey, life is too short to covertly strategize and obsess. Better to find out sooner than later if your affections are reciprocated—and now is the time. During this happy-go-lucky circuit it will be easier to brush off a rejection and keep on swiping. Cross-cultural connections simmer with extra spice, and there couldn't be a better time for couples to take a baecation—or singles to have an irrefutably hot vacation fling! Not able to get away? Find your romantic and artistic stimulation, anywhere BUT the usual places.

11

MERCURY IN SAGITTARIUS

**17 NOV
- 6 DEC**

Let the cat out of the bag! Authenticity is back on trend as Mercury fires arrows into Sagittarius' realm. Defend your principles with the fierceness of a tiger. But *do* leave room for dialogue after you've shared your personal truth. Sagittarius is the sign of global expansion, cross-cultural connections and broad-minded philosophical thinking. Step out of your echo chamber and consider a rainbow of perspectives. Yes, these talks *can* get passionate. Restrict yourself from being reactive if tempers flare. Vent to a neutral third party to sound out feelings instead of unleashing a rough cut of your diatribe. Don't forget Mercury-in-Sagittarius' finest offering: the gift of humor. Mark Twain, who was born under this Sun sign, reminded us that the human race "has one really effective weapon, and that is laughter."

MARS-NEPTUNE SQUARE

**19
NOV**

Is something bubbling below the surface? Pay attention to intuitive hits today. For the second time since October 12, investigative Mars in Gemini locks into a dynamic duel with obfuscating Neptune in Pisces. Want answers? Since Mars is retrograde, you'll need to peel back some layers to find them. Don't rush to form theories based on your first "dig." Just when you think you've cracked the case, more evidence may emerge. This is the second in this series of three Mars-Neptune squares. Until the trilogy wraps on March 14, 2023, key information is bound to be obscured. To use these squares to your advantage, embrace the creative process! Approach perplexing situations with a sense of wonder and curiosity. Be a student of your craft, always willing to learn another technique. Apply tons of self-compassion if you "mess up." Mistakes can be blessings in disguise (call them "studies"), so turn them into teachable moments.

SUN-JUPITER TRINE

20
NOV

Ready to go deep—like, even deeper than what you might be thinking? Love and intimacy aren't always the easiest things to navigate, and the juiciest fruit isn't hanging on the lowest branches. But as the Scorpio Sun trines intrepid Jupiter in Pisces, you'll discover opportunities for connection everywhere. This rare and uplifting angle helps you release the need for control and appreciate things for being exactly the way they are. Want a breakthrough in relationships? Veer away from small talk and bare a bit of your soul. You don't have to trot out stories about your childhood trauma (unless that's appropriate). Share a song that makes you cry, talk about a series that moved you. If you bond over the themes, conversations will naturally flow in a more personal direction.

MERCURY-VENUS MEETUP

21
NOV

'Fess up! Today's audaciously outspoken meetup of candid Mercury and charming Venus in Sagittarius loosens tongues and lifts the veil on anything you've tucked under your vest. Quick, tell your crush that you've caught feelings! Authenticity is an aphrodisiac under these skies. If you're coming out of left field, however, don't expect an immediate response. The object of your affections might need a minute to let this information settle in. Long-term couples can spice things up with an evening adventure or a one-night staycation. Though this transit is a brief one, a change of scenery—like a night at a boutique hotel or a starlit stroll to pick up dinner from a new restaurant—can create a delicious memory that gives you juice for days.

11

SUN IN SAGITTARIUS

NOV 22 - DEC 21

Is there unity in your community? The Sun bursts into horizon-broadening Sagittarius for a month, celebrating the differences that make us all dynamic. "Anywhere but home" always seems like the ideal destination for Sagittarius season, but with travel restrictions in place, you can journey in the metaphoric sense this year. There's always more to learn about cultural sensitivity. Check out books, virtual lectures and inter-office training programs to expand your perspective. Since Sagittarius rules education, what could you learn before the year is through? (Or enroll in now to get your 2023 off to a powerful start?) Find new ways to flex your entrepreneurial muscles, whether you're organizing a mastermind group or hosting a holiday pop-up sale. This sporty solar cycle could get you bundled up and onto the slopes—or onto your yoga mat to warm your body from the inside out.The spirit of transparency is in the air, so if you need to have an honest chat with someone before the holidays kick in, hash it out now.

and in love...

Convinced that you have a type? Guess again. The next four weeks could dispel any such myths as the Sun spreads its wings in broad-minded Sagittarius. You may fall head over babouches for someone's adorable accent or their refreshingly different perspective on life. Unearthing common ground will be equally enchanting. And if surface appearances tell a different tale, your love story could provide inspiration for other couples who believe in freedating. And that's exactly the point. Rather than judging a book by its cover, delve into everyone's story with the spirit of discovery. Do this even if you're half of an "old marrieds" pair. Human beings are dynamic creatures, after all. You may think you know your S.O. inside and out...until you approach them with what the Buddhists call "beginner's mind." Converse with limitless curiosity, as if you were meeting for the first time. You might just fall in love all over again or get so damn real that you establish a whole new level of intimate communication.

11

THE ASTROTWINS

SAGITTARIUS NEW MOON

<table>
<tr><td>23
NOV</td></tr>
</table>

Reach across borders! Today's new moon in Sagittarius bridges divides, setting the stage for multicultural mingling. Better yet? A few minutes after the exact new moon occurs, worldly Jupiter—the ruling planet of Sagittarius—wakes up from a four-month retrograde. That's double the incentive to switch to a wide-angle lens, like, immediately! What are the kids doing in Sao Paulo, Savannah and Seoul? Searches could turn up virtual connections—and there's no telling what these will evolve into. This new moon brings a burst of "cosmic capital" for start-up initiatives. Entrepreneurs, take time to set your six-month intentions today. What benchmarks would you love to achieve by the corresponding *full* moon in Sagittarius on June 3, 2023? Consider today your official launch pad. Take an action to move the needle, now!

and in love...

As if you needed *one* more prompt to open your mind, speak your truth or broaden your outlook on love, well, here you go. The annual new moon in Sagittarius pushes you off the diving board and into adventurous romantic waters. Challenge yourself to try a different approach to dating or the way you communicate in your relationship. Spice up your bond by signing up for a couples' workshop or planning a trip. If you've been trapped in the couple bubble, absence makes the heart grow fonder. Give yourself (and your partner) a little more breathing room in the weeks ahead. You'll have so much to talk about when you're each expanding your personal horizons. Plus, supporting each other's passions can be inspiring and fun!

11

JUPITER DIRECT IN PISCES

23 NOV

Enterprising Jupiter snaps out of retrograde, issuing a worldwide wakeup call! With the galactic globalist reversing through Aries, then Pisces, since July 28, it took some heavy lifting to *not* fall prey to doom and gloom. If you've been fighting the demons of denial, discouragement, and a depressing point of view, hope resumes. But stay in the healing process. The red-spotted planet will be submerged in Pisces' deep waters until December 20. The next four weeks are optimal for tackling trauma, metabolizing grief and getting in tune with the full spectrum of feelings. This doesn't have to rain on your holiday season parade. Philosophical Jupiter in Pisces illuminates life-changing lessons and passes out shiny gold stars to everyone who is willing to do the tough inner work. 'Tis the season for artists, musicians, and creatives to flourish. Deck the halls with handmade treasures—and if you tap into Jupiter's enterprising vibes, who knows? You could soon be taking orders from worldwide customers via Etsy!

MARS-SATURN TRINE

28 NOV

For the second time this year, speed demon Mars gets a "slow down!" warning from sensible Saturn, advising us all to hit the brakes. This time, Mars is retrograde, so as annoying as it is to be stopped in your path, it's also a blessing! There's a real chance you could get blown off course if you don't recalibrate your compass. Do this now, before you get a "citation" for ignoring important rules—or waste hours of time doubling back because you took a wrong turn. Did you make a snap judgment about someone on your team? With both planets in communicative, people-focused air signs, you could finally see what they're made of. For better or for worse, don't sweep your findings under the rug. A genuine compliment—or a necessary correction—can build stronger rapport.

11

WAXING QUARTER MOON IN PISCES

<table>
<tr><td>30
NOV</td></tr>
</table>

Silence speaks louder than words under today's quarter moon in esoteric Pisces. Tune in to subtle cues like body language, intuitive hits and the emotional energy of a room. While it's still important to get the facts, these are reliable guides for assessing the temperature of your environment. Pace yourself accordingly! If you've been an open book (and who hasn't during Sagittarius season?), keep a little more mystery to yourself. It's an alluring trait today, one that leaves people hungry to know more. And since Pisces is the master of illusion, it's a wise security measure. Establishing trust takes time. Pace yourself and let things flow organically. Don't be surprised if this "tuned in" approach leads you to a miraculous discovery! Serendipities are probably *not* "mere coincidences" today. If something seems like a sign, follow that thread.

11

DECEMBER
Moon Phases

SUN	MON	TUE	WED	THU	FRI	SAT
				1 ♈ 11:41PM	**2** ♈	**3** ♈
4 ♉ 6:38AM	**5** ♉	**6** ♊ 3:49PM	**7** ♊ Full Moon 11:08PM	**8** ♊	**9** ♋ 2:49AM	**10** ♋
11 ♌ 3:09PM	**12** ♌	**13** ♌	**14** ♍ 3:46AM	**15** ♍	**16** ♎ 2:49PM 3rd Qtr ♍	**17** ♎
18 ♏ 10:31PM	**19** ♏	**20** ♏	**21** ♐ 2:13AM	**22** ♐	**23** ♑ 2:50AM NM ♑ 5:16AM	**24** ♑
25 ♒ 2:14AM	**26** ♒	**27** ♓ 2:34AM	**28** ♓	**29** ♈ 5:36AM 1st Quarter	**30** ♈	**31** ♉ 12:09PM

KEY: ♈ ARIES ♊ GEMINI ♌ LEO ♎ LIBRA ♐ SAGITTARIUS ♒ AQUARIUS
♉ TAURUS ♋ CANCER ♍ VIRGO ♏ SCORPIO ♑ CAPRICORN ♓ PISCES

FM FULL MOON   **NM** NEW MOON   **LE** LUNAR ECLIPSE   **SE** SOLAR ECLIPSE

MERCURY-NEPTUNE SQUARE

<table>
<tr><td>1
DEC</td></tr>
</table>

Your left and right brain hemispheres battle for authority as tough-talking Mercury in Sagittarius squares off with softhearted Neptune in Pisces. Half of you wants to lay down the law with strict orders. The other half is melting into a giant pile of mush. And with both planets in mutable signs, every option may seem as valid as the next. Although you're conflicted about the right course of action, there *is* a middle ground. Try expert Suzy Welch's 10-10-10 rule for decision-making. Reflect on how the results of your choice could unfold in ten minutes, ten months and ten years. You'll be surprised by the insight! Beyond that, are you having too many "conversations" in your head? Get into dialogue with the so-called offending party. By asking a few open-ended questions, you could unpack their not-so-hidden motives and get to the bottom of the miscommunication. Sweet relief!

VENUS-MARS OPPOSITION

<table>
<tr><td>1
DEC</td></tr>
</table>

War and peace? Combative Mars draws peacekeeping Venus into a lover's quarrel, as the two lock into a somewhat rare opposition. Feelings ricochet between extremes and simmering tension comes to a boil. Bridge-building Venus in Sagittarius can point you to common ground, but that might not be enough to help anyone see eye to eye. Mars is retrograde in nitpicking Gemini, flashing trigger alerts at the slightest provocation. Avoid temptation if you don't want to stray. Lusty vibes may overtake good senses, making it a little too easy to blur the lines. This opposition *can* set the stage for productive conversations, even if they start out as arguments. There's no stepping over BS or sweeping problems under the rug. If you have been, get ready for an explosion. But hey, these issues probably needed to be blown into the open, anyway. Map out your exit strategy *before* you enter the danger zone.

NEPTUNE DIRECT IN PISCES

3 DEC

Zone in! Soothsayer Neptune snaps out of retrograde and powers forward through its native sign of Pisces. After five months of soulful exploration, you can turn your vision quest into tangible action. What have you been quietly developing (or dreaming about developing) since the backspin began on June 28? As the planet of cathartic creativity corrects course, confidence returns for any missions that make the world a welcoming place for everyone. If you've felt adrift from your purpose, add some soul to your goals. Tap into your creative right brain (and the divine flow) with journaling, meditation or visualization exercises. If you delved into shadow work over the past five months, take inventory of your feelings: Do you need to set healthier boundaries? Forgive someone or ask for it from a person you wronged? Extend an olive branch! You might just sort this out before the holidays kick in.

VENUS-NEPTUNE SQUARE

4 DEC

Love goggles: off! We don't want to burst your bubble, but today's tense standoff between romantic Venus and delusional Neptune is *not* the time to rock any rose-colored glasses. Catch yourself before you get lost in a fantasy. See the situation for what it really is, and you'll be far more prepared to navigate the seas. Just wait a couple days before drawing hard and fast conclusions. When these dreamy planets square each other twice each year, reality is a moving target. Take a deeper cut at anything that seems too good to be true. That said, you might get swept away with spontaneity, even if the vibe is more "situationship" than "happily ever after." As long as you know what you're getting into (and you're confident that you'll be able to detach from expectations later) why *not* have a little fun? With Venus in global Sagittarius and Neptune in nomadic Pisces, it's anyone's guess where this fantasy-fueled wave will take you!

MERCURY-JUPITER SQUARE

6 DEC

Ideological debates could flame into shouting matches as feisty Mercury in Sagittarius locks horns with principled Jupiter in Pisces. You can't always be on the same page with everyone. While it's hard to accept on days like this, save your breath. Trying to sway a hothead is a fool's errand today. Are you being overly optimistic or trying to force your agenda? Tunnel vision mixed with stubborn willfulness will make a combustible cocktail right now. Lead by example if you want to open people's eyes or awaken their compassion. They might need to see it to believe it.

MERCURY IN CAPRICORN

6 DEC - 11 FEB '23

Want to wrap up 2022 like a boss? Plan, strategize, and negotiate your way to the finish line! Nimble Mercury puts your mind on your money as it bounds into ambitious Capricorn for the rest of the year. Set emotions aside and think through goals with objectivity and precision. Cut the fluff and keep it simple. Sometimes, the first answer is the best one. Over the holidays, you could get a jump-start on your 2023 resolutions, as the responsible Capricorn influence will have your mind on the future. Just make sure these achievements aren't SO lofty that they feel out of reach. Shop talk could filter into end-of-year conversations. As you mingle amongst the revelers and sip top-shelf champagne, think of clever ways to phrase the question that will be at the top of everyone's mind, "So, what do you do for a living?"

GEMINI FULL MOON

<table>
<tr><td>7
DEC</td></tr>
</table>

What you *say* is what you get. Words are powerful attractors under the light of the loquacious full moon in Gemini. Articulate your dreams, desires and wishes aloud. Post about them on social media, to the degree you feel comfortable. Someone in your circle (or a degree of separation away) could point you toward important resources that help you manifest your vision. With the full moon in the sign of the Twins, a creative partnership could turn into an official dynamic duo. If you've been hustling together for the past six months, plan a drop or debut or get the buzz going! Need a new set of wheels? Since transportation is Gemini's domain, this full moon may light the way to the perfect car or mobile accessory for commutes. What you don't want to do, however, is focus on problems. With Mars retrograde sitting close to the full moon, you risk drawing trouble your way. Keep it positive and proactive. If you're having trouble flipping that switch, start by making a gratitude list. Surround yourself with uplifting people. Good vibes are contagious!

and in love...

Bring some levity into your love game! The year's only full moon in Gemini illuminates lighthearted ways to sync up. Think of your other half as your playmate, or revamp your dating app profile to reveal as much about your extracurricular interests as your long-term life plans. Kindred spirits could unite under this twinning influence. Or should we say *reunite*, since this full moon arrives in close contact to retrograde Mars. For the two weeks that follow, keep yourself in "pairing mode." If you feel that spark of potential (or soul recognition!), make a move. Saying hello never hurt anyone, right? Whether for romance, friendship or a creative collaboration, you might attract your missing puzzle piece. Local searches could be fruitful! Stay out of a tech trance while you're walking around your neighborhood. Your future mate could be waiting in line behind you at the post office or grocery store. Or you might find the perfect date-night option in your very own zip code.

SUN-MARS OPPOSITION

8 DEC

In it to win it? Competition is fierce during today's take-no-prisoners opposition between the Sagittarius Sun and warrior Mars in Gemini. With these articulate signs amplified by the planets, a heated debate could get fiercer than a legendary rap battle. But watch out! With Mars retrograde, the gloves come off quickly, whether you're texting, tweeting or loudly asserting your opinion. And no one's shaking hands after sticks and stones are thrown. Channel aggression into a physical project. Hit the gym hard or power clean your house for the holidays. Sexual tension reaches a fever pitch, but the chemistry could be combustible. Rash moves may bring regret—but good luck telling that to your reptilian brain, which is bound to seize the wheel under these skies!

VENUS-JUPITER SQUARE

9 DEC

People might talk a good game, but can they back up their words with action? That's questionable as heavenly optimists Venus and Jupiter get locked in a sense-blurring square. Both planets have a strict "no negative vibes" policy, but rocking the rose-colored glasses puts you in a gullible position today. To avoid being a victim of this "hustler's holiday," take nothing at face value. Drop your date's name into Google. Ask the tough questions. If they're as legit as they present, background checks will make you *more* confident about moving forward. Besides, even the most solid relationships require periodic reviews. Have a sit-down with your sweetie today, if only to get back on a level playing field. Remember: Assumptions are the enemy of intimacy! Ask the difficult questions and don't interrupt while people are answering. While you may hear a few uncomfortable truths, better to get it all out into the open than to let it fester.

VENUS IN CAPRICORN

9 DEC - 4 JAN '23

What's next for your love life? Sharpen the focus of your relationship goals as amorous Venus shifts into structured Capricorn. Couples can align around your shared future, discussing your 2023 dreams by the fireplace. If you're single and looking, search for someone who is ready for meaningful co-creation, like now. Matters of the heart will get serious...but they don't have to be as serious as a heart attack! Playful, seductive Venus likes to keep the mood light. Defining nebulous situationships could be a fun game of "You show me your bucket list, I'll show you mine!" Or, if you're the type who doesn't even think about bucket lists, well, maybe it's time to write one. With driven Capricorn ruling romance for the next few weeks, couples could achieve something memorable—and profitable—as a pair. No apologies for being attracted to status now. If you're looking to "date up," 'tis the season for strategic mistletoe placement.

SUN-NEPTUNE SQUARE

**14
DEC**

Reflect before you project! Hazy Neptune in Pisces is at loggerheads with the bright Sagittarius Sun, obscuring facts and drawing in untrustworthy types. Check to make sure you aren't dodging conversational bullets or avoiding an uncomfortable topic that's past due for discussion. Hit pause and take stock of how realistic your ambitious ideas are. While nothing outside of yourself may be clear, your inner landscape *will* be illuminated. Seize the opportunity to flip your viewfinder inwards and do some deep introspection. Just don't act on it impetuously. Unless, of course, you pick up some artistic tools and let the divine inspiration flow through you. Keep the critics far away while you're in this zone. Today is about making art for art's sake—and for the pure, therapeutic process!

WANING QUARTER MOON IN VIRGO

**16
DEC**

Don't sweat the small stuff, but don't ignore it either. Fine lines and wrinkles can interfere with plans as the quarter moon in Virgo plays inspector for the day. Proof your work before sending it off, making sure everything's spellchecked, accurate and up to date. Ask a wise friend to read your text before you fire it off in the heat of reactivity. Falling prey to perfectionism? If you find yourself on *that* end of the spectrum, adjust your expectations. Are you asking more of people than they can humanly provide? Today's moonbeams may guide you to more qualified service providers who can help you get the job done to code. But even then, get real. Timelines and budgets may also need adjusting unless you're willing to simplify your strategy.

JUPITER IN ARIES

**20 DEC -
16 MAY '23**

Larger-than-life Jupiter resets its compass, surging into trailblazing Aries for its second of three adventurous passes in 2022-23. Stalled missions pick up momentum—and at warp speed, to boot! Suddenly, you're planning a ceremonial New Year's getaway on the beach when, a week ago, you swore you'd keep it chill and lay low at home. Ambitious projects and passionate attractions heat up, diverting attention from stocking-stuffing duties. When inspiration strikes, record the gems in an audio note before you lose them. People making demands on your time and energy? Not a favorite thing while Jupiter is in self-focused, spontaneous Aries. Don't shirk responsibilities though! No, you don't have to keep *every* promise you made while Jupiter paddled through sacrificial Pisces since October 28. But if you're going to break your word, give people time to devise a Plan B. Make a graceful exit instead of burning bridges.

DEC 21 - JAN 20

SUN IN CAPRICORN

It's beginning to feel a lot like solstice! The Sun enters Capricorn, marking the shortest day of the year for those living in the northern hemisphere. Under the cover of darkness, turn inwards and scan the landscape of your subconscious mind. Carve out space to meditate, reflect and find gratitude for the high points of your 2022. Then, clarify what you'd like to leave behind as you enter 2023—and what evolution you're most proud to bring with you into the New Year. The winter solstice always coincides with the Sun's move into grounding, elegant Capricorn. And since the celestial Sea Goat is the governor of goal setting, how perfect is it that we get to make our resolutions under these solar flares every year? Get a running list going in your Notes app for now, so you can enjoy the holidays pressure-free. Capricorn season rallies on until January 20, so you're not going to lose your momentum (or your "high pro glow") if you start building your supersized visions early next year.

and in love...

Tradition, tradition! After four wild weeks, Cupid slips into an old-fashioned groove. There's a reason why conventional rules of romance, like honesty and fidelity, have lasted through the ages. Whether you're staunchly monogamous, proudly polyamorous or "monogamish" (as sexpert Dan Savage calls it), integrity is key to any successful union. Get honest about where you stand with people, even if a good one slips away because you want totally different things. In a rock-solid relationship? Now's the time to honor your bond by creating cherished memories—and memorializing the ones you've already shared. Assemble photos of your greatest moments into an album or have matching jewelry engraved. (Hello, holiday gift ideas!) Did you break a promise to the one you love? Start making it up to them in tangible, measurable ways. You'll be back in good graces in no time.

SUN-JUPITER SQUARE

21 DEC

Defying gravity? That may be your goal today as daredevil Jupiter in Aries eggs on the ambitious Capricorn Sun. But with these cocky planets locked into a tangled angle, you may not notice the ceiling over your head. (Or the fact, that there's still an "atmosphere" to contend with here on Earth.) By all means, set your sights high. Just don't be impulsive about getting off the launch pad. Would a cooperative dynamic be more useful than a competitive one? Treat everyone you meet like a potential future teammate. Because you never really know, right?

VENUS-URANUS TRINE

22 DEC

Productivity and creativity go hand in hand today, so draw on both sides of the brain. With Venus in can-do Capricorn, practical magic is the name of the game. Even better? A supportive beam from innovative Uranus guides you to tech-savvy solutions that can speed up your efficiency. Why yes, there is an app for that! Speaking of which, since wherever she goes, Venus is the love planet, today's mashup is well wired for digital dating. Don't waste time grumbling about how much you hate the whole process. If at first you did not succeed, swipe, swipe again! All it takes is the one click, and under these spontaneous skies, anything can happen!

CAPRICORN NEW MOON

23 DEC

Ready to wrap up the year with a giant velvet bow? Today's new moon in Capricorn, the only one in 2022, brings a burst of speed to help you crush those end-of-year goals. We realize it's the eleventh hour and you have stockings to stuff. That's more reason to stay nimble and pivot if a better strategy presents itself. Efficiency is the name of the game, but you know what's not? Wearing struggle like a merit badge. What can you delegate and outsource to get the job done? While you're wrapping presents, try visualizing where you'd like your career to be six months from now. (And feel free to beam a psychic wish to Santa.) Can't-stop-won't-stop Capricorn loves the hustle, but this potent supermoon helps you radar in on work that's worthy of your time and energy. Want to pull off a grandiose plan? Create structure and systems. That's how this cardinal earth sign energy supports growth!

and in love...

Set your clocks for a new chapter in bonding. Today's new moon in Capricorn, the sign of the timekeeper, kicks off a fresh six-month cycle. With the Sun and Venus already settled in the Sea Goat's suite, you've no doubt been pondering the future of your love life. Tap into the planning powers of this new moon and write down your relationship and romance resolutions for the next six months. Make them measurable and actionable. For example: "I will swipe right on a minimum of one person a day for the rest of the year," or, "I will coordinate a weekly date night on the shared calendar before January 1." While actions like these are the opposite of spontaneous, they provide a necessary structure to keep you in Cupid's court!

WAXING QUARTER MOON IN ARIES

29
DEC

Today's quarter moon in Aries reminds you that "shiny and new" doesn't tell the whole story. Trailblazing influencers and trendy techniques are easy attractors, which is not a bad thing. Get excited about these discoveries. Then, weigh them against timeless wisdom. The FOMO is real when the moon is in Aries, but it can prevent you from fully enjoying anything you try. These moderating moonbeams recommend easing slowly into any new arrangements. Test the waters with a trial run, 10-day subscription or free day pass. As you immerse yourself in the reality of the situation, you'll see if the dangling carrot is worth snatching up. Be mindful not to spread yourself thin as you dabble. You don't have to try *everything* all at once!

MERCURY-VENUS MEETUP

29
DEC

Cozy up for a sweet little chat. As expressive Mercury and love planet Venus unite in sensible Capricorn, you'll have the ability to talk about your feelings without gushing or overwhelming anyone. Few subjects are off-limits today—except the super triggering ones, since Mercury *is* retrograde. Don't waste this golden hour on lame small talk. With future-focused Capricorn steering the conversation, open up about your bigger dreams, goals and ideal vision for a relationship. Should you discover that you want a loft-style apartment and kids (much!) later but your love interest is *so* ready to be the suburban little league coach, don't panic. The point of this exercise is to share freely and then see if you can't navigate a compromise as life unfolds. Have you been locking horns with your love? Better to clear the air today than during a champagne-fueled crying jag on NYE, in case you needed an incentive!

MERCURY RETROGRADE IN CAPRICORN

29 DEC - 18 JAN '23

Do you hear what I hear? Doubtful. As Mercury spins into a signal-jamming retrograde, they year ends on a muddled note. Good luck getting aligned around NYE plans, 2023 goals, or whose traditions you're going to honor. If you're traveling, leave early for your destination and reconfirm bookings. Think very carefully about your New Year's guest list. Interactions could become heated and divisive, upsetting the general mood of your festivities. If end-of-year plans have grown overly complex, don't force it. Even if you *do* pull them off "perfectly," you could be too resentful (and exhausted!) to enjoy the fun. To use this three-week cycle to maximum effectiveness, start reviewing career goals right after the New Year. Scour LinkedIn and social media. Is a former colleague crushing it? And do you see an opening for a collaboration? Send a hello note or catch up over a cup of cheer. If nothing else, you'll leave inspired, with ideas you can apply to your own ambitious plans.

VENUS-PLUTO CONJUNCTION

31 DEC

Would you care for some hot sauce with your champagne? 2022 wraps on a spicy, sultry note as seductive Venus sidles up to magnetic Pluto in Capricorn for the night. If you're in a relationship, keep celebrations intimate—or end them with quality one-on-one time. Under this soulfully sexy sync-up, a mind-body-soul connection could heat up fast! No matter how you choose to ring in the New Year—or with whom—make it festive. Venus favors beauty, music, art and romance...and a classic LBD. Pluto is the planet of transformation. (Think: phoenix rising from the ashes.) What do you want to leave in the dust as 2022 closes? Write a list, then do a ritual to burn the paper, using a candle or a firepit. (Safely, of course!) Making a vision board or attending a spiritual ceremony are other great ways to set the tone as you welcome 2023.

2022

NUMEROLOGY

UNIVERSAL YEAR

6

In Numerology, each calendar year adds up to a single-digit number, which holds a unique energetic influence & imprint.

We all feel this energy, and it's called the Universal Year. A Universal Year means that everyone on the planet will experience the energy of a particular number during the entire year, from January 1 through December 31.

Whether or not you make New Year's resolutions, most of us intuitively feel a profound energy shift whenever the calendar turns. In Numerology, that transition is a pivot point, marking the passage into a new Universal Year—the collective atmosphere of the world for a 12-month period. Everyone on the planet will feel the energy of a particular number during the entire year, and each number comes with its own unique resonance or theme.

What's the focal point for our collective consciousness during a given year? Last year (2021) was a 5 Universal Year and it demanded that we:

5 UNIVERSAL YEAR:

* INVESTIGATE WHERE WE DID AND
  DIDN'T FEEL A SENSE OF FREEDOM

* REIN IN OUR ESCAPIST AND
  AVOIDANT TENDENCIES

* FOCUS ON THE LONGER GAME RATHER
  THAN INSTANT GRATIFICATION

* TAP INTO OUR SENSUAL SIDES

* FACE OUR FEARS AND BEGIN TO
  DISMANTLE THEM

* OPEN UP TO CHANGE ON EVERY LEVEL

Now we're leaving the frenetic energy of the 5 behind and launching into 2022 with the grounding energy of a 6 Universal Year.

2022

(2 + 0 + 2 + 2 = 6)

This sequence of numbers contains added resonance because it's comprised of repeating 2's, accentuated by the 0.

So while 2022 is a 6 Universal Year, it carries a strong "2" resonance.

The energy of the 2 is all about patience, partnership and diplomacy. This peacekeeping number is highly sensitive and in tune with other people's emotional landscapes.

In numerology, 0 is an intensifier. Whenever a 0 shows up, it amplifies both the optimal and the challenging aspects of the number with which it's co-mingled. So what does this all mean?

KEY CONCEPTS
OF A 6 UNIVERSAL YEAR

HOME

RELATIONSHIPS

SERVICE

RESPONSIBILITY

FAMILY

VISION

In Numerology, the number 6 is the energy of nurturing. It emphasizes relationships, following through on obligations, taking on responsibility, and savoring home and family. There's something innately self-sacrificing about the number 6.

As we bridge from the freedom-seeking energy of the 5 Universal Year in 2021, we're collectively given the opportunity—and the mandate—to turn our focus outward. The 5 opened the door for us to bask in self-indulgence. Now the winds of change blow the weathervane in a different direction as we head into a more "attend to others" Universal Year. What's best for the collective, rather than just the individual?

When you look at the number 6, it resembles a little pregnant belly. The 6 year is truly pregnant with possibilities when the focus is on visionary plans, service to others and justice for all.

Since *service* is a key theme now, get ready to ramp up your caretaking and protective efforts. In the personal sphere, this might mean beautifying your surroundings and strengthening bonds. Globally, this could spotlight issues such as mitigating the climate crisis. Perhaps we'll enter our post-pandemic world with fresh resolve to make a difference and take accountability.

Since the pandemic disrupted lives around the globe, in the 6 Universal Year we'll collectively experience the need to feel settled, nested and "at home," along with the desire to nurture our relationships.

THE ZERO FACTOR

Let's look at the added dimension of the "0" in "2022" and how it will impact the 6 Universal Year.

Numerologically, this year layers the empathic and harmonious number 2 as if it's a beautifully designed cake—with rich, butter-creamy love infused between skillfully baked, rose-flavored sponge.

This configuration brings added significance to finding solutions that focus on the good of all, not just for one person (or country, political party, religion, corporation, et al.) to stand victorious at the end of a brutal battle.

The path forward globally resides in working *with*, not *against*. The 2 always seeks the diplomatic solution and takes the wants and needs of all into account—which means that every group must commit to a "give" for equitable solutions. 2022 is not a "winner takes all" year.

The 6 Universal Year supports the expansion and success of any businesses or organizations whose values are rooted in service. The visionary nature of the 6 supports and bolsters services like renewable energy and innovations in caregiving.

Perhaps there will be more sites like Hogeweyk, a Netherlands nursing home for people with memory issues, where residents live in a village with caregivers but also have free access to the outdoors and other aspects of life—like grocery shopping and evenings at the pub!

Research shows that loneliness is as deadly as smoking and twice as lethal as obesity. In this 6 Year, we can prioritize the reform of social systems that care for people's emotional and mental wellbeing.

Post-pandemic-related health impacts will get more attention this year, with more resolve to make mental health a shame-free conversation. We can envision a kinder environment for schools, workplaces, healthcare facilities and public spaces. The beautifying energy of the 6 can add a healing touch.

HOW TO MAKE THE MOST OUT OF THE 6 UNIVERSAL YEAR

1. Be of service.

The nurturing 6 isn't fully activated unless it's offering support and directing its energies toward the greater good. In 2022, focus on justice and impact investment. But make sure to balance those selfless acts with self-care!

2. Follow through on obligations.

The 6 Universal Year asks us to step up to responsibilities and make good on our noble commitments. We'll need to walk our talk beyond social media and put activism into action.

3. Accept the perfection of the imperfection.

The shadow traits of the 6 Year can be impossible standards and unyielding judgment. This cycle reveals where we hold our loftiest and perhaps most illogical expectations of the world and the people around us. Where do we insert over-the-top idealism and rigid rules? Remember the adage "progress, not perfection" in 2022.

When working with the energy of the 6, keep in mind that there are many ways to resolve issues or mediate conflicts that don't shut down one group or another. Remain open and allow events to play out differently than you think they should.

4. Lead with love.

The 6 puts the focus on family. Globally, this is being developed from the ground up. In the late 1980s, Albert Einstein's daughter Lieserl donated letters her father had written during his lifetime. Among them was a letter that offered these thoughts:

> *"There is an extremely powerful force that, so far, science has not found a formal explanation to. It is a force that includes and governs all others... This universal force is LOVE. Love is light, that enlightens those who give and receive it. Love is power, because it multiplies the best we have, and allows humanity not to be extinguished in their blind selfishness... This force explains everything and gives meaning to life."*

Albert Einstein, master of physics and intuition, was a 6 Life Path (the guiding number based on his date of birth). This is a spirited message speaking directly from the 6, showing its ultimate beauty and purpose.

5. Support versus enable.

One of the key challenges of the 6 Universal Year energy is the delicate balance between supporting and enabling. This year challenges us to offer support while not being in everyone else's business. Tricky stuff! At times, we'll have to allow others to stumble; to witness them struggling as they figure out a solution without judging their pace or methods.

6. But first, dinner!

The 6 Universal Year is saturated in the desire for *nourishment.* How do we feed and nurture our bodies, minds and spirits? How do we fuel and nourish our economies in a way that isn't just a "fad diet" or Band-Aid solution that functions for a couple weeks but can't possibly be sustained long-term?

Conclusion

CREATIVITY & COMPASSION ARE KEY.

The highest expression of the 6 energy is through creative genius, visionary revelations, responsible follow-through, nurturing service and heartfelt compassion.

If we can stave off the desire to control all outcomes, the 6 Universal Year offers a lot of opportunities for connection and renewed relationships. This is a year to keep our promises, reach out and support others on a grand scale, and to sacrifice a bit of personal gratification in order to put the needs of "family" and "community" first. ✺

2022

LUNAR YEAR
OF THE
WATER TIGER

Year of the Water Tiger

Let it flow! The decade's first two years were all about building infrastructure. In 2022, it's time for creativity, innovation and deep insights.

> **The Year of the Water Tiger**
>
> February 1, 2022 to January 31, 2023

Ready to flip from day to night? On February 1, 2022, the systematic Metal Ox passes the yoke to the instinctual Water Tiger. The industrious Ox muscles through duties from sunup to sundown. The clever Tiger hunts at night. Morning people could morph into nocturnal creatures under this roaring transformation. Regardless of your prime productivity hours, get ready to change your beat. The Ox takes its orders from Saturn, the stern and disciplined taskmaster of the skies. Tiger, on the other hand, downloads cues from free-spirited Uranus, a planet whose main mission in life is to disrupt "the system."

There is a link here, however. Both Saturn and Uranus are the co-rulers of Aquarius—and it's the Age in which we are living. Need more proof that 2022 is the Year of the New Abnormal? Stalking through the Water Tiger's jungle is a trek through uncharted terrain. Or make that a swim. After a pair of back-to-back metal years (2020-21), water cascades across the landscape of the next two. Let it go and let it flow.

Water years (which end in 2 or 3) restore fluidity to our lives. Sweet relief! Rigid rules apply during metal years (any year ending in 0 or 1), which can make people feel fenced in and controlled. Metal puts the focus on data, infrastructures and financial security. In a true example of #MetalYearProblems, banks had a coin shortage over the past couple years, due to the rising rate of virtual transactions. And while Bitcoin's value soared, savvy investors also added gold and silver to their portfolios—safe bets at a time where fiat currency's future seems to be so uncertain.

There will be many things "in flux," over the next couple years, in fact, which is the nature of this element. Water flows freely, shapeshifting from frozen to liquid to invisible gas. Seemingly solid situations may go up in smoke, then hover overhead like inescapable cloud cover before raining down again. Paradoxically, the Uranus-ruled Tiger longs to break free from structure. Yet, without a container, water spills everywhere and dries up. Want to be as strong as a rushing river? Carve out your "banks" (i.e., boundaries) and unblock dams (as in, go-nowhere situations).

Have you marked your turf? Wild tigers are territorial creatures, spraying their scent and scratching their claws into trees to stake their claim. In 2022, access to fresh water could be a primary cause of political uprising and wars. Record droughts and floods threatened farming and utilities

in many regions last year, including those along the Colorado River and in the Gulf Stream's path. Dry areas and flood zones may depopulate in 2022, while cities with stable fresh-water resources could see record residential spikes.

Can we, find solutions to the potentially apocalyptic future of melting ice caps and rising sea levels? Here's some very good news: Science is revered during Uranus-ruled Tiger years. (So long to the fearmongering, Saturnian Ox!) From water reclamation to desalination to carbon capture, this Water Tiger year could bring breakthrough innovations that mitigate the effects of the climate crisis on our liquid assets.

Since the intuitive Water Tiger traffics in signs, serendipities and psychic visions, solutions could arrive supernaturally. Such was the case for chemist Dmitri Mendeleev, who "discovered" the periodic table of elements in his sleep. "I saw in a dream, a table, where all the elements fell into place as required," said Mendeleev. "Awakening, I immediately wrote it down on a piece of paper."

Or hey, maybe we will cure COVID in 2022, a watery virus that spreads through respiratory droplets. But given public resistance to modern medicine, it may come down to this: Vaccination or isolation. Since Tiger years tend to be solitary, people may opt out of society rather than play by the rules.

It bears mentioning that wild tigers have become a critically endangered species. In the early 1900s, an estimated 100,000 tigers roamed through 11 regions, including Siberia, India, Sumatra and Myanmar. Their current global count has dwindled to a scarce 3,900, putting these gorgeous big cats at risk for extinction. Among humans, birth rates are dropping globally, bringing conversations about population decline to the headlines. This trend is unlikely to turn during an independent Water Tiger year. In fact, wild tigers interact quite briefly, purely for mating purposes.

Relax! We're not suggesting you'll spend 2022 alone. When it's time to seduce, attractions can get steamier than a mangrove swamp. With this cocky creature helming the operative, fierce fashion may be back with a vengeance. When that "tiger, tiger" is "burning bright," light-up clothing, eye-popping neons and jungle prints could hit the runways. Skin baring, body-con fashions cast a spell suited for this seductively alluring creature.

When you're out prowling the field, lose the phone! The sensory Water Tiger doesn't get off by reading messages from a cold, hard screen. They connect through a complex social system based on visual signals, scent marks and vocalizations. Unleash your raw humanity. This hot-blooded hunter wants to inhale pheromones, brush against silky skin, and penetrate you with its unwavering gaze.

Emotional bonds strengthen during any water year. But during a Tiger year, this is an inside and outside job. Carve out time for soulful reflection. Self-love sets the stage for intimacy. Do your inner work and you're bound to attract people with a high EQ—or raise the vibration in an existing relationship. Water seeks its own level.

Bring on the swagger! Tipping the scales at between 300 and 600 pounds, this animal is a force to be reckoned with. To attract your mate or seal a business deal, you may have to throw a little weight around. But use plenty of emotional intelligence. Painfully obvious advances are not in the Tiger's playbook. Too cool for that school? Emotional detachment might be more your speed. Draw back into observer mode, watching and waiting for qualified "prey" to appear. Failure is not in the Water Tiger's vocabulary. If at first you don't succeed, try, try again.

Bottom line: Transitioning from the Metal Ox's plowed and plotted field to the Water Tiger's deep, dark emotional realm won't be a stalk in the park. And oh, the feels this shift will bring! Get ready to abide by the law of the jungle, which isn't very lawful at all. If the Metal Ox's mantra was "lather, rinse, repeat," the Water Tiger's marching orders are, "observe, strategize, strike!" ✺

2022

EPHEMERIS

JANUARY 2022

January 2022 — Sun, Moon & Inner Planets

Day	Sid.time	☉ (Sun)	☽ (Moon)	☽ +12h	☿ (Mercury)	♀ (Venus)	♂ (Mars)	♃ (Jupiter)	♄ (Saturn)
1 Sa	06:42:30	♑10°31'44	♐15°28'52	♐23°01'50	♑28°10	♑23°17	♐13°05	♓00°32	♒11°54
2 Su	06:46:27	♑11°32'55	♑00°36'37	♑08°11'43	♑29°35	♑22°47	♐13°48	♓00°44	♒12°00
3 Mo	06:50:23	♑12°34'06	♑15°46'09	♑23°18'21	♒00°57	♑22°16	♐14°31	♓00°56	♒12°07
4 Tu	06:54:20	♑13°35'17	♒00°47'25	♒08°11'55	♒02°16	♑21°43	♐15°14	♓01°08	♒12°13
5 We	06:58:17	♑14°36'28	♒15°31'10	♒22°44'04	♒03°31	♑21°08	♐15°56	♓01°20	♒12°20
6 Th	07:02:13	♑15°37'38	♒29°50'21	♓06°49'19	♒04°43	♑20°33	♐16°39	♓01°32	♒12°27
7 Fr	07:06:10	♑16°38'48	♓13°41'05	♓20°25'21	♒05°50	♑19°57	♐17°22	♓01°44	♒12°33
8 Sa	07:10:06	♑17°39'58	♓27°02'35	♈03°32'49	♒06°51	♑19°21	♐18°05	♓01°57	♒12°40
9 Su	07:14:03	♑18°41'07	♈09°59'46	♈16°14'40	♒07°46	♑18°44	♐18°48	♓02°09	♒12°47
10 Mo	07:17:59	♑19°42'16	♈22°27'23	♈28°35'16	♒08°34	♑18°07	♐19°31	♓02°21	♒12°54
11 Tu	07:21:56	♑20°43'24	♉04°39'14	♉10°39'43	♒09°15	♑17°31	♐20°14	♓02°34	♒13°00
12 We	07:25:52	♑21°44'32	♉16°37'36	♉22°33'18	♒09°46	♑16°55	♐20°57	♓02°46	♒13°07
13 Th	07:29:49	♑22°45'39	♉28°27'39	♊04°21'01	♒10°07	♑16°19	♐21°40	♓02°59	♒13°14
14 Fr	07:33:46	♑23°46'46	♊10°14'10	♊16°07'21	♒10°18	♑15°45	♐22°23	♓03°12	♒13°21
15 Sa	07:37:42	♑24°47'52	♊22°01'18	♊27°56'08	♒10°18	♑15°12	♐23°06	♓03°25	♒13°28
16 Su	07:41:39	♑25°48'58	♋03°55'28	♋09°50'21	♒10°06	♑14°41	♐23°49	♓03°38	♒13°35
17 Mo	07:45:35	♑26°50'03	♋15°55'17	♋21°52'13	♒09°43	♑14°11	♐24°33	♓03°51	♒13°42
18 Tu	07:49:32	♑27°51'08	♋27°56'34	♌04°03'12	♒09°08	♑13°43	♐25°16	♓04°04	♒13°49
19 We	07:53:28	♑28°52'12	♌10°12'29	♌16°24'12	♒08°22	♑13°17	♐25°59	♓04°17	♒13°56
20 Th	07:57:25	♑29°53'15	♌22°38'42	♌28°49'12	♒07°26	♑12°53	♐26°42	♓04°30	♒14°03
21 Fr	08:01:22	♒00°54'18	♍04°59'42	♍11°04'18	♒06°22	♑12°32	♐27°26	♓04°43	♒14°10
22 Sa	08:05:18	♒01°55'21	♍17°09'27	♍24°06'48	♒05°11	♑12°12	♐28°09	♓04°56	♒14°17
23 Su	08:09:15	♒02°56'22	♎01°04'09	♎07°39'03	♒03°56	♑11°54	♐28°53	♓05°10	♒14°24
24 Mo	08:13:11	♒03°57'24	♎14°17'32	♎20°39'32	♒02°39	♑11°40	♐29°36	♓05°23	♒14°31
25 Tu	08:17:08	♒04°58'24	♎27°56'34	♏04°03'24	♒01°23	♑11°28	♑00°19	♓05°37	♒14°38
26 We	08:21:04	♒05°59'25	♏11°12'29	♏18°29'18	♒00°09	♑11°18	♑01°03	♓05°50	♒14°46
27 Th	08:25:01	♒07°00'25	♏25°30'55	♐02°38'00	♑28°59	♑11°11	♑01°47	♓06°04	♒14°53
28 Fr	08:28:57	♒08°01'25	♐09°49'27	♐17°04'40	♑27°56	♑11°06	♑02°30	♓06°17	♒15°00
29 Sa	08:32:54	♒09°02'24	♐24°23'31	♑01°45'09	♑27°00	♑11°04	♑03°14	♓06°31	♒15°07
30 Su	08:36:51	♒10°03'22	♑09°09'08	♑16°34'18	♑26°12	♑11°05	♑03°58	♓06°45	♒15°14
31 Mo	08:40:47	♒11°04'20	♑23°59'59	♒01°24'48	♑25°33	♑11°07	♑04°42	♓06°58	♒15°21
Δ Delta	01:58:16	30°32'35"	398°31'07"	398°22'58"	-2°37'	-12°09'	21°36'	6°26'	3°27'

January 2022 — Outer Planets & Points

Day	♅ (Uranus)	♆ (Neptune)	♇ (Pluto)	☊ (Mean Node)	☊ (True Node)	⚸ (Lilith)	⚷ (Chiron)
1 Sa	♉10°57	♓20°40	♑25°56	♉29°31	♊01°12	♊18°27	♈08°30
2 Su	♉10°56	♓20°41	♑25°58	♉29°28	♊01°09	♊18°34	♈08°31
3 Mo	♉10°55	♓20°42	♑25°59	♉29°25	♊01°05	♊18°40	♈08°31
4 Tu	♉10°54	♓20°42	♑26°01	♉29°22	♊00°58	♊18°47	♈08°32
5 We	♉10°53	♓20°44	♑26°03	♉29°19	♊00°51	♊18°54	♈08°33
6 Th	♉10°53	♓20°45	♑26°05	♉29°15	♊00°44	♊19°00	♈08°34
7 Fr	♉10°52	♓20°46	♑26°07	♉29°12	♊00°38	♊19°07	♈08°35
8 Sa	♉10°52	♓20°48	♑26°09	♉29°09	♊00°34	♊19°14	♈08°36
9 Su	♉10°51	♓20°49	♑26°11	♉29°06	♊00°32	♊19°20	♈08°37
10 Mo	♉10°51	♓20°50	♑26°13	♉29°03	♊00°31	♊19°27	♈08°38
11 Tu	♉10°50	♓20°52	♑26°15	♉29°00	♊00°32	♊19°34	♈08°39
12 We	♉10°50	♓20°53	♑26°17	♉28°56	♊00°33	♊19°40	♈08°41
13 Th	♉10°49	♓20°54	♑26°19	♉28°53	♊00°34	♊19°47	♈08°42
14 Fr	♉10°49	♓20°56	♑26°21	♉28°50	♊00°34	♊19°54	♈08°43
15 Sa	♉10°49	♓20°57	♑26°23	♉28°47	♊00°31	♊20°00	♈08°45
16 Su	♉10°49	♓20°59	♑26°25	♉28°44	♊00°26	♊20°07	♈08°46
17 Mo	♉10°49	♓21°00	♑26°27	♉28°41	♊00°18	♊20°14	♈08°48
18 Tu	♉10°49	♓21°02	♑26°29	♉28°37	♊00°08	♊20°20	♈08°49
19 We	♉10°49	♓21°03	♑26°31	♉28°34	♉29°57	♊20°27	♈08°51
20 Th	♉10°49	♓21°05	♑26°33	♉28°31	♉29°45	♊20°34	♈08°52
21 Fr	♉10°49	♓21°06	♑26°35	♉28°28	♉29°32	♊20°40	♈08°54
22 Sa	♉10°49	♓21°08	♑26°37	♉28°25	♉29°25	♊20°47	♈08°56
23 Su	♉10°50	♓21°10	♑26°39	♉28°21	♉29°18	♊20°54	♈08°57
24 Mo	♉10°50	♓21°11	♑26°41	♉28°18	♉29°14	♊21°00	♈08°59
25 Tu	♉10°50	♓21°13	♑26°43	♉28°15	♉29°12	♊21°07	♈09°01
26 We	♉10°50	♓21°15	♑26°45	♉28°12	♉29°12	♊21°14	♈09°03
27 Th	♉10°51	♓21°16	♑26°47	♉28°09	♉29°12	♊21°20	♈09°05
28 Fr	♉10°51	♓21°18	♑26°49	♉28°06	♉29°09	♊21°27	♈09°07
29 Sa	♉10°52	♓21°20	♑26°51	♉28°02	♉29°06	♊21°34	♈09°09
30 Su	♉10°52	♓21°22	♑26°53	♉27°59	♉29°04	♊21°40	♈09°11
31 Mo	♉10°53	♓21°24	♑26°55	♉27°56	♉28°57	♊21°47	♈09°13
Delta	-0°04'	0°43'	0°58'	-1°35'	-2°15'	3°19'	0°43'

FEBRUARY 2022

February 2022

Longitude & Retrograde Ephemeris [00:00 UT]

Day	Sid.time	☉	☽	+12h ☽	☿	♀	♂	♃	♄	♅	♆	♇	☊	☊	⚸	⚷	Day
1 Tu	08:44:44	♒12°05'17	♒08°48'00	♒16°08'09	℞ 25°03	♑11°12	♑05°25	♓07°12	♒15°29	♉10°53	♓21°25	♑26°56	℞ 27°53	℞ 28°46	♊21°53	♈09°16	1 Tu
2 We	08:48:40	♒13°06'12	♒23°24'35	♓00°36'03	♑24°41	♑11°20	♑06°09	♓07°26	♒15°36	♉10°54	♓21°27	♑26°58	♉27°50	♉28°35	♊22°00	♈09°18	2 We
3 Th	08:52:37	♒14°07'06	♓07°42'06	♓14°41'50	♑24°27	♑11°29	♑06°53	♓07°40	♒15°43	♉10°55	♓21°29	♑27°00	♉27°47	♉28°23	♊22°07	♈09°20	3 Th
4 Fr	08:56:33	♒15°08'00	♓21°35'07	♓28°21'27	♑24°22	♑11°41	♑07°37	♓07°54	♒15°50	♉10°56	♓21°31	♑27°02	♉27°43	♉28°12	♊22°13	♈09°22	4 Fr
5 Sa	09:00:30	♒16°08'52	♈05°01'04	♈11°33'47	Ds 24°25	♑11°55	♑08°21	♓08°08	♒15°57	♉10°57	♓21°33	♑27°04	♉27°40	♉28°04	♊22°20	♈09°25	5 Sa
6 Su	09:04:26	♒17°09'42	♈18°00'10	♈24°20'20	♑24°34	♑12°11	♑09°05	♓08°22	♒16°05	♉10°57	♓21°35	♑27°06	♉27°37	♉27°58	♊22°27	♈09°27	6 Su
7 Mo	09:08:23	♒18°10'31	♉00°35'02	♉06°44'35	♑24°50	♑12°29	♑09°49	♓08°36	♒16°12	♉10°58	♓21°37	♑27°08	♉27°34	♉27°55	♊22°33	♈09°30	7 Mo
8 Tu	09:12:20	♒19°11'19	♉12°49'53	♉18°51'20	♑25°13	♑12°49	♑10°33	♓08°50	♒16°19	♉10°59	♓21°39	♑27°10	♉27°31	♉27°54	♊22°40	♈09°32	8 Tu
9 We	09:16:16	♒20°12'05	♉24°49'54	♊00°46'03	♑25°41	♑13°11	♑11°17	♓09°04	♒16°26	♉11°01	♓21°41	♑27°12	♉27°27	D 27°54	♊22°47	♈09°35	9 We
10 Th	09:20:13	♒21°12'50	♊06°40'43	♊12°34'21	♑26°14	♑13°35	♑12°01	♓09°18	♒16°33	♉11°02	♓21°43	♑27°13	♉27°24	℞ 27°53	♊22°53	♈09°37	10 Th
11 Fr	09:24:09	♒22°13'33	♊18°27'52	♊24°21'38	♑26°52	♑14°00	♑12°45	♓09°32	♒16°40	♉11°03	♓21°45	♑27°15	♉27°21	♉27°52	♊23°00	♈09°40	11 Fr
12 Sa	09:28:06	♒23°14'14	♋00°16'31	♋06°12'46	♑27°34	♑14°27	♑13°29	♓09°47	♒16°48	♉11°04	♓21°47	♑27°17	♉27°18	♉27°48	♊23°07	♈09°42	12 Sa
13 Su	09:32:02	♒24°14'54	♋12°11'09	♋18°11'49	♑28°21	♑14°56	♑14°13	♓10°01	♒16°55	♉11°05	♓21°49	♑27°19	♉27°15	♉27°42	♊23°13	♈09°45	13 Su
14 Mo	09:35:59	♒25°15'33	♋24°15'23	♌00°21'52	♑29°11	♑15°27	♑14°57	♓10°15	♒17°02	♉11°07	♓21°51	♑27°21	♉27°12	♉27°33	♊23°20	♈09°48	14 Mo
15 Tu	09:39:55	♒26°16'09	♌06°31'46	♌12°44'57	♒00°04	♑15°58	♑15°42	♓10°29	♒17°09	♉11°08	♓21°53	♑27°23	♉27°08	♉27°21	♊23°27	♈09°50	15 Tu
16 We	09:43:52	♒27°16'45	♌19°01'44	♌25°21'54	♒01°01	♑16°32	♑16°26	♓10°44	♒17°16	♉11°10	♓21°55	♑27°24	♉27°05	♉27°07	♊23°33	♈09°53	16 We
17 Th	09:47:49	♒28°17'18	♍01°45'38	♍08°12'36	♒02°00	♑17°06	♑17°10	♓10°58	♒17°23	♉11°11	♓21°57	♑27°26	♉27°02	♉26°53	♊23°40	♈09°56	17 Th
18 Fr	09:51:45	♒29°17'51	♍14°42'54	♍21°16'08	♒03°02	♑17°43	♑17°54	♓11°12	♒17°30	♉11°13	♓22°00	♑27°28	♉26°59	♉26°40	♊23°47	♈09°59	18 Fr
19 Sa	09:55:42	♓00°18'21	♍27°52'23	♎04°31'14	♒04°07	♑18°20	♑18°39	♓11°27	♒17°38	♉11°14	♓22°02	♑27°30	♉26°56	♉26°28	♊23°53	♈10°02	19 Sa
20 Su	09:59:38	♓01°18'51	♎11°12'47	♎17°56'39	♒05°14	♑18°59	♑19°23	♓11°41	♒17°45	♉11°16	♓22°04	♑27°31	♉26°52	♉26°20	♊24°00	♈10°04	20 Su
21 Mo	10:03:35	♓02°19'19	♎24°42'59	♏01°31'28	♒06°23	♑19°38	♑20°08	♓11°56	♒17°52	♉11°17	♓22°06	♑27°33	♉26°49	♉26°14	♊24°07	♈10°07	21 Mo
22 Tu	10:07:31	♓03°19'45	♏08°22'21	♏15°15'19	♒07°34	♑20°19	♑20°52	♓12°10	♒17°59	♉11°19	♓22°08	♑27°35	♉26°46	♉26°11	♊24°13	♈10°10	22 Tu
23 We	10:11:28	♓04°20'11	♏22°10'41	♏29°08'12	♒08°46	♑21°01	♑21°36	♓12°24	♒18°06	♉11°21	♓22°10	♑27°36	♉26°43	♉26°10	♊24°20	♈10°13	23 We
24 Th	10:15:24	♓05°20'35	♐06°08'10	♐13°10'15	♒10°01	♑21°45	♑22°21	♓12°39	♒18°13	♉11°23	♓22°13	♑27°38	♉26°40	♉26°10	♊24°27	♈10°16	24 Th
25 Fr	10:19:21	♓06°20'58	♐20°14'43	♐27°21'07	D 11°17	♑22°29	♑23°06	♓12°53	♒18°20	♉11°24	♓22°15	♑27°40	♉26°37	♉26°10	♊24°33	♈10°19	25 Fr
26 Sa	10:23:18	♓07°21'19	♑04°29'35	♑11°39'29	♒12°35	♑23°14	♑23°50	♓13°08	♒18°27	♉11°26	♓22°17	♑27°41	♉26°33	♉26°07	♊24°40	♈10°22	26 Sa
27 Su	10:27:14	♓08°21'39	♑18°50'45	♑26°02'35	♒13°54	♑24°00	♑24°35	♓13°22	♒18°34	♉11°28	♓22°19	♑27°43	♉26°30	♉26°02	♊24°47	♈10°25	27 Su
28 Mo	10:31:11	♓09°21'58	♒03°14'42	♒10°26'07	♒15°15	♑24°47	♑25°19	♓13°37	♒18°41	♉11°30	♓22°21	♑27°44	♉26°27	♉25°55	♊24°53	♈10°29	28 Mo
Δ Delta	01:46:27	27°16'41"	-354°26'41"	-354°17'57"	20°12'	13°34'	19°53'	6°24'	3°11'	0°36'	0°55'	0°47'	-1°25'	-2°51'	2°59'	1°12'	Delta

MARCH 2022

March 2022

Longitude & Retrograde Ephemeris [00:00 UT]

Day	Sid.time	☉	☽	+12h☽	☿	♀	♂	♃	♄	♅	♆	♇	☊	☊	⚸	⚷	Day
1 Tu	10:35:07	♓10°22'15	♒17°36'24	♒24°44'31	♒16°37	♑25°35	♑26°04	♓13°51	♒18°47	♉11°32	♓22°24	♑27°46	℞ 26°24	℞ 25°44	♊25°00	♈10°32	**1** Tu
2 We	10:39:04	♓11°22'31	♓01°49'59	♓08°51'49	♒18°01	♑26°23	♑26°49	♓14°06	♒18°54	♉11°34	♓22°26	♑27°48	♉26°21	♉25°33	♊25°07	♈10°35	**2** We
3 Th	10:43:00	♓12°22'44	♓15°49'39	♓22°42'36	♒19°25	♑27°13	♑27°33	♓14°20	♒19°01	♉11°36	♓22°28	♑27°49	♉26°18	♉25°21	♊25°13	♈10°38	**3** Th
4 Fr	10:46:57	♓13°22'56	♓29°30'33	♈06°12'53	♒20°52	♑28°03	♑28°18	♓14°35	♒19°08	♉11°39	♓22°30	♑27°51	♉26°14	♉25°10	♊25°20	♈10°41	**4** Fr
5 Sa	10:50:53	♓14°23'05	♈12°49'42	♈19°20'41	♒22°19	♑28°54	♑29°03	♓14°49	♒19°15	♉11°41	♓22°33	♑27°52	♉26°11	♉25°01	♊25°27	♈10°44	**5** Sa
6 Su	10:54:50	♓15°23'13	♈25°46'11	♉02°06'10	♒23°47	♑29°45	♑29°48	♓15°04	♒19°21	♉11°43	♓22°35	♑27°53	♉26°08	♉24°55	♊25°33	♈10°48	**6** Su
7 Mo	10:58:46	♓16°23'19	♉08°21'12	♉14°31'26	♒25°17	♒00°38	♒00°32	♓15°18	♒19°28	♉11°45	♓22°37	♑27°55	♉26°05	♉24°51	♊25°40	♈10°51	**7** Mo
8 Tu	11:02:43	♓17°23'23	♉20°37'39	♉26°40'08	♒26°48	♒01°31	♒01°17	♓15°33	♒19°35	♉11°48	♓22°39	♑27°56	♉26°02	♉24°50	♊25°47	♈10°54	**8** Tu
9 We	11:06:40	♓18°23'25	♊02°39'45	♊08°36'53	♒28°20	♒02°24	♒02°02	♓15°47	♒19°41	♉11°50	♓22°42	♑27°58	♉25°58	D 24°50	♊25°53	♈10°57	**9** We
10 Th	11:10:36	♓19°23'24	♊14°32'30	♊20°26'59	♒29°53	♒03°18	♒02°47	♓16°02	♒19°48	♉11°52	♓22°44	♑27°59	♉25°55	♉24°50	♊26°00	♈11°01	**10** Th
11 Fr	11:14:33	♓20°23'22	♊26°21'18	♋02°15'53	♓01°28	♒04°13	♒03°32	♓16°16	♒19°55	♉11°55	♓22°46	♑28°01	♉25°52	℞ 24°50	♊26°07	♈11°04	**11** Fr
12 Sa	11:18:29	♓21°23'17	♋08°11'38	♋14°08'56	♓03°04	♒05°08	♒04°17	♓16°31	♒20°01	♉11°57	♓22°49	♑28°02	♉25°49	♉24°49	♊26°13	♈11°07	**12** Sa
13 Su	11:22:26	♓22°23'10	♋20°08'37	♋26°11'00	♓04°40	♒06°04	♒05°02	♓16°45	♒20°08	♉12°00	♓22°51	♑28°03	♉25°46	♉24°45	♊26°20	♈11°11	**13** Su
14 Mo	11:26:22	♓23°23'01	♌02°16'48	♌08°26'13	♓06°18	♒07°00	♒05°47	♓17°00	♒20°14	♉12°02	♓22°53	♑28°04	♉25°43	♉24°39	♊26°27	♈11°14	**14** Mo
15 Tu	11:30:19	♓24°22'50	♌14°39'49	♌20°57'38	♓07°57	♒07°57	♒06°32	♓17°14	♒20°20	♉12°05	♓22°55	♑28°06	♉25°39	♉24°30	♊26°33	♈11°18	**15** Tu
16 We	11:34:15	♓25°22'36	♌27°20'06	♍03°47'00	♓09°38	♒08°54	♒07°17	♓17°29	♒20°27	♉12°07	♓22°58	♑28°07	♉25°36	♉24°20	♊26°40	♈11°21	**16** We
17 Th	11:38:12	♓26°22'21	♍10°18'38	♍16°54'35	♓11°19	♒09°52	♒08°02	♓17°43	♒20°33	♉12°10	♓23°00	♑28°08	♉25°33	♉24°10	♊26°47	♈11°24	**17** Th
18 Fr	11:42:09	♓27°22'03	♍23°34'58	♎00°19'14	♓13°02	♒10°50	♒08°47	♓17°58	♒20°39	♉12°13	♓23°02	♑28°09	♉25°30	♉24°00	♊26°53	♈11°28	**18** Fr
19 Sa	11:46:05	♓28°21'43	♎07°07'20	♎13°58'36	♓14°46	♒11°49	♒09°32	♓18°12	♒20°46	♉12°15	♓23°04	♑28°11	♉25°27	♉23°51	♊27°00	♈11°31	**19** Sa
20 Su	11:50:02	♓29°21'21	♎20°52'55	♎27°49'35	♓16°31	♒12°48	♒10°17	♓18°26	♒20°52	♉12°18	♓23°07	♑28°12	♉25°24	♉23°44	♊27°07	♈11°35	**20** Su
21 Mo	11:53:58	♈00°20'58	♏04°48'29	♏11°48'55	♓18°17	♒13°47	♒11°02	♓18°41	♒20°58	♉12°21	♓23°09	♑28°13	♉25°20	♉23°40	♊27°13	♈11°38	**21** Mo
22 Tu	11:57:55	♈01°20'33	♏18°50'50	♏25°53'36	♓20°05	♒14°47	♒11°47	♓18°55	♒21°04	♉12°23	♓23°11	♑28°14	♉25°17	♉23°39	♊27°20	♈11°42	**22** Tu
23 We	12:01:51	♈02°20'05	♐02°57'15	♐10°01'14	♓21°54	♒15°47	♒12°32	♓19°10	♒21°10	♉12°26	♓23°13	♑28°15	♉25°14	D 23°39	♊27°27	♈11°45	**23** We
24 Th	12:05:48	♈03°19'37	♐17°05'38	♐24°09'59	♓23°44	♒16°48	♒13°17	♓19°24	♒21°16	♉12°29	♓23°16	♑28°16	♉25°11	♉23°40	♊27°33	♈11°49	**24** Th
25 Fr	12:09:44	♈04°19'06	♑01°14'24	♑08°18'26	♓25°36	♒17°49	♒14°02	♓19°38	♒21°22	♉12°32	♓23°18	♑28°17	♉25°08	♉23°41	♊27°40	♈11°52	**25** Fr
26 Sa	12:13:41	♈05°18'34	♑15°22'13	♑22°25'17	♓27°28	♒18°50	♒14°48	♓19°52	♒21°28	♉12°35	♓23°20	♑28°18	♉25°04	℞ 23°40	♊27°47	♈11°56	**26** Sa
27 Su	12:17:38	♈06°18'00	♑29°27'41	♒06°28'53	♓29°22	♒19°52	♒15°33	♓20°07	♒21°34	♉12°38	♓23°22	♑28°19	♉25°01	♉23°38	♊27°53	♈11°59	**27** Su
28 Mo	12:21:34	♈07°17'25	♒13°28'56	♒20°27'11	♈01°18	♒20°54	♒16°18	♓20°21	♒21°39	♉12°41	♓23°25	♑28°20	♉24°58	♉23°34	♊28°00	♈12°03	**28** Mo
29 Tu	12:25:31	♈08°16'47	♒27°23'36	♓04°17'32	♈03°14	♒21°56	♒17°03	♓20°35	♒21°45	♉12°44	♓23°27	♑28°21	♉24°55	♉23°28	♊28°07	♈12°06	**29** Tu
30 We	12:29:27	♈09°16'08	♓11°08'55	♓17°57'05	♈05°12	♒22°58	♒17°49	♓20°49	♒21°51	♉12°47	♓23°29	♑28°22	♉24°52	♉23°21	♊28°13	♈12°10	**30** We
31 Th	12:33:24	♈10°15'27	♓24°41'59	♈01°23'02	♈07°11	♒24°01	♒18°34	♓21°03	♒21°56	♉12°50	♓23°31	♑28°23	♉24°49	♉23°13	♊28°20	♈12°13	**31** Th
Δ Delta	01:58:16	-29°53'11"	397°05'34"	-396°38'30"	-50°34'	28°26'	22°29'	7°11'	3°08'	1°17'	1°07'	0°36'	-1°35'	-2°31'	3°19'	1°41'	**Delta**

Ephemeris tables and data provided by **Astro-Seek.com.** All times in UTC.

April 2022

Longitude & Retrograde Ephemeris [00:00 UT]

Day	Sid.time	☉	☽	+12h☽	☿	♀	♂	♃	♄	♅	♆	♇	☊	☊	⚸	⚷	Day
1 Fr	12:37:20	♈11°14'43	♈08°00'15	♈14°33'10	♈09°11	♒25°04	♒19°19	♓21°17	♒22°02	♉12°53	♓23°34	♑28°23	℞ 24°45	℞ 23°06	♊28°27	♈12°17	**1** Fr
2 Sa	12:41:17	♈12°13'58	♈21°01'57	♈27°26'16	♈11°13	♒26°07	♒20°04	♓21°31	♒22°07	♉12°56	♓23°36	♑28°24	♉24°42	♉23°01	♊28°33	♈12°20	**2** Sa
3 Su	12:45:13	♈13°13'10	♉03°46'25	♉10°02'16	♈13°15	♒27°11	♒20°50	♓21°46	♒22°13	♉12°59	♓23°38	♑28°25	♉24°39	♉22°57	♊28°40	♈12°24	**3** Su
4 Mo	12:49:10	♈14°12'21	♉16°14'14	♉22°22'23	♈15°18	♒28°15	♒21°35	♓21°59	♒22°18	♉13°02	♓23°40	♑28°26	♉24°36	♉22°55	♊28°47	♈12°27	**4** Mo
5 Tu	12:53:07	♈15°11'29	♉28°27'16	♊04°29'02	♈17°22	♒29°19	♒22°20	♓22°13	♒22°23	♉13°05	♓23°42	♑28°27	♉24°33	D 22°55	♊28°53	♈12°31	**5** Tu
6 We	12:57:03	♈16°10'35	♊10°28'25	♊16°25'39	♈19°26	♓00°23	♒23°06	♓22°27	♒22°29	♉13°08	♓23°44	♑28°27	♉24°30	♉22°56	♊29°00	♈12°34	**6** We
7 Th	13:00:60	♈17°09'39	♊22°21'33	♊28°16'26	♈21°31	♓01°27	♒23°51	♓22°41	♒22°34	♉13°12	♓23°47	♑28°28	♉24°26	♉22°58	♊29°07	♈12°38	**7** Th
8 Fr	13:04:56	♈18°08'41	♋04°11'10	♋10°06'08	♈23°36	♓02°32	♒24°36	♓22°55	♒22°39	♉13°15	♓23°49	♑28°29	♉24°23	♉22°59	♊29°13	♈12°41	**8** Fr
9 Sa	13:08:53	♈19°07'40	♋16°02'12	♋21°59'45	♈25°40	♓03°37	♒25°22	♓23°09	♒22°44	♉13°18	♓23°51	♑28°29	♉24°20	♉23°00	♊29°20	♈12°45	**9** Sa
10 Su	13:12:49	♈20°06'37	♋27°59'40	♌04°02'18	♈27°45	♓04°42	♒26°07	♓23°23	♒22°49	♉13°21	♓23°53	♑28°30	♉24°17	℞ 23°00	♊29°27	♈12°48	**10** Su
11 Mo	13:16:46	♈21°05'32	♌10°08'29	♌16°18'29	♈29°48	♓05°47	♒26°52	♓23°36	♒22°54	♉13°25	♓23°55	♑28°30	♉24°14	♉22°58	♊29°33	♈12°52	**11** Mo
12 Tu	13:20:42	♈22°04'24	♌22°33'03	♌28°52'20	♉01°51	♓06°52	♒27°38	♓23°50	♒22°59	♉13°28	♓23°57	♑28°31	♉24°10	♉22°55	♊29°40	♈12°55	**12** Tu
13 We	13:24:39	♈23°03'15	♍05°16'56	♍11°46'50	♉03°52	♓07°58	♒28°23	♓24°04	♒23°03	♉13°31	♓23°59	♑28°31	♉24°07	♉22°51	♊29°47	♈12°59	**13** We
14 Th	13:28:36	♈24°02'03	♍18°22'27	♍25°03'31	♉05°52	♓09°04	♒29°08	♓24°17	♒23°08	♉13°34	♓24°01	♑28°32	♉24°04	♉22°47	♊29°53	♈13°02	**14** Th
15 Fr	13:32:32	♈25°00'48	♎01°50'17	♎08°42'13	♉07°50	♓10°10	♒29°54	♓24°31	♒23°13	♉13°38	♓24°03	♑28°32	♉24°01	♉22°42	♋00°00	♈13°06	**15** Fr
16 Sa	13:36:29	♈25°59'32	♎15°39'19	♎22°40'51	♉09°45	♓11°16	♓00°39	♓24°44	♒23°17	♉13°41	♓24°05	♑28°33	♉23°58	♉22°39	♋00°07	♈13°09	**16** Sa
17 Su	13:40:25	♈26°58'14	♎29°46'38	♏06°55'43	♉11°37	♓12°22	♓01°24	♓24°57	♒23°22	♉13°44	♓24°07	♑28°33	♉23°55	♉22°36	♋00°13	♈13°13	**17** Su
18 Mo	13:44:22	♈27°56'53	♏14°07'47	♏21°21'49	♉13°27	♓13°29	♓02°10	♓25°11	♒23°26	♉13°48	♓24°09	♑28°33	♉23°51	♉22°35	♋00°20	♈13°16	**18** Mo
19 Tu	13:48:18	♈28°55'31	♏28°37'26	♐05°53'36	♉15°13	♓14°35	♓02°55	♓25°24	♒23°30	♉13°51	♓24°11	♑28°34	♉23°48	D 22°34	♋00°27	♈13°20	**19** Tu
20 We	13:52:15	♈29°54'08	♐13°09'59	♐20°25'37	♉16°55	♓15°42	♓03°40	♓25°37	♒23°34	♉13°55	♓24°13	♑28°34	♉23°45	♉22°35	♋00°33	♈13°23	**20** We
21 Th	13:56:11	♉00°52'42	♐27°40'17	♑04°53'09	♉18°34	♓16°49	♓04°26	♓25°50	♒23°39	♉13°58	♓24°15	♑28°34	♉23°42	♉22°37	♋00°40	♈13°26	**21** Th
22 Fr	14:00:08	♉01°51'15	♑12°04'06	♑19°12'29	♉20°09	♓17°56	♓05°11	♓26°04	♒23°43	♉14°01	♓24°17	♑28°35	♉23°39	♉22°38	♋00°47	♈13°30	**22** Fr
23 Sa	14:04:05	♉02°49'46	♑26°18'18	♒03°21'00	♉21°39	♓19°03	♓05°57	♓26°17	♒23°47	♉14°05	♓24°19	♑28°35	♉23°35	♉22°39	♋00°53	♈13°33	**23** Sa
24 Su	14:08:01	♉03°48'16	♒10°20'44	♒17°17'04	♉23°05	♓20°11	♓06°42	♓26°30	♒23°51	♉14°08	♓24°21	♑28°35	♉23°32	℞ 22°39	♋01°00	♈13°37	**24** Su
25 Mo	14:11:58	♉04°46'44	♒24°10'12	♓00°59'45	♉24°27	♓21°18	♓07°27	♓26°43	♒23°55	♉14°12	♓24°22	♑28°35	♉23°29	♉22°38	♋01°07	♈13°40	**25** Mo
26 Tu	14:15:54	♉05°45'11	♓07°46'00	♓14°28'37	♉25°44	♓22°26	♓08°13	♓26°55	♒23°58	♉14°15	♓24°24	♑28°35	♉23°26	♉22°36	♋01°13	♈13°43	**26** Tu
27 We	14:19:51	♉06°43'35	♓21°07'53	♓27°43'30	℞s 26°56	♓23°33	♓08°58	♓27°08	♒24°02	♉14°18	♓24°26	♑28°35	♉23°23	♉22°34	♋01°20	♈13°47	**27** We
28 Th	14:23:47	♉07°41'58	♈04°15'45	♈10°44'24	♉28°03	♓24°41	♓09°43	♓27°21	♒24°06	♉14°22	♓24°28	♑28°35	♉23°20	♉22°32	♋01°27	♈13°50	**28** Th
29 Fr	14:27:44	♉08°40'20	♈17°09'45	♈23°31'33	♉29°06	♓25°49	♓10°29	♓27°34	♒24°09	♉14°25	♓24°30	♑28°35	♉23°16	♉22°30	♋01°33	♈13°53	**29** Fr
30 Sa	14:31:40	♉09°38'40	♈29°50'11	♉06°05'25	♊00°03	♓26°57	♓11°14	♓27°46	♒24°12	♉14°29	♓24°31	℞ 28°35	♉23°13	♉22°29	♋01°40	♈13°56	**30** Sa
Δ Delta	01:54:19	28°23'56"	381°49'55"	381°32'14"	50°51'	31°53'	21°54'	6°28'	2°10'	1°35'	0°57'	0°11'	-1°32'	-0°37'	3°13'	1°39'	**Delta**

MAY 2022

May 2022

Longitude & Retrograde Ephemeris [00:00 UT]

Day	Sid.time	☉	☽	+12h☽	☿	♀	♂	♃	♄	♅	♆	♇	☊	☊	⚸	⚷	Day
1 Su	14:35:37	♉10°36′58	♉12°17′40	♉18°26′48	℞s 00°56	♓28°05	♓11°59	♓27°59	♒24°16	♉14°32	♓24°33	℞ 28°35	℞ 23°10	℞ 22°28	♋01°47	♈14°00	1 Su
2 Mo	14:39:33	♉11°35′14	♉24°33′16	♊00°37′00	♊01°43	♓29°13	♓12°45	♓28°11	♒24°19	♉14°36	♓24°35	♑28°35	♉23°07	D 22°28	♋01°53	♈14°03	2 Mo
3 Tu	14:43:30	♉12°33′29	♊06°38′32	♊12°37′51	♊02°25	♈00°22	♓13°30	♓28°24	♒24°22	♉14°39	♓24°36	♑28°35	♉23°04	♉22°28	♋02°00	♈14°06	3 Tu
4 We	14:47:27	♉13°31′41	♊18°35′34	♊24°31′46	♊03°01	♈01°30	♓14°15	♓28°36	♒24°25	♉14°43	♓24°38	♑28°35	♉23°01	♉22°29	♋02°07	♈14°09	4 We
5 Th	14:51:23	♉14°29′52	♋00°27′08	♋06°21′49	♊03°33	♈02°39	♓15°00	♓28°48	♒24°28	♉14°46	♓24°40	♑28°35	♉22°57	♉22°29	♋02°13	♈14°12	5 Th
6 Fr	14:55:20	♉15°28′01	♋12°16′33	♋18°11′34	♊03°59	♈03°47	♓15°46	♓29°00	♒24°31	♉14°50	♓24°41	♑28°35	♉22°54	♉22°30	♋02°20	♈14°15	6 Fr
7 Sa	14:59:16	♉16°26′08	♋24°07′39	♌00°05′06	♊04°20	♈04°56	♓16°31	♓29°12	♒24°34	♉14°53	♓24°43	♑28°35	♉22°51	♉22°31	♋02°27	♈14°19	7 Sa
8 Su	15:03:13	♉17°24′14	♌06°04′44	♌12°06′51	♊04°35	♈06°05	♓17°16	♓29°24	♒24°37	♉14°57	♓24°45	♑28°34	♉22°48	♉22°31	♋02°33	♈14°22	8 Su
9 Mo	15:07:09	♉18°22′17	♌18°12′17	♌24°21′20	♊04°45	♈07°14	♓18°01	♓29°36	♒24°39	♉15°00	♓24°46	♑28°34	♉22°45	♉22°31	♋02°40	♈14°25	9 Mo
10 Tu	15:11:06	♉19°20′18	♍00°34′50	♍06°52′59	♊04°50	♈08°23	♓18°46	♓29°48	♒24°42	♉15°03	♓24°48	♑28°34	♉22°41	℞ 22°31	♋02°47	♈14°28	10 Tu
11 We	15:15:03	♉20°18′17	♍13°16′34	♍19°45′41	℞ 04°50	♈09°32	♓19°32	♈00°00	♒24°44	♉15°07	♓24°49	♑28°34	♉22°38	♉22°31	♋02°54	♈14°31	11 We
12 Th	15:18:59	♉21°16′15	♍26°20′58	♎03°02′21	♊04°45	♈10°41	♓20°17	♈00°11	♒24°47	♉15°10	♓24°51	♑28°33	♉22°35	♉22°31	♋03°00	♈14°34	12 Th
13 Fr	15:22:56	♉22°14′10	♎09°50′16	♎16°44′25	♊04°36	♈11°50	♓21°02	♈00°23	♒24°49	♉15°14	♓24°52	♑28°33	♉22°32	♉22°31	♋03°07	♈14°37	13 Fr
14 Sa	15:26:52	♉23°12′04	♎23°44′58	♏00°51′19	♊04°22	♈12°59	♓21°47	♈00°34	♒24°51	♉15°17	♓24°53	♑28°33	♉22°29	D 22°31	♋03°14	♈14°40	14 Sa
15 Su	15:30:49	♉24°09′56	♏08°03′23	♏15°20′14	♊04°03	♈14°09	♓22°32	♈00°46	♒24°53	♉15°21	♓24°55	♑28°32	♉22°26	♉22°31	♋03°20	♈14°42	15 Su
16 Mo	15:34:45	♉25°07′47	♏22°41′29	♐00°05′58	♊03°41	♈15°18	♓23°17	♈00°57	♒24°55	♉15°24	♓24°56	♑28°32	♉22°22	♉22°31	♋03°27	♈14°45	16 Mo
17 Tu	15:38:42	♉26°05′36	♐07°33′05	♐15°01′31	♊03°16	♈16°27	♓24°02	♈01°08	♒24°57	♉15°28	♓24°57	♑28°31	♉22°19	℞ 22°31	♋03°34	♈14°48	17 Tu
18 We	15:42:38	♉27°03′25	♐22°30′32	♐29°58′48	♊02°47	♈17°37	♓24°47	♈01°19	♒24°59	♉15°31	♓24°59	♑28°31	♉22°16	♉22°31	♋03°40	♈14°51	18 We
19 Th	15:46:35	♉28°01′11	♑07°25′41	♑14°49′55	♊02°17	♈18°47	♓25°32	♈01°30	♒25°01	♉15°34	♓25°00	♑28°30	♉22°13	♉22°30	♋03°47	♈14°54	19 Th
20 Fr	15:50:32	♉28°58′57	♑22°11′03	♑29°28′05	♊01°44	♈19°56	♓26°17	♈01°41	♒25°02	♉15°38	♓25°01	♑28°30	♉22°10	♉22°29	♋03°54	♈14°56	20 Fr
21 Sa	15:54:28	♉29°56′41	♒06°40′47	♒13°48′25	♊01°10	♈21°06	♓27°02	♈01°52	♒25°04	♉15°41	♓25°02	♑28°29	♉22°07	♉22°29	♋04°00	♈14°59	21 Sa
22 Su	15:58:25	♊00°54′24	♒20°51′02	♒27°48′10	♊00°36	♈22°16	♓27°46	♈02°03	♒25°05	♉15°45	♓25°04	♑28°29	♉22°03	♉22°28	♋04°07	♈15°02	22 Su
23 Mo	16:02:21	♊01°52′06	♓04°40′06	♓11°26′34	♊00°01	♈23°26	♓28°31	♈02°13	♒25°06	♉15°48	♓25°05	♑28°28	♉22°00	D 22°28	♋04°14	♈15°05	23 Mo
24 Tu	16:06:18	♊02°49′48	♓18°08′02	♓24°44′24	♉29°27	♈24°36	♓29°16	♈02°24	♒25°08	♉15°51	♓25°06	♑28°27	♉21°57	♉22°29	♋04°20	♈15°07	24 Tu
25 We	16:10:14	♊03°47′28	♈01°16′11	♈07°43′24	♉28°54	♈25°46	♈00°01	♈02°34	♒25°09	♉15°55	♓25°07	♑28°27	♉21°54	♉22°29	♋04°27	♈15°10	25 We
26 Th	16:14:11	♊04°45′07	♈14°06′38	♈20°25′54	♉28°23	♈26°56	♈00°46	♈02°45	♒25°10	♉15°58	♓25°08	♑28°26	♉21°51	♉22°30	♋04°34	♈15°12	26 Th
27 Fr	16:18:07	♊05°42′45	♈26°41′47	♉02°54′18	♉27°54	♈28°06	♈01°30	♈02°55	♒25°11	♉16°01	♓25°09	♑28°25	♉21°47	♉22°31	♋04°40	♈15°15	27 Fr
28 Sa	16:22:04	♊06°40′22	♉09°04′03	♉15°11′00	♉27°28	♈29°16	♈02°15	♈03°05	♒25°12	♉16°05	♓25°10	♑28°24	♉21°44	♉22°32	♋04°47	♈15°17	28 Sa
29 Su	16:26:01	♊07°37′58	♉21°15′43	♉27°18′12	♉27°05	♉00°27	♈02°59	♈03°15	♒25°12	♉16°08	♓25°11	♑28°24	♉21°41	♉22°33	♋04°54	♈15°20	29 Su
30 Mo	16:29:57	♊08°35′33	♊03°18′56	♊09°17′56	♉26°45	♉01°37	♈03°44	♈03°25	♒25°13	♉16°11	♓25°12	♑28°23	♉21°38	℞ 22°32	♋05°00	♈15°22	30 Mo
31 Tu	16:33:54	♊09°33′07	♊15°15′41	♊21°12′10	♉26°29	♉02°47	♈04°29	♈03°34	♒25°13	♉16°14	♓25°13	♑28°22	♉21°35	♉22°31	♋05°07	♈15°24	31 Tu
Δ Delta	01:58:16	28°56′09″	392°58′00″	392°45′21″	-4°26′	-34°41′	-22°29′	-5°35′	0°57′	1°42′	0°39′	-0°13′	-1°35′	0°03′	3°20′	1°24′	Delta

June 2022

Longitude & Retrograde Ephemeris [00:00 UT]

Day	Sid.time	☉	☽	+12h ☽	☿	♀	♂	♃	♄	♅	♆	♇	☊	☊	⚸	⚷	Day
1 We	16:37:50	♊10°30'40	♊27°07'55	♋03°02'54	℞ 26°17	♉03°58	♈05°13	♈03°44	♒25°14	♉16°18	♓25°14	℞ 28°21	℞ 21°32	℞ 22°29	♋05°14	♈15°27	1 We
2 Th	16:41:47	♊11°28'12	♋08°57'43	♋14°52'21	♉26°09	♉05°08	♈05°57	♈03°53	♒25°14	♉16°21	♓25°15	♑28°20	♉21°28	♉22°27	♋05°20	♈15°29	2 Th
3 Fr	16:45:43	♊12°25'42	♋20°47'25	♋26°43'00	♉26°05	♉06°19	♈06°42	♈04°03	♒25°15	♉16°24	♓25°16	♑28°20	♉21°25	♉22°23	♋05°27	♈15°31	3 Fr
4 Sa	16:49:40	♊13°23'12	♌02°39'45	♌08°37'47	DS 26°06	♉07°29	♈07°26	♈04°12	♒25°15	♉16°27	♓25°16	♑28°19	♉21°22	♉22°20	♋05°34	♈15°33	4 Sa
5 Su	16:53:36	♊14°20'40	♌14°37'48	♌20°40'01	♉26°11	♉08°40	♈08°10	♈04°21	℞ 25°15	♉16°30	♓25°17	♑28°18	♉21°19	♉22°17	♋05°41	♈15°36	5 Su
6 Mo	16:57:33	♊15°18'07	♌26°45'10	♍02°53'29	♉26°21	♉09°50	♈08°55	♈04°30	♒25°15	♉16°34	♓25°18	♑28°17	♉21°16	♉22°15	♋05°47	♈15°38	6 Mo
7 Tu	17:01:30	♊16°15'33	♍09°05'44	♍15°22'10	♉26°35	♉11°01	♈09°39	♈04°39	♒25°14	♉16°37	♓25°19	♑28°16	♉21°13	♉22°14	♋05°54	♈15°40	7 Tu
8 We	17:05:26	♊17°12'57	♍21°43'35	♍28°10'09	♉26°53	♉12°12	♈10°23	♈04°47	♒25°14	♉16°40	♓25°19	♑28°15	♉21°09	D 22°14	♋06°01	♈15°42	8 We
9 Th	17:09:23	♊18°10'20	♎04°42'37	♎11°21'06	♉27°17	♉13°22	♈11°07	♈04°56	♒25°14	♉16°43	♓25°20	♑28°14	♉21°06	♉22°15	♋06°07	♈15°44	9 Th
10 Fr	17:13:19	♊19°07'43	♎18°06'12	♎24°57'50	♉27°44	♉14°33	♈11°51	♈05°04	♒25°13	♉16°46	♓25°21	♑28°13	♉21°03	♉22°16	♋06°14	♈15°46	10 Fr
11 Sa	17:17:16	♊20°05'04	♏01°56'24	♏09°01'34	♉28°16	♉15°44	♈12°35	♈05°13	♒25°13	♉16°49	♓25°21	♑28°12	♉21°00	♉22°18	♋06°21	♈15°48	11 Sa
12 Su	17:21:12	♊21°02'25	♏16°13'26	♏23°31'18	♉28°52	♉16°55	♈13°19	♈05°21	♒25°12	♉16°52	♓25°22	♑28°11	♉20°57	♉22°18	♋06°27	♈15°50	12 Su
13 Mo	17:25:09	♊21°59'44	♐00°54'55	♐08°23'13	♉29°32	♉18°06	♈14°03	♈05°29	♒25°11	♉16°55	♓25°22	♑28°10	♉20°53	℞ 22°18	♋06°34	♈15°51	13 Mo
14 Tu	17:29:05	♊22°57'03	♐15°55'34	♐23°30'35	♊00°16	♉19°17	♈14°46	♈05°37	♒25°11	♉16°58	♓25°23	♑28°09	♉20°50	♉22°17	♋06°41	♈15°53	14 Tu
15 We	17:33:02	♊23°54'21	♑01°07'22	♑08°44'20	♊01°04	♉20°28	♈15°30	♈05°45	♒25°10	♉17°01	♓25°23	♑28°07	♉20°47	♉22°14	♋06°47	♈15°55	15 We
16 Th	17:36:59	♊24°51'38	♑16°20'30	♑23°54'16	♊01°56	♉21°39	♈16°14	♈05°52	♒25°09	♉17°04	♓25°24	♑28°06	♉20°44	♉22°10	♋06°54	♈15°57	16 Th
17 Fr	17:40:55	♊25°48'55	♒01°24'50	♒08°50'48	♊02°52	♉22°50	♈16°57	♈06°00	♒25°08	♉17°07	♓25°24	♑28°05	♉20°41	♉22°05	♋07°01	♈15°58	17 Fr
18 Sa	17:44:52	♊26°46'11	♒16°11'38	♒23°26'20	♊03°51	♉24°01	♈17°41	♈06°07	♒25°06	♉17°10	♓25°24	♑28°04	♉20°38	♉22°01	♋07°07	♈16°00	18 Sa
19 Su	17:48:48	♊27°43'27	♓00°34'45	♓07°36'15	D 04°54	♉25°13	♈18°24	♈06°14	♒25°05	♉17°12	♓25°25	♑28°03	♉20°34	♉21°57	♋07°14	♈16°02	19 Su
20 Mo	17:52:45	♊28°40'43	♓14°31'04	♓21°18'55	♊06°01	♉26°24	♈19°08	♈06°21	♒25°04	♉17°15	♓25°25	♑28°02	♉20°31	♉21°55	♋07°21	♈16°03	20 Mo
21 Tu	17:56:41	♊29°37'59	♓28°00'20	♈04°35'18	♊07°12	♉27°35	♈19°51	♈06°28	♒25°02	♉17°18	♓25°25	♑28°00	♉20°28	♉21°54	♋07°28	♈16°04	21 Tu
22 We	18:00:38	♋00°35'14	♈11°04'31	♈17°28'07	♊08°26	♉28°46	♈20°34	♈06°35	♒25°01	♉17°21	♓25°25	♑27°59	♉20°25	D 21°54	♋07°34	♈16°06	22 We
23 Th	18:04:34	♋01°32'29	♈23°46'54	♉00°01'06	♊09°43	♉29°58	♈21°17	♈06°41	♒24°59	♉17°24	♓25°26	♑27°58	♉20°22	♉21°55	♋07°41	♈16°07	23 Th
24 Fr	18:08:31	♋02°29'44	♉06°11'30	♉12°18'21	♊11°04	♊01°09	♈22°00	♈06°48	♒24°57	♉17°26	♓25°26	♑27°57	♉20°19	♉21°57	♋07°48	♈16°09	24 Fr
25 Sa	18:12:28	♋03°26'59	♉18°22'23	♉24°23'49	♊12°28	♊02°21	♈22°43	♈06°54	♒24°55	♉17°29	♓25°26	♑27°55	♉20°15	♉21°58	♋07°54	♈16°10	25 Sa
26 Su	18:16:24	♋04°24'14	♊00°23'22	♊06°21'10	♊13°56	♊03°32	♈23°26	♈07°00	♒24°53	♉17°32	♓25°26	♑27°54	♉20°12	℞ 21°58	♋08°01	♈16°11	26 Su
27 Mo	18:20:21	♋05°21'29	♊12°17'49	♊18°13'27	♊15°27	♊04°44	♈24°09	♈07°06	♒24°51	♉17°34	♓25°26	♑27°53	♉20°09	♉21°55	♋08°08	♈16°12	27 Mo
28 Tu	18:24:17	♋06°18'43	♊24°08'35	♋00°03'16	♊17°01	♊05°55	♈24°52	♈07°12	♒24°49	♉17°37	♓25°26	♑27°52	♉20°06	♉21°51	♋08°14	♈16°13	28 Tu
29 We	18:28:14	♋07°15'57	♋05°57'59	♋11°52'45	♊18°39	♊07°07	♈25°35	♈07°18	♒24°47	♉17°39	℞ 25°26	♑27°50	♉20°03	♉21°45	♋08°21	♈16°15	29 We
30 Th	18:32:10	♋08°13'11	♋17°48'01	♋23°43'45	♊20°20	♊08°19	♈26°17	♈07°23	♒24°45	♉17°42	♓25°26	♑27°49	♉19°59	♉21°37	♋08°28	♈16°16	30 Th
Δ Delta	01:54:19	27°42'31"	380°40'06"	380°40'50"	24°02'	34°21'	21°04'	3°39'	-0°29'	1°23'	0°12'	-0°32'	-1°32'	-0°51'	3°13'	0°48'	Delta

July 2022

Longitude & Retrograde Ephemeris [00:00 UT]

Day	Sid.time	☉	☽	+12h☽	☿	♀	♂	♃	♄	♅	♆	♇	☊	☊	⚸	⚷	Day
1 Fr	18:36:07	♋09°10'26	♋29°40'26	♌05°38'02	♊22°03	♊09°30	♈27°00	♈07°28	℞ 24°42	♉17°44	℞ 25°26	℞ 27°48	℞ 19°56	℞ 21°29	♋08°34	♈16°17	**1** Fr
2 Sa	18:40:04	♋10°07'39	♌11°37'01	♌17°37'25	♊23°50	♊10°42	♈27°42	♈07°33	♒24°40	♉17°47	♓25°26	♑27°46	♉19°53	♉21°20	♋08°41	♈16°17	**2** Sa
3 Su	18:44:00	♋11°04'53	♌23°39'46	♌29°44'06	♊25°40	♊11°54	♈28°25	♈07°38	♒24°37	♉17°49	♓25°26	♑27°45	♉19°50	♉21°11	♋08°48	♈16°18	**3** Su
4 Mo	18:47:57	♋12°02'06	♍05°51'01	♍12°00'37	♊27°33	♊13°06	♈29°07	♈07°43	♒24°35	♉17°51	♓25°26	♑27°44	♉19°47	♉21°04	♋08°54	♈16°19	**4** Mo
5 Tu	18:51:53	♋12°59'18	♍18°13'34	♍24°30'01	♊29°28	♊14°17	♈29°49	♈07°48	♒24°32	♉17°54	♓25°25	♑27°42	♉19°44	♉20°59	♋09°01	♈16°20	**5** Tu
6 We	18:55:50	♋13°56'31	♎00°50'40	♎07°15'42	♋01°26	♊15°29	♉00°31	♈07°52	♒24°29	♉17°56	♓25°25	♑27°41	♉19°40	♉20°57	♋09°08	♈16°21	**6** We
7 Th	18:59:46	♋14°53'43	♎13°45'51	♎20°21'15	♋03°26	♊16°41	♉01°13	♈07°56	♒24°26	♉17°58	♓25°25	♑27°39	♉19°37	♉20°56	♋09°15	♈16°21	**7** Th
8 Fr	19:03:43	♋15°50'55	♎27°02'36	♏03°49'56	♋05°29	♊17°53	♉01°55	♈08°00	♒24°23	♉18°00	♓25°25	♑27°38	♉19°34	D 20°56	♋09°21	♈16°22	**8** Fr
9 Sa	19:07:39	♋16°48'07	♏10°43'50	♏17°44'08	♋07°33	♊19°05	♉02°36	♈08°04	♒24°20	♉18°03	♓25°24	♑27°37	♉19°31	♉20°57	♋09°28	♈16°23	**9** Sa
10 Su	19:11:36	♋17°45'19	♏24°51'10	♐02°04'29	♋09°38	♊20°17	♉03°18	♈08°08	♒24°17	♉18°05	♓25°24	♑27°35	♉19°28	℞ 20°57	♋09°35	♈16°23	**10** Su
11 Mo	19:15:33	♋18°42'30	♐09°24'06	♐16°49'08	♋11°46	♊21°29	♉03°59	♈08°11	♒24°14	♉18°07	♓25°23	♑27°34	♉19°25	♉20°56	♋09°41	♈16°24	**11** Mo
12 Tu	19:19:29	♋19°39'42	♐24°19'13	♑01°53'03	♋13°54	♊22°41	♉04°41	♈08°15	♒24°11	♉18°09	♓25°23	♑27°32	♉19°21	♉20°52	♋09°48	♈16°24	**12** Tu
13 We	19:23:26	♋20°36'54	♑09°29'51	♑17°08'02	♋16°02	♊23°54	♉05°22	♈08°18	♒24°08	♉18°11	♓25°23	♑27°31	♉19°18	♉20°46	♋09°55	♈16°24	**13** We
14 Th	19:27:22	♋21°34'06	♑24°46'35	♒02°23'44	♋18°11	♊25°06	♉06°03	♈08°21	♒24°04	♉18°13	♓25°22	♑27°30	♉19°15	♉20°39	♋10°01	♈16°25	**14** Th
15 Fr	19:31:19	♋22°31'18	♒09°58'29	♒17°29'12	♋20°21	♊26°18	♉06°44	♈08°24	♒24°01	♉18°15	♓25°22	♑27°28	♉19°12	♉20°30	♋10°08	♈16°25	**15** Fr
16 Sa	19:35:15	♋23°28'31	♒24°55'06	♓02°14'55	♋22°30	♊27°30	♉07°25	♈08°26	♒23°57	♉18°17	♓25°21	♑27°27	♉19°09	♉20°21	♋10°15	♈16°25	**16** Sa
17 Su	19:39:12	♋24°25'44	♓09°28'15	♓16°34'16	♋24°38	♊28°43	♉08°06	♈08°29	♒23°54	♉18°18	♓25°20	♑27°25	♉19°05	♉20°13	♋10°21	♈16°25	**17** Su
18 Mo	19:43:08	♋25°22'58	♓23°33'01	♈00°24'07	♋26°46	♊29°55	♉08°47	♈08°31	♒23°50	♉18°20	♓25°20	♑27°24	♉19°02	♉20°07	♋10°28	♈16°25	**18** Mo
19 Tu	19:47:05	♋26°20'12	♈07°08'00	♈13°44'36	♋28°53	♋01°07	♉09°28	♈08°33	♒23°46	♉18°22	♓25°19	♑27°22	♉18°59	♉20°03	♋10°35	♈16°25	**19** Tu
20 We	19:51:02	♋27°17'27	♈20°14'40	♈26°38'21	♌00°59	♋02°20	♉10°08	♈08°35	♒23°43	♉18°24	♓25°19	♑27°21	♉18°56	♉20°02	♋10°42	℞ 16°26	**20** We
21 Th	19:54:58	♋28°14'42	♉02°56'33	♉09°09'32	♌03°04	♋03°32	♉10°49	♈08°36	♒23°39	♉18°25	♓25°18	♑27°20	♉18°53	D 20°02	♋10°48	♈16°25	**21** Th
22 Fr	19:58:55	♋29°11'59	♉15°18'14	♉21°23'02	♌05°08	♋04°45	♉11°29	♈08°38	♒23°35	♉18°27	♓25°17	♑27°18	♉18°50	♉20°02	♋10°55	♈16°25	**22** Fr
23 Sa	20:02:51	♌00°09'16	♉27°24'48	♊03°23'53	♌07°10	♋05°57	♉12°09	♈08°39	♒23°31	♉18°29	♓25°16	♑27°17	♉18°46	℞ 20°02	♋11°02	♈16°25	**23** Sa
24 Su	20:06:48	♌01°06'34	♊09°21'08	♊15°16'49	♌09°11	♋07°10	♉12°49	♈08°40	♒23°27	♉18°30	♓25°16	♑27°15	♉18°43	♉20°00	♋11°08	♈16°25	**24** Su
25 Mo	20:10:44	♌02°03'53	♊21°11'41	♊27°05'58	♌11°10	♋08°22	♉13°29	♈08°41	♒23°23	♉18°32	♓25°15	♑27°14	♉18°40	♉19°56	♋11°15	♈16°25	**25** Mo
26 Tu	20:14:41	♌03°01'13	♋03°00'17	♋08°54'46	♌13°07	♋09°35	♉14°08	♈08°42	♒23°19	♉18°33	♓25°14	♑27°12	♉18°37	♉19°50	♋11°22	♈16°24	**26** Tu
27 We	20:18:37	♌03°58'33	♋14°49'59	♋20°45'56	♌15°03	♋10°48	♉14°48	♈08°42	♒23°15	♉18°35	♓25°13	♑27°11	♉18°34	♉19°40	♋11°28	♈16°24	**27** We
28 Th	20:22:34	♌04°55'55	♋26°43'07	♌02°41'28	♌16°57	♋12°01	♉15°27	♈08°42	♒23°11	♉18°36	♓25°12	♑27°10	♉18°31	♉19°29	♋11°35	♈16°24	**28** Th
29 Fr	20:26:31	♌05°53'17	♌08°41'26	♌14°42'52	♌18°50	♋13°13	♉16°07	℞ 08°43	♒23°07	♉18°37	♓25°11	♑27°08	♉18°27	♉19°16	♋11°42	♈16°23	**29** Fr
30 Sa	20:30:27	♌06°50'40	♌20°46'12	♌26°51'16	♌20°41	♋14°26	♉16°46	♈08°42	♒23°03	♉18°39	♓25°10	♑27°07	♉18°24	♉19°02	♋11°49	♈16°23	**30** Sa
31 Su	20:34:24	♌07°48'03	♍02°58'31	♍09°07'48	♌22°30	♋15°39	♉17°25	♈08°42	♒22°58	♉18°40	♓25°09	♑27°05	♉18°21	♉18°50	♋11°55	♈16°22	**31** Su
Δ Delta	01:58:16	28°37'37"	393°18'05"	393°29'46"	60°26'	36°08'	20°25'	1°13'	-1°43'	0°55'	-0°16'	-0°42'	-1°35'	-2°38'	3°20'	0°05'	**Delta**

Ephemeris tables and data provided by **Astro-Seek.com.** All times in UTC.

AUGUST 2022

August 2022

Longitude & Retrograde Ephemeris [00:00 UT]

Day	Sid.time	☉	☽	+12h☽	☿	♀	♂	♃	♄	♅	♆	♇	☊	☊	⚸	⚷	Day
1 Mo	20:38:20	♌08°45'27	♍15°19'35	♍21°33'45	♌24°17	♋16°52	♉18°04	℞ 08°42	℞ 22°54	♉18°41	℞ 25°08	℞ 27°04	℞ 18°18	℞ 18°39	♋12°02	℞ 16°22	**1** Mo
2 Tu	20:42:17	♌09°42'52	♍27°50'50	♎04°10'48	♌26°03	♋18°05	♉18°42	♈08°41	♒22°50	♉18°42	♓25°07	♑27°02	♉18°15	♉18°31	♋12°09	♈16°21	**2** Tu
3 We	20:46:13	♌10°40'17	♎10°34'13	♎17°01'06	♌27°48	♋19°18	♉19°21	♈08°40	♒22°46	♉18°43	♓25°06	♑27°01	♉18°11	♉18°26	♋12°15	♈16°20	**3** We
4 Th	20:50:10	♌11°37'43	♎23°32'06	♏00°07'15	♌29°30	♋20°31	♉19°59	♈08°39	♒22°41	♉18°44	♓25°05	♑27°00	♉18°08	♉18°23	♋12°22	♈16°19	**4** Th
5 Fr	20:54:06	♌12°35'10	♏06°47'13	♏13°31'59	♍01°11	♋21°44	♉20°37	♈08°37	♒22°37	♉18°45	♓25°04	♑26°58	♉18°05	♉18°22	♋12°29	♈16°19	**5** Fr
6 Sa	20:58:03	♌13°32'38	♏20°22'10	♏27°17'41	♍02°50	♋22°57	♉21°15	♈08°36	♒22°32	♉18°46	♓25°03	♑26°57	♉18°02	♉18°22	♋12°35	♈16°18	**6** Sa
7 Su	21:01:60	♌14°30'06	♐04°18'58	♐11°25'43	♍04°28	♋24°10	♉21°53	♈08°34	♒22°28	♉18°47	♓25°02	♑26°56	♉17°59	♉18°22	♋12°42	♈16°17	**7** Su
8 Mo	21:05:56	♌15°27'34	♐18°38'08	♐25°55'35	♍06°04	♋25°23	♉22°31	♈08°32	♒22°24	♉18°48	♓25°01	♑26°54	♉17°56	♉18°19	♋12°49	♈16°16	**8** Mo
9 Tu	21:09:53	♌16°25'04	♑03°17'56	♑10°44'10	♍07°38	♋26°37	♉23°08	♈08°30	♒22°19	♉18°49	♓25°00	♑26°53	♉17°52	♉18°15	♋12°55	♈16°15	**9** Tu
10 We	21:13:49	♌17°22'35	♑18°13'47	♑25°45'24	♍09°11	♋27°50	♉23°45	♈08°28	♒22°15	♉18°49	♓24°58	♑26°52	♉17°49	♉18°08	♋13°02	♈16°14	**10** We
11 Th	21:17:46	♌18°20'06	♒03°18'14	♒10°50'39	♍10°42	♋29°03	♉24°23	♈08°26	♒22°10	♉18°50	♓24°57	♑26°50	♉17°46	♉17°58	♋13°09	♈16°13	**11** Th
12 Fr	21:21:42	♌19°17'39	♒18°21'46	♒25°49'56	♍12°12	♌00°16	♉24°59	♈08°23	♒22°06	♉18°51	♓24°56	♑26°49	♉17°43	♉17°47	♋13°16	♈16°12	**12** Fr
13 Sa	21:25:39	♌20°15'12	♓03°14'21	♓10°33'39	♍13°40	♌01°30	♉25°36	♈08°20	♒22°01	♉18°51	♓24°55	♑26°48	♉17°40	♉17°36	♋13°22	♈16°10	**13** Sa
14 Su	21:29:35	♌21°12'47	♓17°47'17	♓24°54'16	♍15°06	♌02°43	♉26°13	♈08°17	♒21°57	♉18°52	♓24°53	♑26°46	♉17°37	♉17°27	♋13°29	♈16°09	**14** Su
15 Mo	21:33:32	♌22°10'23	♈01°54'28	♈08°47'19	♍16°30	♌03°56	♉26°49	♈08°14	♒21°52	♉18°52	♓24°52	♑26°45	♉17°33	♉17°19	♋13°36	♈16°08	**15** Mo
16 Tu	21:37:29	♌23°08'00	♈15°33'05	♈22°11'36	♍17°53	♌05°10	♉27°25	♈08°10	♒21°48	♉18°53	♓24°51	♑26°44	♉17°30	♉17°13	♋13°42	♈16°06	**16** Tu
17 We	21:41:25	♌24°05'39	♈28°43'27	♉05°08'43	♍19°14	♌06°23	♉28°01	♈08°07	♒21°43	♉18°53	♓24°49	♑26°43	♉17°27	♉17°11	♋13°49	♈16°05	**17** We
18 Th	21:45:22	♌25°03'20	♉11°28'12	♉17°42'12	♍20°33	♌07°37	♉28°37	♈08°03	♒21°39	♉18°54	♓24°48	♑26°41	♉17°24	♉17°10	♋13°56	♈16°04	**18** Th
19 Fr	21:49:18	♌26°01'02	♉23°51'38	♉29°56'52	♍21°51	♌08°51	♉29°13	♈07°59	♒21°34	♉18°54	♓24°47	♑26°40	♉17°21	D 17°10	♋14°02	♈16°02	**19** Fr
20 Sa	21:53:15	♌26°58'46	♊05°58'51	♊11°57'59	♍23°06	♌10°04	♉29°48	♈07°55	♒21°30	♉18°54	♓24°45	♑26°39	♉17°17	℞ 17°09	♋14°09	♈16°01	**20** Sa
21 Su	21:57:11	♌27°56'31	♊17°55'11	♊23°50'49	℞s 24°20	♌11°18	♊00°23	♈07°50	♒21°25	♉18°54	♓24°44	♑26°38	♉17°14	♉17°08	♋14°16	♈15°59	**21** Su
22 Mo	22:01:08	♌28°54'19	♊29°45'45	♋05°40'16	♍25°32	♌12°32	♊00°58	♈07°46	♒21°21	♉18°55	♓24°42	♑26°37	♉17°11	♉17°04	♋14°23	♈15°57	**22** Mo
23 Tu	22:05:04	♌29°52'07	♋11°35'11	♋17°30'40	♍26°41	♌13°45	♊01°33	♈07°41	♒21°16	♉18°55	♓24°41	♑26°36	♉17°08	♉16°58	♋14°29	♈15°56	**23** Tu
24 We	22:09:01	♍00°49'58	♋23°27'24	♋29°25'29	♍27°49	♌14°59	♊02°07	♈07°36	♒21°12	♉18°55	♓24°39	♑26°34	♉17°05	♉16°49	♋14°36	♈15°54	**24** We
25 Th	22:12:58	♍01°47'49	♌05°25'30	♌11°27'24	♍28°54	♌16°13	♊02°41	♈07°31	♒21°08	℞ 18°55	♓24°38	♑26°33	♉17°02	♉16°38	♋14°43	♈15°52	**25** Th
26 Fr	22:16:54	♍02°45'43	♌17°31'41	♌23°38'12	♍29°57	♌17°27	♊03°15	♈07°26	♒21°03	♉18°55	♓24°36	♑26°32	♉16°58	♉16°26	♋14°49	♈15°51	**26** Fr
27 Sa	22:20:51	♍03°43'38	♌29°47'22	♍05°58'56	♎00°57	♌18°41	♊03°49	♈07°21	♒20°59	♉18°55	♓24°35	♑26°31	♉16°55	♉16°13	♋14°56	♈15°49	**27** Sa
28 Su	22:24:47	♍04°41'34	♍12°13'17	♍18°30'07	♎01°55	♌19°54	♊04°22	♈07°15	♒20°55	♉18°54	♓24°33	♑26°30	♉16°52	♉16°00	♋15°03	♈15°47	**28** Su
29 Mo	22:28:44	♍05°39'32	♍24°49'46	♎01°11'58	♎02°50	♌21°08	♊04°55	♈07°10	♒20°50	♉18°54	♓24°32	♑26°29	♉16°49	♉15°50	♋15°09	♈15°45	**29** Mo
30 Tu	22:32:40	♍06°37'32	♎07°37'03	♎14°04'45	♎03°42	♌22°22	♊05°28	♈07°04	♒20°46	♉18°54	♓24°30	♑26°28	♉16°46	♉15°42	♋15°16	♈15°43	**30** Tu
31 We	22:36:37	♍07°35'33	♎20°35'27	♎27°08'57	♎04°31	♌23°36	♊06°01	♈06°58	♒20°42	♉18°54	♓24°29	♑26°27	♉16°42	♉15°37	♋15°23	♈15°41	**31** We
Δ Delta	01:58:16	28°50'05"	395°15'52"	395°35'12"	40°13'	36°44'	17°57'	-1°43'	-2°12'	0°12'	-0°39'	-0°36'	-1°35'	-3°02'	3°20'	-0°40'	**Delta**

SEPTEMBER 2022

September 2022

Longitude & Retrograde Ephemeris [00:00 UT]

Day	Sid.time	☉	☽	+12h☽	☿	♀	♂	♃	♄	♅	♆	♇	☊	☊	⚸	⚷	Day
1 Th	22:40:33	♍08°33'35	♏03°45'42	♏10°25'30	℞s05°16	♌24°50	♊06°33	℞ 06°52	℞ 20°38	℞ 18°53	℞ 24°27	℞ 26°26	℞ 16°39	℞ 15°34	♋15°30	℞ 15°39	1 Th
2 Fr	22:44:30	♍09°31'39	♏17°08'51	♏23°55'35	♎05°58	♌26°04	♊07°05	♈06°46	♒20°34	♉18°53	♓24°26	♑26°25	♉16°36	D 15°34	♋15°36	♈15°37	2 Fr
3 Sa	22:48:27	♍10°29'44	♐00°46'12	♐07°40'28	♎06°36	♌27°19	♊07°37	♈06°39	♒20°29	♉18°53	♓24°24	♑26°24	♉16°33	♉15°34	♋15°43	♈15°35	3 Sa
4 Su	22:52:23	♍11°27'51	♐14°38'51	♐21°40'59	♎07°10	♌28°33	♊08°08	♈06°33	♒20°25	♉18°52	♓24°22	♑26°23	♉16°30	℞ 15°35	♋15°50	♈15°33	4 Su
5 Mo	22:56:20	♍12°25'59	♐28°47'10	♑05°56'53	♎07°40	♌29°47	♊08°40	♈06°26	♒20°21	♉18°51	♓24°21	♑26°22	♉16°27	♉15°33	♋15°56	♈15°31	5 Mo
6 Tu	23:00:16	♍13°24'08	♑13°10'10	♑20°26'16	♎08°06	♍01°01	♊09°10	♈06°20	♒20°17	♉18°51	♓24°19	♑26°21	♉16°23	♉15°30	♋16°03	♈15°29	6 Tu
7 We	23:04:13	♍14°22'19	♑27°44'56	♒05°05'09	♎08°26	♍02°15	♊09°41	♈06°13	♒20°14	♉18°50	♓24°18	♑26°21	♉16°20	♉15°25	♋16°10	♈15°26	7 We
8 Th	23:08:09	♍15°20'31	♒12°26'27	♒19°47'35	♎08°41	♍03°30	♊10°11	♈06°06	♒20°10	♉18°50	♓24°16	♑26°20	♉16°17	♉15°17	♋16°17	♈15°24	8 Th
9 Fr	23:12:06	♍16°18'45	♒27°07'57	♓04°26'13	♎08°51	♍04°44	♊10°41	♈05°59	♒20°06	♉18°49	♓24°14	♑26°19	♉16°14	♉15°08	♋16°23	♈15°22	9 Fr
10 Sa	23:16:02	♍17°17'00	♓11°41'48	♓18°53'29	♎08°55	♍05°58	♊11°11	♈05°52	♒20°02	♉18°48	♓24°13	♑26°18	♉16°11	♉14°59	♋16°30	♈15°20	10 Sa
11 Su	23:19:59	♍18°15'18	♓26°00'47	♈03°02'45	℞ 08°53	♍07°12	♊11°40	♈05°44	♒19°58	♉18°47	♓24°11	♑26°17	♉16°08	♉14°51	♋16°37	♈15°17	11 Su
12 Mo	23:23:56	♍19°13'37	♈09°59'11	♈16°49'26	♎08°44	♍08°27	♊12°09	♈05°37	♒19°55	♉18°46	♓24°09	♑26°17	♉16°04	♉14°44	♋16°43	♈15°15	12 Mo
13 Tu	23:27:52	♍20°11'58	♈23°33'37	♉00°11'23	♎08°29	♍09°41	♊12°38	♈05°30	♒19°51	♉18°45	♓24°08	♑26°16	♉16°01	♉14°40	♋16°50	♈15°13	13 Tu
14 We	23:31:49	♍21°10'21	♉06°43'10	♉13°08'53	♎08°07	♍10°56	♊13°06	♈05°22	♒19°48	♉18°44	♓24°06	♑26°15	♉15°58	♉14°38	♋16°57	♈15°10	14 We
15 Th	23:35:45	♍22°08'45	♉19°29'12	♉25°44'15	♎07°39	♍12°10	♊13°34	♈05°15	♒19°44	♉18°43	♓24°04	♑26°14	♉15°55	D 14°38	♋17°03	♈15°08	15 Th
16 Fr	23:39:42	♍23°07'13	♊01°54'50	♊08°01'14	♎07°04	♍13°25	♊14°02	♈05°07	♒19°41	♉18°42	♓24°03	♑26°14	♉15°52	♉14°39	♋17°10	♈15°05	16 Fr
17 Sa	23:43:38	♍24°05'42	♊14°04'20	♊20°04'29	♎06°22	♍14°39	♊14°29	♈04°59	♒19°38	♉18°41	♓24°01	♑26°13	♉15°48	♉14°40	♋17°17	♈15°03	17 Sa
18 Su	23:47:35	♍25°04'14	♊26°02'37	♋01°59'06	♎05°34	♍15°54	♊14°56	♈04°51	♒19°34	♉18°40	♓23°59	♑26°13	♉15°45	℞ 14°40	♋17°24	♈15°00	18 Su
19 Mo	23:51:31	♍26°02'48	♋07°54'52	♋13°50'13	♎04°41	♍17°08	♊15°22	♈04°44	♒19°31	♉18°39	♓23°58	♑26°12	♉15°42	♉14°39	♋17°30	♈14°58	19 Mo
20 Tu	23:55:28	♍27°01'23	♋19°46'05	♋25°42'42	♎03°43	♍18°23	♊15°48	♈04°36	♒19°28	♉18°38	♓23°56	♑26°12	♉15°39	♉14°37	♋17°37	♈14°55	20 Tu
21 We	23:59:25	♍28°00'02	♌01°40'53	♌07°40'50	♎02°41	♍19°37	♊16°14	♈04°28	♒19°25	♉18°36	♓23°54	♑26°11	♉15°36	♉14°32	♋17°44	♈14°53	21 We
22 Th	00:03:21	♍28°58'42	♌13°43'15	♌19°48'14	♎01°37	♍20°52	♊16°39	♈04°20	♒19°22	♉18°35	♓23°53	♑26°11	♉15°33	♉14°25	♋17°50	♈14°50	22 Th
23 Fr	00:07:18	♍29°57'24	♌25°56'20	♍02°07'32	♎00°32	♍22°07	♊17°03	♈04°12	♒19°19	♉18°34	♓23°51	♑26°10	♉15°29	♉14°18	♋17°57	♈14°48	23 Fr
24 Sa	00:11:14	♎00°56'08	♍08°22'18	♍14°40'27	♍29°28	♍23°21	♊17°28	♈04°04	♒19°16	♉18°32	♓23°50	♑26°10	♉15°26	♉14°10	♋18°04	♈14°45	24 Sa
25 Su	00:15:11	♎01°54'55	♍21°02'21	♍27°27'40	♍28°25	♍24°36	♊17°51	♈03°56	♒19°14	♉18°31	♓23°48	♑26°09	♉15°23	♉14°02	♋18°10	♈14°42	25 Su
26 Mo	00:19:07	♎02°53'43	♎03°56'40	♎10°28'58	♍27°27	♍25°51	♊18°15	♈03°48	♒19°11	♉18°29	♓23°46	♑26°09	♉15°20	♉13°56	♋18°17	♈14°40	26 Mo
27 Tu	00:23:04	♎03°52'33	♎17°04'45	♎23°43'32	♍26°34	♍27°06	♊18°38	♈03°40	♒19°09	♉18°28	♓23°45	♑26°08	♉15°17	♉13°51	♋18°24	♈14°37	27 Tu
28 We	00:27:00	♎04°51'26	♏00°25'31	♏07°10'11	♍25°48	♍28°20	♊19°00	♈03°32	♒19°06	♉18°26	♓23°43	♑26°08	♉15°14	♉13°48	♋18°31	♈14°34	28 We
29 Th	00:30:57	♎05°50'20	♏13°57'43	♏20°47'39	♍25°10	♍29°35	♊19°22	♈03°24	♒19°04	♉18°25	♓23°41	♑26°08	♉15°10	D 13°47	♋18°37	♈14°32	29 Th
30 Fr	00:34:54	♎06°49'16	♏27°40'09	♐04°34'47	♍24°41	♎00°50	♊19°43	♈03°16	♒19°01	♉18°23	♓23°40	♑26°08	♉15°07	♉13°48	♋18°44	♈14°29	30 Fr
Δ Delta	01:54:21	28°15'41"	383°54'27"	384°09'16"	-10°35'	35°59'	13°10'	-3°36'	-1°36'	-0°30'	-0°47'	-0°18'	-1°32'	-1°46'	3°14'	-1°10'	Delta

Ephemeris tables and data provided by **Astro-Seek.com**. All times in UTC.